P9-DMJ-316

# Vanessa

## THE LIFE OF
## VANESSA REDGRAVE

# DAN CALLAHAN

PEGASUS BOOKS
NEW YORK  LONDON

VANESSA

Pegasus Books LLC
80 Broad St., 5th Floor
New York, NY 10004

Copyright © 2014 Dan Callahan

First Pegasus Books edition May 2014

Interior design by Maria Fernandez

All rights reserved. No part of this book may be reproduced in whole or in part without written permission from the publisher, except by reviewers who may quote brief excerpts in connection with a review in a newspaper, magazine, or electronic publication; nor may any part of this book be reproduced, stored in a retrieval system, or transmitted in any form or by any means electronic, mechanical, photocopying, recording, or other, without written permission from the publisher.

Library of Congress Cataloging-in-Publication Data is available.

ISBN: 978-1-60598-557-2

10 9 8 7 6 5 4 3 2 1

Printed in the United States of America
Distributed by W. W. Norton & Company, Inc.
www.pegasusbooks.us

# Vanessa

*For My Parents:*
*Cal and Linda*

# Contents

# Introduction

When I was studying acting at the Stella Adler Conservatory in the late 1990s, Vanessa Redgrave was at the Public Theater directing and starring in a production of Shakespeare's *Antony and Cleopatra*. Our movement teacher Joanne Edelmann told us to do something useful with our free time: "Try to see all the films of Vanessa Redgrave," she said. Seeing all of Redgrave's films was a tall order even then, before her resume had expanded further in size and eccentricity, but it remains an eminently worthwhile suggestion to anyone interested in acting or anyone simply interested in daredevil risk-taking.

The Stella Adler studios at that time were right next door to the Public Theater on Lafayette Street in downtown Manhattan. During breaks in our classes in the early winter of 1997, I would sometimes hang around outside if it was a sunny day and would often see Redgrave during breaks in her rehearsals. Her hair was cropped and light red, and she would be walking very slowly up and down in front of the Public Theater in her punkish costume, smiling in an abstracted way and enjoying a cigarette. I drew much happiness and courage just from being in such close proximity to the woman I considered then and still consider the greatest living actress working in English.

I bought a ticket for a matinee of Redgrave's production of *Antony and Cleopatra*. It cost fifteen dollars for a seat with an obstructed view, and it was the first play in New York that I ever paid for and went to by myself. The readings of the verse were clear and vital, and Redgrave's Cleopatra was tomboyish, jaunty, and amusingly capricious. The multi-media elements she had chosen as a director made their modern points without getting in the way of the play, and the startled look on her Cleopatra's face when she was confronted by a news camera was particularly memorable. At one point, Cleopatra and her handmaidens were attacked and thrown on the floor of the stage, and I still vividly remember Redgrave's sense of helplessness at this moment and how these men violated and destroyed the queenly hauteur that she had displayed in her first scenes.

She had little chemistry on stage, though, with her Marc Antony, David Harewood, and this was a problem that only got worse as the play went on, so that she basically had to give her performance of this most difficult and complicated of all Shakespeare's female roles in a void. It was suggested in the press that she was having a romance with Harewood, who was thirty years her junior. "Sometimes, I'll be watching in the wings and get so transfixed by her, I miss my cue," Harewood said.

At the curtain call, Redgrave came out to the front of the company and asked for silence for a moment. "I have just been informed that the director Fred Zinnemann, who directed me in the movie *Julia* . . . has died," she said softly, in her drawling British accent. Her face was uptilted, and she looked like a heroine, like Joan of Arc going into battle. "As a tribute to him, I would like to sing the theme song from his film *High Noon* . . . which was a very brave and indeed very necessary stand against the all-pervasive and destructive McCarthyism . . . of that time and place." A few of the older audience members murmured and snorted a bit, as if to say, "Oh, please don't talk about politics, Vanessa!"

And then she began: "Do not forsake me, oh my darling!" Redgrave sang, in a high, thin voice. "On this our wedding day–ay!" When she got to the part of the song that goes "Gotta get on my horse and ride it," there was a very funny incongruity between her high-toned British pronunciation and this cowboy song of the American West. She tried hard to overcome that gap, so that when she came to that line again, "get" became "git," which had the effect, unfortunately, of being even funnier, objectively speaking. But I didn't laugh, and neither did anyone else. As she kept singing this song as a tribute to Zinnemann and it went on and on, some of the audience started to leave, but I was transfixed by the romantic intensity of her concentration and her need to communicate.

Redgrave's fellow cast members looked at her fondly as she sang, as you would look at a much-loved bohemian aunt, and I moved closer to the stage and focused all of my attention on her as she kept going. The theater was half empty now. When she came again to "Gotta git on my horse and ride it," the "git" sounded natural, finally. This queenly British woman had slowly become an American frontier lady singing a lament for a fallen hero. Through the power of Redgrave's imagination, she had turned something that had started out as vaguely embarrassing and made it into a dignified and heartfelt theatrical gesture of mourning. It was unforgettable. And it is one of the reasons why I am writing this book in tribute to her work.

A few years later, while working on a piece about Katharine Hepburn, a friend got me Redgrave's phone number in London and said I should call and ask her about working with Hepburn in *The Trojan Women* (1971). Foolhardily, I did ring the number one afternoon, and this is what I heard: "Hello, this is Vanessa Redgrave. Please, please don't leave a message here, because I am very busy indeed . . . and if you leave a message . . . well . . . I'll have to answer it . . . and you see I don't really have the time to answer messages here . . . so if you've reached this machine . . . please . . . please . . . don't leave a message . . . please. . . ." I hung up the phone quickly and laughed. She had sounded so put-upon, so plaintive, especially on the repeated "please," and I found this funny. Though, again, I do not think she meant to be funny.

While she was playing on Broadway in *Driving Miss Daisy*, I wrote Redgrave a letter saying that I wanted to write a book about her and her work. I didn't receive a reply, but I didn't really expect to. As I researched her life, it became clear to me that if this book were to have any value, it would need to present a more objective view of her than her own 1994 autobiography could. Redgrave has her own way of looking at things. It was important, I felt, to hear her own voice, her own version of events, and also the voices of others who have known her and spoken about her, particularly when it came to describing her fifteen or so years as a member of the Workers Revolutionary Party and her relationship with its leader, Gerry Healy.

In her art, Redgrave is the most empathetic and nuanced of actresses. In most of her adult life as a political ideologue, she was usually the opposite of that, an absolutist who saw only what she wanted to see. The conflict between these two qualities, or these two poles of her life, is what makes her such an unbelievably rich, touching, humorous, and often baffling character and subject. "It is easy to know the superficial Vanessa, and very, very difficult to know the creature beneath the glowing surface," said her sister-in-law Deirdre. "She's always been the same, never changed," said her friend Thelma Holt. "She's a mixture of a tornado, the daughter of the Empress of Russia, and the ideal stage manager."

Keeping up with her film and TV performances has always been a challenge. Her early career is strewn with hard-to-see TV episodes, shorts, and oddities, and though her choice of material is generally consistent, where and how she worked and for whom can seem quite nomadic and peculiar. Past 1990 or so, her work rate accelerated and became ever more random and wayward. The perilous excitement of Redgrave's acting career is that you never know where she will be next or how she will react to her opportunities. Through impatience or love of risk or sheer perversity, she might utterly fail in a major and worthy role, yet in the most unrewarding small parts she sometimes boldly clarifies all kinds of conflicting ideas all at once and lifts you out of your seat with her creative reach.

Her instinct is always to pick projects that might be of some socially conscious value, something that might improve us. She once said, in all seriousness, "I choose my roles carefully, so that when my career is finished I will have covered all our recent history of oppression." All of it! And she has certainly covered the waterfront in her work when it comes to oppressed people. Such a statement is more than a little comic, of course, but it is also moving. What other performer would say something like that in all seriousness? And what other performer could lighten such a heavy load of persecution and suffering on screen with spontaneous moments of naughty glee and gurgling laughter, with sudden shafts of light and gulps of air in the darkened places she led us into?

In one of her most characteristically unpredictable film performances of the 1960s, *Isadora* (1968), the thirty-year-old Redgrave unexpectedly excels in just the scenes that you would think might give her trouble, the scenes where her Isadora Duncan is older and campy and disillusioned, while in the young Isadora scenes, which seem ready-made for her brand of romanticism, she's rather awkward and flat. You can never tell with her what might activate her truly prodigious imagination.

Many of her colleagues have described how she brings a constant stream of ideas into rehearsal while she is working on a role, a lot of them inappropriate but some of them amazing. She can be very wild and stubborn and wrongheaded when she's creating a part. She can also hit notes and emotions that no one else would have dreamed of attempting. "I give myself up to my roles as to a lover," she told *Time* magazine in 1967. "And so I save myself for work, to lose myself in a role. It is the only way." At another moment, she described her instincts in life thusly: "It's a kinky part of my nature—to meddle."

The Redgrave family is often referred to as an acting dynasty, and Vanessa is the tallest, grandest tree in that particular forest of Redgraves, which runs from her grandfather Roy to her father Michael and her mother Rachel to her brother Corin and sister Lynn to her own daughters, Natasha and Joely Richardson, and her niece Jemma. "Literally all my family is in acting—well, some of the husbands are not, but all the actual family members are," she said in 1999. Magic runs through all the Redgraves, but it runs through Vanessa to an awe-inspiring degree. She is the star of this book, and her family will function as her extremely distinguished supporting cast.

There are times when, watching Vanessa at her best, it is possible to think that there has never been an actor as extravagantly gifted and expressive as she is, not even Marlon Brando. Like Brando, Redgrave is led by instinct. Her failures, like his, are in Mount Everest areas where most actors wouldn't even be able to breathe, let alone create. His instincts led him to renounce his profession for political activism in favor of the underdog and eventually led to self-indulgence and silence. Hers have led her to highly questionable political activity while she continued to practice her art at the highest possible level of skill and daring. "If there existed something like a dream in which a recipe was concocted to create an ideal actress, that dream would end with an entrance by Vanessa Redgrave," said Tennessee Williams.

Asked by Charlie Rose in 1995 if she was satisfied as an actress, she said, "Oh no, because any achievement you may make at any given time, or may know you have made, immediately you arrive at a new state or field. You then perceive whole other fields that you couldn't perceive until you'd arrived at that particular state." Redgrave has brought audiences up to fields and vistas that had never before been seen. "I'm lucky," she said. "When there's a difficult mountain to climb, I sometimes get chosen to make the climb. Growing up with Shakespeare, as I had to, you lived with the challenge of what drama can mean as a social experience for people, how important it can be." Meryl Streep, often called our greatest actress, disagrees with that assessment. She thinks that designation belongs to Redgrave and has referred to Redgrave's work as "the pinnacle."

This is a woman who, at the height of her early movie stardom in 1970 and 1971, decided to make *two* Italian 16mm features financed with her own money and directed by future exploitation director Tinto Brass. With her, you must always expect the unexpected. As time went on, the middle-aged and then elderly Redgrave would work constantly on stage in the greediest possible classical repertoire while doing cameos in socially conscious features, voice jobs and unconventional narrations, miniseries filmed in Russia, bit roles, and even leads in films shot in Argentina and Germany and Sweden that barely got a release of any kind anywhere, but her work is always worth the most adventurous search.

Redgrave's sheer lust for artistic activity can be overwhelming and it can lead to frustration and dead ends, but it can also lead to the discovery of obscured, forgotten, darkened worlds where she erects lighthouses of consciousness for us. This is an attempt to analyze, in part, why she did what she did, how she does what she does, and an examination of her lifelong hope that acting of the highest caliber might cause social or moral change.

# Michael:
# Mask or Face

I n his 1953 book on acting, *The Actor's Ways and Means*, Michael Redgrave emphasizes the difference between actors who merely play for effect and actors who search for the cause of that effect before producing it. He favored an intellectual approach to performing and was sometimes criticized for being overly brainy in the way he tackled his roles. His daughter Vanessa took a similarly intellectual approach to her own roles when she was preparing for them, doing all kinds of research beforehand; when the time came for performance, she would make a leap into the unknown and trust her instincts, whereas her father held on tight to his preconceptions. Michael, in his surviving acting work, can be guarded, careful, cautious, whereas his daughter Vanessa is forever throwing caution to the winds.

Michael's father Roy Redgrave and his mother Margaret Scudamore were both actors. The theater credentials of the Redgrave family went back as far as the mid-1800s when Cornelius Redgrave became a pub owner and theater ticket agent and scalper. Roy's mother Zoe Pym had been a popular stage actress, and Roy himself, known professionally as

"The Dramatic Cock o' the North," was a star name on stage and on film in Australia.

A charming rake and a drinker, Roy was a dab hand at stunts and a chronic womanizer with a continually untidy personal life. He married the wealthy actress Judith Kyrle in 1894, and she bore him three children, but Roy soon moved in with his mistress Ettie Carlisle. Afraid that she would be named in a divorce suit by the furious Kyrle, Carlisle left Roy and married the actor William Parrett, but Roy chased after her and won her back. The understanding Parrett divorced Carlisle while Kyrle divorced Roy in 1905, which temporarily cleared up the mess that Roy had made.

Roy did not marry Carlisle, but they cohabited and he got her pregnant in 1907. He also got Margaret Scudamore pregnant that same year while they were acting in a play called *Their Wedding Day*. Though he felt obligated to Carlisle, the feckless Roy found Scudamore's claim more persuasive. "I know I am not a saint but dear, with the right hand at the helm I can and will steer straight," he shakily promised her in a letter.

Michael was born six months after his parents married. Michael's son Corin thought that Michael may have been illegitimate and that Roy's marriage to Margaret might have been bigamous, and many Redgrave family members have repeated this untrue story through the years because they did not know about Kyrle's 1905 divorce decree from Roy.

In 1908, Roy and Margaret both received favorable reviews in *The Christian*, a play about a woman trying to lead her own independent life, but shortly thereafter the restless Roy went back to Australia, and his wife soon followed Roy to Australia with their son. "He preferred to be a big fish in a small pond," Scudamore said.

Michael made his debut in one of Roy's Australian outback melodramas, which sometimes featured live sheep. Watching Roy on stage, Michael toddled out and cried "Daddy!" Roy scooped the boy up, improvised some lines, and slowly brought his son back to Margaret's arms in the wings, which won vigorous applause from the audience. This is the only interaction Michael ever had with his father, a piece of impromptu business on the stage.

Soon fed up with Roy's drinking and philandering, Margaret brought her son back to England. Michael never saw Roy again. As a five-year-old boy, Michael watched his mother declaim, "My son—my son!" in a stage melodrama. This caused him to cry out, "*That's* not your son—*I'm* your son!" The audience laughed at his outburst, and the tearful Michael was given a box of chocolates by a theater attendant to console him.

Margaret played Lady Bracknell in a revival of Oscar Wilde's *The Importance of Being Earnest* and won some good notices, but Michael felt she overacted a little when she played in Shaw's *Arms and the Man*. A steady worker, Margaret, who considered herself a socialist, was never a star player in the theater. When Michael's son Corin saw Margaret on stage as an older woman, he thought she played too much in the grand manner and characterized her as a drunken bore off the stage. Though Michael suffered from her ill treatment of him, he wouldn't hear a word against his mother and refused to criticize her in his 1983 memoir *In My Mind's I*.

Pointedly, Margaret told her son Michael that a life in the theater was no life for a man, but he had an affinity for acting, or pretending, and he was helplessly drawn to the theater. She left him in the care of relatives and landladies while she toured, picking him up at the age of nine when she became the mistress of the well-off Captain James Anderson, a strict and stuffy tea planter. Margaret wanted to marry her Captain, but Roy never responded to her letters, so Margaret and Anderson lived together without benefit of a marriage license until Roy's death was reported in 1923, which finally allowed them to wed. Down in Australia, Roy had indeed committed bigamy in 1916, marrying Mary Leresche without bothering to get divorced from Margaret.

Michael rebelled against his stepfather's influence, and he struggled to lead his own life on close to his own terms. There were aspects of himself that would always remain repressed in his work, and this repression is partly what his best work was all about. Redgrave played female roles in plays at school, and he could always cry on cue, but later in life he would write that tears on stage are better left unshed if not called for in the text. He was always reining in his more emotional instincts on stage and in film and hoping to hide behind the distant majesty of his intellect.

Michael reached his full height of six feet three inches while at school, a seeming handicap which did not prevent him from scoring a triumph with his performance as Lady Macbeth, which impressed even the critical Margaret, who in her off-stage life was taking more and more to drink.

In his autobiography, there is a long section where Michael describes being drawn to one of his schoolmates, a painted boy who was obviously gay. Afraid of being thought effeminate like this boy, Redgrave wrote that he lost his virginity with a woman in front of a roaring fire. This woman was his mother's friend Margaret Chute, a thirty-nine-year-old journalist, but Michael's most romantic feelings were reserved for boys and men.

Though he was mainly gay, Michael's fear of gayness and shame over his desires meant that he often sought out women, too. When he was seventeen and attending Cambridge, Michael was involved in a two-year romance with a boy named Michael Garrett, and they were known as "The Two Ms" around campus. He befriended the openly gay Oliver Baldwin, the son of the British Prime Minister, and he also tried hard to love an older woman, Mary Coss.

A deep-dyed romantic, Michael was tormented and conflicted about his sexuality. "The two years I have been loving Michael G have not been wasted," he wrote in his diary. "They strengthened me for this most perfect love. My life has been so unbalanced sexually. This is now righted, I am certain. This purely physical sex, which I have so often enjoyed in my life, mostly with men, once with a woman, seems no trouble now, and, moreover, I trace it all to my failings." He proposed to Coss, but she turned him down.

Fear of seeming unmanly, and a desire to be financially independent of his stepfather, meant that Michael resisted acting for a bit and went in for more academic interests. "Too many people go into the theater for what they can get out of it, and not enough go for what they can put into it," Margaret told her son, a remark in favor of artistic selflessness that served as a model for the career of her granddaughter Vanessa.

Michael edited a magazine at school with Anthony Blunt and wrote experimental fragments of prose. He was a schoolmaster for three years at Cranleigh School in Surrey, where he acted in many school productions of Shakespeare before pursuing acting professionally. There would always be something of the schoolmaster in his approach to his craft, a quality that would aid his finest on-screen performance in *The Browning Version* (1951).

In 1935, while acting together in the Liverpool Repertory Company in John Van Druten's *Flowers of the Forest*, Redgrave met and quickly married the actress Rachel Kempson, and they stayed married for the whole of Michael's life, even though he told her outright that there were "difficulties" in his nature. Though she was a virgin and ignorant about sex, Rachel knew what he meant and decided to overlook it. She told him that his desires for men didn't matter to her because she loved him so much. Like many women in her situation at that time, Kempson at first thought she could help to change Redgrave's gayness.

As their nuptials approached, Michael was uneasy. "There were moments when I would have been only too glad to hear that the wedding had been called off," he said. "But I flunked the role of a jilter." Their wedding night was "a moderate success," as Rachel wrote later, but Michael remembered that he got drunk and fell asleep and only managed to consummate the marriage the morning after. Rachel's daughter Lynn said of her mother, "She was the most romantic person I ever knew—always full of romance. My father can be called either bisexual or gay—but he couldn't ever be called my mother's Romeo . . . he had this longing in his nature for something else."

At the start of his stage career, Redgrave had particular successes as Sir Andrew Aguecheek in *Twelfth Night*, as Tuzenbach in Chekhov's *Three Sisters*, and as Orlando opposite Edith Evans in *As You Like It*, all roles that suited his vulnerability, his youthful, slightly silly-looking beauty, and his romanticism. About the eccentric Evans, Redgrave wrote, "Edith always had a habit of falling in love with her leading man; with us, it just went rather further." He began a kind of love affair with Evans, and whatever the exact nature of their relationship, Redgrave fell first for her talent and for her Rosalind, exactly as Tony Richardson would fall in love with his daughter Vanessa's Rosalind in 1961.

Michael was always reproaching himself for his affairs with men and women. "I am shallow, selfish (horribly), jealous to a torturing degree, greedy, proud, and self-centered," he wrote to his friend John Lehmann.

"I have grasped at people's love and done vain and stupid things to get it; I am at times hideously immoral."

Redgrave carried on his affair with Evans while Rachel was pregnant with Vanessa. He also left her alone to go and seek out male partners at Turkish baths, which he told her about. Rachel often admitted that she lacked confidence in herself, and she meekly tolerated all of his varied philandering. "She understands so much, but there is so much to understand," Michael wrote broodingly in his diary. "She always felt very intimidated by my father, whom she worshipped," Vanessa said.

At a party in later life, Rachel reminisced with Noël Coward, who had been Michael's lover in the early years of their marriage. Coward said that he found Michael too charming to resist, and Rachel found that she couldn't help but agree with him. But there was more to Michael than just charm. In his sexual life with men, Michael would sometimes explore very dark areas, aided in his pursuit of sadomasochistic activity by copious amounts of alcohol. John Gielgud joked in a letter that Michael's theme song should be "Someday I'll bind you/Both hands behind you."

Michael would often confess his feelings of love for certain men to Rachel, and she would listen attentively and comfort him as best she could. She liked that she was his confidante. "It's silly, but I feel quite happy about it," she told him once, when he had unburdened himself to her. But these confidences also took a toll on her, and she occasionally didn't like some of his boyfriends, especially Tony Hyndman, a left-wing hedonist and former lover of poet Stephen Spender who was always borrowing money from them and not paying it back.

Their youngest daughter Lynn thought that her father's affairs must have made her mother very unhappy, and she felt that her mother was a saint for putting up with him. Michael did not tell Rachel about his affair with Edith Evans until a biography of Evans was about to be published, and her response was that it was "very wonderful to have been in love with and loved by the greatest actress of our time." In the Redgrave household, talent was the most seductive thing, and talent could also justify just about any behavior.

In the late 1940s, the neglected Rachel took on the actor Leo Genn as a lover, and she later had a steady lover of her own, the married actor Glen

Byam Shaw. "Michael, being tolerant in these matters, was understanding and in a sense relieved," Rachel said. Whenever Rachel would broach the idea of a separation, Michael would become so upset that she would have to comfort him for a week. However unhappy they were at times, Michael needed the stability she provided, and the front of heterosexual respectability. "They had a long marriage, but they had a difficult marriage," their daughter Lynn said. "The difficulty took over and did shut her out."

Michael was a furtive, self-regarding, divided person, yet in his first film, Alfred Hitchcock's *The Lady Vanishes* (1938), he showed that he could summon all the magnetic charm and cute arrogance of Cary Grant if he wanted to. As a musicologist who playfully elects to help lady-in-distress Margaret Lockwood, Redgrave wears a mustache and is bright and quicksilver in his amused handling of his funny dialogue, giving a thoroughly charming performance of a kind of movie dream man who is always up for fun and resourceful in a pinch.

If Redgrave had never done anything else but *The Lady Vanishes*, he would be remembered for it. Though he professed that he was not at ease with Hitchcock's purely technical way of working, it's a shame that he never worked for him again, in *Rope* (1948), say, or *Spellbound* (1945), both of which might have benefited from his light touch.

Redgrave followed his Hitchcock debut with a slapstick farce for Carol Reed, *Climbing High* (1938), where Alastair Sim plays a Communist revolutionary who says "We don't recognize sex in the party." The following year, Redgrave supported the German diva Elisabeth Bergner in *Stolen Life* (1939) and worked again for Reed in *The Stars Look Down* (1940), a film based on an A. J. Cronin novel. In that uneasy movie, Redgrave played Davey, a passionate young intellectual from a mining community who comes out against private ownership of the mines. At one point, Reed cuts to a miner looking on with distaste at one of Davey's showboating political speeches, and the film seems to be saying that Davey's political dramatics look and sound impressive but actually get very little done on a practical level.

*The Stars Look Down* and Redgrave's performance in it made for an ominous harbinger of what the Redgrave family came to stand for politically. In her 1994 memoir, Vanessa does not see the critical side of *The*

*Stars Look Down* in relation to her father's character Davey. To her, it is a story about the miners' struggle against corrupt owners, and that is all.

Michael continued to work on stage, playing Macheath in a production of *The Beggar's Opera* in 1940. In a film of his stage success *Thunder Rock* (1942), Redgrave is briefly overshadowed in the first scenes by a young James Mason, and he can do nothing to transcend the limited play, in which immigrant ghosts come to haunt him.

Redgrave had a success in *Uncle Harry* on stage, and in 1945 he made the anthology movie *Dead of Night*, playing a tormented ventriloquist in the last of its macabre tales. "Some people seem to think this is my best film," he writes in his first memoir, but nothing can touch *The Lady Vanishes* as a film, and his best performance on film is almost certainly *The Browning Version*.

He's a bit overdone in his first scenes in *Dead of Night* (too much under-motivated widening of his eyes), but as the story proceeds, and we take in the demented relationship he has with his dummy Hugo (who may or may not be actually alive), Redgrave's possessed neuroticism makes an unnerving impression, especially when he lets out a long gasp and practically crawls up a wall when Hugo is placed in his prison cell. It's the kind of performance that carries on the tradition of German Expressionist acting, especially when he smothers Hugo and gets very close to the heightened romantic pitch of Conrad Veidt circa 1921 or so. Barely suppressed nervous tension was Redgrave's specialty as an actor, at least on screen.

In the 1940s he made a lot of war films, and he served in the war himself, spending his last night before service with Noël Coward, much to Rachel's chagrin. He acted with Rachel in a film called *The Captive Heart* (1946), where he played a Czech prisoner of war who assumes the identity of a dead British soldier and writes to the soldier's wife, played by Rachel. Her character is surprised to get his loving letters because her marriage had been on the rocks. "Is it too late to recapture the happiness of our first years together?" she wonders, as their exchange of letters gets more intimate and loving. Rachel looks very stiff-upper-lip and refined at first, but as the film goes on she reveals the passion behind this woman's polite exterior. She's particularly fine and truthful in the last scene, when

Redgrave comes to visit her in the flesh. The climax of this film makes it clear that Vanessa didn't inherit her talent only from her father.

After the war, Redgrave made an attempt on Hollywood, but the two films he made there, an adaptation of Eugene O'Neill's *Mourning Becomes Electra* (1947) and Fritz Lang's *Secret Beyond the Door* (1947), were both arty failures. In the O'Neill adaptation, Redgrave joins in a kind of overacting contest with Rosalind Russell and Katina Paxinou, but he can't keep up with their relentless posturing. In *Secret*, he gave himself over to one of the most outlandish stories Lang ever put on screen.

As Crocker-Harris, or "The Crock," a despised schoolmaster who starts to come apart at the seams in *The Browning Version*, Redgrave gives a faultless, virtuoso performance, serving up the perfect blend of technique and emotion in a two-faced role. Crocker-Harris is a man who has had to hide a large part of himself for years, something that both Redgrave and gay playwright Terence Rattigan intimately understood. He speaks in a high, precise voice that is easily mocked by his students. Due to heart trouble, he is being forced into retirement, and he learns that he will not be receiving a pension, which enrages his straying, unhappily shrewish wife Millie (Jean Kent).

All the people around this married couple judge them only by appearances. They wonder why the attractive Millie wound up married to "The Crock," who is referred to as a man who is "dead" by nearly everyone who knows him. Only the sensitive student Taplow (Brian Smith) feels any sympathy for Crocker-Harris, and the combination of Taplow's sympathy and all the other pressures in his life brings this man to the breaking point. There is tremendous nervous tension in Redgrave's voice and especially in his hands as Crocker-Harris begins to collapse and open up.

In one extraordinary scene, the incoming teacher Gilbert (Ronald Howard) carelessly tells Crocker-Harris that some of his boys call him "The Himmler of the Lower Fifth," and when he hears this, the retiring schoolteacher immediately begins to panic. At first he can't remember who Himmler was, and then he chokes out, "Oh, yes, the Gestapo chief," at which point Redgrave takes off on an accelerated downward slope toward this man's long-delayed self-knowledge.

As he walks around his deserted classroom, Crocker-Harris quickly and helplessly talks about how he started out as a young teacher wanting to do his job well, but with the years, he fell into a self-parody or performance of himself as a prim but tough martinet so that the boys, most of whom were "unfeeling," could laugh at him and maybe learn something through laughter. With time, he says, he took this self-parody much too far until it hardened him into the rather awful, joyless teacher we have seen in the earlier classroom scenes.

As he hits each of these gongs of recognition, Redgrave gives us the sense that Crocker-Harris is being made to realize all at once his utter failure as a teacher and as a man. When he sits down and finally jams his hands under his spectacles to rub his eyes, the effect is like a singer finishing a riskily sung aria with a gratifying high C.

After Taplow brings him a gift of his Robert Browning translation of Aeschylus's *Agamemnon*, which they had discussed earlier, Crocker-Harris is so grateful for this bit of kindness that he breaks down and weeps, a pitiable sight, and exactly rendered by Redgrave. He might have rejected how easily he was able to cry on cue, but by 1951 he is able to select just the right *kind* of crying for this proud but now spent and broken man.

Millie spoils Taplow's gesture for her husband, telling him that the boy most likely just wants to insure a promotion in school, at which point she's in danger of becoming merely a villain until Rattigan has Crocker-Harris explain the disaster of their marriage from her side. He was unable to give her the physical love she needed, he tells Gilbert, and he takes himself to task yet again, from an even more personal angle, until he tells the new schoolmaster that this isn't all so serious: "It is usually, I believe, a subject for farce," he finally says gamely, an annihilatingly sad but thrilling moment of total objectivity.

Crocker-Harris realizes that he has nearly become the part he had started to play as a tactic in the classroom, and in his valedictory speech to the school he asks for forgiveness for his failure. "I will not find it so easy to forgive myself," he says. This is one of the great film performances and a precious record of Redgrave's rare skill and intelligence as an actor. It feels like Redgrave is revealing all of himself and his repressions and self-doubt in this role while still keeping safe behind the cloak of "characterization."

This is not the kind of performance Vanessa was ever interested in giving. If she had been given a role like this, she would have made it wilder, more reckless, more exposed. Her father, great as he is and can be, keeps the audience at a distance. Vanessa will always reach out to us with those long fingers of hers, hoping and praying that we understand what she's trying to give us and tell us. Michael hides and keeps himself protected while sending us signals of pure agony. Vanessa shows all of herself and is capable of pure joy and pure grief and risks our very worst response in return.

In the 1952 movie of *The Importance of Being Earnest*, which captured Edith Evans's definitive Lady Bracknell, Redgrave relies too much on his voice and indicates most of his emotions. He was retreating into a realm of unemotional technique, and in the films that followed, his delivery of lines became increasingly stagy, especially in an adaptation of George Orwell's *1984* (1956) where he played General O'Connor.

In Orson Welles's *Mr. Arkadin* (1955), Redgrave wore a hairnet and indulged himself with a campy accent. In this grotesquely enjoyable bit of character work, it's possible to see the genesis of his daughter Lynn's comic stylings, particularly her housekeeper in *Gods and Monsters* (1998). There were a few more unrewarding war films for Redgrave, but one of them inspired an immortal quip. When Noël Coward saw a poster that read, "Michael Redgrave and Dirk Bogarde in *The Sea Shall Not Have Them*," he turned to his friends and said, "I don't see why not—everyone else has."

Redgrave played the lead in Joseph Losey's hysterical *Time Without Pity* (1957), and at this point his nervous tension began to seem miscalculated and uncontrolled, the first signs of the Parkinson's disease which would rob him of many years of his career. There were other issues now, too. "Redgrave is a great actor," said Losey. "And I like him immensely, personally. And his gifts are more than acting: he's an intellectual, a poet, a literary man, an innovator in the theatre. But he's completely destroyed by alcohol. And even at that time there were one or two days when he was actually alcoholic. It was a big problem." Redgrave's character in *Time Without Pity* was also an alcoholic, and when playing the drunk scenes, he abstained from liquor. "One of the remarkable things about him," Losey said, "and this is something every actor will understand and agree with, is that he never ever drank while he was playing a drunk."

He made a decent stab at the role of Thomas Fowler in an adaptation of Graham Greene's *The Quiet American* (1958), but after that, he mainly played small parts in films and withdrew slowly and reluctantly from the stage. His movie career is disappointing, on the whole. Illness and drink and the wrong collaborators stymied the movie-star aplomb he showed in *The Lady Vanishes* and the tragic depth he displayed in *The Browning Version*. The career of his oldest daughter Vanessa would be just as embattled as his, at times even more so, but she has been able to stick to it longer than he could, and her record now practically speaks for itself.

# Vanessa:
# A Great Actress is Born

The story was told often by Vanessa's mother Rachel, and it might even be true. Michael was playing Laertes to Laurence Olivier's Hamlet at the Old Vic on the snowy night of January 30, 1937. While they were fighting a duel, someone signaled to Michael from the wings and said, "It's a girl." At the curtain call, Olivier stepped forward and supposedly said, "Ladies and gentlemen, tonight a great actress has been born." How's that for an entrance into both the world and the profession?

"I think it's true," Vanessa said. "My mother says it's true, but my mother wasn't there because she was giving birth to me. All of the stories come from the people who were in the company at the time, that there were actors in the wings signaling boy, girl, this, that. And I think it's very typical of Larry Olivier that he'd say some extravagant, warm-hearted thing for Michael. They certainly fought the fastest duel Hamlet and Laertes have ever fought."

Olivier always had a sense of occasion for moments like this, whereas Michael lacked this sort of showmanship. Olivier himself never worked with Vanessa on stage, though he acted in three of her films, *The Seven-Per-Cent Solution* (1976), *Wagner* (1983), and *Peter the Great* (1986), but not in scenes with her. He gets points for prescience, of course, and surely as Olivier watched Michael's children bloom he might have looked on with some envy at the idea of a theatrical dynasty. Why not have some daughters for the theater who can be ready-made Cordelias and Gonerils for your Lear? (Vanessa did play Cordelia to Michael's King Lear in a scene for her second documentary, *Vanessa Talks with Farouk Abdul-Aziz* {1978}, and for one benefit performance in the early 1980s). Vanessa was named, at Michael's whim, after painter Vanessa Bell, the sister of Virginia Woolf.

Vanessa's first memory was of an air raid in 1940 and how her mother sang a lullaby to soothe her and her younger brother Corin. The children were soon evacuated to the country, where they stayed with Lucy Wedgwood Kempson, a cousin of their grandfather Eric Kempson. In November of 1940, Vanessa saw the firebombing of the city of Coventry, which killed more than two thousand people, and she has often said that this was the decisive moment in her life. For years she had nightmares about large fires coming and no way of warning people or getting them to safety.

"To actually see a whole city in flames is very traumatic," she said. In a way, as an actress and also in her political work, she has been trying to warn people about that fire ever since. For a sensitive girl like Vanessa, it was a spur, something to never forget, and she has returned to the memory of it again and again in interviews.

From Grandpa Eric, who considered himself a socialist, she heard theories that everyone should have to work. Michael had for a while been a socialist too, even "a red-hot socialist," as he told the *Liverpool Echo* in his first season at the Old Vic: "I believe in everything to do with socialism."

"My father was a very idealistic man, and he had some bitter political experiences that made him draw away, in his idealistic youth," Vanessa said. "The Communist Party of Great Britain had some policies he was asked to sign in support of, as a famous young film star. But he was deceived as to what was actually going on. He went to Communist Party members to ask them to explain, but none of them would, which was characteristic of all the Communist parties . . . it came out of being betrayed as a human being, basically. I was able to inherit a situation in which all the things his generation were deprived of knowing . . . so many of them lost their lives in Stalin's regime and the totalitarianism of Eastern Europe."

What happened was that Michael signed a peace manifesto by the People's Convention, a party that believed that Winston Churchill was as bad as Nazi Germany. He wasn't made fully aware of their position, and he deeply regretted signing the manifesto, which briefly got him banned from working on BBC radio. Churchill himself raised the ban on Redgrave and the other actors who had signed, telling the BBC that they had no right to blacklist performers.

Vanessa began doing a lot of playing and acting out as a little girl, to entertain herself. "I began acting when I was six," she said. "During the war, there wasn't anything my brother and I could do, generally speaking, because we were in the country and we were evacuated. There was a radio show once a week that we listened to, and we used to listen to the news every day. And I used to read, because I learned to read when I was four, so I could read a lot. So what we used to do was play, and really, acting at that point was pretending to have what you haven't got."

Michael remembered that the first character the young Vanessa created was a lady named "Queen Pretoria." To Edith Evans, Michael wrote, "Vanessa grows more and more enchanting. She talks a great deal now, seems to forget nothing she has ever heard." Put outside to play by herself, Vanessa would knock on the window and want to come in and join the adults. "She wanted to go to the nursery and cried a little at being told to stay in the garden," Michael wrote in his diary. "Any attempt to compromise brings on a real temperamental fit of tears." Like her father as a boy, Vanessa wanted attention and often didn't get it. She was raised mainly by nannies, just as Michael was raised mainly by family friends. This perhaps partly explains their intense need for the spotlight on the stage.

"Later on it was possible to see my father in plays, mainly in Shakespeare," Vanessa said. "So my conception of acting was being able to take part in the recreation of great events, even though at that time I was very far from taking part in any great events at all. I always took it for granted that I would act, or I would dance, because my family had acted for generations and generations, so it never occurred to me that I would do anything else."

In 1943 the children were returned to London, and Vanessa came down with scarlet fever. She was taken to a hospital to convalesce, and while there she was comforted by a girl who taught her Cockney rhyming slang and sang "The White Cliffs of Dover" to her, a tale that Vanessa tells in full in Henry Jaglom's film *Déjà Vu* (1997). She soon recovered, and as an adolescent she shot up almost overnight to five feet eleven inches and kept on growing, but she still seriously pursued the idea of becoming a ballet dancer.

Vanessa knew that she was already too tall to be a prima ballerina, but she hoped that she might still pass muster in the back row of the corps de ballet. There's a photograph of Michael holding one of Vanessa's arms as she dances *en pointe*, and her unformed little face looks miserably unhappy to be on top of such an enormously large woman's body.

She really fell in love with the theater at the age of eight when she was taken to see *Cinderella* and when she saw Michael in a play called *The Duke of Darkness*. Before the performance, he took her backstage to show her where his dead body would be flung after his character was killed so that she would know it was all make-believe and wouldn't be scared.

While she was playacting with her beloved younger brother Corin, Vanessa was also developing her social conscience. In 1944, she read about children who were evacuated from their homes and forced into child labor on farms. One story struck her particularly hard. Two boys named Neil and Terry were so hungry on one of these farms that they went into a field one night to scrape up some turnips to eat, and the farmer found them and beat them so badly that Neil, the elder boy, died. This story made such an impression on Redgrave that she recounts it in detail in her autobiography.

From a place of privilege, Redgrave's sympathy and her imagination were always reaching out to the less fortunate, and she wanted to be a witness to their suffering and to try to change conditions that caused such suffering in any way that she could. At the ages of ten and eight, Vanessa and her brother Corin were already developing political opinions. "Corin and Vanessa now rail against [Prime Minister] Attlee and come out with streams of statistics and generally appear to know almost more than any of us about the whole situation," Rachel wrote to Michael.

Vanessa had poor eyesight as a child, and she wouldn't get contact lenses until she was well into adulthood. There is a sense, in some of her early performances, that she is lost in a kind of blur, and this added to the feeling that she was somehow set apart, or not like other people. Her dancing teacher Madame Rambert told her that she was a tight little rosebud, but that she was beginning to open.

Speaking of her time in dancing class, Redgrave said, "I learned to continue when you feel you cannot continue, because in classical ballet, the training is very rigorous, it's very repetitive, and you need energy. You have to repeat things many, many times. And just at the point when you have repeated perhaps forty times a very strenuous exercise, we would have to repeat that another forty times. And you discover, and I learned then, that you can do what you think you can't do, and that in trying to do it, you create the conditions for your body to be able to do it. So this was the first and most important lesson I learned, as well as the discipline of doing it whether you felt like doing it or not. And I found this discipline very valuable, particularly when I went into the theater, to allow myself to not be dominated by my own moods or by anybody else's moods. How to carry out, quietly, calmly, urgently, what you have to do."

It was in Madame Rambert's class that Redgrave learned how to move in space and how to make her first decided gestures with those limitlessly long arms and legs that would prove such assets to her later work. Audrey Hepburn, who was just breaking into films at that point, was in Redgrave's ballet class. By the time Redgrave herself became a star in movies, Hepburn's movie career was nearly over, for Hepburn was a creature of the 1950s whereas Redgrave only came into her own in the radical '60s.

"The great contemporary dance companies from America hadn't come over at that time," Redgrave said. "I didn't realize there was such a thing as contemporary dance, and anyway, my dream was to wear a tutu and dance in *Swan Lake*."

She was a bluestocking who read a lot and felt a lot, and it took a while for her to bloom. Her brother Corin claimed in his 1995 memoir that she saved a girl from drowning around this time, a first signal of her lifelong urge to help others, but the actual story was far stranger. Vanessa said in an early interview that she wanted to prove her courage and got it into her head that she should save someone from drowning. She waited all summer, staring out at the water by the family cottage. Finally, she spotted a man who needed help and raced out and pulled him in. He didn't thank her or even say anything to her.

As an adolescent in 1950, Vanessa went to a dance in a blue-and-green silk skirt, a blue velvet bodice, and a blue-and-green stole. She and a similarly dressed friend were taken aback when they saw the other girls in sweaters and tight skirts, dancing to bebop. Vanessa stood there all evening and no one asked her to dance. She was an outsider, or like someone from another time, an Alice Adams trembling with hope that some discerning person might notice her specialness.

Whenever she would look particularly discouraged, her mother Rachel would always exclaim, "Oh, my beautiful daughter!" to buck up her spirits. When Vanessa couldn't see her head in a mirror, she burst into tears over being too tall, and Michael came into the room to comfort her. "Don't worry about being too tall, Van," he told her. "Hold yourself up and be severe, demanding, and splendid."

Such key encouragement aside, Vanessa, Corin, and their younger sister Lynn grew up missing their father and mother. "My parents and I didn't see a lot of each other when I was young," Redgrave said. "When it did happen, it was a very fleeting couple of hours. That, in part, produces an immense anxiety, but perhaps also it produces an immense appreciation of the moments which come."

Walt Disney asked for Vanessa's photograph because he was thinking of doing a live-action version of *Alice in Wonderland*, and he was pleased with what he saw. With her large eyes and long, straight hair, Redgrave did look like the Alice in Tenniel's drawings, and Disney requested that she be sent to Hollywood for a screen test. Around this time, however, Redgrave began having blackouts and fainting spells, and so she wasn't allowed to go.

At the age of fourteen, at Queen's Gate School, Redgrave persuaded her parents to let her cut her hair short so that she would look right to play Shaw's *Saint Joan* for a production at school. The photographer Angus McBean took a picture of the teenage Redgrave as Saint Joan for a magazine article, laying the groundwork for her entrance into the family profession. They did three performances of *Saint Joan*, and the morning after the last performance, the headmistress of the school warned everyone that they should be glad for the success of the school play but should not lionize any particular pupil.

No doubt Redgrave made a glowingly convincing Saint Joan, even at fourteen, enough to make a headmistress worry about heroine worship. Later on, her younger sister Lynn would say that Vanessa always identified with Saint Joan. Lynn said that there was always "a bit of the touch of the martyr" about Vanessa, and this would have both good and bad consequences in her art and her life. The role of Saint Joan ran in the family, for Vanessa remembered Rachel's attempt at the part in 1954 as very moving and focused, and she would see echoes of it when Lynn played the role in 1977 with the same kind of courage and straightforwardness. Vanessa herself never did a major production of the play, but Shaw's Saint Joan had been assimilated into her attitude toward life.

In 1951 at Stratford-upon-Avon, Michael played *Richard II*, Hotspur in *Henry IV, Part I*, the Chorus in *Henry V*, and Prospero in *The Tempest*, and he also directed *Henry IV, Part II*. Vanessa thought Michael was happier during that season than at any other time in his life, and she was so carried away by excitement on the way to see his dress rehearsal in *Richard II* that she grabbed Corin's green school cap and flung it out of the car. "*What* did you do that for?" asked their mother Rachel, who was hardly ever angry with her children. It feels now like a very Vanessa thing to do, a gesture of celebration and abandonment, a gesture toward freedom, or casting off the shackles.

She was deeply impressed by Michael's Richard II, a difficult part that suited both his vulnerability and his ability to see the various roles he played in life and on stage from an objective standpoint. Redgrave also loved his golden hair and golden beard, how his Richard II glistened on the stage. She thought that his performance had an intimate understanding of betrayal and was backed by his historical knowledge of the way absolute monarchy was coming to an end.

Michael approached his roles intellectually, and he was one of the first British actors to speak about and use Stanislavsky's teachings at a time when Olivier and Gielgud and others of that generation were starting to make unfavorable comments about The Method in the press. He was reproached first by James Agate and then by Kenneth Tynan for playing his roles too much with his brain and not enough with his heart, and Vanessa, in her memoir, thinks that Tynan was just repeating a received opinion from Agate.

She later defended her father's Hamlet: "Perhaps it never occurred to those critics that only an actor who can think can also feel to the extent demanded by Shakespeare's tragedies and histories," she said, "and moreover without any distortion to Shakespeare's blank verse." She thought Michael unequaled in *Hamlet, King Lear,* and *Antony and Cleopatra,* and though perhaps she may have been a bit blinded by a daughter's love, there is no reason not to take her word for it. She herself would prove the great Rosalind of her generation after her father had been Orlando and had loved Edith Evans, the great Rosalind of his generation. The achievements of the Redgrave family in classical theater are almost always connected by tradition, and these are vital connections that feed and nourish each other.

Vanessa attended a dress rehearsal of her father's Hamlet. "When he heard from the ghost that his father had been killed," Vanessa said, "and how he'd been murdered, I froze with anguish and belief that this had happened, that this man, who I now suddenly didn't know, had had this dreadful news. That is my favorite Shakespeare moment, if we're talking about theater." Watching her husband play Hamlet, Rachel later said that she felt all of his personal suffering shining forth on stage, and she was able to feel closer to him after that, and to forgive him his trespasses.

Michael and Vanessa both shared a tendency to neurasthenia while performing that needed to be fought off at various points. With her brother Corin, she watched her father's dress rehearsal for *Antony and Cleopatra* and was alarmed when Michael forgot every other line. She herself wondered if she could remember any of her lines during her mid-1960s run on stage in *The Prime of Miss Jean Brodie,* and only technique got her through. Similarly, Rachel had had a panic attack while playing *The School for Scandal* in 1937, forgetting her lines and where she was for a spell, an episode that had further dented her confidence.

Michael had been having difficulty memorizing the part, and he asked advice from Olivier, which was not a good idea. Unable to resist prodding a rival who was in trouble, Olivier said he was surprised and said that, for himself, memorizing Antony had been easy. After the scare of this dress rehearsal, Michael went on the next night and gave a definitive performance, according to Vanessa. The physical limitations of Parkinson's disease restricted his career as Michael got older, but he fought against this valiantly. As an older man, doing Shakespeare recitations, he was still capable of enthralling his daughter with the resonance of his voice and his phrasing.

At fifteen, Vanessa went abroad to Italy with her schoolfriend Tasha and fell in love with the country. When she talked to an Italian soldier at a frontier station, he unexpectedly kissed her, and this speeded her transformation from moth into butterfly. She drank in all the beauty of Italy and feasted on the Italian food after a childhood of tasteless English boiled beef and watery boiled potatoes. An older man whose mother cooked them pastries looked at Vanessa and said, "Sweets for the sweet," and she was charmed by that. A sheltered girl was starting to come to life and feel its possibilities.

Back at Queen's Gate School, Vanessa studied poetry and talked with her friends about T. S. Eliot and Ezra Pound, and her literary contribution to the school magazine had a morbid turn: "As the sun disappears, its last glow fading from the villa, I see Death appear, embodied in this house." She went back to Italy and lived with a family in Tuscany for a summer, where she learned Italian and learned to idolize Garibaldi, whom she compared later, in one of the most reckless passages in her memoir, to Palestine Liberation Organization leader Yasser Arafat.

Redgrave took singing lessons from Jani Strasser, who had coached Michael when he needed help with the role of Macheath in *The Beggar's Opera*, and he taught her not to listen to the sounds she made. "If you listen to the sound, you start correcting the sound," he told her, and he coached her to never plan the way she would sing or say a line.

Strasser's influence on Redgrave and her first stage success as Rosalind in *As You Like It* was decisive and long-lasting. He shepherded and molded her into the most spontaneous of actresses, so in-the-moment that she would have to trust everything to her talent and her instincts. Redgrave learned to distrust instant results and the kind of technical expertise that can produce something expected in a short period of time. She felt that the real work of acting was letting go, or letting loose, and the passage where she writes about this in her memoir is right next to a radiant photo of her 1961 Rosalind, smiling and dancing and seemingly airborne, drunk on poetry and romantic exaltation.

Though he had doubts at first about her succeeding as an actress because of her height, Michael soon wanted Vanessa to study singing and dancing so that she might be able to go into musical comedy. It was a musical household, where all the Redgraves would often gather around the piano while Michael played through Schubert songs, Noël Coward tunes, and their favorite, "The Trolley Song."

Vanessa longed to see America, picturing it as the country of Danny Kaye, Betty Grable, and Ethel Merman, whose records she listened to over and over again, but she was most impressed with what she had seen at Stratford-upon-Avon and particularly with the work of Peggy Ashcroft, and so she stayed at home and auditioned to get into the Central School of Speech and Drama. The principal of the school, Gwyneth Thurburn, told Vanessa not to expect any kind of regular employment in the theater until she was in her thirties due to her extreme tallness, and she accepted that as her fate.

In January of 1955, Redgrave began her first classes at the Central School. She did hours of voice lessons with a whale bone clamped between her teeth, and began to grow nervous over the school's emphasis on technique alone. The movement classes were old-fashioned affairs where she was made to pretend she had a teacup in her hand, the polar opposite of what was happening in America, where Lee Strasberg had his students drinking a cup of imaginary coffee until they could taste every bit of it.

Animal exercises, which are now standard in acting classes, were shunned at the Central School as distastefully experimental. Michael had advised her not to go to drama school, and he was probably worried that she would acquire only outmoded techniques that might impair her burgeoning creativity. Vanessa was enthusiastic about her training, but she also knew that something was missing from the teaching she was getting at the Central School. Fellow students remembered her as awkward, disorganized, and rebellious.

Michael sent Vanessa to a performance of *Richard II* done by the Theatre Workshop, a new company that presented the play in a realistic, stripped-down manner. Her head filled with what she was learning at the Central School, Vanessa returned home outraged, and when her father asked her what she had thought of the production, she let out a tirade against it. A pained Michael told her to never go to a production with expectations of what it should be. He told her to focus first on what the production was trying to accomplish before describing its failures. It was a lesson in sensitivity and objectivity, a message against prejudice and closed-mindedness that Vanessa took fully to heart.

Michael was fond of repeating the words of Ellen Terry, one of Vanessa's heroines, who had pledged always to be "a useful actress," and that became Vanessa's credo as well. All of Vanessa's background was incomparably fertile soil for the making of a great and useful actress, and now she received a much-needed jolt from America when Michael had her come over to New York for three weeks when he was playing in Harold Clurman's production of Jean Giraudoux's *Tiger at the Gates*. While there, she saw Arthur Miller's *A View from the Bridge* and Julie Harris in *The Lark*, and she attended classes at the Actors Studio for a week.

Observing these Actors Studio classes, Redgrave instinctively felt the wrongness of what Lee Strasberg was teaching when she watched an actress concentrating on her own feelings of fear rather than imagining the given circumstances of the scene she was playing. When she asked Strasberg about this, he told her that the actress's own feelings were the most important element on stage. Redgrave was not convinced by this, but she admired the fact that Strasberg was not interested only in repetition and the acquiring of technique.

Unsatisfied with the extremes of the Central School and the Actors Studio under Strasberg, Redgrave began to formulate her own path. The Central School gave her some technique, and Michael's teaching gave her the fundamentals of the Stanislavsky Method, and she fused these tools into her own imaginative brand of acting, the kind of imaginative work based in research and emotional truth that was the backbone of what Stella Adler had taught to Marlon Brando and all of her own students of that era.

Back at the Central School in 1956, Redgrave founded a quarterly magazine about acting called *Encore* with her friend Clive Goodwin, and she discovered Stanislavsky's book *An Actor Prepares* on her own. Already searching for dogma, when she had finished that book Vanessa raced to Central and exclaimed to everyone, "It's all here! IT'S ALL HERE!" only to be met with condescending indifference by the staff.

She attended a lecture in which Arthur Miller, flanked by his wife Marilyn Monroe, said that the English theater was based too much on the assumptions of English middle-class life and neglected the real problems in society. This was the time when the Angry Young Man kitchen-sink plays started to make their noise on the English stage, and the first such play, John Osborne's *Look Back in Anger*, would be directed by the man who would become Redgrave's first husband, Tony Richardson. Redgrave recognized the limitations of *Look Back in Anger*, but she loved its sense of rebellion and its humor.

This was also the year when Peter Hall's production of Samuel Beckett's *Waiting for Godot* made its first appearance on the English-speaking stage, and the Bolshoi Ballet made their first London visit—Vanessa and her fellow students waited all night at Covent Garden to be the first in line in the morning for tickets to the ballet. With her mother Rachel, a young Vanessa made a silent appearance on the television series *Men, Women, and Clothes: Sense and Nonsense in Fashion* (a program that also featured a young Benny Hill), and she continued to study at Central.

In October of 1956, Vanessa's full attention fell on the developments of the Hungarian revolution, and she left Central to volunteer to sort and pack clothes for Hungarian refugees who were fleeing across the Austrian border. "I said to my parents, I can't go on studying *acting* when people are being crushed by Soviet tanks," she remembered. She worked all day and night at this activity, but felt that she could do more. "I felt very inadequate, needless to say, and I didn't know Hungarian, but I did learn an awful lot from that," she said. "I couldn't understand why the West hadn't intervened. What did we have any weapons for, or politics for, or politicians for? Why not to help these Hungarian people?" She could do little for them, but she wanted to give them "my eyes, and the warmth of my hands, and a cup of tea." Redgrave was out of place at this refugee shelter, certainly, but it was a gesture, and of such gestures would her political life be made.

Walking home and staring at the Christmas decorations in Knightsbridge and Kensington, Redgrave felt the gap between her own country and class and what was happening to the people of Hungary. When the Hungarian revolution was crushed by the Soviet Union, Redgrave felt discouragement both at what had happened and at her own limited knowledge of world affairs.

Her social consciousness was one more decisive trait that set Vanessa apart from her fellow students and from her father. Michael had been politically active in his youth, even recording a song for the Workers' Music Association called "A New World Will Be Born," but he was forced into political caution after signing his name to the People's Convention manifesto. Vanessa would take her father's yearning for political action much further than he could have ever dreamed. Speaking about the radical leftism of Vanessa and her brother Corin in the 1970s, Michael said, "I do not understand their politics, but I like the revolutionary flavor."

After three years of study, Vanessa graduated from Central alongside classmate Judi Dench. In their first year, they had been made to share a costume when both were playing Portia in *The Merchant of Venice*, which made them laugh because Dench was just over five feet tall. Vanessa envied Dench's ease and vivacity on stage and in life. Next to Dench and some of the other free-living students, Redgrave felt unattractive and old-fashioned, but she found the necessary confidence when it mattered most. The graduating students performed in a public matinee for producers and agents on June 5, 1957, a sink-or-swim situation where Vanessa's principal role was as a forty-five-year-old society mother.

Redgrave rented a white wig for the occasion. Before going on, she put her head on a towel and put her feet up above her head, a trick to increase circulation of blood to the brain. She got up and jogged a bit from foot to foot and let her long arms and neck go limp, in the tradition of most actors from this era forward. Then she took a deep breath, grasped a door handle, exclaimed her entrance line, and took the stage with such boldness that she won the Sybil Thorndike prize and eventually got a job in rep at the Frinton Summer Theatre playing a raft of elderly ladies in commercial comedies.

When Corin saw her in one of these plays, he was impressed, telling her that he hadn't known that she could be funny. From a very early age, she had a reputation for high seriousness. "Vanessa is great on gravity," Michael said. In Robert Beulah's portrait of her as a little girl, she looks severe, almost cross. "Gravity can be mistaken for severity," he observed, trying to make a distinction for her. He thought that Vanessa had inherited her joyous smile from her mother Rachel.

"I was told very early on and then later on in my life that I had a gift, and I kind of resisted that idea," Vanessa said. But eventually she saw that she was "born with a gift, and whether you develop that gift and really work on it or not is partly up to finance, partly up to encouragement, and partly what gets born in yourself, a desire to develop."

Her father guided her carefully. "He trained me, but I didn't realize it at the time that he was training me," Vanessa said. "He worshipped her talent as if it had nothing to do with his own—and yet he was always very watchful and objective," observed her brother Corin.

# Rosalind and Tony

n 1958, Michael secured Vanessa a film role as his daughter in a medical drama, *Behind the Mask*. To prepare for her screen debut, Michael insisted that she lose weight, putting her on a drastic diet so that she went from 156 pounds to 119 pounds fairly quickly. She gets a special credit, "Introducing Vanessa Redgrave," but the movie is more of a grueling debutante-coming-out party than a proper film launch.

Redgrave thought that her part was what Stanislavsky would have called "a stencil," a girl who did nothing but arrange flowers and pour cups of tea. She noted that there were two roles for young actresses in British films of this period, the English rose and the peroxide-blonde bombshell, and she didn't fit into either category.

Cast as the English rose, she's all done up with bright red lipstick and her hair is pulled back in a repressive chignon. It's fun to see her this young, at twenty-one, but it's also clear that she doesn't fit the prevailing female norms of the 1950s and will have to wait for the 1960s for her real chance in movies.

The rarely seen *Behind the Mask* is a standard British program film, and Redgrave is still green in it. She hasn't turned into a swan yet and seems worried about her looks and hemmed-in emotionally. Redgrave was told to flick her eyes back and forth when she looked at her scene partner to keep them lively, and this drove all other thoughts out of her head.

*Behind the Mask* does contain a sweet moment between father and daughter. "Aren't you afraid they'll accuse you of wanting to found a dynasty?" asks Vanessa of Michael at one point. He seems delighted with this notion, clinking the glass she's holding and kissing her forehead and saying, "To the dynasty," as if he might just make out the impact that his children and his grandchildren were going to have on the art of acting.

"I prefer the word 'family' than 'dynasty'," Vanessa said. "Scientists stress that it's the combination of DNA and RNA, what you're genetically born with and what gets input during the development process. And they insist, and I'm sure they're right, that it's the two . . . you see the work that your parents do and you get fascinated by it, at least I did. I had a lot of training, thanks to my father. If I'd been anything else, I would have been a teacher. But you do what you're born to do." In the mid-sixties, she put it more poetically when speaking of herself and her siblings: "We are the sprigs of a great and beautiful tree."

She played Sarah Undershaft in a production of Shaw's *Major Barbara* at the Royal Court Theatre, then read for the role of Michael's daughter in N. C. Hunter's play *A Touch of the Sun*. Director Frith Banbury remembered "How exciting it was when Vanessa walked on stage and we saw that particular quality of vulnerability, power, and beauty. She read three or four lines at an audition, and I turned to Binkie [Beaumont, the producer] and said, 'We obviously won't get anybody better, and I can really, truthfully say that. There will be no charge of nepotism.'"

Michael taught his daughter not to make her negative feelings known during a rehearsal, because such feelings affect the whole company. Vanessa was living in the family flat, and she would walk home from rehearsals and discuss her work with her father. "I learned very, very important lessons from acting with him," she said. "And later on, I learned more about the contribution that he had made to my work. A very important part of professional work and a very important part of political work is to be able to consider each day what developments have taken place and how you're going to do what you're going to do tomorrow, how you're going to change what you've been doing if it seems necessary.

"My father is a very special actor," she said. "There are many other actors who could be said to outstrip him in this, that, or the other quality, but he has a quality of acting that I have always aimed for. He feels very deeply about what he's thinking about, and he thinks very deeply about what he's doing, about what the play is about, about his part in the play, about the significance of the events that take place. But when he comes to perform, at his very best, whether it's in Shakespeare or whether it's in a modern play, it seems to be purely spontaneous, what he's doing. He seems to be living that moment and the words that he's saying seem to be said for the first time, not written in a script. Not to have been considered, but to have come from a living human being who is in the middle of a struggle that is taking place only on a stage."

Years later, speaking about how intimidating it was working with her father, Vanessa said, "When I say intimidating, I mean literally, like you know you're going to maybe play one ding on one bell in an enormous orchestral piece and one of the great conductors of the world is conducting and you think, oh my God, if I mess up this ding!" There were times when she wished that Michael would stop being the critical master actor and more the supportive father, but she came through this trial by fire. "Most people would have been broken by this, but not Vanessa," Corin said.

A much more destructive dynamic of criticism between parent and child was playing out at this time in the family. Banbury remembered a day when an embittered Margaret, roaring drunk on gin, came to visit Michael and began to lay into him and cruelly criticize his work. "She was just dreadful, and he was in an agony in her presence," Banbury said. Michael took refuge from her attack with an annihilating series of gins of his own. Margaret was so far gone with drink and disappointment in the last ten years or so of her life that even Rachel, who had the patience of a saint, could barely put up with her.

During the run of *A Touch of the Sun*, Vanessa began to explore the contradictions in certain characters as expressed by their given circumstances and changes in those circumstances, which make them behave in ways that might seem antithetical to their own personalities. At a certain point, Michael confessed to feeling thrown by the power of his daughter's concentration on stage, and he knew then that he had a real actress on his hands, one who might one day stand as the tallest tree in the family.

"Dare to be big," he counseled his daughter, as if she were a part of himself that had been repressed that could now get full expression. "If you're going to cry, cry buckets." Later on, when she had become a political radical, Vanessa was fond of a quote from Russian writer and activist Alexander Herzen: "There is nothing so vulgar as the bourgeoisie love for moderation."

Vanessa fell in love with Dinsdale Landen, the actor playing her brother in *A Touch of the Sun*, but nothing came of it when she learned that he was engaged to be married. Her own brother remained of the greatest importance to her. "I will never find for myself a man like Corin," Vanessa told her sister-in-law Deirdre.

Ian McKellen attended King's College with Corin, and he remembered a day when he was walking with Corin and Vanessa along the avenues by the River Cam. "I idly asked, 'What's that tree?'" McKellen remembered. "Immediately he pronounced, 'It's an oak, Ian.' I knew he was wrong and showed him the evidence of a fallen leaf that was not oak-shaped. 'Ah, that's because it is an unusual type of oak; one you haven't seen before.' I protested and he persisted. Perhaps sensing some verbal violence, Vanessa took my arm and quietly said, 'Corin is always right, you know.' I wasn't sure she meant it."

Vanessa played at Stratford for a season and got to be Helena in *A Midsummer Night's Dream* in a production directed by Peter Hall, with Charles Laughton playing Bottom and Ian Holm playing Puck. Hall remembered that Laughton was "like some kind of mad dog that had come into the rehearsal room—a wet dog, too, shaking all over the place." Fellow actor Michael Blakemore felt that in rehearsal Laughton was "evading the moment when he actually had to commit to a view of the scene." Surely observing the ever-questing Laughton rehearse had some kind of influence on Redgrave's own approach to rehearsal going forward.

An abridged version of the production that ran for seventy-five minutes was shot for TV but never properly shown. Simon Callow found Redgrave's performance in this recording as Helena "so startlingly exaggerated that only a huge natural gift could have sustained it without self-consciousness." Already, and perhaps spurred by Laughton's example, Redgrave was shooting for the moon and not at all afraid she might not hit it.

In 1960 Vanessa played Michael's daughter for a third time in *The Tiger and the Horse*, a play by Robert Bolt about nuclear disarmament that got her going on that issue. She helped to organize marches against nuclear arms and for the first time began to be arrested at protests, led to jail, and then let out after paying a fine. Michael worried about this activity and Vanessa did her best to reassure him. She said she wanted to work for peace, but she also wanted to act in the classics for the rest of her life. Michael warned Vanessa against her heavy smoking habits, but she told him that it was her one indulgence and that she planned to keep it.

Vanessa began seriously dating forty-year-old businessman Gavin Welby, and she planned on marrying him, much to Rachel's chagrin. "I only pray we can prevent this marriage," Rachel fretted to Michael in a letter, but Michael saw that the relationship would come to a natural end, which it did, mainly because Welby wanted her to pull back from her career. "For various reasons, I know it wouldn't work," Vanessa wrote to Michael afterward. "I feel relieved, but also sad, because he does love me, and in many ways I love him and have had some very happy days with him."

At the New Watergate Club in 1960, Vanessa appeared opposite Gladys Cooper in Joan Henry's *Look on Tempests*, playing the wife of a homosexual man who accepts her husband's sexuality but hopes to change it. Vanessa does not mention this production in her memoir, but her acting in a play so close to the difficult home life of her parents is an early signal of both her instinctive daring and her need for perilous challenges.

Early in 1961 at the Queen's Theatre, Redgrave made her first appearance in the Ibsen play *The Lady from the Sea* as the eldest daughter Boletta, winning fine reviews, particularly from the exacting Kenneth Tynan. Margaret Leighton played the lead, Ellida, which Vanessa would one day make her own.

Peter Hall called Vanessa in the spring of 1961 and asked her to be Rosalind in *As You Like It* at Stratford, and she accepted his offer with excitement and also some trepidation. During rehearsals, she listened to recordings of Michael as Orlando and Edith Evans as Rosalind, saying later that she felt as if she were going on a complicated cross-country journey and needed a good map.

On the day of the first night of the production, her director Michael Elliott took Redgrave out to lunch and looked at her seriously for a moment. He told her that the production was going to be a failure if she didn't give all of herself to it. She had been holding back in rehearsals, he said, and he reiterated that the production would be a failure if she didn't give all of herself that night to Rosalind.

It was a bold thing to tell an actress on the day of her first performance. "The director of *As You Like It* told me I erected a wall between me and the audience, and I felt a chill of fear," she said. "Rosalind was the first fantastic part I ever played, and I supposed it was the kind of fear you might feel the first time you make love. I was shocked rigid. I lay in bed all day, I thought I would go mad. It is such an extraordinary thing anyway to go out on a platform and be what you are not emotionally. The wardrobe lady finally put me straight. She said, 'You have to go on with it, haven't you, dear?'"

Redgrave realized that she had been too cautious and too intent on getting it exactly right, even down to copying Edith Evans's phrasing. All at once, she knew that she had been approaching the role in a spirit that was totally wrong, and totally un-Rosalind. And so she got dressed, went into the wings, and then bounded on stage and took a leap into the unknown.

She forgot all about *how* she wanted to play Rosalind and threw herself into actually playing her full-out. Redgrave might have made a modest success as Rosalind if she had kept doing the role cautiously, but when she gave up her control and gave herself up to instinct and spontaneity, she knocked everyone sideways with the scope of her talent. That first night as Rosalind was the night that Vanessa Redgrave came into her own as the most magical of come-fly-with-me lyric actresses who might lead you anywhere.

"The Redgrave girl is very charming and talented, though dreadfully tall," wrote John Gielgud at the time. "She will have the same difficulties as Phyllis Neilson-Terry had—no leading man capable of topping her. No Shakespearian joke intended!" The usually sharp-tongued critic

Bernard Levin was besotted with her in *As You Like It* and even began to take Redgrave out on dates after the show. He called her "a creature of fire and light, her voice a golden gate opening on lapis lazuli hinges, her body a supple reed rippling on the breeze of her love. This was not acting at all, but living, breathing, loving."

Nigel Andrews vividly wrote about the galvanizing effect of Redgrave's Rosalind in 2007 in the *Financial Times*:

> The audience at the Royal Shakespeare Theatre, Stratford-upon-Avon, rose ten feet from their seats and cooed and gibbered like cherubs. We had known nothing like it; we had discovered theater could be like falling in love. I was a teenager. But the hardboiled drama critic Bernard Levin became, famously and for weeks, a driveling loon, journalism's answer to Rosalind's lovelorn Orlando. With Vanessa Redgrave's starring debut in Michael Elliott's *As You Like It*, Shakespearean performance was reinvented. The twenty-four-year-old actress didn't speak the lines, she breathed them. They danced to her meaning, not to Shakespeare's meter. Yet, 400 years old, Shakespeare's words became as new and true as the day he wrote them. It was 1961 and even the Bard was allowed to swing. Redgrave was the poster girl for a revolution already beginning. We who had grown up with Olivier's Titanic diction and Gielgud's crooning artistry couldn't believe it could happen: that by going for clarity, meaning, and "simple" passion, a player could let the poetry take care of itself—or rather find the deeper, more human poetry of a great playwright's intent. The kick-on effect transfigured classical theatre. It legitimized performers who were already trying out the "meaning comes first" principle (Judi Dench) or inspired ones who were just beginning (Ian McKellen). Schoolkids could relate to this high-octane street rap, which also happened to be Tudor blank verse. Vanessa transformed revolutionary theory into spellbinding praxis. She was the star, the genius, who turned a reconfiguration in the culture into a phenomenon for all seasons and spectators.

As a new star, Redgrave was besieged with interview requests. She fell in love with her Orlando, Ian Bannen, though, again, nothing came of it. Redgrave recorded her Rosalind for radio in 1962 and got to play Rosalind again on film for the BBC in 1963, and it serves as a vital record of her work. Her Rosalind, who, like Redgrave, is "more than common tall," is naughty, delicate, vulnerable, impulsive. Redgrave takes a lot of risks with the verse, never just reciting it or "singing" it. She's alive to the words she is speaking and is unconcerned with the tradition of fine verse speaking, so that this is still a very modern Shakespearean performance. It remains the definitive preserved Rosalind.

Redgrave sometimes glides recklessly over her lines and then takes daring, lingering pauses in between phrases but still manages to keep her energy driving the play forward. In the filmed version for TV, she looks extremely young, with puppy fat in her cheeks, and it is clear from moment to moment that this Rosalind is living as dangerously as possible, skating on thin ice and sometimes palpably scared that she might fall through and perish. Above all, her voice is suffused with emotion.

This is a young woman who prefers a fool to make her merry rather than a man who might bring the sadness of adult experience. Wooing the beautiful young Orlando, she runs through all the problems they might have, but she does so with such playfulness and wit that she kills their possibility with her imagination of them, and her intelligence. Redgrave chooses to read the last farcical lines in Act V, Scene 2 quite seriously, and then bounds back into full-on flirtatiousness for the epilogue, where she teasingly thinks over kissing every man she sees in the audience. This is the most purely romantic performance this very romantic actress ever gave, and probably the sexiest, too.

Her Rosalind had an enormous effect on practically everyone who saw it. Director Richard Eyre said, "I saw a production on the BBC of *As You Like It* with Vanessa Redgrave. I was absolutely enraptured by it. It changed my life. Up to that point I had been more interested in science, had thought that I would be a chemical engineer, but seeing that production capsized me."

Redgrave was making do with dates with Levin, but she was soon swept up by the wickedly smart and entertaining director Tony Richardson, who was gaga over her Rosalind and told her that she alone could play Shakespeare's heroines. She was "like a sinuous golden flame," he said, and Redgrave received his compliments appreciatively.

Redgrave was with her mother Rachel when Richardson first went backstage, and so he felt constrained. Two days later, Richardson saw Redgrave's towering figure in a restaurant, where she was dining with Levin. Richardson handed his waiter a note for her. Vanessa, who wasn't wearing her glasses, passed it to Levin to read. It was a short love letter, which ended with the command "And tell Mr. Levin to go fuck himself."

In 1958, Redgrave had auditioned for Richardson's film of *Look Back in Anger* and he had turned her down, but now her Rosalind excited him both personally and professionally, and he whisked her off to dinner after her performances in *As You Like It* in his red Thunderbird. "I knew that he had fallen in love with me because of my Rosalind," Redgrave said. "And I also knew the difference between watching someone in a play and being with them in real life. I wasn't confident at all—I felt illiterate, stupid. But with guidance, I could act. And then of course Tony and I did fall in love."

*Look Back in Anger* playwright John Osborne was Richardson's flatmate at that time, and he was impressed by the violent chemistry between this young theater couple. After Richardson and Redgrave had spent a night together in the flat, Osborne surveyed an unholy mess: cigarette burns everywhere, empty champagne and whiskey bottles on the carpet, and a curtain hanging down as if it had been torn.

Osborne insightfully marveled in his diaries that Richardson and Redgrave "seemed to compound a piranha-toothed androgynous power within each other." (In Osborne's play *Time Present*, the character of Abigail, a dizzy actress, was thought by some to be a satirical portrait of Redgrave.) Rosalind, of course, spends a lot of time in *As You Like It* dressed as a boy, and Redgrave's mixture of male and female qualities very much stimulated the bisexuality in Richardson.

Continuing on with the classics on stage, Redgrave played Katherine in *The Taming of the Shrew* for Peter Hall and got some more rapturous reviews. While she was playing in *Shrew,* she marched for nuclear disarmament and spent a night in jail after a protest at Trafalgar Square. Like many people, she felt that nuclear disarmament was the most important issue of the day.

Richardson cast Corin as Lysander and Lynn as Helena in his poorly reviewed production of *A Midsummer Night's Dream* at the Royal Court, so he was happily swimming in Redgraves at this point. Vanessa felt that Richardson knew everything about everything, and she was in love with his intellect and his sense of fun. She thought that Richardson knew even more than her brother Corin, and knowledge always turned her on.

Richardson was ten years older than Redgrave, and he was riding high both in the theater and in film. While Redgrave was playing in *Shrew*, Richardson was filming *The Loneliness of the Long Distance Runner* (1962), a film where Michael was playing a small but key role. One night, Richardson came back from the set so tired that he placed his head in Redgrave's lap and closed his eyes. It was at this moment of vulnerability that Redgrave knew that, more than anything else in the world, she wanted to look after him. Richardson sleepily proposed marriage to her. The next day, she asked if he had been serious, and he said he was, and so they were engaged. While at Cannes, Richardson took Redgrave water-skiing, and when she fell into the water, the towrope on the boat caught her star-sapphire engagement ring. It sank to the bottom of the sea and was lost.

They were married on April 28, 1962. "How long do you give them?" Michael asked Rachel. "Oh, five years, at a guess," she replied. "I was on tour with a company at that time," said critic Michael Billington, "and somebody in the company very knowingly said, 'Ah, she's making the same mistake as her mother.' Meaning, obviously, that she was marrying an attractive bisexual man. What's always struck me is how recklessly in love Vanessa was with Tony Richardson."

The newly married couple vowed to name their first daughter Natasha because *War and Peace* was their favorite novel. By July, Redgrave was pregnant and playing Imogen in *Cymbeline* at Stratford under the direction of William Gaskill, who staged the play on a bare set. Her former beau Bernard Levin complained of the production's stark quality and Brechtian alienation effects, but he and most of the other critics cheered Redgrave's work.

Redgrave and Richardson were separated for a time due to their work schedules, but she went on location with him while he filmed *Tom Jones* (1963), which was a modish success in America, winning an Oscar for Best Picture. Richardson told her that she was too upper-class-looking to play in the film, so she disguised herself as an old man and joined some of the extras one day. "Tony discovered me in the movie too late," she said, "in the foreground, overacting as usual."

Redgrave found herself right in the center of what was to become Swinging London, and her marriage was rocky from the start. "Difficulties started at that time, when—perhaps because of the separations—Tony not always discreetly took up with this or that member of the crew or actress or actor," Rachel said. "Vanessa told me this later; if she was aware of it at the time, she kept still about it."

Redgrave labored to keep her head together with more organizing and political work for nuclear disarmament with Bertrand Russell. Michael went to watch her speak at a rally, carefully hiding himself from her view. "I remember thinking that she was perhaps more persuasive as an actress than as a public speaker," he candidly said.

Eventually Redgrave grew a bit disenchanted with protests that didn't have a clear aim in mind beyond the date of the next protest. She longed for something specific politically, something like when she found the book *An Actor Prepares* and exclaimed, "It's all here!" at the Central School. Redgrave also realized that if she went all the way with her protests she would lose momentum in her career, and if she wasn't a well-known actress, who would listen to what she had to say? So she scaled back on her political activity for a bit.

Redgrave went with Richardson to New York, where he was directing John Osborne's *Luther* on stage, and she found inspiration in Simone de Beauvoir's second book of memoirs, *The Prime of Life*. Reading de Beauvoir's book *L'Invitée*, Redgrave was particularly struck by the scene where the heroine cannot enjoy a beautiful view and good coffee because "the workers" are unable to enjoy these luxuries. Redgrave and Richardson traveled to Cuba, and she was impressed by what she saw, though she later said that the people were obviously not living under what she thought of as an ideal socialist state.

Back in England, Redgrave organized a one-night program called *In the Interests of the State: A Historical Guide for the Modern Agitator*, which was an attempt to put together the history of political radicalism and clarify her own intentions on this subject. She delivered a speech by Elizabeth II juxtaposed with the demonstrations of schoolchildren against British troops in Cyprus.

Slowing down momentarily, Redgrave gave birth to Natasha Richardson by caesarian section in May of 1963. In her memoir, Redgrave rails at length against caesarian sections and thinks that they are often suggested because they cost more money. As a natural woman of the '60s, she had refused all painkillers.

Richardson took Redgrave, their nurse Viola, and baby Natasha to the South of France for a holiday. Lynn soon joined them there, and the two sisters sang all the songs from the hit musical *Gypsy* well into the night. Lynn had just come from playing in a revival of Noël Coward's *Hay Fever* with Maggie Smith and Edith Evans, and her own theater career was burgeoning. As with the Gish sisters, it was clear from the start that drama was for one sibling (Vanessa) and comedy was for the other (Lynn). "Lynn is better at giving of herself in social situations," Vanessa said. "I'm afraid I'm not too good with groups of people." She saved herself, very guardedly, for her work.

Corin remarked on Redgrave's need to sometimes absent herself from social situations, so that her face went blank. "She just switches off," he said. "It's a very strange thing—she's done it for as long as I can remember." Corin's wife Deirdre found Redgrave "extraordinarily guarded . . . it is easy for her to veer from extremes of chill disapproval to extremes of warmth and charm." In these extremes of behavior, Vanessa was much like her father Michael, who could be convivial in social situations if he was in the right humor but totally unapproachable if he was not.

Redgrave wrote a song, "Hanging on a Tree," and sang it in Trafalgar Square to protest South African apartheid. She also participated in a protest against apartheid while she was rehearsing her Nina in Richardson's production of Chekhov's *The Seagull* at the Queen's Theatre, with her idol Peggy Ashcroft as Arkadina. Late in life, Redgrave related that Ashcroft had confessed while they worked together on this play that she was tired of acting at this point in her career. Ashcroft hoped that this would never happen to Vanessa.

Her Nina in *The Seagull* won many fine reviews, though some critics felt she was too strong and capable-looking to be convincing as a tragic victim and an aspiring actress who is not good at her work. But John Gielgud found Redgrave "splendid" as Nina, "especially in the last act." Richardson told Redgrave that working with her was everything he had dreamed of when he first saw her Rosalind. He even allowed Redgrave and Peter Finch to move any way they liked during their scenes together, to do away with standard blocking so that they could surprise each other.

Pregnant again, Redgrave then began rehearsals with Richardson for Brecht's *Saint Joan of the Stockyards*, but she was forced to drop out of the production when she began to hemorrhage and needed to rest for the arrival of the baby. While Richardson shot *The Loved One* in Hollywood in 1964, Redgrave took classes in political science at the University of California, and she sat for a drawing by Don Bachardy, the lover of Christopher Isherwood, who co-wrote the screenplay for *The Loved One*.

Back in London, Redgrave worked around the clock for the Labour Party, but she began to see them as too wishy-washy for her own more revolutionary taste. Her second daughter Joely Richardson was another difficult birth, and Redgrave was about to ask for painkillers until Richardson whispered to her that she looked absolutely beautiful, just like Italian actress Monica Vitti (he knew that Redgrave idolized Vitti), and this gave her the courage to go the distance without drugs.

When the Labour Party came into power, Redgrave said, "I was thrilled to bits. Subsequently, in the course of the next six months, I realized, alongside millions of other British people, the workers and wagers that had done everything they could to get Labour elected, that this government supported the war in Vietnam in spite of everything that they said. I had personally assured housewives in the flats that I had visited that the Labour Party was different from the Conservative Party. Women had said to me, 'It won't make any difference what we vote.' I firmly believed that this party was not like the Tory Party. This party will change everything, they will lower the rent, wages will go up. And of course, it broke every one of the pledges that it had made. So I tore my party card up and left the Labour Party."

A disillusioned Redgrave was often left alone with her two children, for Richardson loved to socialize and cruise for men. In her professional life, Redgrave was a tireless searcher after truth and insight, but in her personal and political life, she was capable of extreme myopia, not so much not seeing the forest for the trees as not even recognizing or admitting that she was in a forest at all. She believed what she wanted to believe. This sometimes led to unhappiness or disaster, personally and politically, but it was exactly this quality that led her to scale the steepest of heights as an actress.

On film, she had done only a few television episodes at this point, including a version of Marguerite Duras's *La Musica* in 1965, and a miniseries of Hemingway's *A Farewell to Arms* (1966) with George Hamilton as her unlikely Lieutenant Henry. She had stayed out of movies. This was about to change. At nearly thirty, Redgrave's slightly round face had begun to lengthen, which made her eyes more noticeably lyric and striking. Movie people began to take notice of her, much to her conflicted delight.

# Swinging Vanessa

n 1966, Redgrave was re-introduced to film audiences in *Morgan: A Suitable Case for Treatment* (also known simply as *Morgan!*), a mod comedy directed by Karel Reisz about the non-conformist, monkey-aping Trotskyist Morgan (David Warner), who is trying to win back his rich ex-wife Leonie (Redgrave).

"I first met Karel through my husband Tony Richardson," Redgrave said, "when we went to a party at the Royal Court—wine and cheese, all dressed up, looking quite nice, actually—and Karel saw me there. Then I got word he would like to see me for *Morgan*. I was excited when I got the part, but then it was postponed for a while and anyway I was pregnant just then." Reisz cast her in the film after she had had her second baby.

Richardson advised Redgrave in how to behave on a movie set. "The first thing he taught me when I was about to do my first serious film was 'Remember, the director is always right,'" Redgrave said. "'And why is he always right?' I asked, obedient pupil that I was. And he said, 'Because, for better or worse, the film is his, and it better be his vision. If there's a tussle at any point, you may be right, but you're only going to muddy things.'"

Time has not been kind to *Morgan*, which was a hit in its day. It flattered the youth audience with its unruly, obscure leftism and it flattered male egos with a story about a man who ruthlessly stalks his former mate because he knows she wants him to. In 2002, Redgrave spoke thoughtfully about Reisz's merits and demerits as a director. "He had this patience and he took endless time to explain things," she said. "There was a standing joke on the set that when Karel said 'excellent' you knew he was going to do a lot more takes. He kept your spirits up, but it was all a sort of tenacity to get the best out of you. People can be meticulous in different ways, but you felt Karel's sort was Czech.

"There was a fantastic humanity to the work, though his films insisted they didn't have a manifesto," she said. "Perfection is not the aim, they said, and I thought that was difficult to understand—I'd grown up with classical ballet where perfection was always the aim. For me now, though, Lindsay Anderson and Karel and Tony begin to seem right in their doubting of perfection. Life is not full of perfection. They were holding a mirror up to nature, in that old Shakespeare way, showing the sordid, the joyful, the grey despair, and the farcical."

Redgrave is beautifully dressed, made up, and presented in *Morgan*, and she does all-out star acting: darting, birdlike, both spontaneous and "spontaneous," the sort of thing that Julie Christie had cornered the market on in this Swinging London era. Right away, with Richardson's mentoring, Redgrave realized that a film is in many ways an improvisation and that it has an organic life that cannot be over-controlled or premeditated.

In their first scene together, Redgrave's Leonie undresses and teases Morgan until he starts to pretend to be an ape for her, whereupon Redgrave gently beats her chest for him, a shy, exciting bit of private sexual behavior that is deeply charming, as is her wondrous scene where she sings and cavorts with her new, stable lover Charles (Robert Stephens) in a convertible, behaving like a large and playful goose/swan.

Redgrave is extremely vivid in *Morgan* and very Carole Lombard-like at times. It's an atypical start for her in the movies, for she never again did this kind of sexy comedy playing, and this is something of a shame, because she's quite good at it. A few more comedies might have given some variety to the nearly unrelieved solemnity of her subsequent film work.

Tickled by the idea of a fight between Morgan and Charles, Redgrave's Leonie cries, "The winner will drag me off and *have* me!" She's a kind of dream girl in *Morgan*, a fantasy figure, and the film seems to know this, but by the time that Morgan has kidnapped Leonie and brought her out to a lakeside wilderness, it's clear that this movie is romantic in the worst possible way.

"Nothing in this world seems to live up to my best fantasies, except you," Morgan tells Leonie before kissing her, and he winds up in an asylum after crashing her wedding to Charles. Leonie visits him there, and the film's penultimate shot is a lingering close-up of Redgrave's open-mouthed laugh, as if to proclaim that a new star has been born. As a record of Redgrave's charismatic youth and beauty, *Morgan* is treasurable, but her glamorous, dirty-minded performance is defined by the strict limits of her role, and it looks now like an anomaly in her work, an easy road not taken.

After shooting *Morgan*, Redgrave was asked if she wanted to go to Vietnam. She knew that if she went it would mean the loss of the career in films that *Morgan* had ushered in for her, and so she declined, reasoning that she could accomplish more politically if she continued to be known and celebrated for her movie work.

"Vanessa's just sensational—and so sexy," Reisz told journalist Peter Evans. "Those people who thought I was off my head for casting her are going to have to think again. They'll be queuing up to sign her after they see this." In the newspapers now some of the headlines for Redgrave read "Shakespearian Turned Sexpot" and "The Sexiest Socialist."

"Before, men never spoke to me as someone they might like to go to bed with," Redgrave told Evans. "*Never.* I was not considered a bedworthy person, I suppose. Of course, I'm so near-sighted I might have missed one or two of the more subtle passes," she joked. "I feel myself flowering. It is an enormous, enormous pleasure. I now know I want to be a film star with all the capital letters. Yes, I do. I know that filming is very much for me, more than the stage. Though I'm nearly thirty, which is late to start a new career in movies, I've made up my mind. Just you wait and see. Wait and see."

While her film career was getting its real start, her personal life was unhappy and her fragile marriage started to collapse. Richardson was bewitched now by the French actress Jeanne Moreau. After Richardson's first meeting with Moreau in Paris, Redgrave told her sister-in-law Deirdre, "Tony came back literally elated. It frightens me because

I recognize that feeling. I've felt it myself. She must be extraordinary—Tony seemed transformed, set alight."

Richardson and Moreau collaborated on the Jean Genet-based *Mademoiselle* (1966), perhaps his best movie, certainly his boldest. It was filmed in a French village called Le Rat in the Corrèze, a wooded area of France, and Richardson installed Redgrave and their two daughters in a small house above a river during the shoot. As his feelings for Moreau became more evident, Richardson and Redgrave started sleeping in separate rooms.

Moreau would come over to their place for dinner and their chef, Monsieur Le Bonnet, who was also smitten with Moreau, would go all out for her with special soups and roasted rabbits. Given the fraught situation, there doesn't seem to have been any overt animosity between Moreau and Redgrave at this point or at any other point as Richardson made a switch between them. In fact, Redgrave was openly admiring of Moreau, whereas Moreau looked on Redgrave with cryptic curiosity.

"Tony Richardson told me that Moreau was the only woman he had ever known who could elevate and eroticize virtually any activity," said Tennessee Williams. "Her mind was so alive and curious and experimental. She was, he said, the most preternaturally developed two-year-old on the planet. Her perpetual refrain was 'Why not?' followed by 'What's that?' Diabolically hungry, reading everything, eating everything, exhausting everyone, then sighing at the end of the day and putting everything into perspective better than most writers. She was afraid only of boredom, so she moved constantly."

Shortly after *Mademoiselle* was completed, Richardson offered Redgrave a thankless role in his second film starring Moreau, a version of a Marguerite Duras novel, *The Sailor from Gibraltar* (1967), which used a screenplay co-written by Christopher Isherwood. "Tony later apologized to Chris for the film being so bad," says Isherwood's long-time partner Don Bachardy.

And bad the film is, in spite of its promising source material, a cameo from Orson Welles (it's almost impossible to understand a word he says), and a front-lined Moreau, who sings a song, does her iconic "sudden smile" mannerism, and opens herself up to shivery melancholy when she talks about her vanished sailor from Gibraltar, all to no avail—this is probably the nadir of her 1960s star vehicles. Redgrave wanted to hold on to Richardson in any way she could, and so she accepted the small part he gave her.

During a hiatus in filming, Redgrave was offered a trip to China with a delegation of artists. Trying to save her marriage, which had started to come apart, Redgrave cut short the trip, but Richardson, still besotted with Moreau, told his wife that she should have stayed away.

In *The Sailor from Gibraltar*, Redgrave plays a gawky optimist who is thrown over by her fiancé (Ian Bannen) for the glamorous Moreau, something Richardson did to Redgrave in real life, apparently, which makes her participation here feel cruel on his part, or at least insensitive. "We knew that Jeanne Moreau and Tony were engaged in an affair," says Bachardy, "and that was Tony's excuse for failing as a director. He said that he was so involved with Moreau that he wasn't attending properly to the film. I think Moreau was very powerful, and I think he was very pleased with himself having an affair with her."

Redgrave thought that Richardson's feelings for Moreau were completely understandable. They had both fallen in love with her, in fact, when they saw her in *Jules and Jim* (1962). It seems clear that the bisexual Richardson fell in love with a woman's talent first and foremost. "I think that's what Tony used for 'being in love,'" says Bachardy. "I don't think he was really capable of being in love like other people are. So he had to whip himself up in some way, and so his admiration for certain actresses sometimes did the trick, especially if they were famous."

Redgrave cried a lot over her broken marriage, but she later said that she wasn't sad that Richardson loved Moreau, only that he didn't love her anymore. She said it was a tragedy. Richardson answered, "It's not a tragedy, it's life." Redgrave praised what she saw as his objectivity, and she tried to assimilate his cool emotional attitude for herself, to bring herself closer to him.

This is a curious episode in her career, not least because Moreau is one of her few female peers, in every way equal to her size as an actress in films. It all feels like a bit of a cover story for something even more complicated that Redgrave herself might not have been aware of. The director Peter Glenville told Richard Burton a more complex version of this love triangle. Burton wrote in his diary:

> Lots of gossip . . . about Tony Richardson, Jeanne Moreau, and a Greek gigolo. Apparently Tony R. thought he was in love with Moreau and assumed she was in love with him, left his wife Vanessa Redgrave for that reason. In the meantime Neil Hartley (Tony R's producer, assistant, and procureur) had produced a very handsome Greek boy as off-duty entertainment. Glenville then re-enacts the scene of the boy's first appearance on the set: Mouth pursed, eyes narrowed, Moreau says to herself, "I want that." And with ten days free from the picture takes the boy to Greece and later announces she will marry him. Peter says, "Tony R of course doesn't know which way to be jealous." [The Greek boy actor who caused all this trouble was named Thodoros "Theo" Roubanis.]

Speaking of Redgrave and her feelings for Richardson, Bachardy says, "I think she was very much in love with Tony at that time, and I think she still is. I mean, he's very dear to her heart still. In fact, she wanted to buy three drawings that I did of Tony from the early '60s."

Redgrave insisted that she really liked her role in *The Sailor from Gibraltar*, and later said that she saw playing that role as the most important test of her life. Was this a test of humility? A test of love? Her meek acceptance of the part's limitations and obvious parallels to her own situation feel almost masochistic on screen, whatever the admirable merit of her objective viewpoint off-camera. For his part, Richardson told Redgrave that she was wonderful in an emergency but not so reliable for day-to-day living.

And so Richardson exchanged one great actress for another romantically, and still tried to have his boys on the side. It sounds an ideal life, in a way, but it had its drawbacks. "He placed his female lovers center stage and relegated his male lovers to the wings," said writer Gavin Lambert, who also said that Richardson once told him, "The price of repression is extremely high."

"There was always drama around Tony," says Bachardy. "He created drama to keep himself entertained. If there wasn't something happening naturally, he would make something happen artificially. He was very talented, both on stage and on film as a director, but he was just so at the mercy of his whims that he couldn't always be relied on to do his best work."

The success of *Morgan* boosted Redgrave's confidence when she badly needed it. She took some pleasure in being thought of and written about as beautiful and even posed for some high-fashion photographs in glossy magazines. She got fitted for contact lenses so that she could finally see something without her glasses, but sometimes she didn't wear them, and this enhanced her other-worldliness.

Alone now with her two daughters to take care of, Redgrave returned to the theater and began a successful run in *The Prime of Miss Jean Brodie*, in which she emphasized the most romantic aspects of Muriel Spark's charismatic and politically dangerous schoolteacher. After a performance as Jean Brodie, she was asked by Michelangelo Antonioni to be in his film *Blow-Up* (1966), and she accepted, acting for Antonioni during the day and playing Miss Brodie at night.

Redgrave was on the edge of a nervous breakdown while playing Miss Brodie. She began to get self-conscious about the lines. When she first came out on stage, she would think, "How is it, why is it, that I actually know every word I am going to say?" A doctor gave her shots of B12 and Librium, but nothing seemed to calm her panic, which she later thought was partly caused by overwork.

She got rave reviews for her performance in *The Prime of Miss Jean Brodie*, but Redgrave felt she didn't deserve them. Her problem here was that she disliked the woman she was playing and couldn't get a grip on her or deal with the implications of the Spark material. Redgrave had tried to back out three days before they opened because she realized she didn't like the play. Unable to leave it, she put together a performance that was all external, in the old-fashioned way of British stage acting, and came to grief.

"I had to construct the entire part around the outside with me somewhere in the middle," she said. She felt that the performance was just a kind of machine that she turned on, and she later firmly turned down the film version. Perhaps the material and this character were too close to home for her. She refused to identify with this hypocritical, politically deluded woman and came perilously close to physical collapse trying to play her without involving herself on any level.

As if she didn't have enough to do, on weekends she was also filming a musical short film for Richardson called *Red and Blue* (1967), which was originally supposed to star Moreau before she dropped out and Redgrave took her place. She played a singer in a nightclub who is always getting dumped by men and who tells the story of her life with seven songs, all of them by Serge Rezvani, who had written Moreau's signature song "Le Tourbillon" for *Jules and Jim*.

*Red and Blue* was meant to be a part of an omnibus film with other shorts directed by Lindsay Anderson, who completed his segment *The White Bus*, and Peter Brook, who was doing a segment with Zero Mostel, but that film never came to fruition because Brook dragged his feet over finishing his contribution (it was going to be called *Red, White and Zero*). *Red and Blue*, which runs forty minutes, has been a sort of orphan short ever since.

"It's about Vanessa, who's a nightclub singer," said the film's cinematographer Billy Williams. "And she has various lovers in her life, going from Michael York to Douglas Fairbanks, Jr., and each lover relates to a song . . . I got along very well with Tony. He was an absolutely delightful personality. I remember that each morning for breakfast, we'd have champagne! Well, that was a great start. Although he was separating from Vanessa at that time, they still seemed to be on really good terms, and she was game for anything that Tony wanted."

*Red and Blue* played as a featurette with Mike Nichols's *The Graduate* at the London Pavilion in 1968, but it was pulled before the run finished due to public complaint. It was judged too old-fashioned for those counterculture times, and Rezvani's wordy songs on the soundtrack album seem more suited to Moreau than to Redgrave, who has some trouble sustaining musical notes and also with sustaining the hard sophistication the songs call for.

On stage in *Miss Brodie*, Redgrave relied on the memory of the play in the muscles of her face rather than trusting that the lines were in her head. At times, she was very close to the abyss that swallows up actress Elisabeth Vogler (Liv Ullmann) in Ingmar Bergman's *Persona* (1967), who one night cannot remember her lines on stage and falls into a life without words. After the fact, Redgrave also felt that guilt over not traveling to Vietnam had spurred on this crisis. Since she had shut out reality, her artistic life, she felt, had begun to seem unreal.

Antonioni, surely one of the major artists of the twentieth century and one of the most articulate of all artists, had an unlikely commercial success with *Blow-Up*, which contained all or most of the hallmarks of his poetic, existential art cinema but also featured an engrossing thriller plot and some playful sexuality. David Hemmings gives the performance of his life as a fashionable young photographer who finds himself pulled in by Redgrave's woman of mystery. "I adore her," Hemmings said of Redgrave, "but like all actresses, she's insecure. She is really a gentle person."

"I like the protagonist," Antonioni said later. "I like his life. When I made the film, I also lived his sort of life and enjoyed it. It was a fun lifestyle, which I led only to follow the character, not because it was my own life." This sounds a lot like an actor preparing to play a role, yet Antonioni's cinema is resistant to the kind of theater-based acting that Redgrave was trained for. What he was interested in was the visual, the surface, which his poetic camerawork would study for unusual signs of life.

Redgrave wanted to be blond for the film, like Monica Vitti in Antonioni's *L'Avventura* (1961) and *L'Eclisse* (1963), but the Maestro had other visual ideas. He made Redgrave dye her hair black and shave an inch off her hairline to give her a higher forehead. She later said, "With Michelangelo the camera angle, its movement, the frame, the objects in the frame, their color, position, and movement, whether human or inanimate, told his story. . . . Trained as a dancer, I was able to appreciate this. I learned to look sharply and precisely at the shapes and colors around me. Exact positions, angles of the body, the head and shoulders, exact tempo of movement, were vital to him. I had never encountered such an eye in the cinema."

Redgrave was cinematically discerning enough to know just what she was dealing with with Antonioni. She knew that she had landed herself into something entirely different creatively, and *Blow-Up* is probably the best and most meaningful film, as a *film*, she ever appeared in. Her own contribution to it, however, can be a bit tricky to read.

It begins with groovy Herbie Hancock music under mirror-like credits, and the dominant initial colors on screen are blue and gray. We see a clownish group of kids driving along in a car down rather isolated streets. Though Antonioni keeps his distance from the more exuberant sides of Swinging London, his camera captures certain spaces and buildings so vividly that it feels like you are there, in 1966, in the middle of all the fun, which has an edge of disquiet in his uncanny lensing of it.

Hemmings's Thomas walks wearily out of a flophouse where he has just spent all night taking photographs. In his famous sex scene-ish photo shoot with the model Veruschka, where Hemmings kisses her twice and goads on her sexual poses for him, Antonioni catches a kind of morning-after hedonism, the kind that doesn't mind a bit of red wine as a breakfast pick-me-up. The sexual tension between photographer and model in this scene is of the "why not?" variety, and it's not particularly heated. It's as if too much unreflective, easy pleasure has begun to dull the senses of these Swinging London people.

Thomas looks like a jaded little boy who has been drinking and whoring for weeks on end. He is a bit of a tyrant with his other "birds," his models, treating them like waxworks. When they dissatisfy him, he orders them to close their eyes and then leaves them to walk around outside until he finds himself in an eerie sort of park. The park is deserted except for a woman and an older man. The woman looks to be pulling the man along. Thomas takes photos of them, and when the woman sees him she charges right up to him and demands the photos back and then looks trembly and guilty.

The woman is Redgrave, nearly unrecognizable with dark hair and subtly altered hairline. In this first scene, she does a few Katharine Hepburn-ish "shaking with umbrage" mannerisms, and it's clear that she's "acting," or indicating feeling, in this first scene, which rather upsets the movie's balance, momentarily. It's only in the long sequence in Thomas's studio that Redgrave yields to Antonioni's vision and becomes the model that he wants and needs.

She still uses a few little huffy-puffy pieces of Hepburn-like behavior when she enters the photographer's studio, desperate for the photos. "My private life's already in a mess," she says. "It would be a disaster if . . ." she continues, trailing off. Thomas toys with her like a cat with a mouse, or a cat with a jumpy thoroughbred horse. "Show me how you sit," he says. He is used to beautiful women doing anything he tells them to.

Thomas puts on music and asks her to move to it, and Redgrave is very funny and gawky as she tries and fails to move to the rhythm of this music. Thomas tells her to move against the beat while she smokes a cigarette, and she does this perfectly well. For a few moments, Redgrave forgets to "act" and search for a character to play and simply is a kind of dancer in Antonioni's *mise en scène*, a proper English girl persuaded to let her guard down, and the effect is extremely sexy.

She tries to run out with his camera but gets caught. Finally she takes her shirt off and gives Thomas an angry look. We never see her breasts, only her arms folded across them, and her bare back, all spine, as she walks through the studio, a sort of vanquished queen refusing to give up her dignity. (A few fully topless photos of Redgrave in *Blow-Up* ran in *Playboy* magazine, and it must be said that she looks extraordinarily beautiful in them.)

When Thomas gives her the film, she kisses him in a wholly spontaneous way, and at this moment Redgrave makes this woman seem truly mysterious. Who is she? Why does she need Thomas's photos so badly? Antonioni frames Redgrave against a purple backdrop with her dark hair and her pensive look, and this makes for an indelible picture of her, a glimpse of something both totally real and totally artificial, or created.

She smokes some pot with Thomas and then disappears from the movie, never to be seen again except in the still photos he blows up. Thomas thinks he sees her briefly in front of a building, but is it her or just someone who looks like her? He sees what he thinks is a murder in his photographs and then discovers a corpse when he goes back to the park at night, but the corpse is gone when he checks again. Why did she want the man in the park killed?

Thomas falls back on old habits, pulling down that purple backdrop for a slightly coerced romp with two aspiring models in tights. "It is fresh, light, and, I dare hope, funny," wrote Antonioni of this scene, which set new standards for sexual frankness on screen.

Thomas's apprehension grows, but he isn't mature enough to process what he's experiencing until he learns to throw an imaginary ball back to the kids from the opening scene, in that park he keeps coming back to. Redgrave haunts *Blow-Up*, and though it might seem outside her usual ken, the sequence in Hemmings's studio is as revealing of her own haughty, dazed, but bold nature as anything she has ever done.

This was Redgrave's busiest period as a young actress, and the acclaim she was getting sat uneasily with her growing awareness of the world around her. "I was in a West End play," she said, "which was very successful, and I was told that I'd won the Cannes Film Festival Award for Best Actress for *Morgan*. That night, someone brought in the evening paper to my dressing room and said, 'Oh, look, there you are on the front page, you got this prize.' And I looked at the paper and the picture of myself and I looked at the story next to it, which was the story of a massive bombing attack on North Vietnam. This was what was happening every day. And you get a measure of what you are, and the measure is intolerable between what is being demanded of the situation and what you're doing. I'm not saying I wasn't pleased to get that award, I was very pleased indeed, but at the same time, what did such things mean? Nothing when you're thinking of the bombing attack."

Higher stakes and salaries awaited her. Produced by studio head Jack Warner himself, the film version of *Camelot* (1967), an Alan Jay Lerner and Frederick Loewe musical that had starred Richard Burton and Julie Andrews on stage, was a mammoth production entrusted to Joshua Logan, who had directed films but was mainly a theater man.

Millions of dollars were spent on what Logan called "texture," so that the first scenes of the film seem to be taking place in a Macy's Christmas floor display filled with gray spray-painted trees and tons of fake snow. There are moments, especially in the first half of this movie, when the camerawork feels so uncertain, so bumbling and senile, that we seem to be viewing unedited rushes. Logan's film of *Camelot* is a ruination of a delightful show, which was at least captured with its unbeatable original cast in some scenes for television, and also on a treasurable cast recording where Andrews really outdoes herself, bringing unexpected drive and attack to all of her witty lyrics.

Warner had insisted on casting Audrey Hepburn in the film of *My Fair Lady* (1964), depriving Andrews of her stage role, but then Andrews had won an Oscar that year for *Mary Poppins* while Hepburn was snubbed for her uneven but heartfelt performance. Once bitten, Warner thought of casting Andrews as Guenevere, but Logan hadn't liked her stage performance. When Logan's son Tom saw *Morgan*, he told his father, "Dad, I've found your Guenevere. Her name is Vanessa Redgrave, and she's acres of beautiful."

Logan went to see her in *Morgan* and he got excited because he wanted a "ravishing bitch" for the role, and he felt that Redgrave's Leonie more than fitted that bill. He went to meet her while she was still acting in *The Prime of Miss Jean Brodie* in Brighton, and she played him two records she had made of folk songs, including the anti-war song "Where Have All the Flowers Gone?" His mind was made up about casting her. "She was so extraordinary to look at that I was entranced," said Logan.

They hit a snag when *Brodie* was a hit and Redgrave was contracted to stay with it for six months. "Do we really have to wait for that tall Communist dame until November?" Warner asked Logan, who insisted that they stick with her. Redgrave wrote Logan letters that seemed to argue for some simplicity: "I've got a wonderful idea, Josh. Why don't I wear one costume the entire time? Never, never change. Wouldn't it be terribly chic and original?" Logan wrote back that he didn't think that this idea would work, and he got into a bit of a back-and-forth exchange with her. "I learned later that the best thing to do was just to read her letters, answer them sweetly, and forget her ideas," he said.

Redgrave's performance is the only thing that makes this *Camelot* even barely watchable now, aside from her obvious romantic chemistry with her Lancelot, beautiful Italian Franco Nero, whose love-struck blue eyes match up ideally with Redgrave's own startled blue peepers. She had been offered Richard Lester's *Petulia* (1968) but Richardson, who remained her career adviser, told her to take the more commercial venture, saying that she would be able to do anything she wanted after making *Camelot*.

Nero wasn't at all impressed when he first saw the bespectacled Redgrave off the set: "I was walking in a corridor with Logan, and this girl in jeans had her back to us. Logan said, 'This is Vanessa,' and I said, 'Hello'

... but when she was gone I said to Logan, 'Are you crazy! She's so ugly!'"
Logan told Nero to wait until he saw her in full makeup. He also noticed
the way she looked at Nero. "So help me God," Logan remembered, "it
occurred to me at that moment, she's been looking for someone to have
another baby with and here's this good-looking Italian."

Redgrave left a note for Nero, in Italian, inviting him to dinner at the
house she was staying in in the Pacific Palisades. Curious, Nero went and
he saw "a pretty woman cooking in the kitchen. I rang the bell and asked
for Miss Redgrave and she said, 'I am Miss Redgrave!' She was very lovely,
and I understood what Joshua meant."

According to her sister-in-law Deirdre, Redgrave was also accepting
the attentions of the serial Hollywood seducer Warren Beatty, who was
of course intrigued with this new British star. Deirdre also claims that
Redgrave had a brief romance with George Hamilton while they filmed
their BBC *A Farewell to Arms*. Her information on Redgrave's love life of
this period should probably be taken with a grain of salt, for Deirdre
complained that Redgrave couldn't remember her name even after several meetings. For what it's worth, Redgrave doesn't even rate a mention
in Hamilton's cheerful 2008 memoir *Don't Mind If I Do*, even though he
brags about bedding the seemingly carnally omnipresent Jeanne Moreau.

Nero had an Italian girlfriend at that point. "My girlfriend got tired of
LA and flew home, so I was alone," said Nero. "Then Vanessa asked me to
drive a professor friend of hers to the airport. We all drove out and when
we were alone, when he had gone, she said, 'Are you working tomorrow?'
I said, 'No, and you?' She said she wasn't and suggested we do something
together. So we caught a plane and went to San Francisco and got to know
each other properly." Nero said that they were "close like a family, forever."
He fell in love with her, and he basically stayed in love with her. He has
been a kind of rock for her in the storm of her life.

Redgrave enters Logan's white and silver sets on a bed of white feathers,
and she's flanked by a wasted but welcome Estelle Winwood. When she
goes into her first song, "The Simple Joys of Maidenhood," it becomes
clear that her singing voice is thin and that she's going to try to act her way
through all the tunes, and that's a fearsome duty for any musical as song-
heavy as *Camelot*. She looks slyly at her surroundings and then widens

her eyes with excitement, and it's unclear whether she is actually exposed emotionally or just "exposed," really dangerous or just "dangerous," or smartly unconvinced by all this wasteful Hollywood outlay of money.

It's easy to miss Andrews's sure touch with the humor of the part and her crystal-clear singing, and there are times when Redgrave just refuses to see the fun in Guenevere, a lady with a lust for setting male violence in motion. It's an easy part to score in, but she doesn't take the easy way with it, instead insisting on locating Guenevere's genuine emotions, moment by moment, so that her performance doesn't pay off in the expected ways in her first scenes but begins to gather power as she continually builds it.

As is usual with her, Redgrave is working without a net and skating on thin ice. With her slow-dawning smile and gurgling laugh, she does seem like a fantasy princess, or at least someone we would never meet in daily life. Richard Harris labors beneath lots of heavy eye makeup as her King Arthur, and his performance starts out badly and gets steadily worse as the film plods on. Logan allows Harris to mug and linger over words in his monologues until it seems like the actor is putting together a catalogue of hammy, empty line readings.

Arthur and Guenevere marry amid much soft focus and a sea of candles, and though this wedding scene is typically overproduced it's an improvement over the Santaland funeral-home look of the first scenes. Redgrave's wedding dress costume alone cost $12,000. "The feeling one had was of every attention lavished upon the smallest detail," Nero said.

Harris was fond of ribaldry while they were filming. When Redgrave was supposed to bathe him, he came onto the set stark naked with an erection. "Everyone howled, particularly Vanessa," said Logan. "She was delighted, except she had to think of something to top him. It was all we could do to keep her from going to Richard, grabbing him by the handle, and leading him to the tub."

Logan found that though Redgrave was "maddeningly perverse as well as aggressive, she's a most beautiful and accomplished actress and a live, throbbing woman." When she came to sing "Then You May Take Me to the Fair," Logan was disconcerted when she began singing one of the verses in French. "Isn't it marvelous!" she told him. "I sat up all night making the translation. It's marvelously funny. It's hilarious."

Logan felt otherwise. "Why on earth are you singing this delightful song in a foreign language?" he asked her. "It's not a foreign language, it's French," Vanessa replied obstinately. "We're making fun of Lancelot, aren't we? And he's French. Well, the whole idea is that by singing it in French we're making more of a joke of him." Logan humored her and asked her how the audience was supposed to understand this concept. "They'll *know*," she insisted.

Trying a new tactic, Logan said that Warners could be sued by Lerner and Loewe for changing their song. "Oh, I don't believe that," Redgrave said. "I'm sure everybody would go along with a gentle spoof. Certainly, Alan Lerner can persuade Mr. Warner that it would be all right, because I'm going to sing it in French no matter what! What's Alan's number? I'll call him." Logan deliberately gave her a wrong number so that she couldn't reach Lerner, and her harried director persuaded her to shoot a version in English.

"Oh, Josh," she told him. "I thought you had more imagination than that!"

The trouble she gave Logan was made up for by her performance on screen. The morning after Guenevere's wedding night, Redgrave wakes up flushed and tousled, as fetchingly beautiful as she would ever be in the movies, and she pronounces Arthur "the greatest warrior in the land" in a sighing way that conveys that she also considers him the greatest lover. When Arthur worries aloud about "might being right," Guenevere interjects, "To be right and lose couldn't possibly be right," and on that line, Redgrave hits a pure Brechtian note, standing both entirely inside and entirely outside of her character's blinkered point of view, a technique that would stand her in good stead in many performances to come.

Redgrave does sometimes make Guenevere's obliviousness funny in her distinctive dazed, out-of-it way, but she is made to do her sensual rendition of "The Lusty Month of May" with some of the most miserable-looking extras imaginable. She'll be drawing us into a space made only for pleasure, drumming her ultra-long fingers on her head and lolling her eyes around like an alien being discovering the joys of the flesh, and then Logan will cut to a man and a woman in stiff costumes grimly kissing each other because that's what they've been told to do.

Redgrave's thinking-through of all her lyrics does tend to blur their humor, but her coyness gives way to true danger when Guenevere sets her sights on Nero's Lancelot and decides that she wants to punish him for his knightly egotism. She acts by instinct, and so we can believe Redgrave's Guenevere as a woman who could unthinkingly bring down a whole kingdom, and that's what both Logan and Warner wanted when they cast her instead of Andrews. "In our first two months in Spain we shot wonderful stuff, none of which ever reached the screen," said Nero. "In our last one week in Warner's Burbank studios we shot almost an hour of used screen time."

The chemistry between Nero and Redgrave makes the film come alive in spurts, even when they're made to do battle with absurdly clichéd imagery during his "If Ever I Would Leave You" serenade to her, a song sequence that has a backlit-to-the-teeth Guenevere entering Lancelot's room while a wind machine off-camera nearly *blows* them into each other's arms. In certain close-ups, Logan holds the camera on Redgrave as she weeps and her nose starts to run, and this glistening mucus in her nostrils gives her an air of emotional authenticity in a mega-production that flattens out and uglifies almost everything else in its path.

At the end of the song "What Do the Simple Folk Do?" which sees Arthur and Guenevere dancing around the room and trying to forget their troubles, Redgrave drops this woman's forced gaiety and accesses an enormous kind of despair, and this same epic despair is there in her last scene with Arthur. Watching this *Camelot* is a trial, but Redgrave is so deeply upset when her Guenevere asks Arthur for forgiveness that she almost makes it seem as if we have been viewing an intense psychological study of a woman in love with two men and not one of the worst of all Broadway musical movie adaptations.

Redgrave accepted a CBE from the British government with much ambivalence. When journalist Peter Evans told her he felt her acceptance of the honor was rather schizoid considering her politics, she told him, "Actors are always prone to schizophrenia—which is always worrying! People laugh at the old socialists, those people who refused to go to Buckingham Palace or, if they did, went in cloth caps. But they were right because they knew what they had to do to defend their principles . . . and integrity is so perishable in the summer months of success."

"And so I had to find a good excuse to accept my CBE. I finally told myself it would make the things I was doing more defiant if I had the CBE. That it would make people take more notice. But I was kidding myself, of course. What I really wanted was the recognition, and I feel ashamed of that because I was weak and gave in."

She could be disarmingly childlike off-screen. "The Christmas Day lunch was at Gladys Cooper's house, which Vanessa has rented," wrote Christopher Isherwood in his diary. "There really is something very sweet about her. She had taken the trouble to compose individual verses for each one of about a dozen grown-up guests—there were also swarms of children."

Both Vanessa and Lynn were nominated for a Best Actress Oscar in 1966, Vanessa for *Morgan* and Lynn for *Georgy Girl*. There was never any rivalry between them. They were far too different for that, and far too complementary, even if they did have their disagreements in later years. Vanessa enjoyed the fact that her little sister, who had always been treated as something of an also-ran in the family, was now coming into her own on screen but also on stage, where she was starring on Broadway in Peter Shaffer's *Black Comedy*.

Vanessa wore a stylish green dress and large 1960s hair to the Oscar ceremony, but she also wore her thick glasses and very little makeup, and the total effect was a bit visually perverse, or conflicted, a bit of Hollywood and a bit of radical England. She and Lynn lost the award to Elizabeth Taylor for *Who's Afraid of Virginia Woolf?* and there were no hard feelings, as there were whenever sisters Olivia de Havilland and Joan Fontaine competed for Oscars in the 1940s.

Attending the Cannes Film Festival, where *Blow-Up* was showing, Nero told Redgrave that he loved her, and he gave her a golden bracelet with a little disk that read: *"Francesco e Vanessa—per sempre,"* which means "for always." But she still had time for her ex-husband, creatively speaking. Concerning Tony Richardson's version of *The Charge of the Light Brigade* (1968), Redgrave wrote in her memoir that she thought the film a masterpiece. It was the most expensive British movie made up to that time.

Richardson uses black-and-white cartoons to set the political stage for his movie and also to comment on the action, and the cartoons do work beautifully as exposition and also in and of themselves (a turkey plays Turkey, a large bear is Russia, Britain is a sleeping lion, etc.). Richardson insisted that the women in his film wear no makeup, which has an unflattering effect on poor Jill Bennett, but Redgrave's natural radiance shines through on her clean-scrubbed face here. It's one of the few times on screen we can see her freckles, and they don't detract in any way from her poetic appeal.

Redgrave plays Clarissa, a young woman who gets married but then falls passionately in love with Captain Nolan (David Hemmings). Richardson shoots her with obvious affection, especially in her open-mouthed smiles in the wedding scenes. Trevor Howard dominates most of the film with his likable crudeness, and Redgrave counterbalances this with her own rarefied capturing of light and feeling. She has a kind of up-in-the-clouds spaciness here punctuated by moments of diamond-like clarity of thought, and she creates a character out of practically nothing and makes us care about her.

When Clarissa kisses Captain Nolan, Richardson films her so that the camera lingers over the beauty of her jutting white chin, and he also lingers over her trembling emotion as she weeps by a door, and her joy as she dances a bit at a distance, pregnant with Nolan's child. Redgrave is a lyric actress, made for heroines, and Richardson uses this quality as a bit of hope amid the senseless militarism at the center of his film. As a period recreation, *Charge* is superb and the cast is unbeatable, particularly Howard and John Gielgud.

Her co-star Hemmings said of Redgrave at this time, "I don't know how she does it. I've seen her be a queen, a posh bird having a bit on the side, and a Swinging Sixties dolly bird, a real piece of loose elastic—and she still finds time to save the whole fucking world, and not have a single hair out of place. But I don't think she's a very happy lady. She has her priorities all wrong. I feel sorry for her—and her daughters."

In the summer of 1968, Redgrave went to Sweden with her daughters in tow to do a film of Chekhov's *The Seagull* directed by Sidney Lumet, with Simone Signoret as Arkadina, James Mason as Trigorin, and her *Morgan* co-star David Warner as Treplev. Redgrave has often spoken of this summer as an idyllic experience, though she gently chided herself for shutting out all that was happening in the world in 1968 as she filmed Chekhov's play.

They shot it in twenty-seven days after ten days of rehearsal. Lumet was effusive about Redgrave's talent and nearly unable to put his feelings into words. "She has lyricism which is extremely rare . . . a combination of strength and delicacy . . . and a complete intangible . . . just the depth of the talent itself."

It was a very happy set. "We were in the process of going completely mad with shared tenderness and mutual comprehension," said Signoret. "We didn't make love together, but we kissed, we held hands, we were becoming Russified as fast as we could. We never wanted to leave one another."

Happy sets, alas, often make for unsatisfying movies. After seeing the finished product, Redgrave felt that it fell short as a film, and that is sadly true. In fact, this little-seen Lumet movie, which is called *The Sea Gull* in the credits, is a disaster where every choice of framing and staging feels totally, even overwhelmingly wrong. The open-air Swedish locations are striking but Lumet flatly observes them without any discernible visual viewpoint. He lets the actors simply say their lines, and they never connect with the material or each other. Surely there have been better college productions of *The Seagull* than this movie with its starry cast. There's no Chekhovian humor, no tender melancholy, only an insensitive, graceless recitation of the play, which is not understood or illuminated by Lumet at any point.

Vincent Canby in his *New York Times* review felt that the film was "so uneven in style, mood, and performance that there are times when you could swear that the movie had shot itself . . . Lumet's way with this adaptation by Moura Budberg is implacably straightforward. It plows ahead, scene by scene, act by act, in which there always is first an establishing long shot and then cuts to individual actors as they act and react. This kind of *Secret Storm* technique inevitably flattens out the nuances and the pauses that give depth to the tangled personal relationships . . . all of the actors seem to be on their own."

Lamentably, Redgrave is the chief casualty of Lumet's lack of care and judgment. He destroys the impact of her entrance by filming her Nina in long shot and then keeping her in long shot for the entirety of Treplev's play. We only manage to get a good look at her acting choices when she speaks to Signoret's Arkadina after the play, and Redgrave is disappointingly low-key, as if she's a bit tired or her mind is on something else. She's so poorly directed and poorly shot that a role that should suit her perfectly and a film that should be a triumph of her early career is instead a bewildering failure.

Warner declaims all of his lines without thinking through them, and Signoret suddenly seems lost in the English language, even though she had done fine work in English in previous years. Mason is the one takeaway from this film, offering a major interpretation of a Trigorin who sincerely believes what he tells Nina about himself until he is revealed in the end as a fluent self-deceiver and devouring pro. In the penultimate scene, where Nina talks about her failure as an actress, Redgrave is at least competent, and in her final close-up, she opens up her face and at last shows us what her on-screen Nina might have been, but it's far too little and far too late.

The 1975 Williamstown production of *The Seagull*, with Blythe Danner as Nina, is the gold standard for filmed versions of this play, and Danner's vividly lyric, risky work leaves Redgrave's film Nina looking all the more pallid and uncertain. Still, this version of *The Seagull* remained in Redgrave's memory for personal reasons. "I remember it not because it was a good film," she said, "but because of the fun we had as a family, the long summer, white nights, and the jokes we had."

# Isadora

B efore *The Seagull*, Redgrave had shot *Isadora* (1968), a biopic for Karel Reisz on the life of Isadora Duncan, the godmother of modern dance (it was released after the Lumet film). "The gods sell their gifts dearly," warned Isadora toward the end of her life, and few artistic paths are as suggestive or as troubling as hers.

As a girl, Isadora was drawn to Greek culture, and she was similar to Redgrave in her attraction to philosophic extremes that led her from Walt Whitman to Nietzsche to Bolshevism. Her first major love affair was with the son of actress Ellen Terry, Gordon Craig, a theatrical visionary whom she worshipped and subsidized during most of their affair. Isadora had always been a bohemian in outlook and pledged to the idea of free love, and so she had no qualms about bearing Craig's child out of wedlock.

When the womanizing Craig moved on, Isadora set her sights on finding a millionaire to pay for her dreamed-of school of dance for young girls, and she hooked Paris Singer, an heir to a sewing-machine fortune who helped her throughout her life. She was an artist who had an ideal, and many commented on her naïveté, both on and off the stage, but the woman who emerges in Peter Kurth's definitive biography *Isadora: A Sensational Life* (2002) has surprising moments of mocking self-knowledge and wit.

Reading Kurth's book, it becomes clear that Isadora only played the fool and the sexual clown as roles that amused her. In reality, as proven by her letters and many of her interviews, she was a highly intelligent person who was able to see straight to the heart of many subjects.

Her merriness was brought to a vicious halt when her two children were drowned with their nurse in a car accident. Isadora reacted to this news with shock and calm, consoling the people around her. She said that she died then: "What is surprising is that the body still lives," she reflected. After a hiatus, Duncan returned to dancing during the height of World War I, and her work took on a patriotic fervor and darkness. In 1916, she performed perhaps her most famous dance, "Redemption," which saw her prostrate on the floor of the stage and very slowly raising herself up.

A period of relative peace was followed by a sojourn in Russia, where she began a dancing school for Russian children. She fell in with Sergei Esenin, a punk poet who saw what her fame could do for him. Isadora spoke almost no Russian and Esenin spoke little English, but they spent years together making scenes all over the world. He would drink and slap her around, and she would take his abuse like a guilty mother. She called him a genius. "All my lovers have been geniuses. It's the one thing upon which I insist," she said, in that weirdly self-aware, lightly self-mocking way she had. Robert Edmond Jones said that her voice was "oddly absent" as she made her habitual speeches from the stage for money for her school of dance: "It is an American voice, an Irish voice, and in some curious way it is a humorous voice."

In Boston during an American tour, Isadora danced bare-breasted and shouted, "I'm red!" to her scandalized audience. When asked about communism and whether it would succeed, she answered, "What is right or wrong cannot be measured by its success." Isadora herself laid out what she had learned in an interview with George Seldes:

What mankind calls love is only hatred in another form. In the flesh there is no love. I have had as much as anyone of that sort of thing . . . men foaming at the mouth—men crying they would kill themselves if I didn't return their love. Love—rot! I had just barely come on the stage when it began. . . . From all sides I was besieged by all sorts of men. What did they want? Their feelings, I know now, were the feelings they have for a bottle of whiskey. They say to the bottle, "I'm thirsty. I want you. I want to drink you up. I want to possess all of you!" To me they said the same things. "I am hungry. I want you. I want to possess you body and soul." Oh, they actually add the soul, when they plead for the body.

Was that love? No. It was hysteria.

When I was in Moscow I saw little children lying huddled asleep in doorways and on rubbish heaps. Would this be possible if there was love in the world? . . . Was that love? . . . If there is such a thing as love in the world, would people allow this sort of thing? Could they go to their comfortable houses knowing that there are children in such distress? So long as little children are allowed to suffer, there is no true love in the world.

Isadora finally crashed down on the Riviera, fluffing F. Scott Fitzgerald's hair, fighting over sailors with Jean Cocteau, and dictating her memoirs. "If I had been a man, I might have done for dancing what Wagner did for music," she told Sewell Stokes. Self-pitying one minute and full of plans the next, Isadora zeroed in on a handsome chauffeur who took her for a ride in his car. A long shawl she wore got caught in the spoke of a wheel on the car and it broke her neck, pulling her out of her seat and dragging her body twenty to thirty feet. "Isadora's end is *perfect*," wrote Cocteau, "a kind of horror that leaves one calm."

Ken Russell made one of his best television films for the BBC about Isadora in 1966. It starred Vivian Pickles, who is quite funny when telling off bourgeois communists and memorable when wandering through a Siberian plain filled with her scattered love letters. Whenever a serious mood builds, however, Russell breaks it with a crude joke, and there are moments when Pickles camps Isadora, but she dances well and survives Russell's frequent lapses in taste. Two years later, Redgrave had her chance to play Isadora for the big screen.

*Isadora* was a large, ambitious project filmed mainly in Yugoslavia, and it earned Redgrave her second Oscar nomination as Best Actress. She did not think that the film was a success, mainly because Madame Furtseva of the USSR Ministry of Culture refused to let Oleg Tabakov play the role of Esenin. And indeed, Zvonimir Crnko (billed as Ivan Tchenko) is faintly silly in the part, not quite dangerous enough.

The movie suffers from the miscasting of all the male roles. James Fox is made to look like Gordon Craig when he first stalks into a theater and watches Isadora dance, but he has none of Craig's sexual magnetism and drive. Much worse than Fox is Jason Robards, a major actor totally at odds with the role of Paris Singer. Because Robards is a name player, the Singer scenes are given prominence in the middle of the film, and they're all duds that don't even get the basic relationship details right. Reisz himself later called the film "a disaster" because he was unable to take in all of Duncan's life in one movie.

There are several different versions of *Isadora*. The original roadshow release ran 168 minutes, but the film was soon cut and then re-released as *The Loves of Isadora*, which ran 131 minutes. This version loses many of the grace notes in the first half of the movie, but *Isadora* doesn't really work at any length, including the 153-minute director's cut that restores some scenes.

The movie begins in 1927 on the Riviera, where we hear Isadora's voice dictating her memoirs. A curtain is blowing in the breeze behind her, an evocative visual touch (one of the few in the film, alas). "I was born under the star of Aphrodite, goddess of love," says Isadora, in the twangy American voice that Redgrave uses for the role. This voice takes some getting used to. It's very extreme, all "r," a bit overdone, but true to what Isadora's friend Gretchen Damrosch said about her "curiously flat little voice."

Isadora starts to sing "Bye, Bye, Blackbird," living for the moment until her gay amanuensis Roger (John Fraser) gets cross with her. As Isadora sips champagne, Redgrave exactly catches the slightly camp, self-mocking tone of her grand but humorous manner of this time: "Roger, dear," she says, "I will never have the pen of Sir Walter Scott!"

The film then makes an awkward transition to a scene from Isadora's youth where she dances in a music hall. The tone of this scene is so crude and false that Redgrave can do nothing to transcend it, but Reisz soon cuts back to the Riviera and the colorfully ruined middle-aged Isadora, and as this older woman Redgrave is always on firm ground. She's so magically in sync with Duncan in decay that it would have been far better if the film had stayed with Isadora on the Riviera instead of forever jumping back and forth in time.

Reisz shows us a young Isadora dancing in Greece, and Redgrave strives to catch the imagery of the famous Edward Steichen photos of Isadora from this period. She does a lovely little dance with a piece of white material for a salon of rich society people, but in the dances that she recreates on stage, Redgrave is not always physically graceful. She is, however, totally committed to the dances emotionally and makes evocative use of her swan-like neck and incredibly long arms and legs as she feels and embodies the music of Schubert and Alexander Scriabin. "The thing about dancing is that it's a tremendous struggle," Redgrave said. "And out of that struggle comes great joy. And the history of dance is a history of millions of people over some billions of years expressing their life and their death and their struggles, their converts and their achievements and their sorrows in dance as well as in song.

"Isadora revolutionized dance, and she revolutionized dance because she studied nature, and discovered, therefore, that nature is revolutionary," Redgrave said. "And she tried to express nature in her dance. She tried to express music rather than impose concepts upon music, which was in itself a revolution at that time."

Redgrave makes her face moldy with age and sorrow as the aged Isadora remembers her dead children. She *is* this woman, this wreck, without any fuss, and it's her empathy that gets her there so instantaneously to a place of grief where angels and others would fear to tread. When Isadora returns to her senses, Redgrave captures her mordant wit through sheer imagination. Judging from her autobiography and her interviews, this kind of wit is totally foreign to Redgrave, but she gets it exactly right, even sounding a bit acidic and Maggie Smith-like in her scenes as the older Duncan.

When Isadora starts her affair with Craig, Redgrave makes her face completely open and vulnerable as Fox's Craig lowers her tunic. Reisz films her from overhead as she sprawls out her arms and legs to their full length on the floor, dropping her right knee to the beat of the music playing, and Redgrave never looked or seemed as much like a mythological goddess as she does at that moment when her knee hits that floor. She dances the lovemaking between Isadora and Craig very sensually, but innocently too, and this really captures the spirit of Duncan. Redgrave is *acting* great dancing, mainly with her face when her body can't quite do what she wants it to do, and she's willing to go as far as possible emotionally, even to the trembling brink of Isadora's first orgasm with Craig, which is expressed with frank and naked trembling on Redgrave's face as she finishes her dance.

"The choreographer, Litz Pisk, and I had been working together all summer and rehearsing every night after filming," Redgrave said. "One day, we were shooting Isadora dancing to Beethoven's Seventh Symphony. By the lunch break, I am exhausted. I do not believe I can walk, let alone do six or seven more takes of a two-minute dance sequence. Our director, Karel Reisz, sits me on a chair. 'Listen to this,' he says. The orchestra plays a piece from a Dvořák symphony. Every muscle in my body melts. Karel says, 'Right, now we will shoot.' As I stand in position, Beethoven's wild stream of notes takes off, and so do I. I have been taken outside myself. The energy in my body seems to know no limits. I am not commanding my body; the music is. I do not know whether Karel and Litz put their heads together to find this solution for my exhaustion; I imagine so."

From this romantic peak, Reisz quickly brings us back to the self-consciously embarrassing older Isadora on the Riviera. Cynthia Harris is far too young to be playing Isadora's best friend Mary Desti, looking more like a new secretary than Duncan's oldest friend in the world. The casting of Harris was most likely a choice made so that Redgrave would seem older in these scenes, but it's one more flaw that upsets the balance of the movie. Yet when Mary tells her friend that they can go to Paris tomorrow, Redgrave is dead-on Isadora when she says, "Tomorrow is a hypothesis," just lethally tossing out this darkening thought in that flat voice she's found for this character.

At her best here, Redgrave imposes her large body on screen in just the way Isadora imposed her own body on stage. Duncan and Redgrave are kindred spirits in so many ways, but Reisz's prosaic film lets both of them down. *Isadora* was the last movie silent screen icon Louise Brooks saw in a theater, and she thought Redgrave "superb," but was chagrined by the clunkiness of the film itself. "There will never be another Redgrave, perfect in acting, poetry, fire, body, and dancing, to bring Izzy to life," she wrote. "If I were she, I would challenge the writers to a wrestling match and pound their brains out."

Redgrave goes full-out in the scene of Isadora's agony during her first childbirth. Her eyes have gone blank with an almost demonic suffering, and it's the same madness we see in her eyes when she dances, the flip side of that aesthetic exaltation. After this scene, unfortunately, the film sputters and dies out completely for the Robards/Paris Singer section, which feels aimless, coarse, and heavy-spirited.

When we get back to the Riviera scenes, Redgrave is as inspired as ever, letting out a witch's cackle as she deals tarot cards. She keeps uncannily capturing parts of Isadora's middle age and her youth, but Reisz's film never lets her synthesize all of these parts so that we can make out the shape of Isadora's rise and fall. If the film could have fused together these moments, Redgrave's performance in this movie might be as monumental as the picture of the artist and the woman that emerges in Kurth's harrowing biography. What we're left with in *Isadora* is bits and pieces of insightful pretending from Redgrave that can never form a whole.

The loss of Isadora's children is done in soft focus, a visual choice by Reisz that feels very vulgar and unfortunate. Isadora Duncan could be the most vulgar woman on earth when it came to manners and civilized social behavior, but she was an aristocrat in her art, and surely she would have recognized the pernicious vulgarity of Reisz's cinematography here, which trivializes an event of such sickening weight and unfairness. He has Isadora writing the deaths of her children out on paper in her room at night by candlelight, and Redgrave is unerringly precise in what she's doing here. This is not the first shocked grief she's showing us, or even the grief of the years that came afterward, but the exhausted grief of a woman who has lived too long and knows it.

The scenes set in Russia give a lift to the film, but they traffic in Soviet kitsch visually and Crnko's Esenin has a sketch-comic quality, yet Redgrave blasts through these obstacles and plays out three outstanding scenes. Her Isadora is a drunken, dissolute mess after a night in bed with Esenin, and when he starts smashing her photos and memorabilia, she smashes away with him with all of her game spirit desperate but intact. The scene builds and builds until he grabs a photo of her children and destroys it before she can stop him. In this scene, there is a nauseating sense of the real-life abusive push and pull between Esenin and Isadora.

When Isadora gives a disastrous American press conference with her Russian husband, Redgrave gets across the idea that Isadora herself is trying to believe in her own bright prattle and failing. Best of all is Redgrave's recreation of Isadora's scandalous Boston concert, where she dances the holy hell out of Tchaikovsky's "Marche Slave" and then finally tears off the top of her dress in front of the outraged audience. The extras were not told that Redgrave would be ripping her top off and baring her breasts, and so the camera catches their actual shocked reaction.

This is such a vivid scene that not even Reisz's crude cutting away to a street corner sermon outside the theater can destroy the rhythm of Redgrave's daring and full identification with her role. "We were wild once!" she shouts to a nearly empty house. "Don't let them tame you!" she cries, right at the top of Redgrave's vocal register, in a voice so harsh and sharp that it could cut you.

"In *Isadora*, the two most important dances I had, and they were difficult, and I think I made a primitive effort, was the dance of the Russian working class and peasantry emerging from slavery under the Tsarist autocracy to winning the revolution," Redgrave said. "I had to express this in a dance and I had to conceive this dance with my coach as well as carry it out."

*Isadora* ends with a kind of wish fulfillment on the Riviera, as the older Isadora does a slow dance with her angel-of-death chauffeur, taking a playful Apache slap from him and craning her glorious neck back in a way that the aged, corpulent Isadora herself could never have done in 1927. As she rides away in the death car, Isadora is jubilant, foolish but also playing the fool, and when her scarf gets caught in the spokes of the car wheel, Reisz cuts to a grotesque close-up of Redgrave's face as she screams in horror and surprise. He then cuts to her corpse in the car, her eyes wide open in death and her tongue jutting stiffly out of her mouth.

This ending is daring and almost comic, and it works, but Redgrave must have known that she hadn't been able to really give the performance she was capable of. In the early 1990s she played Isadora again on stage and won awards in Martin Sherman's play about her years with Esenin, *When She Danced*. Duncan's biographer Kurth said of this performance, "I remember thinking it was lucky Martin's play was closing, because if too many more people saw Vanessa as Isadora—live, in the flesh—I wouldn't need to write a word." Poetically enough, there is no film of Redgrave's definitive stage stab at Isadora Duncan, just as there is little film of the dancer herself, only a few photographs of her arms reaching for the heavens.

When she was nominated a second time for the Best Actress Oscar for *Isadora*, Redgrave went to the ceremony with Nero. A protester outside held a placard that read, "A Vote for Vanessa is a Vote for the Vietcong." Again, she let the television camera catch her looking serious and wearing her glasses. It was a very competitive race that ended with a tie between Katharine Hepburn for *The Lion in Winter* and Barbra Streisand for *Funny Girl*.

There were filmic odds and ends from this period: Redgrave did a seven-minute short for Swedish director Bo Widerberg called *A Mother with Two Children Expecting Her Third* (1970). She made a cameo as suffragette Sylvia Pankhurst in Richard Attenborough's lummox of an anti-war movie, *Oh! What a Lovely War* (1969), preaching for peace harshly and passionately: "War cannot be won, no one can win a war!" she cries in the sharpest possible voice to pierce her unsympathetic audience.

Attenborough stages the film's fifty musical numbers in a stately, dignified fashion, making the same points over and over again, but his cast, filled with the best of British actors, picks up a lot of slack: Ralph Richardson, John Gielgud, Laurence Olivier, and Redgrave's father Michael stomp around as dopey generals, and Maggie Smith does a scarifying music-hall turn as a singer who bullies men into enlisting that overshadows everything else in the film with its precision and authority.

Smith and Redgrave were often up for the same roles all their working lives, even though they couldn't be more different as performers. Whereas the formidable Smith is all angles and elbows and wrists and boxed-in, brutally sharp comic and dramatic timing, Redgrave is all loose, flowing movement and radiance and open air. It is possible to imagine Redgrave playing most of Smith's roles—though surely not *California Suite* (1978) or any of the other parts that called for Smith's razor-like way with bitchery—but it is hard to picture Smith in most of Redgrave's parts.

Smith doesn't idealize herself in the way Redgrave does, working instead in an extremely potent vein of English snobbery, hypocrisy, and ruined hopes. Smith looks at the world critically, caustically, as if her mind is made up against it, whereas Redgrave sees enormous possibilities and vast space for improvement. After Smith won an Oscar for *The Prime of Miss Jean Brodie* (1969), Nero told Redgrave, "That Maggie Smith is a real actress. She doesn't waste her time on politics like you, Vanessa."

Great as she is, Smith doesn't give a lot of herself on screen, relying instead on a rather mysterious and steely kind of technical command, whereas Redgrave scorns technique and always offers all of herself to us. Smith, who is Redgrave's nearest rival, has no technical limitations, but she does have some temperamental limits, and this was pointed up when she got older and what little warmth she had was chilled out of existence by most of the stereotyped, huffy matron roles she was given to play. Smith's view of the world is essentially cold, while Redgrave's is always warm or blazing hot. "I am in awe of what Maggie Smith does," Redgrave said. "She is kind of unique."

Parenthetically, but maybe worth keeping in mind, when Smith was playing with her husband Robert Stephens in *Private Lives* in London in 1972, it was reported that there was a "dressing room fracas" between Smith and Redgrave when Redgrave visited Stephens backstage. Smith allegedly took a swing at Redgrave and missed, hitting Stephens and knocking out his two front teeth. The marriage between Smith and Stephens was volatile and embattled, and so something like this might have happened, though it was probably less dramatic than what hit the papers.

With Nero again, Redgrave made the Italian *A Quiet Place in the Country* (1968), a flashy psychological thriller directed by Elio Petri with a brooding Ennio Morricone score. After the fragmented credits, we see Nero all tied up. A mod, swinging London-like Redgrave enters and brags about some of her esoteric purchases, including "an erotic electromagnet." She's soon nude and stabbing him and saying, "We had nearly everything, nearly everything, what a pity," and then he wakes up—this whole first scene has been a dream. When asked about nude scenes, Redgrave said, "One spends an awful lot of one's life naked, so what's extraordinary about spending a little bit of film naked?"

Nero's character looks at upsetting photos and then paints, and we see the couple reading sex magazines and laughing over them. Bourgeois to the core, Redgrave's character cares more about the money she makes from Nero's art than the art itself. She knows she's losing him and clings to him physically. "I may be a practical woman, but I love you," she says, trying to reconcile her consumerist nature with his artistic one. He reassures her, but their house itself starts lashing out at her, and we finally see him beating her to death with a shovel, which proves to be another dream (he's eventually led off to a madhouse). This was a second philistine-wife role for Redgrave, and just as essentially thankless as *Morgan*.

Robert Altman offered Redgrave the lead role in *That Cold Day in the Park* (1969). After reading the script, Redgrave said that it was more suited to Sandy Dennis and that Altman should try to get her, and this resulted in one of Dennis's best performances. After an interval of three years, Redgrave returned to the stage to play Gwendolen Harleth in a Michael Elliott production of George Eliot's *Daniel Deronda*, a book that was partly meant to strike a blow against English anti-Semitism with its sympathetic portrayal of its Jewish characters and their need for a homeland. It was only because she trusted Elliott implicitly that she took the plunge after all the terror she had felt during the run of *The Prime of Miss Jean Brodie*.

In her first scene, Redgrave's Gwendolen kissed her reflection in a large mirror. "It is Miss Redgrave's triumph that she shows us all this, all the devouring egotism, yet also shows us in her pale, graceful, wavering presence the glimmer of better things which flicker beneath the carapace of selfishness, struggling upward," wrote J. W. Lambert in the *Christian Science Monitor*.

Redgrave took a large flat with seven other members of the company and cooked for them after every performance. "She does have the rather old-fashioned idea that if you all eat together, you probably won't kill each other," said her friend Thelma Holt. "So she cooks for everyone in her house." Redgrave carried a copy of the first page of Eliot's manuscript on her person during the run of the play. Whenever she had a twinge of her old *Jean Brodie* stage fright, she would simply take out this page, this calm beginning to a major novel, and it would make her calm in turn.

During this production Redgrave discovered that she was pregnant with Nero's child. Their son Carlo was born out of wedlock and out of love. "When women say to me, 'I'm going to have your baby,' I'm always skeptical," said Nero. "But when Carlo was born, I saw he had a whorl of hair above his temple just like I have, and I said, 'That's my boy.'"

After having her third baby, Redgrave was denounced as immoral by the conservative newspaper columnist David Astor in the *Observer*. She went with her agent Robin Fox to see Astor and demanded an apology in print, and they got one. She spent most of 1970 taking care of her three children, but her vocal protests that year against the Vietnam War heralded a new decade when politics would come to define Redgrave until it nearly swallowed up her film and stage career.

# Trojan Women
# and Devils

The title card that opens Michael Cacoyannis's film version of Euripides' *The Trojan Women* (1971) calls the play "a timeless indictment of the horror and futility of all war," and the silent credits that follow reveal the starry cast: Katharine Hepburn as Hecuba, Geneviève Bujold as Cassandra, Vanessa Redgrave as Andromache, and Irene Papas as Helen of Troy.

It was thought in the press that there might be conflict between Hepburn and Redgrave, but they got along very well on location in Atienza, Spain, some eighty miles north of Madrid. They were similar in many ways, stubborn and also endlessly curious—both began to learn Spanish while they worked together. Hepburn had been particularly taken with Redgrave's Rosalind, a role she herself had played in the early 1950s when she was just a bit too old for it. In fact, Hepburn considered Redgrave the most accomplished young actress of her time. "A thrill to look at and to listen to," she said. When a film was proposed of her 1987 memoir about the making of *The African Queen* (1951), Hepburn wasn't interested until she heard that Redgrave might play her. "I don't know who else could possibly do it," she said.

Rex Reed went up to interview Hepburn on location. "I drove three hours north from Madrid," Reed wrote, "past hydroelectric plants and empty gas stations until the road hit the parched and open plains, arid and dead as the Dakota badlands. Following a lonely telephone cable in the Castilian mountains, the car began to climb. Up past the castle walls of ancient Roman ruins, through dwarfed Hieronymus Bosch villages where crones draped in black raised sunburned arms to chase the ravens from their granaries."

At the end of his trip, Reed was on top of a mountain and found himself "surrounded by a herd of bearded goats, a band of gypsies from the nearby caves leaning against a rock and eating a stolen melon, and Katharine Hepburn, bent over a washtub, shampooing Vanessa Redgrave's hair. She charged the film company $5.00 for doing it.

"Nearly blinded by the rubber tire smoke from the burning of Troy, she hobbled up and down hills between scenes like a rabbit collecting fossils," Reed wrote. "Everyone in the cast suffered from sunstroke, diarrhea, nausea, and every kind of local disease imaginable, except for Kate, who nursed them all. 'I'm working as hard as any human being can,' she said, wiping bloodshot eyes. 'The climate hates me, and there is no money, but I am hired to deliver the goods no matter what the circumstances, so I'll do the best I can. I owe it to the people who have supported me through the good years and bad.'"

Cacoyannis had made some excellent films in his native Greece, like *Stella* (1955) with Melina Mercouri, and he had staged *The Trojan Women* in Italy, New York, and Paris in the early 1960s. "For me," Cacoyannis said, "the play is particularly pertinent and real. What the play is saying is as important today as it was when it was written. I feel very strongly about war, militarism, killing people . . . and I haven't found a better writer who makes that point more clearly than Euripides. The play is about the folly of war, the folly of people killing others and forgetting that they are going to die themselves."

Cacoyannis periodically freezes the film into still images in the first scenes of chaos but soon abandons this awkward device. We see Hepburn raising herself off the ground, speaking in low, precise tones and then letting loose with great big guttural bursts of anger. Bujold goes all-out as Cassandra, but Cacoyannis impedes her work with graceless fast-cutting as she exits. No amount of editorial over-indulgence, however, can get in the way of Redgrave's interpretation of Andromache, which stands as one of the very best of all her performances.

It helps that Redgrave has never been more beautiful than she is here. She enters with her young son, standing on a wagon, stately, proud, noble, her blond hair blowing in goddess-like tendrils around her face. When she comes down to earth and mingles with the despairing women, Redgrave knows exactly how to play the elemental quality necessary for Greek tragedy. She *leaps* right up to towering heights of sorrow and rage, and her emotions are so focused, so blade-like and clean, that she makes Hepburn look like she's showing off without giving enough thought and imagination to the situation.

To Redgrave, Andromache isn't just a role to be played to test her mettle as a classical actress but a real and specific person from long ago. She might have sprung right from Ancient Greece, and yet Redgrave also mixes in fleeting moments of contemporary emotion, like the almost-humorous "um-hum" she uses when Andromache realizes the full unfairness of her plight as a royal woman reduced to slavery. "Oh, shame, oh!" she cries, rolling her head from side to side, viscerally feeling the torment of her future in bondage. When this Andromache raises her eyes to the sky and talks to her dead husband Hector, it's almost possible to see and hear what he must have been like. Redgrave scores so decisively in this most difficult of material because she is able to so fully imagine life in this period.

A soldier speaks to her gently, and she freezes: "Evil follows words like those," she says quietly, creating a sense of burgeoning fear right before the soldier tells her that her son is to be killed. Cacoyannis keeps his camera on Redgrave as a harsh little rattle in her throat starts to expand upwards into a larger sound. Her blanked-out face begins to fill with muscle-tensing panic as her mouth opens wider and wider and the sound she's making gets bigger and bigger until it ends in a static kind of cry of anguish that is unlike anything else in the cinema. The closest equivalent to it, on an acting level, is James Cagney's breakdown scene in the mess hall in *White Heat* (1949) after he's just been told his beloved mother is dead, where he throws himself all over the space as he makes ugly grunts of tear-soaked despair. Redgrave, by contrast, holds herself totally still as she makes her sound of grief. She lets the emotion take possession of her until she looks like a woman turned to stone. There finally are no words to describe just how far Redgrave gets with this cry. It's the ultimate expression of classical Greek despair.

Andromache tries to shield her son, but she can't keep this up for long, and at last she winds up spent on the ground, clutching his little body, her face white and pulled back like a corpse who looks surprised by death. "How sweet the fragrance of you," she says to the boy, before letting him go and burying her face in the dust. She rubs the dust all over her head as she says, "The gods have destroyed me, I cannot save my child from death."

Thinking of the splendors of her past, Redgrave's Andromache stares up at the sky again and asks, "All nothing then?" She is led away standing on a wagon and, heroically, she has regained her full composure. Redgrave has done nothing better than this Andromache, and Irene Papas has her work cut out for her following Redgrave, but she makes her own vital impression as a scary-strong Helen. By the end, Hepburn's energy has faded, though she makes a good stab, overall, at Hecuba. On the set, Redgrave was so concentrated that she couldn't speak much to reporters, but she did say, "I see Andromache from the point of view of a mother, not an actress."

Redgrave made two psychedelic movies co-starring Franco Nero for Italian director Tinto Brass, *Dropout* (1970) and *La Vacanza* (1971), neither of which did much good or harm to her career because they were barely seen. Brass's film *L'urlo* (1968) had been banned, which aroused the interest of Jane Fonda, who arranged a private screening of the movie. After the lights came up, Brass was approached by Redgrave and Nero, who asked him to write a script for them. He happily obliged.

Carlo Ponti was supposed to produce *Dropout*, but when he declined, Brass said to Nero and Redgrave, "Let's do it anyway!" and the three of them paid for it themselves. They had such a good time making it that they did *La Vacanza* the following year, also financing it on 16mm with their own money. When asked why she was working with Brass, Redgrave said, "I saw his last film. He is a fantastic director. It's the first film I've been around which is on every level that I am concerned about and that we are all concerned about. It's Tinto's own story and the writer's, Roberto Lerici's." (Italian scenarist Franco Longo also collaborated on the script.)

Redgrave found herself attracted to the no-frills style of much Italian filmmaking as a kind of relief after the overproduced *Camelot*. "In Italian movies it's very good, you don't work along the Anglo-Saxon principle that it is film acting," Redgrave said. "It's filming. We are part of what goes together just as paints and brushes are part of an artist's canvas. And there is an element in it—we are that element and you put yourself into it as an element in the director's hands. With this kind of filmmaking you can see that the actors revolve around the camera. It's the first time I have worked with these principles. When it works, it works very fast. . . ."

Their shooting schedule for both films was six or so weeks. "We always do this in Italy," Brass said. "It's how films are made. We are not a rich country." Redgrave also enjoyed Brass's appreciation of her looks. When they were alone one evening watching the day's rushes, Brass went up to the screen and traced the pattern of her lips with his finger and then kissed her mouth, a paying of homage that surprised and moved Redgrave.

The consensus on these two MIA pictures is that they are "very much of their time," and the footage circulating online from *Dropout* looks home-movie-like and amateurish. Of the second film, Thomas Quinn Curtis wrote in the *New York Times*, "*La Vacanza* stars Vanessa Redgrave and Franco Nero and has to do with a peasant girl who suffers more outrages at the hands of the Establishment than were visited on de Sade's Justine. One must have a heart of stone not to laugh at her humiliations, all of them grotesquely pictured." Brass went on to direct mainly sleazy cinema like *Salon Kitty* (1976) and *Caligula* (1979).

*The Devils* (1971) is clearly the best or at least most presentable film directed by the reliably outrageous Ken Russell, and Redgrave herself thinks highly of it, ranking it in her memoir with *The Charge of the Light Brigade* as the two chief works of genius in the postwar British cinema. That might say something about the postwar British cinema more than the relative merit of these two movies, but her view is understandable.

Pregnant with a second child by Nero, Redgrave took on the role of the hunchback Sister Jeanne, a nun who causes a wave of sexual hysteria in 1634 France. She accepted the part only after Russell's usual star of this time, Glenda Jackson, turned him down because she didn't want to go mad and take off her clothes again for Ken so soon after their labors on *The Music Lovers* (1971), a sensationally vulgar attempt on the life of Tchaikovsky. *The Devils* would not be as potent a film if Jackson had played Sister Jeanne in her usual hard-bitten style. Redgrave brings the role a romantic obsessiveness as well as a quite unexpected wicked humor, both of which she somehow manages to keep in perfect balance.

"I wrote the script," Russell said. "John Whiting wrote the play *The Devils*, which was done with Robert Johnson and Dorothy Tutin. There was a book by Aldous Huxley, *Grey Eminence,* a study of Richelieu's adviser Pere Joseph. Both were inspirations, especially the book. The background of all the events was so well-documented. The dialogue in the play was also excellent. So I amalgamated the two."

*The Devils* is certainly the best-written of all Russell's films, the most disciplined, the only one that can claim a real horror at how twisted human beings can become. He makes a few mistakes, especially in falsely portraying Louis XIII (Graham Armitage) as a woman-hating homosexual who, in the first scene, does a "Venus on the Half-Shell" routine for Cardinal Richelieu (Christopher Logue), but Russell seems inspired by Derek Jarman's extremely suggestive sets, especially the convent, which resembles a vast black-and-white bathhouse.

"I know originally they had them looking for medieval times in France, to shoot on location," said Redgrave. "And I remember vividly that when I heard we'd be shooting in Pinewood studios, I had a sinking stomach and thought, 'Oh dear, oh dear, oh dear.' But of course, when I saw Derek Jarman's designs I knew that we were into something really extraordinary because Ken and he obviously had a very, very marvelous synthesis going between the links with the white tiles that meld with the meticulous costumes of the court and so on."

"All detail is sacrificed to scale as I want the sets as large as possible, and as forceful as the sets from an old silent," wrote Jarman in his journal *Dancing Edge.* "We started filming after months of preparation. The great white city is nearly complete on the lot and has become a tourist attraction. You could almost pay for it with visitors' fees. It cost £97,000.

"Rushes are like bingo," Jarman wrote. "Each of us votes for a favorite—one, two, three, four, or whatever. Ken sits at the back with the lighting cameraman, [David] Watkin, who usually gets his way. Watkin, who always wears plimsolls, reminds me of a bad-tempered sportsmaster. One expects him to take out a whistle and blow it. He doesn't like me very much, probably because everyone calls me 'the artist,' and the sets, rather than his lighting, are the continual topic of conversation." During a row about the sets, Jarman thought that Russell was like "the mad empress from some B-movie—waving his cane, his long hair flowing, wearing a smock and enormous rings on every finger."

"Why have you left your devotions?" asks Redgrave's Sister Jeanne of her fellow nuns, making her first entrance into the film with her head crooked to the right as she schleps into view. Redgrave chooses to let out a high, completely disconnected laugh in between some of Sister Jeanne's orders to her charges, and this feels very Off-Off-Broadway, or like something from a comic sketch, yet she is able to pull you right back into the seriousness of this woman's demented, feverish existence. Sister Jeanne speaks ill of "sen-soo-al delights," with Redgrave caressing the first word (for she is the most sensual of actresses), and then naughtily fondling a key. She makes for a highly disturbing and funny madwoman.

This nun is the very picture of disbelieving cynicism when she receives Madeleine (Gemma Jones) behind the bars of the convent's front door. "You have the face of a virgin martyr in a picture book, very pious," Redgrave sneers, making the "p" in "picture" land with contemptuous force. "Downcast eyes," she continues, gazing at the girl with a hard, amused expression on her face. "Hiding what? Virtue, or lechery?"

Redgrave is certainly one of the least cynical people possible in her public life, but she is able to imagine a kind of cynicism unto madness for this wretched and lethal Mother Superior. She keeps this woman's opposing qualities in play without once descending into caricature or one-note satire. Sister Jeanne tells Madeleine that most of the women in the order are only there because they are unmarriageable girls. This is the one scene where Sister Jeanne seems fully aware of her situation and fully able to laugh at it, in her habitual way, as if she's sneering at the God who gave her a pretty face and a hump on her back to go with it.

Judging from her other work, surely Redgrave would have preferred a more sober accounting of this woman's cracked personality, but she enters into Russell's engrained bad taste and vulgarity, using it when it is useful to her and discarding it entirely when she wants us to feel the depth of this woman's depravity and pain. If *The Devils* is a major film, it is Redgrave who makes it so. No other actress of her time could have given such an extreme and dirty and comic performance while still remaining somehow immaculately pure and so sad at the core.

"God bless you," Sister Jeanne says to Madeleine as the girl goes. Uttering just these three words, Redgrave rapidly gives them a contemptuous feeling, as if Sister Jeanne is following a familiar impulse for derision, but then she dims the contempt within a split second until we see and hear Sister Jeanne's disappointment, and even her wish that she might believe these words. The kaleidoscopic quality of this woman's madness allows Redgrave to give virtuosically blended line readings like this. Not one choice followed by another, as another highly skilled actress might have managed, but several choices all at once expressing the roiling mess of this woman's mind and soul.

Redgrave had a miscarriage of her second child by Nero during the filming of *The Devils*. It would have been a boy. In one of the most touching sections of her autobiography, she wrote that she buried the dead baby under a bush that would flower in the spring. And then she went back to the set to enact her character's huge anger and even larger longing.

Sister Jeanne stares at her beloved priest Urbain Grandier (Oliver Reed) and then has a hallucination where her wimple is off so that we see her long red hair as she cleans his feet with her tongue. He discovers her hump, and she screams, "Don't look at me! Don't look at me!" and then, "I'm beautiful! I'm beautiful!" What could be merely a camp sneer at her character, as it might have been in just about any other Russell movie, comes across as upsetting and deeply humiliating because Redgrave is so in touch with her own inner freak and so empathizes with Sister Jeanne's cursed freakishness. In scenes like this, Redgrave is very close to Katharine Hepburn at her best, and she's even more lyrical in the midst of the kind of bold, filthy, sexual material that Hepburn would never have touched in her time.

Speaking of the film's blasphemous imagery, persistent Russell critic Alexander Walker said, "It looked like the masturbation fantasies of a Roman Catholic boyhood." Walker was later bopped on the head with a newspaper by Russell on TV after the critic unfavorably reviewed the film.

"Where is love?" asks Reed's pregnant mistress as he casts her aside, and it's a question that haunts *The Devils*, a vision of hell on earth that Russell does not spoil with his usual boy-like need to shock and go too far. "It's about the degradation of religious principles," Russell said of the film. "And about a sinner who becomes a saint." He films heaps of human corpses and barbaric medical remedies with an austere kind of outrage much removed from the relentless jokiness of his other work.

*The Devils* almost has an air of Hermann Hesse's best novels as it opens a barely stylized window on a particular time and place. Working on the film, Redgrave said, "It was fairly exhausting, but it had its moments of hilarity." Especially amusing to her was the scene where she had to spew "endless mouthfuls of Heinz vegetable soup" out of her mouth when Sister Jeanne is made to vomit out her devils. She spoke up for her character with sharp psychological acuity. "It's only my own opinion, but I think that it was a sort of continually changing texture and combination of contradictions running through her. I'm sure the wet dreams that she must have had made her feel intensely guilty, and she probably went into denial and placed her own longings onto the other, outside herself. It's a very common mechanism that happens in those kinds of situations."

Sister Jeanne leads the sisters in prayer and has another hallucination about Grandier where he comes down off the cross as a substitute for Christ. When she learns that Grandier has married Madeleine, Sister Jeanne bites down hard on her crucifix and lashes out at Madeleine when she returns to the convent gate. Meanwhile, Richelieu wants to pull down the town's fortifications to quell Protestant rebellion and Grandier rails against this. Sister Jeanne's embittered talk of devils possessing her through Grandier's form are eventually taken up by Richelieu as a political ploy, and her confused accusations against Grandier are capitalized on by the insane Father Pierre Barre (played by an actor named Michael Gothard, who might have been cast by Russell for his name alone).

Everyone laughs at Sister Jeanne when she is asked about her possession in front of a crowd of onlookers, and Redgrave is not able to hold
on to our feelings in the sequence where Russell runs her nun through
a gauntlet of sexual abuse at the hands of Barre and his minions. The
"oh boy!" nastiness of the tone here feels too close to Russell's worst
impulses for sensationalism, but Redgrave's sensuality is at its height when
she describes bathing with her imagined lover "in a sea of stars" while
stretching her body out on the ground of Jarman's infernal lavatory set.

Russell is back to the more severe tone of the earlier scenes when Louis
XIII enters and says that he can cure Sister Jeanne and her order with a
box that supposedly contains a vial of Christ's blood. After Sister Jeanne
and the other nuns claim they have been cured by exposure to the box,
Louis opens it up and reveals that it is empty, which makes Sister Jeanne
laugh her most cynical laugh. It might be said that Redgrave's outstanding
performance in *The Devils* is a catalogue of Sister Jeanne's laughter, which
she cannot control and which exposes her in all her multi-leveled and
violent humanity, in both her meanness and her suffering, which are
sometimes intertwined and sometimes not.

The American release of *The Devils* saw the loss of the so-called
"Rape of Christ" sequence, when the nuns defile a statue of Jesus. "In
the end, Warners went bonkers and cut it," Russell said. "They said I'd
changed the script. I went through it line for line and it was exactly as
I'd written it." But what he had put on the screen was too disturbing
for the studio brass.

The "Rape of Christ" sequence has never been shown in a complete
cut of *The Devils*, and it can only be glimpsed in documentaries about
the making of the film. Sister Jeanne looks on as the nuns take down a statue
of Christ, her face hard and suspicious as she licks the face of a man lying
underneath her. The mad naked nuns dry-hump the statue in many
inventive ways, and their cavorting is intercut with shots of Grandier
taking communion. This juxtaposition is meant to show the contrast of
Grandier's growing faith with the utter depravity of the religious order.
"They've been exploited to the point of absolute, total blasphemy of their
religion," said Russell, "and that's what the authorities wanted, that's what
eventually led to the destruction of the city."

Some of the girls who were extras really put themselves on the line. They were given the script and instructed to read the nude nun hysteria scenes, and if they felt unable to do them, they were told not to accept the job. Russell tried to lighten things up with naughty-boy antics. "Ken's attitude to naked women is one of joy," said actor Dudley Sutton. "They were dancing around naked in the rain and it was very cold, and Ken gave me a hairdryer and said, 'Warm their tits when they come off!'" But a few of the girls just weren't prepared for these scenes. Extra Lee Fyles said, "Some of the younger girls got rather upset with all that frenzy and all the things that were going on. Some of the men extras got carried away and they were pawed rather a bit, and I do remember a couple of them coming out crying."

"A lot of the cut scenes were important to explain the trauma—especially the torment of Sister Jeanne in the convent," Russell said. "There's a scene where she pushes her deformed body through a tiny window to watch out for her fantasy lover. So much of the film is gone now that it doesn't make a lot of sense. Every scene was important to balance the rest of the film."

"The wilder scenes in the film are fueled with champagne, which sometimes arrives with breakfast," wrote Jarman. "In the cathedral, Ken has a drum kit brought in and drums away loudly to whip up fervor." Jarman disapproved of the "flip jokes" that sometime intrude on *The Devils* and all but dominate Russell's other films. Before shooting the scene where the walls of the town are blown up, Russell inadvertently set off the explosives while the camera wasn't running, and they had to wait ten days to rebuild the set and get the shot.

Reed often said that he never gave a better performance than as Grandier, especially in the final scenes, where he defends himself eloquently in court and gets his head shaved. The bullish actor really does outdo himself here, and he never had better lines to speak. After Grandier tells Sister Jeanne that her soul will be damned if she continues with her lying, the nun looks apprehensive, but when she tries to recant, Barre holds her in check with the promise of sex.

As Grandier is being driven to be burned at the stake, he sees Sister Jeanne one more time, a woman he barely knows, a woman who has condemned him to death, but a woman for whom he has a kind of compassion, even kinship, for he is as complicated as she is. He tries to reach out to her, but she just cries, "Devil! Devil!" This is the moment when *The Devils* attains a real tragic power.

Reed said that he had a hard time recovering from making *The Devils*: "You see the film and it lasts for an hour and thirty minutes, but we were working on it for four months." When Grandier came to be burned at the stake, Russell went for absolute realism. "The direction of the wind changed," said Reed, "and Russell kept throwing petrol on the fire, and I really almost burned!"

Reed defended the film's subject. "We weren't trying to afford any-body proper niceties, any proper little entertainment," he said. "We were showing them the bigotry that goes on and all that humanity is capable of. This is the way it happened—those nuns were used for political ends, toted around France as a side show for a year," he said.

In her last scene, Sister Jeanne prays and seems tired-out after all the commotion. Given a bone from Grandier's body, she uses it to masturbate, a scene that is also missing from the American cut of the film. The bone is made to look very much like a dildo, and Sister Jeanne lovingly kisses what look like the bone's balls before stretching out on the floor and con-summating her lust for Grandier with the last physical trace of his body.

"It's a very, very terrifying sequence as written and naturally as filmed," said Redgrave. "I don't think it was done in anything that wasn't simply an accounting of the pitiful, terrifying fact that Sister Jeanne took this bone and she was . . . fucking herself with it. I was quite frightened of the sequence, but at the same time I thought that it expresses in the most pitiful way the depths of her dementia and the depths of her need for . . . humanity." The scene makes for a daring last note of perhaps the most daring performance from this most daring of actors.

"*The Devils* is my favorite amongst my feature films," Russell said. "I think it has a lot more to say than the others, which were more or less just biographies. *The Devils* was about brainwashing, the manipulation of the masses and all that."

Redgrave spoke out against the censorship of the finished work. "I think every director should have the right to show their film in the way they want it to be seen," she said. "A film can't be special without the conception of the story and the conception of the cinematography, the camera set-ups, the lighting of the environment, without it all coming together to make a single whole. And sometimes, even with wonderful people, they sometimes don't succeed in making a single whole. And in the case of *The Devils*, I think all the people who took part in it around Ken, including the actors, did contribute to making a single whole, a masterpiece." It was not a financial success in America in its cut version, but it has become a cult film that still creates controversy wherever it is shown, in whatever watered-down edit.

Redgrave realized that Russell had his ups and downs as a director. "The films Ken made were the work of a genius," Redgrave insisted. "Sometimes his films were much less than genius. You can't be a genius unless you're tops and bottoms, I think." As a risk-taker, she responded with alacrity to his terminal outrageousness.

Seeing the film again after forty years at a Lincoln Center screening during a Russell retrospective, Redgrave spoke afterwards with Russell on stage. "I am even more astonished now," she said. "It's like you took cinema into another world." She then made reference to the movie's "extraordinary images of the kind of brutal chaos that certainly happened at that time, and is still happening in other times." Russell said in response, "That's why I wanted to make it. I mean, I thought it was a tale that needed retelling every few years, because nothing changes."

At the end of this first flurry of movie work, Redgrave won a third Best Actress Oscar nomination for *Mary, Queen of Scots* (1971), an unexceptional costume picture. The film pits Redgrave's loose, lyrical Mary against Glenda Jackson's tense, biting Elizabeth I, and it moves at a fast pace. In many ways this is Jackson's movie, for Elizabeth is always the better part in this story, and when she is missing from the middle of the narrative her absence is keenly felt.

Jackson had just played Elizabeth to rave reviews in a TV series, *Elizabeth R*. "I shot *Mary, Queen of Scots* after *Elizabeth R*," says Jackson. "There was no link between them. The series was factual. They never met, Elizabeth and Mary Stuart never met. The series and the film weren't comparable in that way, if you see what I mean.

"I think the reason I did it was the opportunity to work with Vanessa," says Jackson. "She's terribly shortsighted, so I don't think she ever actually sees the people she's working with, which makes it a fascinating process, actually, and it's one of the reasons why I think she's so marvelous. She is so concentrated, and that concentration and that energy she has, both people can use it. I had met her before, though not working with her. We were in the same studio, though on different films, in the past."

Asked if she can define what makes Redgrave special, the no-nonsense Jackson demurs. "Oh, that's an impossible question to answer," she says. "I mean, obviously, talent. I mean, how do you define it? She's just great. No, no, come on, I did one scene with her in a crappy film, you know, so no, you can't make assessments like that. Her record is her work and the quality of her work."

Redgrave had broken with Nero after a quarrel over taking Carlo to visit Richardson with her daughters. "The Redgraves were quite an imposing family," Nero said. "But our relationship was damaged by her friends; they were enemies to me." Nero at that time wanted an Italian housewife like his own mother, and Redgrave was certainly not going to be that for any man. But there were other problems, too. "You are a fanatic in your politics, and you are ruining your life!" Nero told her.

Timothy Dalton, who played the sybaritic, bisexual Lord Darnley with Redgrave in *Mary, Queen of Scots*, soon made a tempestuous match with her off-screen. He was a severe critic of her work, but she knew that if he ever paid her a compliment it really meant something. One of their first arguments was a five-to-six-hour marathon on what Hamlet's "To be or not to be" speech might mean. Dalton provoked and challenged her, and she responded to that. They would fight and break up and get back together again for most of the 1970s and 1980s.

In *Mary, Queen of Scots*, Redgrave makes sure that we can feel how flighty and pampered Mary is, and the role suits her out-of-it queenliness. In 1936, Katharine Hepburn had been stuck in this part in John Ford's *Mary of Scotland*, and she was as well cast as Redgrave, but both actresses, fine as they are, can do nothing to add much interest to a woman who always seems muddleheaded in any telling of this oft-told tale. "I never cared for Mary," wrote Hepburn in her autobiography. "I thought she was a bit of an ass."

Late in life, Redgrave said, "I loved playing Mary, Queen of Scots, because she was a historical heroine of mine and I loved learning a song that she wrote. I learnt to play the mandolin just for that. You could read Mary like your hand. She was very open. Mary led from the heart and Elizabeth was forced by circumstances to lead from her head, at a great cost to herself. But Elizabeth managed, for her country, to survive under great difficulties." Redgrave's mind seems to be elsewhere a lot of the time in this film, and Mary's wavering motivations sometimes feel foggy because clearer acting choices haven't been made in some scenes. *Mary, Queen of Scots* marked a break in her film work.

"I had continued to act because I didn't know what else to do and I had to earn my living," Redgrave said. "To continue to act without being able to make a decision about the political way forward was useless. I became to a certain extent paralyzed in trying to fight to find some political answers." Her activism against the Vietnam War had won her many enemies who sent her nasty letters. "The minute you realize it is a poison pen letter, put it down immediately," she told her sister-in-law Deirdre. "If you read on, the disgusting threats and abuse somehow stick in your mind, no matter how crazy you know the people are who wrote them."

In the autumn of 1971, while in Los Angeles for a brief run of Berlioz's *Béatrice et Bénédict* with the Los Angeles Symphony Orchestra, Redgrave helped to organize a GI antiwar newspaper called *PEACE* and gave her support to striking schoolteachers. Due to her protests against the Vietnam War, she was unable to get a multiple-entry visa to the US and was branded a member of the Communist Party. "I wouldn't be a Communist for the world," she said at the time. "If there was a decent Communist party, I'd be in it—but there isn't one."

Charlton Heston was able to get Redgrave a work visa to play with him in LA in *Macbeth* in 1974, and Richardson got her one to play in New York in *The Lady from the Sea* in 1976, but Redgrave was not able to get a multiple-entry visa to the US until 1985, the same year, coincidentally or not, that the Workers Revolutionary Party fell apart.

"I'd known of the Workers Revolutionary Party, because even before I'd been an MP I'd been engaged in the political life of my country and also the politics of my union, Equity," says Glenda Jackson. "So we all knew about the WRP. They were hardly hiding their views. I was never as far to the left as they were."

# Keeping Left

Redgrave turned down the plum role of Alex Greville in John Schlesinger's *Sunday Bloody Sunday* (1971), a woman who shares her lover with another man, thereby handing Glenda Jackson one of her best film parts. At the Young Vic in 1971, Redgrave appeared in Robert Shaw's play *Cato Street*, which was about a group of radicals who infiltrated the Tory government in 1820. A backstage candid from this time shows Redgrave wearing granny glasses and looking like a strapping young boy with large arms in her tight tank-top shirt.

The following year she took tap and singing lessons to play Polly Peachum in Tony Richardson's slick version of *The Threepenny Opera* in London at the Prince of Wales Theatre. The great jazz singer Annie Ross played Jenny in this production. "At Christmastime in London, I used to go and sing in the jails and entertain the prisoners, because that's when they need it, at Christmastime," says Ross. "I took my group with me, and I told them that afterward I had to go see somebody about doing a show. I told them it was kind of an opera. I didn't know much about Brecht or *The Threepenny Opera* then.

"I went to Tony Richardson's house, and I was wearing a full-length white cape, quite spectacular," Ross says. "And nobody came to the door after I rang the bell. And then finally the door opened and it was Tony, and he said he had just come in the back way. I told him I didn't want to do theater, but he said he wanted me and he would protect me. And then he said he had a wonderful cast, and he said the name 'Vanessa' and I said, 'Really? Vanessa?' I mean, I was impressed. I think she might be the greatest actress living, you know? So I said yes right away."

Ross remembers that Redgrave and Richardson did a lot of rehearsing by themselves. "He was always in her corner," she says. "I remember that night after night I would watch her from the wings in a certain scene where she says, and I'm paraphrasing here, but she says something like, 'I'll never see him again.' And the way she said that every night made me just dissolve, you know? I saw her later at Tony's house in the south of France, where everybody would pitch in and make food and eat, and Natasha, their daughter, was there."

"Vanessa Redgrave tried to sing but hits only eight notes out of ten," wrote Jonathan Kemp in the *Catholic Herald*. "This is unfortunate particularly because apart from the song her performance is excellent. Her dance at the wedding is a fine piece of comic movement. Tony Richardson's production is consistent in tone and emphasizes Brecht's detached and ironic attitude to his characters."

Redgrave took part in protests against the Bloody Sunday massacre of thirteen Irish civilians by British paratroopers. She very much admired Bernadette Devlin, who spoke of the need to unite Catholic and Protestant workers in their struggle against British rule.

She did a brief run as Viola in *Twelfth Night* in 1972 at the Shaw Theatre in Camden and started to build a nursery school for disadvantaged children in a poor section of London with all of her money from *Camelot*, *Isadora*, *The Devils*, and *Mary, Queen of Scots*. This was one of her most selfless and positive actions for change. The Vanessa Nursery School was officially opened on September 16, 1973, and it remains open to this day.

Restless and dissatisfied, Redgrave was looking for political alternatives to salve her disillusionment with organized protest, and she soon found a group that she felt would give her all the answers. The Workers Revolutionary Party was run by Gerry Healy, a small man, only five foot two or three inches, but a large personality. Her brother Corin had joined the party, and he kept trying to get his sister involved with it.

Redgrave wasn't interested in the WRP at first. Her friend C. L. R. James told her that Healy was really a Stalinist, and this scared Redgrave off for a time, but Corin and Healy kept putting pressure on her. During a lull in her relationship with Dalton, when she was feeling particularly vulnerable, Redgrave finally joined the WRP.

Healy was excited about attracting a star to his group, telling Redgrave that he was glad to have Mary, Queen of Scots join his fold. He had set his sights on her a while back, and now he carefully reeled her in. She was completely captivated by Healy. "I have always loved fanatics," Redgrave told her sister-in-law Deirdre. "They are the only truly genuine people in the world."

Redgrave admitted that she had been drinking too much "cheap wine every morning to get the fuzzy obliteration of alcohol" in this early '70s period. This drinking was due to depression, she said later, over labor and union conditions imposed by Prime Minister Ted Heath. She and fellow members of the WRP thought that a series of car-bomb attacks in London on March 8, 1973 were not the work of the IRA but a deliberate provocation by the ruling Tory government. Redgrave and the novelist Edna O'Brien and a few others wanted to post bail for the Irish youths arrested for the car bombings, but their offer of bail was refused.

The Workers Revolutionary Party, which was known as the Socialist Labour League until November 4, 1973, was run like a cult. Many of the members were encouraged to cut themselves off from their families. The party had grown out of a faction of the Revolutionary Communist Party headed by John Lawrence and Healy, who had insisted that all members of his faction be educated according to his dictates. One of his main objectives was the replacement of police in England with a workers' militia. In Healy's mind, revolution by the workers was always imminent.

"Corin impressed me," said party member Tim Wohlforth. "He seemed extremely interested in Marxist theory and quite willing to do everything other members did. He would go out at five in the morning to sell papers at plant gates and deliver papers door to door in working class neighborhoods. It was Corin who brought his more famous sister around the organization. I met Vanessa on several occasions and she seemed equally as serious as her brother and more than willing to carry out any party task she was asked to do. . . . Clearly, I told myself, these two can make a real contribution to the movement." Today Wohlforth says, "At the time I first met her, she was trying to pretend that she was not Vanessa Redgrave but some regular militant in the group. And she was going to go out on her paper sales, and so on."

Redgrave made her first attempt at Shakespeare's Cleopatra for Richardson in 1973 at an open-air theater called the Bankside. Richardson set the play in the late 1930s and had Redgrave play Cleopatra like a spoiled movie star, but some critics compared her to an alley cat and a gangster's moll because her first Cleopatra had a tendency to be physically violent with anyone within reach. Redgrave was clearly in no mood in 1973 to portray a queen as anything but a bully and a harpy. This production was apparently not one of the finer efforts for anyone involved.

When she acted in Noël Coward's *Design for Living* with Jeremy Brett and John Stride, which opened in November of 1973 at the Phoenix Theatre in London, Redgrave tried in vain to discern some political message in it about the social crises of the '30s. Her instincts and intelligence as a performer on stage, however, according to most reports, remained as sharp and unusual as ever. "It is wonderful, wonderful, wonderful," wrote Sandy Wilson of the very sexy production in *Plays and Players*.

"I was trying to get over the echoes of the Noël Coward productions I had seen many, many years before, at drama school or in the West End or even films," Redgrave said, "in which all of the actors were performing in a way that was said to be 'Noël Coward comedy.' Everybody talking extremely fast and rather clipped and holding in all their emotions very tightly. Perhaps because I knew Noël Coward when I was very young, and I knew that his concern was for human truth. These had to be people that had actually lived and weren't brilliant stereotypes, even brilliant Noël Coward stereotypes." She emphasized her character's "sense of impending disaster."

Much of Redgrave's time at this point was spent getting deeper and deeper into the thinking and management of her political party, which was chiefly run by Healy's righthand men Mike Banda and Alex

Mitchell. Wohlforth told in his memoirs about the rapid rise of the Redgraves in the WRP: "I was shocked when I next met them," Wohlforth said of the Redgraves. "It was at an International Committee meeting held in 1973 and Corin and Vanessa were the SLL's delegates to the conference! This seemed unreal to me as Vanessa had been in the movement barely a year and Corin only a couple of years basically as a rank-and-filer. They had become Healy's special pets, the mask of humility was being dropped and a kind of arrogance emerging. Both made rather lengthy and totally hollow presentations to the meeting, asserting—as if they had just discovered something—the critical importance of the revolutionary party and theory in the next period of the capitalist crisis, etc., etc., etc."

Wohlforth today sees a connection between Healy's cult and another cult that was coming into its own at the time. "Healy to me was on a parallel track with Scientology," Wohlforth says. "He did the same thing that the Scientologists did. In order to reach someone like Tom Cruise, or like Vanessa, they set up a whole special world for them that has been adapted to the artist or actor. Healy had started this class, and actors started to come to it, and Corin Redgrave became involved in that and then he got Vanessa involved. It was a whole dog and pony show just for her. Healy spent a lot of time with her, and he had these special classes that met every week just for the artists, actors, and actresses. He wanted to make her feel that she was doing the right revolutionary thing.

"It was similar to Scientology and other cults like that, where actors have this need that is fulfilled in a cultic way by gurus," Wohlforth says. "It comes out of some kind of self-doubt, I guess. They need that kind of support in order to prove themselves as being more than an actor." Healy would use Redgrave as bait at various meetings. "I remember they had this big labor conference in Birmingham, I think, and they had maybe a couple thousand trade unionists there," Wohlforth says. "And she performed at it, she did 'Diamonds Are a Girl's Best Friend,' this little song and dance routine."

WRP member Norman Harding claims in his memoir *Staying Red* that Redgrave drove her car into another party member's moped and that the damages to Redgrave's car were paid for by the WRP while the party member with the ruined moped had to pay for her own repairs. Redgrave was treated as a special case in the WRP, with special privileges. Harding had a low opinion of Redgrave. Once they were canvassing for votes for the party and stopped to talk to a harried mother with children clinging to her skirts. Harding writes:

> I asked her if there was a tenants' organization on the estate that she could approach for advice and help. At this point Vanessa pushed past me, and started to tell her about the need to change the system. The only way to solve her problems, said Vanessa, was to demand a general strike, and so on. Then out came the membership application form. The young mother was left with "Vote for the WRP!" ringing in her ears. . . . VR told me she severely disagreed with my initial approach and that she was going to raise it at the report-back meeting as an example of how important it was to fight against social democracy. That evening I received a great deal of verbal abuse from Healy, Mike Banda, Mitchell and Co.

Redgrave had gotten back together with Dalton, but he broke with her again when she insisted on going to a rally for trade unionists in Manchester rather than spend a Sunday afternoon with him. She went to the rally and sang at a concert after it, and she vowed to herself not to give up her struggle, but she cried on a train coming back from the meeting, and she cried the next morning at breakfast. Her young daughters Natasha and Joely put their arms around her, and when she told her daughters why she was crying, they did their best to comfort her.

The children felt neglected too, especially Natasha. Redgrave tried to explain to Natasha that she was working to make a better world for her and for all the children of her generation in the future, to which Natasha replied, "But I need you *now*. I won't need you so much then." Redgrave tried to tell Natasha that many children couldn't enjoy happy lives with their parents because of "the injustice and cruelty of our society." To work for all the suffering children she did not know, like the boy she had read about in the newspaper who had died when a farmer beat him to death in the 1940s, Redgrave sacrificed much of her early relationship with her own children. She would grow to keenly regret this as an older woman.

In this period when Healy and the Workers Revolutionary Party consumed almost her whole life and she cast about for causes, sniffed out injustice, and helped to publish a magazine for the party called *Keep Left*, Redgrave also acted in *October*, a play about the start of the 1917 Russian Revolution, and she spent a lot of time getting out her party's main newspaper, *Workers Press*, which later became known as *The News Line*.

She played writer Katherine Mansfield on TV in *A Picture of Katherine Mansfield* (1973), a six-part BBC series opposite Jeremy Brett as Mansfield's husband, John Middleton Murry. In each episode, she would act out a bit of Mansfield's life and then there would be a recreation of one of Mansfield's stories. It sounds extremely interesting, but this is practically a lost performance from Redgrave that remains just about impossible to see. Even the various Katherine Mansfield societies do not own a copy of it. "That BBC TV series is notoriously hard to locate," says ace Mansfield scholar Gerri Kimber. "Even I have never seen it." David Thomson found Redgrave's performance in this Mansfield series "mannered but intriguing" in his first *Biographical Dictionary of Film*.

During her daily life off-screen, Redgrave's absentmindedness could be exasperating. "It was typical of Vee that she would find a revolutionary, fall in love with both hero and cause, drag the revolutionary home with her to start the business of changing the world together with him, then find she had other things to do," her sister-in-law Deirdre said. Redgrave would pick up a revolutionary like Black Power leader Hakim Jamal and then drop him off with Deirdre and Corin or other interested parties while she went off to do a play or a film. Her energy was enormous, but there was never enough time to do all she wanted to do.

Redgrave ran for parliament on the Workers Revolutionary Party ticket in 1974 in Newham North East, a working class neighborhood in the East End of London. She had only three weeks for her campaign, but she and her colleagues held meetings where they warned against a burgeoning military dictatorship in Britain and repeatedly called for a workers' militia to take the place of the army and the police. They canvassed tirelessly from door to door, but Redgrave garnered only a little over seven hundred votes.

She got more and more deeply involved with her guru, but she saw only one fatherly side of him. "Healy could really affect people," says Tim Wohlforth. "He could get people momentarily to believe that some kind of revolution was going to happen. He had this personality where at one moment he would be extremely bitter and attacking you—not Vanessa, of course, but everybody else—and then the next moment he was like a father figure, where he'd be very concerned with you. He was very effective operating that way."

Redgrave went to Los Angeles to play Lady Macbeth opposite Charlton Heston. The diligent Heston began rehearsing the Scottish Play around his pool with the director Peter Wood, who had directed Redgrave in *The Prime of Miss Jean Brodie*. "When Vanessa arrived, a few days before rehearsals began, she joined us by the pool," Heston said. "As Peter had predicted, she did not like any of my redactions in her scenes. I wasn't such a fool as to cut any of her lines, of course, but she preferred them arranged exactly as the Old Gentleman wrote them, as was surely her privilege." Wood told Heston, "It will take her time to realize that you have not suggested these changes to improve your own part."

After a few days of rehearsal, they came to an agreement on the text of the play, and Heston described Redgrave as "patient" as they staged the banquet scene. "Well, at least Lady V doesn't give you any of the standard great-actress behavior," Wood said to Heston. Describing her in the role, Heston said, "She had an icy passion that was at the same time alienating."

"Vanessa was doing the Scottish Play with Charlton Heston, and she said, 'Come and see it,'" says Shirley Knight. "And every time I saw the Scottish Play at that time it was just a disaster. I had seen Simone Signoret in it, and it went badly. And this was dreadful. Vanessa was fine, but Charlton Heston, he was all right on film, but on stage you just couldn't find him. He would talk, and you'd have to look for him. He had no stage presence.

"Afterward, Vanessa said, 'I have to go and talk at this Communist Party meeting, do you want to come?'" says Knight. "And I said, 'Okay, I've never been to a Communist Party meeting, why not? I'll go.' And so we go, and she gives a talk, and it was kind of . . . rambling. And this young black woman finally shut her up and said, 'Oh, that's just bullshit, you don't know what you're talking about. You don't understand the situation.'

"My husband John and I lived in the Village, and Vanessa would often call for money for various projects," says Knight. "And John and I always gave her money. She was starting a thing out in the country with her brother. Sort of . . . teaching people things."

Redgrave gave lectures on Marxism while in LA in order to raise money for a WRP school of Marxist education. In a meeting that almost sounds too hilarious to be true, Redgrave actually approached Groucho Marx and discussed Marxism with him. "There's one thing I don't like about Britain," Groucho told her. "On second thought, there are several things. But the thing I like least is the monarchy." Groucho actually promised some money for the Marxist school, but his donation went missing after his death in 1977. Was he putting her on? Vanessa Redgrave as Margaret Dumont?

She was disappointed in her *Macbeth* with Heston, which she felt was decent but uninspired—in the production photographs for the play, she looks dutiful and rather miserable. Redgrave went back to England to help build the Marxist school for her party. From 1974 to 1985, she spent at least two weeks at the school every year immersing herself in a study of history and social problems.

"Commitment to the party was total," said former member Gary Younge, who joined the WRP as a teenager. "If Britain was about to explode into revolution, then it followed that a revolutionary party had to be ready and waiting in the wings. And if the party was to be ready then its members had to be at battle stations at all times, with no excuses and definitely no time off for good behavior. It meant that everything—births, deaths, marriages, exams, you name it—had to take second place to the preparations under way for the glorious and imminent day when we would not so much inherit the earth as nationalize it, collectivize it, and then forbid anyone from inheriting anything ever again."

Younge offered a vivid description of Healy's speaking style: "He would shout and scream into the microphone, ranting fluent gibberish. And as he prodded the air with his little finger, his face would get redder and redder until his entire bald head was a small, round pate of scarlet." Of the older members of the group, Younge observed, "They were socially disabled—incapable of talking about anything else but the party because they had long since shut everything else out of their lives." Paranoia was a constant in this group. Members were always on the lookout for MI5 British agents who might be trying to breach and infiltrate the party walls.

"Tony [Richardson] said that Vanessa has become a sort of Trotskyite— I forget what it's called nowadays," wrote Christopher Isherwood in his diary. "Whenever she gets a job in a play, she tries to indoctrinate the entire cast. The young impressionable inexperienced actors and actresses are terribly flattered at first to be asked to attend meetings after rehearsals by this great star. But soon she bores them to death and they try to wriggle out of it. According to Tony, Vanessa is completely under the influence of her brother Corin, who is even more fanatical than she is."

While working relentlessly for the WRP and helping to build a school for the party called White Meadows, Redgrave was one cameo among many in the Agatha Christie adaptation *Murder on the Orient Express*, where Ingrid Bergman was the stand-out as a slightly crazed Swedish missionary and Lauren Bacall sucked up a lot of the air around her as an abrasive traveler. Redgrave smartly chooses to hold back and underplay amid the hammy performers surrounding her, and the eye almost always goes to her because she seems to have some kind of perverse secret that keeps her half-smiling at all times.

She rang up Actors' Equity on the *Murder* set when director Sidney Lumet suggested that the cast take only a half-hour lunch break. Redgrave argued that if they agreed to this then the crew would also be forced to accept it eventually. The cast disagreed with her and voted in favor of the half-hour break. The stories that appeared about this incident in the press only increased Redgrave's image of being difficult to handle, or a political crank. In the late summer of 1974, Redgrave gave an impassioned speech at an Actors' Equity meeting for the inclusion of performers in pornographic films into their union, but her plea was ignored.

On Saturday, September 27, 1975, one hundred policemen with dogs raided White Meadows, the WRP school. They were looking for weapons, and they found bullets, but no guns. Trying to get support from actor friends after the raid, Redgrave was outright rebuffed in some cases. Laurence Olivier even came out against Vanessa and Corin and called for a defeat of "the extremists" in a letter to the *Times*. Stewing in Healy paranoia, Redgrave later said that she thought this raid was a political frame-up.

Vanessa and Corin filed a libel case against the *Observer*, which had run an article about the raid on September 28. This article contained a story about the actress Irene Gorst, who had been Corin's mistress. Gorst claimed that she had been held against her will at the WRP school and interrogated for six hours. She had not severed relations with people outside of the party, which was what Healy advised for all new party members, but she still wanted to attend a two-week class at White Meadows designed specifically for theater people. Gorst missed a bus she was supposed to take, and when she arrived the following day, she said that she was grilled from 9:30 A.M. to 5:30 P.M. by Corin, Vanessa, and two other members.

"They started in on me," Gorst said. "How long had I been working for the Special Branch? Where had I planted bombs and drugs? Why did I miss the coach? Who had told me where the school was? . . . After about an hour, I decided to leave. But when I tried to get off my chair, I was pushed back by Vanessa, who said, 'Sit down,'" Gorst alleged.

The Gorst story had been in the hands of the *Observer* for two weeks before the raid. They waited to run it on the day of a Labor Party conference, when it would have the most impact. This newspaper scandal effectively ended Corin's shaky marriage to his wife Deirdre.

It was thought that Gorst had been instrumental in getting the police to investigate the WRP. The WRP denied Gorst's interrogation claims, saying only that there had been discussions about Gorst's former boyfriend John Gale, who had made threats against the party and wanted Gorst to quit it. The libel case was co-filed with director Roy Battersby, scriptwriter Roger Smith, actor Michael Harrigan, and Healy.

Battersby said in a later documentary about the raid, "One has to say that we were legal, we were public, there were no secrets in what we thought. So in a sense you say, well, how does that make me a subversive? My politics are not about to bring down the state." But Healy and Corin and many of the others thought that the WRP could help to bring down the state, however misguidedly or delusionally.

A Special Branch agent named Tom had been recruited to spy on the WRP by MI5. Speaking of Redgrave, he said, "Sometimes she can be very rude, and she would be outspoken. And many times it was said that we should get this government out." Battersby felt that the bullets found at White Meadows had been planted by police.

"With Irene Gorst, this was a typical kind of thing," says Wohlforth. "Healy had what they called the Red House, this estate that the Redgraves had given Healy. And he'd bring people up there for these classes and indoctrination sessions. When those sessions were going on, it was almost like an armed camp. There were guards, and everything was very intense. I fully believe Gorst's story. She wanted to leave and they wouldn't let her leave. This was very common. We had the same thing when we had these camps up in Montreal, when Healy would come and we'd have these guards and so on."

Healy was not above using physical force to keep his members in line. It was well known within the group that when he was in a temper he would physically abuse the women who were working for him. He kicked a party member named Dot Gibson until she developed ulcers on her legs. "I had to take her to hospital to receive treatment over a period of weeks," said party member Norman Harding. "Dot insisted—and others, including me, agreed—that Healy should not be told of the damage he had done because it would upset him. He had to be protected from this kind of pressure. We had to sneak out secretly to make our trips to the hospital."

"Norman Harding worked at the WRP and I alongside him, albeit a few hours a week—on my part—up to 1971 when I left the organization, or cult," says former party member John Manix. "Norman was there in the print finishing area and did an enormous amount of dirty jobs, literally and metaphorically. I can vouch for all he says about Healy being a tyrant, megalomaniac, and monster."

Healy once broke a chair over the back of his secretary Aileen Jennings, causing permanent damage to her. This abuse was tolerated and hushed up at the time, but former members have made their grievances known in a steady stream of articles and full memoirs detailing just what a wretched man he was.

"I have a couple of good friends that I'm still in contact with, and they were beaten up," says Wohlforth. "Healy had these camps in England, and I used to bring people over to them. There would be sometimes up to a thousand working class kids camping out in these tents. And they had Party people running around trying to keep order, many of whom were intellectuals who were not necessarily the most skilled at that kind of thing. Late at night, when everybody was bleary-eyed, Healy would have people taken into his tent and, in at least two cases I know of, he would hold these people and have them beaten up. One of them was Robin Blick, and I know his wife Karen very well, and this happened to him. Robin was a brilliant guy, he did a lot of work for their paper. I felt very afraid when Healy moved in on me in his camp in Montreal and accused the woman I was associated with then of being a CIA agent. The camp had all these guards, and all I wanted to do was just get out of there. I was really worried about what might happen to me.

"I think Vanessa just thought this was about being tough and being a Bolshevik," Wohlforth says. "She was playing an acting role as a Party member. When we were having an international gathering in this little hotel in Clapham someplace, Healy sent Vanessa and Corin as his delegates. And Vanessa turns up with a Lenin hat on with a red star on it. It was acting, you see, but I think as you'd realize since you write about actors, the best acting is also sincere. She was definitely acting, but she was sincerely playing that part at that point."

# Ellida and Julia

er mind clearly and understandably elsewhere, Redgrave appeared
in the dank *Out of Season* (1975), where she plays a grimly
repressed hotelkeeper who has an irritable relationship with her
bratty daughter (Susan George)—at one point the daughter calls her "a
dried-up cow, all puckered inside!" Redgrave's character keeps threat-
ening to "sell this place," and the drama in the film is almost amusingly
half-assed.

She did a fragrant small role in the handsomely designed *The Seven-
Per-Cent Solution* (1976), playing a German stage star, a patient of Freud,
addicted to drugs, who winds up with Nicol Williamson's neurotic Sher-
lock Holmes. Robert Duvall makes a fine (if American) Watson, and
Laurence Olivier has a ball as a Uriah Heep-like Moriarty. "A woman as
beautiful as I has seen everything fearful by the age of seventeen," Redgrave says, speaking in a goofy accent, looking potent but fragile, bringing
her magic to a marginal part.

Her colleagues on set were not happy with her metamorphosis into a
revolutionary. "Vanessa used to be what they called a card," said costume
designer Diana Pengwell. "The critics still slobber all over her, but she's
really become a tiresome person, I do wish she'd shut up." A reporter

observed Redgrave on set and she told him some pretty wacky things. "I don't think much of the Women's Movement in America, why should I?" she asked. "After all, it was founded by the CIA and the FBI . . . everybody knows that." During a break in shooting she said, "If I do go to lunch, perhaps I should go eat in the canteen . . . with the workers." When she visited Andy Warhol's Factory, Redgrave hit Warhol up for a donation to the WRP. He gave her twenty cents.

In 1976, Redgrave acted for the first time in one of her favorite roles, Ellida in Ibsen's *The Lady from the Sea*, which she performed at Circle in the Square in New York under Tony Richardson's direction. Redgrave never attempted Ibsen's two most famous roles for women, Nora in *A Doll's House* or Hedda Gabler, but she was always drawn to the much simpler, almost parable-like *The Lady from the Sea*, in which the married Ellida clings to her ideal of a perfect sailor lover, always staring out over the water as she waits for his ship to return.

It was Redgrave's first appearance on stage in New York, and the rehearsal period with Richardson was stimulating. Pat Hingle, who was engaged as her leading man, grew impatient with her Ellida as they rehearsed at one point, and Richardson told him to think of his own wife. "If she was my wife, I'd hit her," Hingle said, which seemed to enthuse Richardson. "Go on, hit Vanessa!" Richardson cried. "Hit her hard! It'll do her good!"

This is a squirm-inducing story, and Hingle didn't actually hit her, but it would do well to remember just how exasperating Redgrave could be, especially in this period, and how well Richardson knew her at this point. He once supposedly joked, "Vanessa Redgrave is controversial, her enemies hate her, and her friends dislike her!" Redgrave could be temperamental as a child, and Edith Evans had actually counseled her parents to give her a good smack to keep her in line, but sense couldn't be knocked into her, of course, by physical force or otherwise.

She was back together with Dalton at this point, and he was critical of her work in the rehearsals that he saw for *The Lady from the Sea*. This acted as a jolt, just as Michael Elliott had jolted her into Rosalind in 1961. By all accounts, Redgrave was at her very best in this production of *The Lady from the Sea* when it opened at Circle in the Square. It ran for several months.

Peter Hall went to see her in the play when she did it again in 1979, and in his diaries he wrote: "Her face appeared naked of makeup, and naked of guile. You could see right through the skin to the emotions, the thoughts, the hopes, the fears underneath. But here's the paradox. What Vanessa says politically is, to me, insane, and I believe that to her lies *are* truth if they support her ideology. So how can she express such truth, such sincerity, such lack of hypocrisy in her art? In life, which is true, she is false. In art, which is false, she is true."

Hall also noticed that she was unhampered by her lackluster fellow players, and he had an idea as to why that was the case: "She acted to the others as if they were what they ought to be. Part of her belief extended to them too. Mind you, I have never thought it mattered to Vanessa whom she was acting with. She is so shortsighted she can't see who it is anyway." How different, how earthbound her career might have been if she had always worn her contact lenses.

"One of the five most memorable performances I've seen by an actor on stage was her performance in Tony's production of *The Lady from the Sea*," says Don Bachardy. "She did something really supernatural in that. She was possessed in some way, it really worked. It was just something spooky she did. I remember at one point, she was in the audience at the top of the aisle at the back of the theater, and she let out a cry, and she ran down the aisle and onto the stage, and it was really spine-tingling. I still remember the excitement of that all these years later—something was really happening on that stage."

"She brings an atmosphere with her on stage always, she brings a prior life with her," says Simon Callow. "I saw her in *Lady from the Sea*, and when she made her first appearance, drenched, it was simply heart-stopping, because you felt as if you'd seen somebody come out of a dream at you. She's a very disturbing person, spiritually and mentally. She has the ability to let herself get taken over completely by an image or by a kind of poetic notion, and certainly in *Lady from the Sea* she had an idea of this woman who was half human and half aquatic, and she went further than any other actor would have gone with that."

Walking into Circle in the Square one night, Redgrave was given Lillian Hellman's book *Pentimento* by a young usherette named Pam, who told her that it should be made into a film and that Redgrave should play the role of Hellman's special political goddess Julia. Excited by *Pentimento*, Redgrave fought to play the title role in Fred Zinnemann's *Julia* (1977), a prestigious costume drama based on a story in Hellman's memoir. Hellman had spun a tale of a beloved childhood friend who went to Europe, studied medicine, and fought the Nazis, and she also put herself into this story, claiming to have been on a smuggling mission into Nazi Germany that sounds like something out of a 1940s Hollywood movie.

Zinnemann first thought of American actresses to play Julia, but soon came around to Redgrave's fairy-tale size as an actress. "The person who seemed to combine all the essential qualities of style, breeding, and an almost mystic dedication—Vanessa Redgrave—is English," Zinnemann said. "Because of her politics, there was strong opposition at the studio to casting her, but she was undoubtedly the right actress for the part and she kept her political convictions pretty much to herself, until a memorable moment at the Academy [Awards] when, being warmly applauded upon receiving her Oscar, she made a political speech. In thirty seconds the temperature dropped to ice while she, smiling happily, descended the steps, gave me a big kiss, and sat down."

It's fairly certain by now that Hellman appropriated the life of Muriel Gardiner, a woman who had actually worked in the Resistance, for her Julia story. Hellman heard about Gardiner's life from their mutual lawyer, Wolf Schwabacher, and she took the details from Gardiner's story that she wanted. After *Pentimento* was published and *Julia* was released and she was confronted with her lies by Gardiner and others, Hellman made up even less convincing lies about this supposed childhood friend.

"It is believed that a man who knew both ladies might have told Lillian the story," wrote Zinnemann in his memoirs. "The mystery remains—if it is, indeed, a mystery?" he wondered hopefully. In a later interview, he was less diplomatic. "She would portray herself in situations that were not true," he said of Hellman. "An extremely talented, brilliant writer, but she was a phony character, I'm sorry to say. My relations with her were very guarded and ended in pure hatred."

When Mary McCarthy said that every word Hellman wrote was a lie, "including 'and' and 'the'," on Dick Cavett's talk show, she found herself in litigation with Hellman, but history has proved McCarthy close to correct. You have to admire, at least, the sheer chutzpah of Hellman, but it's difficult to figure out what issues she is trying to work out in this Julia story, which is written in a disarmingly tough voice that falls back on a lot of "in my day" and "in my time" observations meant to give her fabrications some authority. The fictional Julia congratulates Hellman on her anger and tells her never to lose it. Anger is important to Hellman, who strives to see everything in good versus bad terms.

Redgrave was predictably drawn to Hellman's fantasy leftist heroine, who comes from money and privilege but refuses to live the life of the rich, and who finds a calling in anti-Fascist activity. She still refuses to believe that Hellman lied, or that Julia did not exist. When she met Hellman in 1984, Hellman insisted to Redgrave that the story had happened. "I knew that *Julia* was a true story before Lillian Hellman confirmed it," Redgrave said. "Every line in her book told me that."

The film *Julia* was a decisive success for Redgrave, and so she is loath to believe that it is based on an outrageous theft and falsehood. This might not matter if Hellman's tall tale worked on screen, but it's a fastidiously arranged, obscure, phony movie, and not even Redgrave's full iconographic impact and Jane Fonda's most Bette Davis-like exertions as Hellman can do anything to enrich the material.

Fonda had always been impressed by Redgrave, so much so that she named her daughter Vanessa Vadim after her. "There is a quality about Vanessa that makes me feel as if she resides in a netherworld of mystery that eludes the rest of us mortals," Fonda said. "Her voice seems to come from some deep place that knows all suffering and all secrets. Watching her work is like seeing through layers of glass, each layer painted in mythic watercolor images, layer after layer, until it becomes dark—but even then you know you haven't come to the bottom of it."

The talented Fonda realized that Redgrave was at the same level of creation as Marlon Brando, a whole other level of invention. "When we worked together I recall never being sure where Vanessa was drawing her inspiration from, what choices she was working off of, and this invariably threw me slightly off balance—which worked in the film," Fonda said. "The only other time I had experienced this with an actor was with Marlon

Brando in *The Chase*. . . . Like Vanessa, he always seemed to be in another reality, working off some secret, magnetic, inner rhythm."

*Julia* marked the feature film debut of an American performer who would come to be thought of as Redgrave's rival for the title of finest living actress working in English: Meryl Streep. "I can't really emphasize enough the effect that Vanessa had on her little sisters, the little sisters of our generation, the actors," Streep said. "If she was going to be in a play, you read the play, and if it was going to be a film, you read everything about the film. Because she's going to ask something of you. She's going to give more than anybody else, of course, but she was also going to call something up, so you had to be ready, emotionally, intellectually, and even spiritually.

"In my first film, *Julia*, I was twenty-seven, and I didn't have any scenes with Vanessa," Streep said. "But I got to share a car with her. I was right out of drama school, and I thought, 'What am I going to say to her, what am I going to say to her?' I was completely tongue-tied, but it didn't matter, because the minute she got into the car, she did all the talking. From the time we got into the car to the time we got out. And it was all about politics, and things about Trotsky. I didn't know anything about Trotsky. I mean, I was really dim, I admit it, I was concentrating on, you know, my hair in the movie. So I never made the connection I'd dreamed of making with my goddess."

Fonda's Hellman narrates most of *Julia*, seemingly from a kind of fishing boat. We see her chain-smoking, drinking, and typing her first hit play *The Children's Hour* as the patient and ever-wise Dashiell Hammett (Jason Robards Jr.) looks over her. *Julia* paints an extremely cozy and romantic view of a writer's life and of the relationship between Hellman and Hammett, which was Hellman's core myth and just as difficult to believe or verify as her others. As Gore Vidal once remarked, "Did anyone ever *see* them together?"

"I know when the truth is distorted by some drama or fantasy," says Fonda's Hellman on the soundtrack, and that would certainly come as news to Muriel Gardiner. All Hellman knows of "the truth" in this movie comes from nothing but her own dramatized fantasies, so that her insistence on herself as a truth-teller begins to seem comic.

The young actresses playing Lillian and Julia as girls are only adequate, but the film picks up a bit when Fonda plays out some soft-focus scenes with Redgrave's Julia where they are supposed to be young women. They have chemistry with each other, and Fonda looks at Redgrave with highly convincing love. As Zinnemann's camera lingers on Redgrave's newborn, speculative eyes and patrician nose and jawline, we hear Fonda's voice say that Julia had "the most beautiful face I had ever seen."

Redgrave lives up to that description, but the trouble with the role of Julia is that this visual display of what can only be called star power is all that is asked of her. She strides toward the camera with a kind of madness in her eyes when Lillian meets Julia at a Viennese college, and when Julia is all broken up in a hospital bed after fighting the Nazis, Redgrave unfurls what have to be the longest fingers in show business as she tries to tell Lillian something.

We don't see Julia for a while as Fonda's Hellman has a success with her play and starts living the high life with Dorothy Parker (Rosemary Murphy) and Alan Campbell (an oddly cast Hal Holbrook). Hellman's smuggling mission on board a train is not overly interesting, and we're made to wait for quite some time before we get to Redgrave's one long scene in the movie, where Julia meets with Lillian in a café.

Julia has lost one of her legs, and she talks about having a baby while the camera lingers again over her huge, vulnerable blue eyes. She is set up as a kind of beauty that cannot be saved, and there isn't much that Redgrave can do to complicate or enrich this straight-ahead, idealized Hellman heroine. Redgrave was cast by Zinnemann to look otherworldly and noble, and that's it.

There was a lot more to her work in *Julia*, but it was left on the cutting-room floor. "I got to know Fred Zinnemann quite well at the end of his life when he lived in London," says director Tony Palmer. "He confessed that he felt very bad about having to cut most of Vanessa's scenes out of *Julia*. 'I was ordered by the studio to keep the film under two hours, and the only thing I could think to do was to cut out many of Vanessa's scenes,' he told me. He left in just the bare minimum. He then took her out to lunch to warn her of this, in the nicest possible way, and he waited for an explosion and cutlery being thrown around, you know. And all

Vanessa said to him was, 'Fred, it's your film. If that's what you want to do, I'm content.'"

"It is marvelous if performances come up to ninety percent of what one has been hoping for," said Zinnemann. "But sometimes there are actors who give you 120 percent, who will bring so many unexpected facets to their characters that their work is a constant source of surprise and delight. Vanessa is one of those rare people. Watching her I was sometimes so riveted by her performance that I would forget to say 'Cut' at the end of the scene. She never seemed to be acting; like Spencer Tracy, she was just there."

It's interesting that when Fonda and Zinnemann reached for comparisons they went for major male actors at opposite ends of the spectrum, from the wildest (Brando) to the most grounded (Tracy). But the facets Zinnemann talks about do not show up on screen. The relationship Julia has with Lillian is not a complex one. Even hints of a deeper kind of love between the women are scuttled in an ugly scene where a depraved society man (John Glover) is smacked by Hellman after suggesting that "everybody knows" about her and Julia. Any notion of lesbianism here has to be firmly and angrily repudiated, and this is certainly the oddest part of Hellman's fantasy.

Julia is stabbed discreetly, in half-light, while Hellman seems to sense her murder as she sits in a theater. We hear that Julia's face has been badly slashed, but we do not see the damage, or feel it. *Julia* is a respectable Oscar-entry sort of item that looks like a good, solid film on its carefully produced surface but is really a bad, flimsy film in disguise that has not been thought out on practically any level.

According to her memoir, it was while living with a couple in Paris as she filmed *Julia* that Redgrave met a Palestinian man who told her about his people's plight at the siege of Tel al-Zaatar, a Palestinian refugee camp in Lebanon that right-wing militias had bombarded for months, leaving many men, women, and children dead. Redgrave vowed to do all she could to bring attention to the situation. But there were other forces at play in her conversion to the Palestinian cause. "Healy was the one to make that connection and bring her around to do this film with the Palestinians and carry out that whole campaign, there's no question about that," says Tim Wohlforth. "He was using her, and he was the contact person to develop that, because he was getting money from them."

The Palestinians were offered a ceasefire, but Yasser Arafat ordered his followers to attack, and they suffered the consequences. This was reported at the time by John Bulloch in the *Daily Telegraph* and later by Yasser Arafat biographer Robert Fisk. Bulloch and Fisk believe that Arafat wanted martyrs for his cause, to the point that Arafat even opened a "martyrs' village" for camp widows. On his first visit to see them, the widows pelted Arafat with stones and rotten fruit. Journalists were ordered away from this scene at gunpoint.

Redgrave sold her two houses in London to make *The Palestinian* (1977), a documentary film directed by WRP member Roy Battersby in which she was seen dancing with a Kalashnikov rifle over her head with the Palestine Liberation Organization. She interviewed right-wing militia leader Pierre Gemayel and went to Tel al-Zaatar to speak with survivors of the siege, including the two doctors who had run a single clinic for the wounded. Redgrave also visited more Palestinian refugee camps in Beirut and was impressed by the Palestine Red Crescent Society, which tended to the injured with very primitive equipment. She interviewed Khalil al-Wazir, a PLO leader, and she also spoke to Yasser Arafat himself.

Wherever *The Palestinian* played, marchers held placards reading, "Redgrave Supports Terrorists" and "Redgrave Is a Murderer." The Jewish Defense League wrote to Twentieth Century Fox in late January of 1978 to say that they would be picketing theaters showing *Julia* unless the studio blacklisted Redgrave and condemned her political activities. When this had no effect, the League released white mice into theaters showing *Julia*. When that had little effect on attendance and Redgrave was nominated for a Best Supporting Actress Academy Award for *Julia*, the JDL said that they would picket the Oscars.

On June 15, 1978, the Doheny Plaza Theatre in Los Angeles was bombed because they were showing *The Palestinian*, which caused a thousand dollars in damage, but the film continued to be shown at that theater the following night. Redgrave's most vocal opponent at this early stage of her commitment to the PLO was the Rabbi Meir Kahane of the Jewish Defense League, who even wrote a slender self-published book called *Listen, Vanessa, I am a Zionist.*

Redgrave's secretary Sandra Marsh showed her a news clipping that reported on a meeting of the Jewish Defense League where one speaker waved a bunch of dollars and said, "Who will get rid of a Jew hater?" The day before the 1978 Oscar ceremony, Howard Koch, the chairman of the Academy Awards committee, urged Redgrave to only say "Thank you" if she happened to win the Oscar.

Outside the Dorothy Chandler Pavilion the following day, seventy-five members of the Jewish Defense League burned Redgrave in effigy as "Arafat's whore." Meanwhile, two hundred PLO supporters marched in her favor outside the Pavilion. To bypass all of this activity, Redgrave was taken to the entrance of the theater in an ambulance and sneaked in with her bodyguards. There were armed plainclothes security backstage and police sharpshooters stationed on the roof of the building.

Best Supporting Actress was the first award of the evening, and it was presented by John Travolta. Redgrave's competition was weak: Tuesday Weld for a small role in *Looking for Mr. Goodbar*, Melinda Dillon for *Close Encounters of the Third Kind*, Leslie Browne, the ingénue in *The Turning Point*, and Quinn Cummings, the little girl in *The Goodbye Girl*.

When Redgrave won her Oscar for *Julia*, she kissed Fred Zinnemann and confidently strode toward the stage in a large black dress with red strings hanging from the shoulders. Jane Fonda was seen applauding, and the applause lasted for a good while. Then Redgrave made her acceptance speech, where she referenced the "Zionist hoodlums" of the Jewish Defense League who were protesting her outside the ceremony. Her speech stirred up trouble and dismay that followed her for the rest of her life:

> My dear colleagues, I thank you very, very much for this tribute to my work. I think that Jane Fonda and I have done the best work of our lives and I think this is in part due to our director, Fred Zinnemann. And I also think it's in part because we believed and we believe in what we were expressing—two out of millions who gave their lives and were prepared to sacrifice everything in the fight against fascist and racist Nazi Germany.
>
> And I salute you and I pay tribute to you and I think you should be very proud that in the last few weeks you have stood firm and

you have refused to be intimidated by the threats of a small bunch of Zionist hoodlums whose behavior is an insult to the stature of Jews all over the world and to their great and heroic record of struggle against fascism and oppression.

And I salute that record and I salute all of you for having stood firm and dealt a final blow against that period when Nixon and McCarthy launched a worldwide witch-hunt against those who tried to express in their lives and their work the truth that they believed in. I salute you and I thank you and I pledge to you that I will continue to fight against anti-Semitism and fascism. Thank you.

After she says "Zionist hoodlums" on the broadcast, there are loud gasps from the audience and one particularly loud male shout of outrage, but Redgrave does not flinch and she does not falter, although she does take a brief pause after "whose behavior" to let the gasps die down, repeating "whose behavior" and then fearlessly pressing on. She betrays a slight tremor of nervousness on the word "salute," which comes out strangely, but she is human, after all. An extremely experienced actress at this point, Redgrave must have known a large segment of the audience was against her and did not understand her position or why she felt the need to speak about it.

When she mentions Nixon and McCarthy, there are very angry sounds coming from the audience and some old-fashioned hissing (led by host Bob Hope backstage?), yet even this does not seem to affect her. As she continues with her speech, some of the audience actually comes around to her, and she leaves the stage to a burst of applause.

"As my friend Jane Fonda pointed out on various occasions, the audience stopped listening after I uttered the two words 'Zionist hoodlums,'" she said at the time. "How would *you* feel if you were threatened, your life and family threatened, if a fine, pro-Jewish film like *Julia* was boycotted and you were burned in effigy outside the Dorothy Chandler Pavilion and called things like 'the Palestinians' whore' and worse?" Two years later, Redgrave said, "To have been given the Oscar is a sign of the moral strength of Jews and others who voted for me in spite of the slanderous propaganda aimed at them by the JDL."

Thirty-five years later, speaking to the *Telegraph* in 2012, Redgrave still had no real regrets about this notorious speech. She had prepared it beforehand: "The basic line. Just in case I won, I thought I'd better. You do what you feel is right. People get it or they don't. I did what I thought was right—and whether that would have any effect on my career or not was quite beside the point."

To the *Guardian* in 2011, she clarified exactly whom she was referring to: "I was saying I pledge myself to fight anti-Semitism and I'm totally opposed to Zionist hoodlums because one had waved a whole lot of dollar bills at a public meeting in Los Angeles at which I wasn't present, saying 'Who will get rid of a Jew hater?' So, you know, it was a pretty nervous context for the Oscars." There was a real fear that night that someone from the Jewish Defense League might assassinate her, but her words were taken as a blanket denunciation of Israel. The specificity of her phrase "small bunch" was not heard and the words "Zionist hoodlums" entered the lexicon.

Later in the show, writer Paddy Chayefsky dramatically spoke out against Redgrave's speech: "Before I get on to the writing awards, there's a little matter I'd like to tidy up, at least if I expect to live with myself tomorrow morning," he said, getting all puffed up with umbrage. "I would like to say, personal opinion of course, that I'm sick and tired of people exploiting the Academy Awards (there was loud applause at this point) for the propagation of their own personal propaganda. I would like to suggest to Miss Redgrave that her winning an Academy Award is not a pivotal moment in history, does not require a proclamation, and a simple 'Thank you' would have sufficed."

Chayefsky later said that he had been asked to say something by the show's producer Daniel Melnick, and he came in for his own share of criticism for pontificating against her speech. Redgrave reiterated backstage that the Jewish Defense League "do not represent the Jewish people and their behavior is an insult to Jewish people all over the world. Of course, I'm on the side of the Jews who have struggled in a most glorious struggle against fascism." When a reporter asked why she made a political speech at the Academy Awards, Redgrave claimed that hers was not a political speech at all.

Many in town were very upset by her speech and vocal about it. "I am the Zionist hoodlum she was talking about," said comedian Alan King. "It's just a pity I wasn't on the platform tonight. I would have gone for the jugular." But she found a supporter in Moshe Mizrahi, the Israeli director of *Madame Rosa* (1977), who was quoted as saying "Basically, she's right."

Jack Nicholson tried to make light of it all: "What are these Zionists? Are they reds? There've been threats? I've been skiing." Redgrave tried to speak to Chayefsky backstage, but he proudly reported that he "cut her dead." Sidney Lumet later said that some in the audience had thought her reference to "Zionist hoodlums" was anti-Semitic but that "she went on . . . with great passion thanking the Academy membership for not being influenced by . . . her politically controversial position. And at the end of the speech, I remember an enormous, enormous burst of applause."

Further on in the evening at the Governor's Ball, Academy president Howard Koch observed, "I felt sorry for Vanessa because at the party afterwards she was sitting all alone with just her two bodyguards. No one else would sit with her and here it was her big night." But Chayefsky thought that she was unbowed, going from table to table to kiss friends. "This is disgusting," he said. "Vanessa thinks she can get away with anything. How can she have the nerve to come here?"

She was now on extremely shaky ground professionally. "I thought about firing her when I heard what she said," said Lester Persky, the producer of her upcoming movie *Yanks* (1979). "But that would have been suppression of free speech." In the years to come, there would be producers and others in charge of film production who would not have Persky's principles.

For so many people, this acceptance speech is what they remember first about Redgrave, and that's a shame. She should have phrased things more specifically and not driven on as she does with her eyes blazing, but whatever we make of her political stand, there can be no doubt about her near-lunatic courage or her obstinate need to communicate what she feels. "I regret where I wasn't able to clarify calmly enough," she told the *Telegraph* in 2010, "but nevertheless I don't regret saying what I said as best I could." What many people didn't understand then and some still don't understand today is that Redgrave was referring specifically to the Jewish Defense League and their threats against her.

Her Oscar speech rippled out into pop culture. The April 8, 1978 episode of *Saturday Night Live* begins with a scathing send-up of her speech with Jane Curtin playing Redgrave. "I don't know where to begin," Curtin says in an English accent. "There are so many people and things to condemn." She then goes on to denounce Zionist hoodlums, British imperialists in Northern Ireland, and imperialists in South Africa, before having Yasser Arafat (played by John Belushi) take the stage and accept her Oscar for her.

Redgrave had no feature film for release in 1978. The scandal of her awards speech and the negative press it occasioned had a destructive effect on her acting opportunities that would last for years to come. At an Equity meeting in June 1978, Redgrave and the WRP proposed a boycott on English artists working in Israel. She later clarified that she did not support a blacklist or boycott of Israeli artists, only a boycott of English artists working in Israel, which she likened to the similar boycott on Equity members working in South Africa under apartheid.

Redgrave was also still embroiled in her libel case against the *Observer*, and she was made to explain many of her positions in court. Terrorist acts, she said repeatedly, are acts of violence against civilians, and she compared the IRA and the PLO's military actions to the partisan actions in France against Nazi Germany. They proved the libel but lost the case. The jury felt that their reputations had not been materially damaged, and the judge ordered the WRP to pay the huge legal fees. While this was going on during the day, she was playing in *The Lady from the Sea* again with Terence Stamp at the Royal Exchange Theatre in London under the direction of Michael Elliott.

Redgrave made a second documentary on the Palestinians called *Vanessa Talks with Farouk Abdul-Aziz* (1978), in which she spoke to the director of the Kuwait Cine Club. "I had the opportunity to meet Vanessa for the first time in March of 1978," said Aziz. "Fresh from south Lebanon, slightly before the Israeli war machine hit the region, she flew into Baghdad to premiere her timely and sweeping three-hour documentary *The Palestinian* at the Third International Film Festival in Palestine. In my first interview with her, produced for Baghdad Television, I asked if someone had told her that the three-hour format is a bit of an unusual duration for a documentary. She looked me in the eye and bluntly put it: 'Do you think that three hours is a long duration to finally tell the story of a people so long ignored for thirty years?'"

In this second film, she showed Aziz the school that had been built for WRP members. "I feel very proud indeed of this place," Redgrave told him. "This is the most important achievement of our party, this school." Speaking of her career, she told Aziz, "The first prize I was really proud to win was the Oscar, because when I won it, I won it as a political actress. I was a revolutionist and an actress, together," she emphasized, crossing two fingers in front of her. "Everybody knew what I was, and what I was was contributing to what had to be done, and my party did it.

"I didn't know how you came into politics," she told him, speaking of her early life and her outrage at injustices she was reading about. "Politics came into me. I wanted to go over there to Hungary to fight, but I didn't know how to fight and I wasn't trained as a nurse, I was useless in that way . . . so I went and helped sort clothes out."

Vanessa talked about her father Michael: "I saw him last year on the stage when he recited one of Shakespeare's sonnets, one of the most well-known of all the sonnets, 'Shall I compare thee to a summer's day.' And when he began to speak it, it was as if nothing had been pre-conceived about it. It just came out of him, and every word was shining and full of life and light . . . I don't know what words to use," she said, looking overcome through her habitual facial expression of worried reverie. "I can't imagine it being said more simply and more perfectly, and completely stripped of all efforts of actors to say things in a certain tone of voice and present them in a certain way. With great thought and with great feeling. It was really remarkable.

"Both my parents were always very firm about the sort of life an actor should lead if they were going to do considerable work," Redgrave said. "An actor must consider what they're doing seriously and they must lead a life which will enable them to do their best work in the evening when they have to do it. They were very severe about this, saying 'This is what you must do.' I took this very seriously indeed. When I was twenty-two, I used to rest two hours in the afternoon before going on the stage, which I laugh about when I think of it today. But the approach was right. When you've got something important to do, you prepare to do it."

Redgrave acted with Michael in this movie, doing the scene from *King Lear* where Lear is reconciled with Cordelia. In that brief scene, which he plays seated, Michael's reading of the verse is strong and lyric and vocally undiminished, and Vanessa looks at him with steady love. Her father, ill with Parkinson's disease, told her that he finally understood the relation between her political and her artistic life.

We also see Redgrave working with WRP members in Aziz's film. "Why do we have to train our senses?" she asks them. "We know we have five senses. Why do we have to train them?" A girl tries to answer her, and Redgrave says, "But why isn't this automatic? Why do we consciously have to train?" Capitalistic conditioning seems to be the answer she is fishing for. "What is man's relationship with nature under the capitalist system? Why must we start with nature? Why don't we start with what we're thinking?" This peek into the WRP headquarters does make it look like a cult where mental conditioning was part of the overall training.

After speaking about her involvement in anti-nuclear marches in the 1960s, Redgrave told of her disillusionment with that form of political engagement. "Imperialism was not going to be defeated through pacifistic protest," she says. "After the Bay of Pigs, you cannot sit down in the streets of a city anymore when you see this." She speaks of how impressed she was with the socialist revolution in Cuba. "When I got back to England, I was very amazed, because my husband, being in the cinema, he would constantly be meeting with writers and directors. In their discussions, I felt very dismayed, because they didn't seem to have any concept of what was going on in the world at all. Their vision seemed limited to their careers and what was happening in Britain. They didn't see the world events that were taking shape. So I was looking outwards, and I was considering big political questions. But I didn't have a party. What party was I going to have?"

In spite of all the controversy surrounding her, Redgrave won the title role in *Agatha* (1979), a handsomely photographed commercial film about the disappearance of mystery writer Agatha Christie, for which she was only paid £25,000. After deducting for taxes and agents' fees, she had

£7000 to live on for the year. "Actually, I have some very bourgeois likes," Redgrave admitted. "For instance, I adore Agatha Christie."

Redgrave makes Christie a painfully shy, red-haired frump with staring, crazy eyes, pursuing her straying husband (Timothy Dalton) with no sense of pride. During the ten or so days Christie went missing in 1926, the film has Redgrave's Agatha go to a spa where she plans revenge on her female rival for her husband's love.

There is also a contrived romance between Redgrave and Dustin Hoffman, who plays a reporter intrigued by the Christie case. In a scene where they dance, Redgrave is a whole head taller than Hoffman, and when she kisses him goodnight, she has to stoop down for him, which has a comic effect. Redgrave uses a high, furtive voice for the role, and she makes a striking initial impression in her scenes with Dalton, but the film gives her no chance to sustain or develop a character.

Redgrave's second film from 1979, John Schlesinger's *Yanks*, is a broad tale of culture clash between Brits and American soldiers during World War II held together by a brassy score by Richard Rodney Bennett. Redgrave seems to enjoy showing how the upper class Englishwoman she is playing loses some of her inhibitions when exposed to William Devane, her sly romantic partner. "Before we began shooting, John took me aside and said, 'I want you to know you will be playing my mother in this film,'" Redgrave said. They strove to personalize her role, and she comes off well in the movie.

"Vanessa is without question one of the best actresses I've ever worked with," Schlesinger wrote in his diary. "She is the consummate actress, able to take direction, really a wonderful musical instrument, so to speak, for a director to play." But he was wary of her politics, especially when she began distributing the WRP newspaper to the crew. "I was worried about working with her because of the political animal which has loomed rather large. Her political activities we agreed somehow tacitly we would never mention," Schlesinger said.

It was while they shot the film that Redgrave gave her Oscar speech, but then she came right back to work as if nothing had happened. "I thought her politics would get mixed up with the work," Schlesinger said. "It never has for one second." She is excitingly alive to emotions when she comforts her son in *Yanks* and, in one fine scene, thrills to a slot machine.

"Vanessa and John had wanted to work together," says Schlesinger's long-time partner Michael Childers. "They had known each other for years. She's eclectic, a little eccentric, a little left, you know, when she was running around with her little brother. John would be on the phone and he'd get off and say, 'It was Vanessa again, asking for money for one of her causes!' and we'd laugh.

"She was totally professional, she was a one- or two-take Charlie," Childers says. "You know, she'd come around with the newspaper from her party or whatever and it was kind of a set joke, 'Oh, here comes Vanessa with her paper again.' And people would take it to be polite, and whether they read it or not didn't matter. But she's really wonderful and sweet. She'd come to our parties through the years, and she loved to laugh. When John had had a stroke, she said, 'We must see John,' and she and her sister Lynn came to see him. That meant a lot to him."

Redgrave then did a shaky Scandinavian accent in *Bear Island* (1979), an Alistair MacLean adaptation and commercial adventure movie that proved a total flop and ended the decade on a low note. It was filmed mainly in Alaska in fifty-below-zero temperatures that froze Redgrave's contact lenses in her eyes while she was wearing them, and it was a bad shoot all around. A helicopter pilot died when he missed his landing on a mountain, and director Don Sharp and some of the crew got stuck on a glacier for three days during a blizzard.

On one of her days off, Redgrave was helicoptered up to where the second unit was shooting real Arctic footage so that they could get some shots of her for the film. A blizzard struck that trapped everyone on a glacier for twenty hours. Redgrave sat in a tent with two crew members and the second-unit director, and at a certain point they just stopped talking and listened to the wind howling outside. Redgrave finally raised her head and said in her lingering voice, "I shall never complain . . . about my Winnebago . . . again."

A commenter on BritMovie.co.uk wrote, "I had the misfortune to see *Bear Island* (in part) on a cross-sea ferry coming back from Sweden. The onboard cinema was packed with young Scandinavians, and me and my brother. When Vanessa Redgrave opened her mouth for the first time the whole place was in an uproar, laughing themselves silly." Accents have never been Redgrave's strong suit, though that has never stopped her from recklessly trying all manner of them.

Her character in *Bear Island* is one of many leading a UN delegation in the arctic when they stumble upon hidden Nazi gold. Addressing Redgrave at one point, Donald Sutherland says, "I'm not here to listen to the questionable views of a nomadic Norwegian shrink." Lines like this aside, *Bear Island* isn't much fun. The camera seems stunned by all the snow on view, and Redgrave herself looks gloomy and preoccupied. "Below freezing and beyond fear . . . will anyone survive its terror?" asked one of the taglines for the film. A larger question at this point was whether Redgrave's acting career was going to survive in any but the most marginal of ways as she pursued her ideal of revolution.

"I would deliver her papers to her house in Hammersmith," says ex-WRP member John Bird, who went on to more solid and useful things in his own political life as the founder of *The Big Issue* magazine, which is published by street vendors who have been affected by homelessness. "She was a leading party member, and as I and a small cohort could not see her intellectual or cultural worth, let alone her sketchy grasp of revolutionary politics, I don't think I can add to her increasing luster. To me she represented a tragic crisis of the middle classes who sincerely wished to do something other than wallow in their plenty. I can only see the tragedy of a particular part of the acting profession who genuinely did want to do something more than postulate dissatisfaction with monopoly capitalism.

"Alas, Vanessa needed guidance and leadership, rather than what she was offered by the WRP, awash as it was with promises of the revolutionary upsurge on the morrow," says Bird. "But God, did we learn! Stuck as we were in a period when clarity was hidden behind a brouhaha of vacant promises."

Redgrave ran again for parliament for the WRP in 1979, for Moss Side, Manchester, while Corin ran in Lambeth. Vanessa garnered only 572 votes. BBC news cameras caught her trying to look stoic but seeming fairly upset when she lost and had to endure some light jeering. "May I speak?" she quietly asked Reginald Prentice, the Conservative Party winner. When she got the go-ahead, her face became hard and her eyes grew fixed. Her voice was low and monotonously insistent as she addressed the crowd.

"Mr. Chairman, friends and comrades, we stood, the only party to stand of all ten candidates, in this campaign, on a socialist program," she emphasized. "The only program to answer this crisis, the only program to meet the needs of the working class in this crisis. A socialist program on food, on jobs, on wages, on education, on health service." At this point, there were a few in the assembly who started to jeer her loudly. "A socialist program to answer the crisis must be for the working class to take over the means of production without compensation under workers' control," she said.

As she continued on, there was loud rhythmic clapping in the crowd to signal their disapproval. "The working class must now prepare for the greatest battle in the whole of its history!" she announced in metallic, harsh, ringing tones that she never used for any of her film performances. "In two hundred years of struggle, the working class must now build a mass revolutionary party to take power and carry out a socialist program. Our party will stand with the working class indissolubly through this crisis!" For those who only know Redgrave's acting work, this footage is a startling example of just how single-minded she could be at this point in her political life. She looks and sounds like a fierce street-corner fanatic who has all the answers and will not listen to anyone else.

Derek Jarman wrote about marching with the WRP around this time and then getting a call from Redgrave. It was New Year's Eve, 1980, and she asked him what he was doing. "She caught my indecision and announced she would be around in a half hour and we would go out selling the party's daily newspaper, *News Line*," he wrote.

"We drove up to the flats in Marchmont Street, near where I had lived in 1963, and worked our way down the dimly lit corridors in the freezing cold. . . . The reception at each flat was unexpected—a small bald man cautiously peeped round one door, and when he recognized Vanessa his eyes popped. He quickly disappeared, and we heard an excited, whispered conversation. Then he re-appeared, with the words—'Go away Vanessa, we don't want your type around here. We vote Conservative.' And closed the door firmly. I couldn't help smiling, and I think Vanessa caught me. Later, she abandoned me outside the Aldwych [Theatre] with an armful of papers and a collection bucket. While the usher boys eyed me suspiciously I made a spirited attempt to sell the cause, and got two customers."

# Playing for Time

R edgrave spent most of her time as an actress in the 1980s on television, often playing in worthy or prestigious projects, and none was worthier than *Playing for Time* (1980), an adaptation by Arthur Miller of Fania Fénelon's memoir about being a member of the women's orchestra that played at Auschwitz. Other members of the orchestra disputed some aspects of Fénelon's version of what happened in the camp, particularly her unflattering characterization of the orchestra's leader, Alma Rosé, the niece of Gustav Mahler, but it was clear that her memoir could make a strong basis for a film.

When producer Linda Yellen cast Redgrave as Fénelon, there was an outcry from many people who believed that such an outspoken supporter of the PLO should not play a Jewish heroine, and Fénelon herself was not pleased with the casting. She felt that the role should have gone to someone who might have captured her own gamine-like spirit.

After the film played on TV, Fénelon decried its lack of gallows humor, which she felt was such an important survival tactic for women in the camp. "I do not accept a person to play me who is the opposite of me," Fénelon said. "I wanted Liza Minnelli. She's small, she's full of life, she sings and dances. Vanessa . . . doesn't have a sense of humor, and that is the one thing that saved me from death in the camp."

"I wasn't aware of what an activist she was," Miller said of Redgrave. "She's a Marxist; this is a political matter. Turning her down because of her ideas was unacceptable to me; after all, I suffered the blacklist myself." And later he said, "If this attack is solely upon her past views and actions it ought to stop short, it seems to me, at trying to drive her out of a role which can only lift the suffering of the Jews, especially Jewish women, to a new ground of understanding."

"We all had death threats and the head of CBS had death threats," said Yellen. "There was a lot of controversy because of the casting of Vanessa and how people felt about her political views. When we came to cast it we didn't even think about that. We were just thinking about who were the greatest actresses in the world who could possibly be part of this, and she was one of the greatest."

Yellen is of German-Jewish descent and lost two of her aunts to the Nazi death camps. Responding before shooting to the request by Jewish groups to have equal time to make their case, Yellen snapped, "They would have to put on a piece that is pro-Hitler." Speaking of Redgrave, she said, "Regardless of her politics, Vanessa cares about humanity and suffering."

When the actresses who were cast were asked to shave their heads for their roles, all of them resisted at first except for Redgrave. "They wanted their hair short, but not all the way," Yellen said. "I wouldn't compromise the artistic integrity."

Tony Richardson was asked to direct, but he dropped out early because he didn't like the location in Pennsylvania and he didn't think the budget was high enough. He came to his former wife's defense in her right to take on the role of a Jewish heroine: "Vanessa may have made mistakes," he said, "but there isn't a drop of anti-Semitic blood in her body."

Joseph Sargent directed *Playing for Time* for three weeks before he was fired by the producers. Daniel Mann took over for the second half of shooting. Sargent goes unnamed in Redgrave's autobiography, but she mentions that she was not happy when he called a certain scene too melodramatic.

"I personally don't understand why Sargent was fired," says Shirley Knight, who was engaged to play the camp leader Maria Mandel. "But something went on between Vanessa and Joe. And I guess the producer Linda Yellen thought that it was creating a lot of problems, because we were all there to make a good film, as I'm sure Joe was, because he was a very meticulous director."

"Joe was on for I think a week or two," says Melanie Mayron, who played the role of Fania's young friend Marianne. "He was why I got hired, actually, because I had worked with Joe on a TV movie called *Hustling* [1975], and he hired me for the part because of that, because he knew my work. He and Vanessa, they were kind of batting heads. They didn't get on that well. So that's probably why he was fired. He was a terrific director, but there was just a personality clash."

Mayron found the change of director fairly easy to adjust to. "It was pretty seamless, because Daniel Mann was a very experienced guy who had done a lot of big movies," she says. "I remember we were shut down for about three or four days because of what had happened and then Daniel Mann came in, and then we started again. I was pretty new, it was one of my beginning jobs, so I just rolled with it."

"I don't know what the situation was, whether Vanessa didn't like Joe Sargent," says Knight. "I know that when I first arrived they had already started filming, and I think about a week or so after I got there, they let him go. We were out in Pennsylvania, and we were filming in a facility that had been a German prisoner-of-war camp during the Second World War, which was so ironic and bizarre."

Knight was uncomfortable about some of the protocol on this shoot. "When I first arrived, it was very strange," she says. "I got onto the set, and they said, 'You have to go and get a dog tag with your name on it. Everyone has done this.' And I said, 'Why?' They said with all the trouble they'd been having with the Jewish Defense League they were concerned for our safety. So I said to the guy, 'Well, are you going to be here every day?' And he said yeah. And I said, 'Well, I'm Shirley Knight, and every day I'll be coming in, so I don't need a dog tag.' And he said, 'But everyone has one.' And I said I didn't want to do that.

"It was fascinating, because I was playing a Nazi, and I was the only woman who said no to the dog tag," says Knight. "All the other women who were playing inmates had agreed to this. And I said, 'Am I the only woman who said no to this?' Because I figured Vanessa would have said, 'Don't be ridiculous.' But they all said, 'Okay.' It was almost like 'Stamp my arm, put a number on my arm,' you know?"

"When we were driving through the gate of this camp every morning, there were people protesting," says Mayron. "They wanted to make sure that everybody in the vans were part of production. I remember hearing that there were people in Nazi uniforms trying to get in, and they were *real* people who were Nazis themselves who had got in by accident. So that's why they wanted us to be identified, because they didn't want any nutcases on the set. We wore identification tags, I don't know if they were dog tags, I don't remember that . . . that's a little . . . but maybe it was."

"Vanessa and I were very attuned politically, because I'm very, very far to the left," says Knight. "I'm a pacifist. But it was difficult, and I don't want to be critical, but it was difficult because Vanessa did continue to sell the pamphlets for her political party for a quarter on the set. And a lot of the women did not respond well to that. They felt that that was not something that should be going on on a film set.

"My children were on the set," Knight says, "and Vanessa came 'round one night with a pamphlet and asked for a quarter, and I gave her a quarter. And she started talking, and my youngest child who was maybe ten said, 'If you're going to talk to my mom, you will have to do it tomorrow, because my sister and I need my Mommy now.' He told her to go away, basically. And Vanessa just laughed and went away."

"She didn't really sell her paper on the set, she'd sell it off the set," says Mayron. "Like at the hotel. I remember she knocked on my door and sold me a paper, and she came in and we talked about . . . her thoughts, and her politics and everything. I don't remember her selling the paper on the set at all, because she was very much in character, and very professional. It was more on the weekend. At least in my experience, she would do that in our downtime. I don't remember her doing that while she was working."

Like many of her fellow cast members, Redgrave had her head shaved for the role. "They shaved my head with Vanessa on camera," says Mayron. "We were both sitting naked and they had three cameras on us, and they shaved our heads together. The only one who didn't go all the way was Marta Heflin, but she had it cut to only an inch, so at that point, I mean, you've cut off all your hair, you might as well go all the way. Basically, the gals who played Jewish prisoners were shaved, but Christine Baranski who sat next to me in the orchestra, she played a Polish gal who was Christian, so she got to keep her hair. Like in real life."

Redgrave went even further than this for realism when she felt that makeup wasn't convincing enough for a necessary large cut on Fania's mouth. So that the cut looked realistic, Redgrave had a doctor put a safety pin through her upper lip. She would do whatever it took to inhabit this role on the deepest level possible.

Anyone who has seen even a photograph of Redgrave as Fania Fénelon will remember the impression of a starved bald woman with a wound on her lip, her two big blue haunted eyes staring up like Falconetti in Carl Theodor Dreyer's *The Passion of Joan of Arc* (1928), as if only these eyes are still alive. Fania was only sixty pounds when she was liberated from the camps.

*Playing for Time* begins with a brief prologue of Redgrave's Fania in full cabaret singer regalia entertaining Parisian night-clubbers and Nazi officials, promising her audience that she will try to make them feel better if they are far away from home. In just a few moments, Redgrave makes an impression of a sophisticated, tender woman, not the more Piaf-like singer that Fénelon was herself, and she is still this woman when we see her trapped in a crowded train headed to the concentration camp. She had been a spy for the Resistance, and now she has been caught.

In the stifling train car, Fania befriends Mayron's sheltered young Marianne and accepts a compliment from an older man who tells her that her music is "the soul of Paris." As Fania and Marianne talk, we keep seeing the train wheels moving inexorably forward, and enormous tension builds because the people inside the car obviously have no conception of what is in store for them. In stray moments, Redgrave's Fania looks apprehensive, but she holds herself like a woman of the world, sitting there in her fur coat with her long blond hair still fashionably styled.

Brad Fiedel's grunting, synthesized music adds to the atmosphere of growing fear and dread as the people on the train start to complain that there is no air. A pail of excrement is spilled, and everyone reacts with horror and disgust. Fania notices that a man is dead, and still no one opens the cabin for them.

Standing with her group of fellow travelers at the camp, Fania still doesn't understand the straits she's in: "Is this where we get our things back?" she asks with a kind of haughty obliviousness. Eyeglasses are taken from faces and the group is ordered to strip. Huddling naked, Fania is forced to sit down as a woman starts to shave all of her hair off.

At this point Fania suddenly realizes *exactly* what kind of situation this is, and Redgrave takes a deep imaginative plunge into terror and disbelief. Her eyes look like a trapped animal's eyes, and that's because the Nazis are stripping her not just of her clothes but of her individuality. When a guard insults her, she responds, "I'm not Jew crap, I'm French," and she gets smacked hard in the head for talking back. This is the end of the line, a terminus for any kind of humanity.

Fania and Marianne are led into a barracks where the women sleep, and they are met with the kind of ravaged faces familiar to anyone who has looked at photos of the liberated camps. Fania embraces Marianne and tries to cheer her up by telling her a story (Redgrave uses a very light French accent, so light that it isn't even really an accent but more a nod to a kind of all-embracing French spirit).

We see images of fire, and then we see the inmates shoveling. At every point of *Playing for Time*, we are placed in the prisoner's point of view so that we're never quite sure where we are or what indignity might happen next. We don't see many of the horrors going on at Auschwitz, but we feel the presence of them. "I tried to treat it as a story meaningful to the survivors—by which I mean all of us," Miller said. "I didn't want it to be a mere horror story."

The film runs 150 minutes, and in that time we begin to feel what day-to-day life must have been like for these women as they waited and steadily deteriorated both physically and mentally. Watching *Playing for Time*, you get the sense of this pitiless duration, of waiting with these women, even of being jailed with them, and this makes for a kind of ordeal that enhances our understanding of such a new low in human suffering. A film of this quality, about an event like this, is a rarity in any case, but the fact that it was made for CBS television in 1980 is more than surprising. There had never been and might never be again a film made for television that reaches this high level.

In the middle of the night, the women are asked if anyone can sing *Madame Butterfly*, and Marianne says that Fania can, and so she is brought in to audition for Alma Rosé (Jane Alexander), the leader of the women's orchestra at Auschwitz. The sardonic Etalina (Robin Bartlett) warns Fania that Alma is "a fantastic talent, but not a warm heart, be careful." Fania plays the piano and sings a bit of *Madame Butterfly* for Alma, and Redgrave catches the absurdity of a theatrical audition in this blasted context.

Fania can barely bring herself to make music, and this means that she and the more practical Alma are always butting heads throughout the film. They are both proud women, but Alma is a proud musician, whereas Fania is a proud human being, and the film hints at the fact that art can be an aid to evil. A Nazi commandant who gasses children all day can go home and listen to Schubert songs with fully enlightened cultural sensitivity. Nothing beautiful can survive at Auschwitz, not even Schubert.

The women of the orchestra live under constant threat. We spend most of our time in their rehearsal room, and we hear the cries of the people being killed outside their window (12,000 a day, a man says at one point). When Fania sits down to play for Dr. Mengele (Max Wright), Maria Mandel (Knight), and Frau Schmidt (Viveca Lindfors), a few of the half-mad leaders of the camp, Redgrave first bares her teeth at them in total hatred, then sings a popular French song and smiles nastily at them when they applaud her. Fania gets away with this partly because there is a kind of hate that we all accept in certain kinds of show business performance, a theme that Miller predictably leaves un-dramatized.

Outside the barracks, as the orchestra plays while the inmates march to work, a woman spits in Fania's face. Fania confesses later to Alma that she can't get used to being so hated by the other prisoners. The pragmatic Alma counsels Fania to lose this kind of sensitivity, but this is not possible for her. She has to remain open to it all, and she lets her soul get brutalized in the process. Redgrave herself has always insisted on this kind of empathy for her fellow creatures in her work, and in *Playing for Time* this insistence is put to its severest test.

Ravaged by hunger, Fania says that she refuses to become an animal for a potato peel, and she's dismayed and outraged when she sees Marianne prostituting herself for more food. When the defiant Marianne leaves a piece of sausage in front of Fania and departs the rehearsal room, the camera holds on Redgrave's face for a punishingly long time as she stares at this piece of food, then licks it, then finally eats it. Even while she's chewing the food, Fania knows that she has now lost a part of herself that she will never get back, and Redgrave experiences the full depth of this realization beat by beat until she finally covers her mouth with her hand and gently bangs her head against a wall. She has become only an animal. Auschwitz has killed the idea of human enlightenment and human possibility. It has killed the soul of Paris, and everything else worth fighting for.

After this defeat, Fania grows more passive, more cynical, but the women in the orchestra continue to look up to her and tell her their troubles. "What Arthur [Miller] has Fania say is, 'The problem is they are human,'" Redgrave emphasized in 2010 at a Paley Center panel on the film. "And that is the major problem. We are all apparently human beings. And if we start saying, well, the ones who are doing terrible things are not human, we are completely misunderstanding the core of the problem, and we've missed any possibility of finding ways to be human together on however small a scale it might be. . . . Inside all of us is a capacity to betray, to kill, to murder humanity, whether physically or spiritually."

Redgrave in this panel discussion on *Playing for Time* has been building to a height of indignation, but then she stops herself and tries to be humble, which is her most habitual conversational mannerism, the instinct to be queenly and authoritative mixed with guilt over being so sure of herself and her dismay at her own ego: "It sounds a bit arrogant for me to say that I have been obsessed, but it's true, I have, since we were in the Second World War and being bombed in London. It was small stuff compared to what was happening in the rest of Europe, but it was enough to give one a different view of the world."

*Playing for Time* weakens whenever Miller seems to put his own thoughts into words for these women. Speaking of Mandel, Fania says, "She's human, like you, like me. You don't think that's a problem?" Alma opens up to Fania and talks about how a lover "warmed me like a coat," and Alexander's performance suddenly becomes stagy for the duration of this too-theatrical scene. Fania says at one point, "I've seen too much, too much, too much," when one "too much" would have sufficed, and her line, "We know a little something about the human race that we didn't know before, and it's not good news," sounds like someone who's reading about these atrocities in the newspaper rather than a woman actually stuck in a concentration camp.

But the actors ride over these problems in the writing. After the Zionist Giselle (Marcell Rosenblatt) talks about her hopes for Israel, Redgrave allows herself a nuanced look of confused sympathy, but her own personal political position is clear on her face as well. When Fania dares to emphasize that her father's name was Goldstein after pleasing Dr. Mengele with another music recital, Redgrave uses a voice that is hard as stone for this brief spurt of courage and righteousness, but there can be no lasting triumphs of the human spirit at Auschwitz, and she steadily details Fania's descent into apathy and discouragement.

Knight and Lindfors offer contrasting Method performances of confused evil and petty evil. "It was the second Nazi I played," says Knight. "I am very white and blond. So, you know, it's 'Let's hire Shirley. She looks like a nice person but she actually isn't!'" she jokes. Bartlett is the one actress here who manages to insert the kind of dark humor that Fénelon wrote about in her book (and she also manages to be memorably pathetic when reacting to a brief bit of male attention). Over the film's long running time, however, it is Mayron who makes the deepest impression, starting off as an innocent girl and then gradually becoming a hardened whore who is able to save the women by coming on to a Nazi officer, an action which gets her corralled with the Nazis themselves.

"That's why Joe wanted me," Mayron says. "He said, 'You're so likable and you're so vulnerable that nobody will have a clue where your character is going.' That's the whole reason he wanted me for the part. He said, 'For someone like you to get to that end,' well, that's what he wanted to depict, what could happen to people, just good, regular people, nice people, that they could get pushed to that point. I knew that was my part and that's where I had to go. That's acting, as they say."

In the film's most devastating moment, Marianne strikes the gray-headed, decrepit Fania during a moment of extreme confusion and despair, and when her ruined friend is led away, Fania looks at Marianne like you would look at a beautiful child who cannot be saved from suffering and ruin. Some things are far worse than death.

A narrative film about any aspect of the Holocaust is always going to be inadequate to the size of what happened. Alain Resnais's *Night and Fog* (1955), a short documentary about the camps that views them after the fact with clinical voice-over, is still probably the most powerful cinematic testament to the Holocaust, and there is a case for *Playing for Time* as the most powerful narrative film about the camps, even if Miller cannot always resist pontificating in some of his dialogue.

The film ends with the near-dead Fania singing the "Marseillaise" over a radio transmission, and when she finishes the song, Redgrave opens Fania's face and for a brief moment substitutes her own feelings about this event that so changed her life and the lives of so many people of her generation. Her face seems to insist that with such knowledge comes responsibility, and with such knowledge also comes a wondering tenderness that blooms again like a flower opening out of barren soil.

Redgrave won an Emmy for *Playing for Time*, but she continued to put her career on hold for her political work, traveling to Iraq and speaking out again and again for "the Palestinian struggle for the right to self-determination," a phrase she used like a mantra. She worked night and day for the Workers Revolutionary Party, finding locations for youth training centers in London, Liverpool, and Manchester. When the WRP opened their first two youth centers in January 1981, some of the press characterized them as "bomb factories" where kids would be brainwashed, and Redgrave tried her best to answer every one of these accusations.

In that year, she produced yet another documentary for her chosen cause, *Occupied Palestine*, and she tried to get the Palestinian Ministry of Culture to buy the rights to *Playing for Time* and show it on television. It had been banned in Israel because of Redgrave's participation, but Israelis might have seen it if it had played on Jordanian TV. They turned her down, refusing to see, as Redgrave did, the common experience between persecuted peoples that she has insisted on her entire life.

She spent six months on the road showing *Occupied Palestine*. It was said that she had a younger Palestinian boyfriend. "I may have a driving, unromantic image, but I'm still a woman, and I have a need for masculine companionship and affection," she told George Haddad-Garcia, a reporter she trusted. She finally came home to her children exhausted. One night her son Carlo recorded her talking on a tape recorder at their kitchen table. When Redgrave fell asleep, she went right on talking to him in her sleep, which made Carlo laugh.

# TV and the Boston
# Symphony Case

F eature film offers had stopped coming in for Redgrave. In many cases, producers who had hired her for TV films would come under fire because it was feared that most of the money she made from her work would go directly to the Workers Revolutionary Party.

Derek Jarman described her at this time draped in red at Kensington Town Hall, sitting under an enormous portrait of Lenin and selling the party's newspaper from a briefcase. "She carries on talking as she discovers more pamphlets: Trotsky on art, Trotsky on internationalism," Jarman wrote. "She hovers on the edge of her seat desperate to share this vision; she shakes as she speaks of conspiracies."

The films she made from this period can be difficult to find, but they are more than worth the search. From 1980 to 1992, Redgrave consistently gained in confidence, depth, and imaginative power as an actress. In many ways, this was the golden age for her talent.

*My Body, My Child*, made for TV in 1982, casts Redgrave as Leenie, a Catholic Italian-American teacher. The film was written by Louisa Burns-Bisogno, a forty-five-year-old high school teacher who developed the project first as a play. "I had several points to make," said Bisogno. "The first is that medical facilities are often too casual with drugs. It's a fact. Second, we often do many things with consequences we really don't understand . . . because of the subtle interference in our lives by the scientific community. All of a sudden we find ourselves in situations that should never have happened in the first place."

Redgrave's Leenie visits her mother in the hospital, and when she hears of her mother's death, Redgrave rushes right to such an extreme expression of grief that this flimsy television context can barely handle the size of what she's doing. Tears *shoot* out of her still, frozen face, and the most broken sound keeps coming and coming out of her mouth as she runs back and forth in her kitchen. It's a deeper and somehow more domestic sound of total grief compared to her more queenly cry in *The Trojan Women*.

Redgrave's face in other scenes here is like a clear pool of water where small ripples of emotion keep disturbing the surface, and she guides us over the rudimentary writing of this film and the fact that her young daughters are played by Sarah Jessica Parker and Cynthia Nixon, which causes unavoidable *Sex and the City* associations today.

*My Body, My Child*, which is based on a true story, is a tale of hospital ineptitude leading to a moral quandary. Though Redgrave's character is pregnant, her doctors misdiagnose her and pump her full of pills. When the pregnancy is finally discovered, the baby has become deformed, and her character has to make the decision to have an abortion.

The whole middle of the film is very draggy, with lots of time-filling shots of cars slowly driving up to buildings to park. When Redgrave's Leenie confronts her doctor (James Naughton), she has all the angry force, alas, of Stan Laurel. Rage, pettiness, and sarcasm generally give her trouble as an actress, and Redgrave doesn't seem too Italian here, but within a range of romantic vulnerability no one can touch her depth of feeling. In her last scene, as her husband tries to comfort her, Redgrave insists on emphasizing the tragedy of the situation. Her face is grim and stark as she says that she will never be the same, like a child who doesn't understand why they are being abused. Everything she had has been lost, and she just stands there in her final close-up, trembling and bereft.

Redgrave was billed as "Queen" in a little-seen Sergio Corbucci comedy, *Sing Sing* (1983), and she played the role of Cosima Wagner opposite Richard Burton in the lofty, obscure, spectacle-heavy nine-hour miniseries *Wagner* (1983). The cast included her brother Corin and Franco Nero in small roles, and the three English knights of acting, Laurence Olivier, John Gielgud, and Ralph Richardson, all of whom ham it up as ministers tut-tutting over Wagner's heavy spending. Starring as the wife of one of the most notorious anti-Semites of all time did not do much to alleviate the perception of Redgrave's relation to the Israeli/Palestinian conflict.

"I was a very great friend of her brother Corin," says *Wagner* director Tony Palmer. "I worked with him a lot. He said to me one day, 'Are you ever going to risk working with my sister?' By which he meant Vanessa, not Lynn! And I said, 'I wouldn't think of it as a risk, I would think of it as a challenge!' And certainly a privilege. She was an absolute joy to work with. Challenging, yes. You can't just cruise with Vanessa."

"We knew it was one big film," says Palmer. "We never thought of it as a miniseries, ever. Later it was divided up so it could be shown as a miniseries on television at the request of one of the distributors. It was shown in the cinema a lot in the '80s."

*Wagner* has an elaborate structure. There are flashbacks, flash-forwards, and flashes to it's hard to tell what. A scene will start, and then Palmer will cut to an exterior or another scene or some imagery inspired by Wagner's operas, and then he will cut right back to the scene he started with. "When you start editing, you do change a certain number of things, but the basic structure was absolutely in the script, which Charles Wood and I worked on for four or five years," says Palmer.

"I sat through six and a half hours of *Wagner*," Gielgud wrote Burton after shooting. "Very sad that all the beauty and many good performances are nullified by the length and endless abstract shots which slow everything up just as one is getting interested in the story and the characters."

Cinematographer Vittorio Storaro is allowed to indulge himself with all kinds of chiaroscuro effects of lighting that are at first impressive and then just alienating. Major scenes are played with the actors almost totally in the dark, so that it becomes hard to follow or care about what's going on or being said because Storaro is only interested in creating painterly compositions. At one point, Joan Greenwood comes on to play a scene and you can barely see her; only her inimitable slurry voice is recognizable. "I took Storaro to see various paintings by Vermeer, and I told him that that's what I wanted it to look like," says Palmer. "I wanted to use as much natural light as possible. I didn't care how dark it was or black it was, that didn't interest me at all, but basically the visual model was Vermeer.

"When you're dealing with great actresses like Vanessa, you stand back and let them do their thing," says Palmer. "It was very stimulating. She liked to discuss things. One of the most interesting things with her happened even before we started filming, when she went off to look at the various costumes that we'd chosen. Shirley Russell was the costume designer, and she told me later that Vanessa flicked through them, and I think she didn't like one costume out of about twenty.

"And Shirley asked her, 'Do you want to know which costumes are for which scenes?' And Vanessa said, 'Absolutely not. This is my wardrobe. Depending on what mood I get up in in the morning will determine what clothes I put on.' Now, obviously our continuity was a consideration and she wasn't willful about continuity, but essentially, if she felt bright and sunny she'd put on a bright and sunny costume, and if she felt black and gloomy she'd put on a black and gloomy costume.

"It was filmed almost entirely on location," Palmer says. "Vanessa would arrive very early on the set all dressed up and ready to go, and if it was a room where Cosima and Wagner were living, she would go around the room and arrange the furniture as she thought Cosima would have arranged it."

Redgrave's Cosima is first seen looking majestic as she leads Wagner's funeral cortege, and then we don't see her again for quite some time. After Wagner's first marriage plays itself out, we next catch a glimpse of her Cosima as a painfully shy younger woman as she sits next to Wagner. She doesn't say a word, but Redgrave gives you every iota of this woman's self-mesmerized consciousness and strained, passionate soul in just those few silent moments.

Well cast as a fanatic and paranoid loyalist, Redgrave physically uses her own feelings about being too tall as Cosima marches from place to place and haggles for money for Wagner, much as Redgrave herself was always searching for money for the WRP. The married Cosima will even falsify her sexual relationship with Wagner just to serve his cause, but the film does not let Redgrave explore this self-revealing vein.

Redgrave is asked to give most of her performance in this series in silent reaction to others, and there's a limit to even her resources when it comes to doing nothing but standing and observing. She is sometimes able to communicate volumes with just a few stares, but often enough she looks like she'll do anything to hold our attention: stick her tongue in her cheek, nod her head, smile, quiver. "Richard [Burton] came up to me one day and said, 'I'm not sure I can do this scene,'" Palmer says. "I said, 'Why, Richard?' And he said, 'I'm being acted off the screen. Just look at her sitting there! She's not doing anything and I'm acting like a demented windmill trying to catch your attention!'"

"If possible, she always wanted the music played that I was going to use at that point in the film," says Palmer. "I explained to her that like Wagner himself I was going to use themes and motifs. There would be a musical motif that was Cosima and several musical motifs that were Wagner and so forth. I told her, 'When this music plays, there's no narrative, no dialogue, no commentary, just the music, so it's really down to you what you do.' We would play the music over and over again before doing the scene, and then I would let her do her thing."

Left to her own devices and lost in Storaro's dark, Redgrave seizes her one opening, taking what she did as she gave birth in *Isadora* and building on it for an incredible childbirth scene that she plays as a kind of horror tableau, eyes popping and mouth gasping and body rolling and heaving for breath, over and over again, making for a true Wagnerian moment if ever there was one. She goes so far out on a limb in this scene that what she reaches for winds up being almost non-human. Any other actress would have looked absurd going for such an extreme effect, but Redgrave achieves her goal by sheer belief in her own imaginative capabilities.

"One of our sparking points, if you like, was that I had produced the TV film about Isadora Duncan with Ken Russell," says Palmer. "And I used to say to Vanessa that she had copied endless things from our film and we'd never given her permission, and she thought that was a great joke. So when it came to the childbirth scene, I said, 'I saw that rubbish childbirth scene you did in *Isadora*, and my God, what were you supposed to be giving birth to, a peanut?' And she laughed and said, 'I get your point.'" And so Palmer in a sense gave her a dare to go bigger, and she always responds with her very best work to dares like that.

As far as politics went, Redgrave kept her work and her WRP leanings as separate as possible on this set. "There was no peddling of her WRP paper on the set, she was incredibly professional," says Palmer. "But what she did do, and she always asked me first, on a couple of evenings when we were well into the filming, she asked if she could give a talk about the Palestinians. And I said, 'Absolutely, I'm sure we'd all be very interested to learn.' And in the second of those talks, to which Richard came, there was fairly heated discussion, but she was perfectly capable of giving as good as she got."

"She and I and Richard spent an entire Sunday arguing about the extent to which anti-Semitism was still prevalent today," Palmer says. "We all agreed that it was as prevalent now as it always had been. And after all, we were filming in Austria, one of the most anti-Semitic countries on earth. We discussed Wagner's anti-Semitism, and Vanessa had very strong views on that. She felt it was not a sufficient excuse that anti-Semitism had been common among most intellectuals of the nineteenth century. She felt that nothing could excuse Wagner's two anti-Semitic pamphlets, 'Judaism in Music Part 1' and 'Judaism in Music Part 2.' And she was very aware that the chief anti-Semite of the partnership was Cosima, who was virulently anti-Semitic."

Redgrave was not being offered much work and now she was even losing work she had already been hired for. In 1982, she was fired, due to her politics, from an engagement to narrate Stravinsky's *Oedipus Rex* with the Boston Symphony Orchestra, and she took them to court for breach of contract. She saw the firing as a case of blacklisting that could set a precedent, and so she fought against this on principle.

As a counterbalance, the Arab American Institute in Washington, D.C. sponsored two performances in Boston, a matinee and an evening, where Redgrave would do some scenes from *As You Like It*, *The Seagull*, and *Isadora*. Feeling harassed and totally alone, Redgrave asked Tennessee Williams to read from some of his work with her on stage. She wasn't sure that Williams would come and was very relieved and happy when he did show up to be with her in her time of trouble. Williams had often called Redgrave the best actress alive, and he felt he needed to support her, whatever her politics. Redgrave has been fond of quoting his definition of happiness as "insensitivity, I guess."

Writer James Grissom knew Tennessee Williams at that time and remembers how much she intrigued him. "Tennessee would say, 'I would love to see the magically deluded Amanda Wingfield she could become,'" Grissom says. "In 1982, she would have been an ideal Amanda, so they spoke about *The Glass Menagerie*. He had so many dreams about work that Vanessa might play and work that he wanted to create for her."

Grissom remembers Williams saying, "There's always a bit of pamphleteering about Vanessa. She always has a cause, and before we talk about any plays, she asks for help for this cause, and so I will write a check or give money. It's almost like an admission fee. If there's ever another blacklist, I'll probably see my name on some kind of pro-Palestinian list, because I don't know where the check goes to."

But Williams felt she was worth the price of admission. "Tennessee had a protective sense about his women," Grissom says. "He felt that Vanessa was dangerously taken advantage of, and he felt that way about Jane Fonda as well. He felt they both had an intellectual and moral insecurity, and they subsumed their identities to certain men."

Redgrave was heartbroken over being denied the opportunity to exercise her art. "If I'm not good at living and being a real person, I do now know enough to make it real when I act," she said. "When I act I can be a pretty highpowered transmitter, even if I'm all wrong inside. I make out of acting a mystical experience that is essential to me. I lose myself in a hole when I'm acting. It is true, I'm unhappy a lot of the time, but that's not a negative thing, to be unhappy. I can create best out of unhappiness."

During the trial, the Boston Symphony Orchestra head Peter Sellars told the jury that Redgrave had the "ability to charge a very small amount of material with a very great amount of meaning, which is a special quality that some performers have and is very crucial in the case of *Oedipus Rex*." After they had engaged Redgrave, the BSO was put under pressure right away. They were told that the local branch of the Anti-Defamation League would be meeting soon to discuss whether or not to censure the BSO. Irving Rabb, who was a symphony trustee, called the general manager of the BSO directly and asked him to break Redgrave's contract.

Judith Gassner, the assistant director of promotion at the BSO at that time, found the calls she was getting "upsetting, unsettling." One caller told her: "You will mourn for this. You will be sorry." Another protester told Gassner that his parents had died at Auschwitz and that the PLO was committed "to the destruction of the state of Israel and the Jewish people." Another caller had said: "This will haunt you. You will mourn. There will be trouble. There is trouble wherever this woman goes."

"Historically at the symphony there had been some problem of anti-Semitism, and they were extremely proud of the fact that progress had been made in this area and that there were now Jewish people on the board of the symphony and actively participating," said BSO chief executive Tom Morris. "This decision could have serious consequences and there could be a backlash that would damage the advance that had been made in relations with the Jewish community."

Morris asked Sellars if he could stage the event without Redgrave, saying that she "might be the thing that would sink the whole ship, and it might be best to throw her overboard." Sellars was not at all happy with this proposed action. "I felt it was a hideous idea," he said. "On no moral grounds was the act of removing Ms. Redgrave acceptable. It was fully the equivalent of [what happened] in 1933, because of a certain political climate, saying at the Vienna State Opera, let's not have a Jewish person sing the role of Siegfried. . . . It was a form of blacklisting."

Boston Police Commissioner Joseph Jordan told Morris that if the Jewish Defense League decided to protest or disrupt the event, the police would not be able to prevent the disruption. Morris himself felt that "the basic political problem here is the use of Miss Redgrave's art to express her political beliefs. She is strong-minded and unpredictable and is likely to turn the BSO situation, in whatever way possible, to her advantage."

Morris was convinced that they needed to break her contract, but Sellars fought him on this. "As of yet, no threats had been received, and there was no reason to suppose that such a situation was even probable. . . . I felt that such an extreme reaction was completely premature," said Sellars.

Morris insisted on removing Redgrave's name from an ad for the concert and unsuccessfully tried to draft an acceptable press release about his decision. Sellars remained adamant that Redgrave be kept on, feeling that the worst they would face would be picketing and that the picketing would only enhance the message of the musical piece, which to him was about "extremely large and profound human issues of an ability to prejudge another human being."

Conductor Seiji Ozawa also felt that Redgrave should be let go, saying that he had to be politically neutral and that his "only concern could be music." Which does, of course, have the ring of an artist trying to function in Nazi Germany. The conductor later testified that he feared Redgrave might talk back to the audience and give a political speech as she had at the Academy Awards in 1978.

BSO Artistic Administrator William Bernell called Redgrave to tell her about the protests, and according to him she received the news "dispassionately." She told him that there had been a bomb scare before the showing of her film *Occupied Palestine* in Australia but that the film had been shown regardless. "How do you think you would feel if you were shot dead on the stage of Symphony Hall?" Bernell asked her. "And her response was, 'I am sure that the Boston police will apprehend my killer.' She said, 'Let's get on with it.'"

If this conversation did indeed take place as Bernell says it did, it shows both Redgrave's cool resolve and stubbornness and also her detached welcoming of martyrdom, which her sister Lynn had once commented on. But she also believed that such violence had small chance of taking place. She told Bernell that she did not think "that there are barbarians who would start screaming and shouting in Symphony Hall during *Oedipus Rex.*"

Morris kept on trying to draft a press release about the situation, "but there were no statements that were finally adequate or defensible that could be issued." At last they just released a statement that the concert was cancelled due to "circumstances beyond [the Orchestra's] reasonable control." This was the first time Redgrave had been successfully fired from a job because of her politics. And she could not let it stand, for herself or for others. She told attorneys that this firing "must not be overlooked.

The Boston Symphony Orchestra has denied me participation in a purely artistic performance for purely political reasons."

Redgrave herself took the stand at her trial and told the BSO's attorney Robert Sullivan that she opposed Zionism but not the state of Israel itself. "I never said there is no room for Israel," she insisted. "I never said that the State of Israel should be liquidated or overthrown. I don't believe it. That's not what I advocate."

It was a tough case to win, because it hinged, according to Judge Robert E. Keeton, on proving that the BSO as an organization deliberately deprived her of her right to perform. The BSO, however, had actually wanted her despite her politics, at least initially. It had caved in to outside pressures, and these outside pressures could not be brought to trial.

Under Keeton's influence, the jury reluctantly found for the BSO on one of Redgrave's claims based on the Massachusetts Civil Rights Act, or MCRA, which was enacted in 1979 and which prohibits "any person or persons, whether or not acting under color of law, from interfering or attempting to interfere by threats, intimidation or coercion, with the exercise or enjoyment by any other person or persons of rights secured by the constitution or laws of the United States, or of rights secured by the constitution or laws of the commonwealth."

They did award Redgrave consequential damages for breach of contract in the amount of $100,000 (in addition to her $31,000 fee). This decision was reached on the grounds of Redgrave's own testimony that her work offers had diminished in the wake of the BSO firing. Producer Theodore Mann testified that he had dropped plans to employ Redgrave in an Off-Broadway production of Shaw's *Heartbreak House* because of her BSO firing. Redgrave's secretary Silvana Sammassimo said in a deposition that Redgrave's offers of work had totally dried up after the BSO decision.

Judge Keeton overturned the jury's findings and stripped Redgrave of the $100,000. He refused to consider what had taken place as blacklisting. The BSO itself, when it discussed firing Redgrave, talked about what they were doing as a kind of blacklisting, but Bernell argued against this thinking: "I was furious. . . . I said, 'Peter, this is not a blacklisting issue. . . . If we wanted to blacklist Vanessa Redgrave, we wouldn't have engaged Vanessa Redgrave.'"

When Sidney Lumet testified for her, he spoke of the blacklist of the 1950s: "The memory of the event that actually created a problem tends to fade, except, of course, this was not true during the McCarthy time . . . a period lasting all through the '50s in which the blacklisting of actors, directors, and writers was official—a list actually existed in movies and television and those people could not find any work."

But there was no actual list here. "The burden of the affidavit is black-listing," Keeton wrote. "There is no conceivable way that what occurred here would constitute blacklisting. Blacklisting involves concerted action. There is no charge, there is no evidence that the BSO has engaged in concerted action with anybody else. . . . So insofar as there is evidence in this affidavit regarding blacklisting, it's totally irrelevant to this trial and would be highly prejudicial."

Redgrave had paid to defend herself, but a large part of her legal fees ($150,000) had been paid by the influential Prince Bandar bin Sultan, the Saudi Arabian ambassador to the United States who worked on arms deals for his country and was closely involved in the Iran-Contra affair. He went on to be tight with both Bush presidencies, so much so that George W. Bush referred to him affectionately as "Bandar Bush."

Pursuing radical politics, as Redgrave did, sometimes made for uncomfortable and shady bedfellows. But a lesser actress and person might never have recovered from a trial like this. Redgrave was perhaps the best or most daring or most well-rounded and complete actress working in English, a queen, an example, a lightning rod. Her talent was such that she could not be successfully blacklisted for long. Ismail Merchant and James Ivory felt that only Redgrave could play the Henry James heroine Olive Chancellor in their film *The Bostonians* (1984).

# The Bostonians

Describing Olive Chancellor, the feminist heroine of his novel *The Bostonians*, Henry James wrote: "She expected to suffer intensely—the prospect of suffering was always, spiritually speaking, so much cash in her pocket." James seems only out to satirize Olive at first, but when she falls deeply in love with Verena Tarrant, a pliable young performer who does speeches on women's rights with her father, James gives his entire repressed soul to Olive and her "power of suffering." (Katharine Hepburn might have made a fine Olive on screen in 1950 or so.)

Most of James's bitchiness drains away as Verena is taken from Olive by Basil Ransom, a failed writer and bitter Southerner with views on women and blacks that are "three hundred years out of date," but James leavens his almost romantic identification with Olive by dramatizing the full irony of this battle over a girl who is nothing but a cipher, a puppet who does what she is told by the strongest person in the room. This irony reaches its height when James details how Ransom's cruelty fulfills Chancellor's confused masochism—these two were meant for each other, a natural oppressor and a natural martyr.

Redgrave was understandably a bit put off by James's tone when she was offered the role of Olive by Merchant and Ivory. Unlike her father and her brother Corin, she was not a James enthusiast, and she felt that he wrote about Olive and her comrades cynically and maliciously. But she also realized that despite himself, James was drawn to the woman he was portraying.

She declined to play Olive at first, and Christopher Reeve, who was attached to the project to play Basil Ransom, recommended Glenn Close as his co-star. When Close got a chance to be in the backlit baseball saga *The Natural* (1984), she dropped out of the film, and director Ivory approached Redgrave again. She was more open to the role now after having given it some serious thought, but she knew that she had to understand James's contradictory view of Olive in order to play her, and she had lively arguments with Ivory on just how to be this woman on screen.

Her political crusade came to the fore with Ivory at one point. They stopped talking about the novel and suddenly Redgrave was asking the director for a donation to the Workers Revolutionary Party. "Her voice got deep and remote," Ivory said. "It was like an oracle coming out of a cave. I found myself in this grotesque position of writing out a check for fifty dollars for a political party whose whole mission was to overthrow practically every institution in Western civilization. But there was no way around it." This was something, of course, that Olive herself might have done for her own cause. Redgrave pushed screenwriter Ruth Prawer Jhabvala to make Olive more heroic and Ransom more villainous, and again, this is something Olive herself might have contrived. She fought like Olive for Olive, and the result was one of her best and most apt performances.

As is his wont, Ivory does nothing to control or inflect his material here, but most of his cast is so good that *The Bostonians* is one of the better Merchant Ivory literary adaptations, securely based in an early, lively James source. At its heart is Redgrave's Olive, a woman she plays with all of her wilder instincts firing at once yet held in check by the character's pride and self-delusions; this is some of the most excitingly layered work that she has ever done on screen. As her opponent Ransom, Reeve is surprisingly sharp sometimes, but he doesn't have the skill to layer his own part the way Redgrave does. Reeve can only play one emotion at a time, whereas Redgrave whips up whole symphonies of thought and feeling while standing in a room, unmoving, her eyes scanning the distances ahead of her.

In her first scene with Ransom, Redgrave's Olive is shrill and insecure as she talks about women's suffrage, and when she realizes that he is not on her side, she snubs him at a suffrage meeting without any compunction: "He's *only* a distant cousin," she emphasizes. The distinctive thing about Olive is that she cannot hide her feelings in public.

During the most Jamesian scene in the movie, where Olive is forced to do drawing-room war with Mrs. Burrage (Nancy Marchand) over the marriage prospects of Verena (Madeleine Potter), Redgrave almost chokes on her tea. Her Olive is a freak, and she knows it, and she knows, too, that she is "dry" and has no charm. Olive is aware of so many things, but she cannot admit to herself the true nature of her love for Verena, not in 1875, even though Redgrave's Olive is always fondling and caressing this girl she loves, clutching at her, and even, at one point, unconsciously moving a hand down one of her breasts.

This Olive is drained of all color, pallid. Even her blond hair looks drained of life, and her cornflower-blue eyes stare out beseechingly from a face that seems to have never had any light on it. Yet underneath this timid exterior is the furnace-like emotion of a woman who is always feeling too much—when she weeps, her whole face gets moist, as if all her pores are crying too. "Will you be my friend, my friend of friends?" she asks Verena outright, the second time they meet. "Forever and ever?"

Verena is impressed by Olive's need and passion, and it's made clear that Olive buys Verena from her odious father (Wesley Addy), continually writing him checks and sending the old mountebank away. Redgrave brings this literary character to life in all of her complexity, and she also keeps a kind of guard over her, going against James's ironic instincts in order to preserve the best parts of Olive's personality. She doesn't use her hard American accent for this role but a kind of lyrical, blended voice that keeps the best of her British phrasing without ever quite sounding British. This careful voice work is as impressively maintained as the rest of the performance.

Olive feels her oppression as a woman as "one feels a stain upon one's honor," and Redgrave gives this line just the right tone of lofty outrage. Confronted with Ransom after a performance by Verena, Redgrave's

A young Vanessa acting with her father Michael in Robert Bolt's 1960 play *The Tiger and the Horse*, which dealt with the issue of nuclear war.

Redgrave as Imogen in William Gaskill's stark, Brechtian 1962 production of Shakespeare's *Cymbeline*.

Swinging Redgrave became a movie star as dream girlfriend Leonie, seen here with Robert Stephens, in Karel Reisz's 1966 counterculture hit *Morgan*.

Redgrave played a sexy woman of mystery in Michelangelo Antonioni's existential masterpiece *Blow-Up*.

Redgrave won her second Oscar nomination as the daring modern dancer Isadora Duncan in Karel Reisz's *Isadora*.

TOP: Redgrave fights for the life of her young son in Michael Cacoyannis's 1971 film of Euripides's *The Trojan Women*. BOTTOM: As the sexually frustrated Sister Jeanne, Redgrave delivered one of her most complex performances in Ken Russell's outrageous, tragic *The Devils*.

Radical Redgrave at a protest against the presence of British troops in Northern Ireland on August 16, 1971.

During a rehearsal for Tony Richardson's 1972 production of Brecht's *The Threepenny Opera*, Redgrave dances for Joe Melia and Barbara Windsor.

A rare photo of Redgrave's brief 1972 run as Viola in Shakespeare's *Twelfth Night*, with actress Nyree Dawn Porter.

Seen here at a press conference in 1974, Redgrave announces the first of her two runs for political office for the Workers Revolutionary Party.

Redgrave won an Emmy as Fania Fénelon, a survivor of Auschwitz, in *Playing for Time* (1980).

As repressed suffragette Olive Chancellor, Redgrave won her fourth Oscar nomination for Best Actress in *The Bostonians* (1984).

Redgrave did her best to enliven *Steaming* (1985), the last film directed by Joseph Losey.

Redgrave demonstrated her enormous imaginative empathy in *Second Serve* (1986) a TV film about the transsexual tennis star Renée Richards.

As literary agent Peggy Ramsay, Redgrave was at her sexiest and most spontaneous in *Prick Up Your Ears* (1987).

Redgrave scored one of the biggest triumphs of her career on stage in 1989 as Lady Torrance in Tennessee Williams's *Orpheus Descending*.

Redgrave was at her androgynous best as the harsh and lonely Miss Amelia in Simon Callow's film of Carson McCullers's *The Ballad of the Sad Café* (1991).

Redgrave haunts the 1992 film of E.M. Forster's *Howards End* as the gorgeously vague and delicate Mrs. Wilcox.

Redgrave consults with director Jane Anderson on the set of *If These Walls Could Talk 2*, which won her a second Emmy.

Olive pulls back into a chair and says, "These occasions leave me ex—exhausted," stumbling over the word to get her real meaning across to her enemy. Like Redgrave herself in her public, political life, Olive can sometimes be in the wrong, or mistaken, but our heart must go out to her because her intentions are so large and so pure.

Olive is sensitive to noise, covering her ears when children yell or when a dinner gong sounds. Her over-sensitivity inspires a kind of awe in others: "How you suffer," Verena says to her wonderingly, helplessly impressed with this woman's capacity for emotion. Though the visionary Olive is right about the emancipation of women, she can be highly neurotic about her own righteousness, yet Redgrave refuses to ever make Olive a figure of fun, as James does early in his novel. For her Olive is a heroine, and since this is the way Olive likes to see herself, the casting of romantic Redgrave in the role has a certain irony that might have tickled James himself.

The second hour of the film is repetitive as Ransom keeps stealing Verena away from Olive, and Ivory does nothing to help Redgrave in the somewhat monotonous scenes where she has to feel the loss of the girl she loves, but he does give her the whole ending, which departs from the tone and tenor of the novel's sarcastic conclusion. At the end of James's tale, Olive is left alone on a stage, having lost Verena to Ransom for the final time, and her capacity for suffering is filled to the breaking point by the boos and catcalls of the assembled crowd, which eventually descend to a respectful Bostonian hush.

In Ivory's film, some of the audience leaves when Verena fails to perform and goes off with Ransom, but when Redgrave's Olive comes out, she finds her own eloquent voice for the few sincere people who want to listen to her point of view. This last scene is a kind of triumph for Olive, and it is richly deserved and believable. Redgrave puts across the idea that her Olive will hold on for as long as it takes to see women get the vote, even if she has to live as long as Miss Birdseye (Jessica Tandy), an abolitionist and grand old lady of causes.

Ivory paid a price for employing Redgrave at this point in her life and career. "People called us up all the time and threatened to bomb us," said Ivory. "Special premieres we had set up were canceled. Snively, stupid things." Redgrave received her fifth Oscar nomination for *The Bostonians*, her fourth for Best Actress. She did not attend the ceremony.

Ismail Merchant testified at Redgrave's BSO trial that the filming itself was not ruined by protesters when they shot on location in Boston in the fall of 1983, in spite of publicity about the shoot and crowds of onlookers who gathered round to observe. "Christopher Reeve was rather shy," Merchant said, "and Miss Redgrave would take the autograph books and get Christopher Reeve to autograph them." Redgrave appeared with Reeve in James material again in 1984, on stage in London, in her father Michael's adaptation of *The Aspern Papers*.

Asked in 1998 about her ability to morph into different people, Redgrave said, "I've seen a chameleon change color, which is just a natural, physical, biological process. It doesn't involve the chameleon's mind. But there are some works of art or a character in a great novel that, as you get close to them, your mind comes up and merges with what the writer's written. Your whole mind changes color, and you become part of that. It's a simplistic analogy, I realize, but that's as close as I can get to explaining it." Speaking of Vanessa's father, her mother Rachel said, "He always had a chameleon quality, and he changed according to whom he was with, even to altering his intonation of voice and his pronunciation."

# Michael

Redgrave announced her appeal of Judge Keeton's decision on her BSO blacklisting case on March 21, 1985. The appeal argued that no motive from the BSO needed to be proven and that caving in to outside pressure was enough. The appeal also argued that the jury had not agreed with the BSO's contention that under the first amendment they had a right to cancel the concerts if they feared that disruption would interfere with the "artistic integrity" of the performances.

Half an hour before she was to talk to the Los Angeles Press Club about her appeal, Corin called to tell her that their father Michael had died. Redgrave wanted to cry and cancel the conference, but she went ahead with it anyway, feeling that her father would have approved. Michael's youngest daughter Lynn recounted in her one-woman show *Shakespeare for My Father* that Michael on his deathbed had thought that he was about to go on stage. He asked her, "How's the house?"

It's difficult to say just how much of Redgrave's political activity might have been meant, at least when she started out, to impress her father. By the end of his life, Michael was impressed, but he kept himself in the dark about the specific details of her actions. One of his last major lead roles was in Joseph Mankiewicz's version of Graham Greene's *The Quiet*

*American*, but the import of that tale of dangerous idealism does not seem to have entered the Redgrave consciousness.

In his personal life, Michael had always had to be secretive. When Corin was helping to write Michael's autobiography, he broached the subject of his father's male lovers, and Michael said, "I shall certainly write about that," but he was too afraid to when the time came. Even at an elderly stage of his life, when he was ill with Parkinson's disease, Michael still had a male lover named Alan. He called Alan his "friend" to Corin, which was the parlance of his era. When Corin discovered a note about a boy called Tommie in a book, he realized that this was Michael's lover, or "friend," from around 1940 or so.

In the 1950s, Michael's friend and lover was Bob Michell, who lived in a studio next door to the Redgrave house for years and charmed all of Michael's children. At the age of eleven, Vanessa was in love with Michell, but she does not speak of him as her father's lover in her own memoir. There is one brief, painfully discreet paragraph about Michell in Michael's memoir, and it has the effect of a cry of agony at both love lost and also love that cannot be spoken outright. Michell himself married and had a son whom he named Michael.

Michael confined himself as an older man to what he wrote about in his diary as "necessary degradations" with men he picked up in train stations. He could never see his own gay desires in any but the most negative terms. Vanessa does not write about either her father's bisexuality or her first husband's bisexuality in her memoir, but her experience with both of these men has surely informed all the splendid work she has done playing gay characters and acting in stories that involve gay issues.

Corin thought that Michael was over-indulged and over-adored by the women in his life. As a father, Michael could be harshly critical of Vanessa and Corin, especially when it came to standards in the family acting profession, but he went a bit easier on Lynn.

Before he died, Michael had seen Vanessa's daughter Natasha play Ophelia at the Young Vic. Taking him back to his nursing home after the play, Redgrave noticed her father's preoccupation, which looked to her like deep melancholy and even boredom. Finally, right before they reached the home in Denham, he turned to Redgrave and said, "She's a true actress," passing on the Redgrave tradition to his granddaughter.

Natasha Richardson and Ian McKellen read at his funeral, and Ian Charleson sang "My Time of Day," a Sky Masterson song from *Guys and Dolls* that had been Michael's favorite. "He was what he was, for better or worse, a difficult, tortured man who could be the joy of people's hearts or the nightmare of your life," said Lynn.

Michael had given perhaps his most impressive stage performance in *Uncle Vanya* at the Old Vic, opposite Olivier, in 1962. "In Redgrave's Vanya you saw both a tremulous victim of a lifetime's emotional repression and the wasted potential of a Chekhovian might-have-been," said Michael Wilmington. Simon Callow wrote of Redgrave in the 1963 film recording of that play: "He does what only the very greatest acting does— he opens up the secret places of the human heart, allowing us to glimpse truths about ourselves that we can barely acknowledge, in Vanya's case the overwhelming sense of waste, the impossibility of love, the death of hope. Redgrave knew about such things."

After that triumph on stage in *Uncle Vanya*, the slow onset of Parkinson's disease began to debilitate him physically. He was unable to make an impact in Ibsen's *The Master Builder* in 1964 at the National Theatre opposite Maggie Smith, and he was insensitively treated by Olivier, who fired him and took on the role himself the following season.

As his disease grew worse, Michael did what he could on stage and on film in increasingly restricted roles. It seemed to many people that he was never able to reach his full potential, and the same would be true, most regrettably, in the case of his granddaughter Natasha. Corin's career was consumed by political action, and Lynn's often frittered away into odd places, as if she had the worst agent in the world. In this justly fabled family, only Vanessa would be able to do everything she was capable of doing as an actress, and she has achieved this against the steep odds that she set for herself politically.

# Healy's Ouster

R edgrave followed Olive Chancellor with an enjoyably hammy appearance as The Evil Queen in *Snow White and the Seven Dwarfs* (1984), an episode of Shelley Duvall's *Faerie Tale Theatre* series for Showtime. She looks to be wearing Sister Jeanne's hallucination wig from *The Devils* but with a 1980s crimp perm, and her spicy overacting is overseen and matched by Vincent Price, who manages to be hammy himself even though he's stuck immobile as the Queen's disapproving mirror. When she throws herself to the floor at the end in a tantrum, it proves just how outsized Redgrave is willing to be as an actress in material for children. She catches the exact comic tone of Duvall's eccentric series and goes as far as she can with it, which is very far indeed.

In her court appeal against the Boston Symphony, Redgrave and her lawyers worked against the original judge's contention that what had happened to her was not blacklisting. It was her job to prove that an organization bowing to third-party pressure was just as liable, if not more so, as an organization that chooses not to employ people for political reasons. And proving this took time. The case caused much back-and-forth argument among judges and lawyers for most of the 1980s.

While Redgrave pitched in to help striking miners, the Workers Revolutionary Party collapsed financially and Gerry Healy was ousted for sexual misconduct. His former secretary, Aileen Jennings, alleged in a letter that Healy had sexually assaulted twenty-six female members of the party, and her allegations were confirmed by an inner-party investigation.

"Many women in the WRP had mistakenly believed that the revolution—in the form of the 'greatest' leader—demanded this, the most personal sacrifice of all," said WRP member Brian Pearce. "They were not coerced . . . physically, but every pressure was brought to bear on them as revolutionaries." The dynamic between Healy and his women, Pearce said, was "not so much rape but . . . sexual abuse by someone in a position of power and trust." It was "wholesale sexual corruption in a manner analogous to those religious sects. There's a very close parallel," said WRP member Dave Bruce.

Jennings's letter denouncing Healy's sexual opportuning was read to a Political Committee meeting on July 1, 1985, and it caused a confusing uproar. "Vanessa Redgrave was screeching at the top of her voice that this was the work of the Black Hundreds [supporters of the Russian Romanov monarchy]," member Richard Price recounted. "That's a memory I cherish. And Mike Banda gave this bizarre, rambling speech about how all sorts of great leaders had had little vices . . . that Tito had been a bit of a womanizer, and Mao as well. . . . You had one wing of the Healyites saying this is lies, lies, lies, and another wing—Banda in particular, and to some extent Alex Mitchell—working out excuses. And the weirdest thing of all was Healy himself, because at one point he was saying, 'This is a provocation,' and at another point, like a harpooned whale, he spread his hands and said, 'Well, I have many friends'!"

"Not all of the women were willing partners," admitted Mike Banda later. "He told them they would be disciplined by the Party if they did not do what he wanted. He gave them the impression that they could not have a political relationship unless they also went to bed with him." Some of the girls Healy picked on and forced into sex were only teenagers and some were well below the age of consent.

Healy's predatory sexuality had been known within the party for years, and now it was used strategically to get rid of him once and for all.

Redgrave saw this as a "witch-hunt." She listened, as always, to Healy, and she felt that he had been framed. Corin said at a party meeting that he was "neither for nor against corruption" but "for the socialist revolution," which points up the blinkered callousness of this radical state of mind. Anything is acceptable if it leads to the longed-for revolution.

In his confused, grandiloquent way, Healy himself was quoted in their paper *News Line* as saying that his situation "cannot be separated from the brutal incarceration of Nelson Mandela, the Israeli Zionist bid to eliminate Yasser Arafat, and the Tory state's relentless attacks on [trade unionist] Arthur Scargill."

Redgrave professed to be hurt that former party members had repudiated their studies in "dialectical materialist philosophy" and Healy's teaching that Britain was a "Bonapartist state," and she refused to believe that her treasured teacher could be a sexual predator. "I don't care whether it's twenty-six, thirty-six, or 236," she said. "They're all liars." She also called the accusers "demented middle class women," presumably because they had betrayed, in her view, their revolutionary ideals.

Former members would say that Healy himself was a fearsome Bonaparte in their organization, so that the WRP fell to a dictator just as countries that tried to implement socialism or communism fell to dictators and totalitarianism. "Healy dominated the organization in an unchallengeable rule sustained by both ideological and physical terror against anybody who dared to disagree with him," wrote former member Sean Matgamna in 1994 for *Socialist Organizer.* "Living the life of a millionaire, if not a pasha, while members of the WRP often went short so that they could finance the organization, and it was not unknown for full-time workers for the organization to go hungry, Healy concentrated more and more on expounding a pseudo-Marxist, pseudo-Hegelian gobbledegook reminiscent, despite its verbiage about 'dialectics' and so on, of nothing so much as L. Ron Hubbard's *Dianetics.*"

Matgamna called the WRP "a farcical caricature of Stalinism despite its verbal 'Trotskyism.'" Of Healy's 1985 ouster, Matgamna writes, "With Vanessa Redgrave—a splendid actress politically short of more than a few of the pages necessary for a full shooting script—playing Cordelia to his Lear, Healy fled from the wrath of his political children."

The way he treated women was not the most serious charge against Healy. "My friends in England sent me all the internal bulletins from the party once Healy was expelled," says Tim Wohlforth. "So I have this huge file of these internal bulletins. That's the source I have for where he was getting the money, flying out to meet with Muammar Gaddafi in the desert in a tent. Basically, these Arab pontiffs, or whatever you want to call them, were supporting Healy in one way or another. He was convincing them that people actually read his newspaper, and they were giving him money to sustain the paper.

"And so the paper supported these regimes, including Saddam Hussein," Wohlforth says. "As far as Hussein is concerned, one of the major accusations against Healy was that Healy exposed the Communist Party people in Iraq, and they were then executed by Saddam Hussein. Whether that particular charge is true or not, I don't know. But he made this adaptation. He developed this theory of the permanent revolution and convinced himself that these people were progressive and against imperialism and therefore deserved his support."

According to Healy's long-time deputy Cliff Slaughter, Healy accepted at least £542,267 from Libya in return for information about prominent supporters of Israel in Britain, and contributions from Kuwait (£156,500), Qatar (£50,000), Abu Dhabi (£25,000), the Palestine Liberation Organization (£19,997), and Iraq (£19,697).

Slaughter claimed in a 1985 article for their *News Line* newspaper that Healy sent a photographer to the Iraqi Embassy with photos of communist protesters of Saddam Hussein's regime. One of the WRP members, whose name was redacted from the internal files, supposedly refused to do this for Healy.

The party paper did support Hussein's execution of twenty-one Iraqi dissidents. Explaining the thinking behind this support, Slaughter said that the party felt "they were only Stalinists." In his own memoir *Come the Revolution*, former WRP member and Healy adviser Alex Mitchell admits to small amounts of money being received from Gaddafi and the PLO.

A former member of the WRP who spoke to me under the condition of anonymity says, "I have always thought there was some probably deliberate confusion here. After the film *The Palestinian* was made, it was toured 'round the Arab world and sold in various Arab countries, including various Gulf States, Libya, Iraq. When the International Committee under the direction of David North conducted its investigation of the party's finances, its investigators, who were not there as friends of any of the WRP factions, rummaged through some of the heaps of paper in the so-called Central Committee Department and unearthed a document listing monies apparently received from various countries.

"The document I saw was an undated single page with no heading. It had the names of countries on the lefthand side and sums of money on the right. In the eyes of the investigators it showed that the party had sold itself to Arab regimes. You have to bear in mind the hysterical atmosphere in which the split took place.

"This document bore out for the likes of North and Slaughter that Healy had gone beyond verbal approbation for Arab nationalism and had actually been taking backhanders. I think this is implausible for a number of reasons. First, the sums involved mostly were in the tens of thousands, as I recall. Second, the countries listed included Kuwait and, I think, Jordan, and some Gulf States, which would have been very unlikely sponsors of British Trotskyism.

"The list didn't indicate who had paid the money, whether the ruler or some rich resident(s) or some local film distributor, if indeed it had been paid. Third, the total amount listed would not have sustained the party apparatus and *News Line* for more than a few weeks. I suspect that what Slaughter was quoting from was actually a list of the proceeds of sale of *The Palestinian*. The film was made with the approval and support of the PLO and was undoubtedly intended as a means to raise the party's profile among rich Arabs to win allies for the PLO as well as more generally in the Arab world. Its production and distribution was an act of solidarity with the Palestinian cause. It wasn't made in secret."

In response to a 2004 article by Kevin Myers in the *Telegraph* condemning Corin and the WRP, Redgrave insisted, "The WRP never received financial backing from Saddam Hussein. The WRP totally and publicly opposed Saddam Hussein's regime from September 1980, when he declared war on Iran. Corin and I were appalled by that war, and all the terrible things that followed. You will remember that the US and Israel supported that war. In the case of Libya, Colonel Gaddafi never financed the WRP." Her letter plaintively wanders off to a conclusion with a tribute to Corin's 2004 performance as King Lear, as if their artistry might wipe away all shadows of their association with the WRP.

"Gerry never said or did anything for personal advantage," Redgrave claimed. "His life was a single piece of steel, and that was why he was feared and hated by the state and by political opportunists." Redgrave and her brother Corin believed, along with party member Ken Livingstone, that Healy was brought down in 1985 due to an MI5 and CIA plot.

Tim Wohlforth wrote of Healy's expulsion: "There were political issues involved. For example, the close political relations Healy established with Arab governments conflicted with the group's generally hardline orthodox stance on other political matters. Yet most members realized the explosion was over more than politics. It was a break with cultism itself."

Redgrave stayed devoted to Healy in exile, paying for a hiding place for him and even occasionally stopping by to cook him meals. She went to court to repossess some of the things she had loaned the WRP.

"Staying with Healy after what happened was a very shameful thing on her part, I think," says Wohlforth today. "It just showed that her connection was this idealizing of Healy and she believed anything he told her. And he had a couple of prominent people in the English Labour Party that supported him, like Ken Livingstone. So he said that the whole business of his sleeping with all of these young girls was just a CIA plot. And when the dust had settled, all that was left was this little group that they called the Marxist Group around Healy of maybe twenty or thirty people, and they were all from this acting milieu.

"Vanessa in that post-split period, she was still like an acolyte," says Wohlforth. "She would bring over a fish and cook it for him. You know, this world-class star cooking this smelly fish for this ugly guy. He had the kind of charisma that a really good guru or cult leader has. He would make it very personal. He knew how to flatter and he knew how to manipulate people and how to control their emotions, their psyche, and their thinking. Vanessa was searching for something, and he provided it for her. They had this very simple way of explaining everything. Anything that came up, they would just say it was all a matter of the CIA."

# Features Again and TV

During all the turmoil over Healy, Redgrave played Arkadina to her daughter Natasha's Nina in *The Seagull* at the Queen's Theatre in London, passing the torch in a play that, like *The Lady from the Sea*, has been a talisman in her artistic life. Both mother and daughter won stellar reviews.

"I'm conscious, in a sense, of my daughters standing on my shoulders as I stood on my parents' shoulders," Redgrave said. "As I grow older, I'm more and more aware of people's work that has gone into my work and that, through my work, will go on into other people. I'm fantastically lucky for the experience that was passed on to me through my father, and not only in a family sense.

"My father insisted that I see American actors, whom he hugely admired," said Redgrave. "I watched Marlon and Tony Franciosa, Eli Wallach, Anne Jackson, so many others. What I've learned from American actors is incorporated in me. It's in theater that you really stretch, because you have to sustain and re-create for an audience, communicate each night. All actors who want to develop as actors will turn to the classics, as musicians do."

She spoke of wanting a second try at the Everest of Shakespeare's Cleopatra: "I want to climb *Antony and Cleopatra* again because I never got there. I did a production in 1973 . . . well, I fell so far short of Cleopatra, I'm embarrassed to say it out loud. It was a beginning, a beginning, not much more than that. It was a sketch. . . . That and *King Lear* and *Hamlet*, incontestably the three great plays. The only part of that stature Shake-speare wrote for a woman was Cleopatra, so I've got to do it. I don't think there's any actress who hasn't felt absolutely daunted by what's said about Cleopatra in the play. If you read Enobarbus's speech: 'Age cannot wither her, nor custom stale her infinite variety.'"

She still had her ambitions in the theater, and movie work started to come her way finally. David Hare wanted her to be the lead in his film *Wetherby* (1985). "She says she's going to do your project, and then when you ask around, you find she's got five others she's planning to do," Hare said. He had to wait for her to focus on just his film and set aside the other directors and claims on her time. "Her bad eyesight physically heightens the impression that she is someone wandering around in a fog," he said.

There have been some critics, notably David Thomson, who have seen a great deal in Hare's *Wetherby*, and it might have seemed like it caught a mood in Britain at the time, but it now looks too academic in its camera placement and too literary in its writing. When a cop talks about a boy who shot himself in front of schoolteacher Jean (Redgrave), he speaks of the boy's "central, disfiguring blankness." An academic (Tom Wilkinson) imagines "a fantasy life of singular intensity" before the boy's suicide.

Redgrave has some fine moments of preoccupation here, when Jean has to really pull herself away from her own internal monologue and get back into social conversations, but her character is too passive, and there aren't many ways into Hare's very pre-determined material, which keeps throwing out random thoughts in dialogue and doing little with them. "Do we become the way we look, or do we look the way we really are?" Jean asks her class, a question that isn't followed up on in any way.

The repressed schoolmarm side of her character is a cliché that Red-grave can only partially redeem. There is an attempt to catch a certain type of hyper-literate, middle-aged British intellectual complacency, but this keeps getting jettisoned by an intrusive synth score and a lack of overall focus. *Wetherby* is more of a notion of a film, or a short story, than a film itself, but critic Andrew Sarris was a fan of the movie, noting:

"I would have given the Oscar to Vanessa Redgrave for *Wetherby*, but I don't know if I would have waited around for her acceptance speech."

Redgrave then played in a two-part drama about the Salem Witch Trials, *Three Sovereigns for Sarah* (1985), for the American Playhouse on PBS. To prepare for her role, Redgrave read three volumes of the court proceedings and steeped herself in the trials and the atmosphere of one of the deadliest literal witch-hunts of all time. "There is still a tremendous amount of mystical demagoguery around," Redgrave said during a break in the shooting. "There are still people who believe in astral bodies," she cautioned, which was a key source of "evidence" at the trials. Redgrave said she admired *The Crucible*, Arthur Miller's version of this story, but she was excited to work on this project because "it's based on the real history of what happened."

Victor Pisano, who wrote the screenplay for the film, originally intended to focus on the trial and death sentence pronounced on Rebecca Nurse, the oldest of the three sisters who were brought to trial. "But after I came across the scene of Sarah storming out of the church, I knew then that she was the real story," said Pisano.

The film, which was also produced by Pisano, was funded in part by the National Endowment for the Humanities, and it was filmed in many of the original locations of the witch-hunt, just north of Boston. A direct descendant of Rebecca Nurse, Herb Lear, was used in a bit part in the film. "In the scenes we're doing in the meeting house, I can feel his eyes urging me on," Redgrave said. "It's a connection to history."

We first see Redgrave's Sarah being driven into town in a wagon. Her right eye is permanently semi-closed and disfigured, and the sight of Redgrave denied one of her big blue eyes has an unsettling effect. When she faces judges to try to exonerate her two murdered sisters from charges of witchcraft and we finally get a good look at Sarah's ruined face, Redgrave offers up a burst of rage.

This is obviously a woman who has been so thoroughly brutalized in body and spirit that she has almost nothing left of herself to hold on to except righteous anger. She is also clearly a woman who is used to being interrogated and outraged. Redgrave uses an incisive voice here, all New England consonants, very specific and very different from her own default speaking voice with its lingering vowels.

Sarah narrates flashbacks to what happened in Salem, and the TV production feels like PBS costume fodder until we take up with Sarah as a younger woman who watches as one of her beloved sisters, Rebecca Nurse (Phyllis Thaxter), is sacrificed to the hysteria of a witch-hunt and blindly incriminates herself. These courtroom scenes are fairly well acted and staged, and Redgrave is formidable as she fights for herself and her sisters: "I shall expose them if it takes all eternity," she says bravely and stubbornly. Sarah reacts coolly to the "possessed" theatrics of a group of wrought-up, accusing girls, standing up for herself and spitting out the word "Tomfoolery!" at them, but her common sense cannot compete with their dramatics. She is led to jail with Rebecca Nurse, and they are soon joined there by their third sister, Mary (Kim Hunter).

As an older woman still trying to clear her family's name, Sarah tells her judges, "I'll give you more than *spectral* evidence," and Redgrave's voice is filled with contempt here at how wicked the world can be. Confronting a corrupt minister in his church, Redgrave has only to stand and look at him silently, her face upturned in a "Why?" expression à la Falconetti in *The Passion of Joan of Arc*. This is one of Redgrave's strongest, angriest performances, detailed and sharp, confronting injustice and steep odds but refusing to go down without a fight.

Redgrave worked with a major director, Joseph Losey, on his last movie *Steaming* (1985), a play by Nell Dunn that was adapted by Losey's wife Patricia. After they saw the play, Patricia Losey was certain it should be a film. "I was so enthusiastic and certain about it that I asked Joe that night to let me do the adaptation," she said. "He read the play carefully and felt enthusiastic, although not initially with such certainty."

When she got to work on the script, there was trouble right away. "Our whole relationship was conflict and we certainly argued a lot," she said. "After all, the film is about women, a subject of perplexity for Joe." The financer John Heyman was unhappy with Patricia Losey's first drafts of the screenplay. She was inexperienced, and the script she wrote retained almost all of the dialogue of the play, only making a change for a happier ending, which Heyman insisted on.

*Steaming* is probably Losey's poorest film, unfortunately, a mistake on every level that sets new standards for dreariness as drab middle-aged women complain about their lives at a Turkish bath-style establishment where buxom blonde Diana Dors, who was dying as she shot the film, advises them to "have a steam" to forget their troubles.

"In my experience," Losey told his cast, "cinema can be used in many ways. One of them is to increase enclosure rather than the Hollywood cliché of 'opening up.'" Which is a reasonable position for making a film of a play, but an untenable one when the play is as limited as this one is. In an article on *Steaming* at David Cairns's invaluable film site *Shadowplay*, Judy Dean comments, "What surprises me is that Patricia Losey, who seems to have been totally dependent on her husband for employment in the film industry, didn't see the irony in choosing a piece of feminist polemic for her first screenplay."

Losey wanted distinguished cameraman Douglas Slocombe for the project, but Slocombe couldn't stand the script. Not wanting to offend Losey, he told the director that his asthma couldn't stand the damp atmosphere of the setting. "I thought it was a nasty, cheap thing for Joe to do," Slocombe said, "and I thought, doing this will kill him. It did kill him. Sad to end on that note."

The cinematographer Losey found for the project, Christopher Challis, even thought that the set itself was a disaster. "We repainted it, but nothing could float, you couldn't move anything," he said. "It was wedged in with backing. The script described atmospheric weather outside, but it was impossible to get it from inside." Consequently, *Steaming* seems to take place in some kind of void where it is difficult to tell how much time is passing.

"The days were long and hard in a long, hard winter," said Patricia Losey. "The schedule was extremely complicated as three of the actresses had commitments made prior to *Steaming*, so the shooting had to be organized according to their availability. There wasn't much time either. The film had to be made in seven weeks because the stage was needed for another film."

When Redgrave first comes on screen in *Steaming*, she seems to be assessing how she can rescue this movie, but even she starts to look restless when forced to listen to the constant stream of intimate details that the women in this steam bath divulge without any prompting; the ravings of a discontented Cockney woman, played by Pattie Love, are particularly hard to take.

There's exactly one fine moment in this film when Sarah Miles stares wonderingly at Redgrave and calls her "a romantic." Otherwise, *Steaming* is far removed from the best Losey movies like *Blind Date* (1959) or *The Servant* (1963), with their ultra-sensitive dissection of the British class system. In *Steaming*, the different classes of women all discover their sisterhood in the most sentimental, unbelievable fashion.

Redgrave appeared briefly in Bill Douglas's lengthy, Terrence Malick-like *Comrades* (1986), a three-hour tour of workers fighting for a living wage in nineteenth-century England, perhaps the most straightforward leftist political tract she has ever been associated with. The workers have only a crust of bread to eat, and they are told to stay in line by their church, but any outrage Douglas might be going for is watered down by the arty pictorialism of his film's imagery. It's a far too pretty-looking movie, and it was a big flop when it was released.

"Douglas's screenplay for *Comrades* is consistently perverse," wrote Vincent Canby in the *New York Times*. "Everything of importance happens off-screen. What we see on screen is a series of short, anticlimactic scenes that are held no longer than the time one would spend looking at a lantern slide. Characters are dressed in appropriate period costumes but are otherwise largely uncharacterized." Perhaps it was Douglas's perversity as well as his political aims that drew Redgrave to the project. As Mrs. Carlyle, a discontented wife, Redgrave makes an unnerving visual impression in her brief appearance, but it leads nowhere much. She would have been much better suited to playing one of the fighting workers.

Redgrave then portrayed the scheming Sophia in the epic six-hour miniseries *Peter the Great* (1986), a huge production that cost close to thirty million dollars, employed two directors, and retained Vittorio Storaro on camera. Lead Maximilian Schell became ill toward the end of shooting and had to fulfill another commitment, so some of his scenes are played by a double, Denis DeMarne.

It was the first American-based production allowed to film in the Soviet Union, and it was heavily promoted. A million dollars was spent to bring Schell, Redgrave, and producer Marvin Chomsky together with a flotilla of TV critics, who were treated to a lavish Russian meal. When Redgrave was asked about her support of the PLO, she said, "This isn't a political conference, so I won't take any political questions." The critic persisted. "It's a pertinent question," he said. Redgrave wouldn't budge: "Perhaps you'd like to write a letter to the press office and put forward a request for a political interview, and then we'll think about it, but not now." She was fond of telling journalists to write letters to her lawyer at this point.

Working on *Peter* was an opportunity to do what Redgrave enjoyed best: delving into the past. "It was a chance to learn about that fantastic piece of history," she said. "I didn't know anything about Peter the Great. They didn't teach a thing about him in school, not in my schools. But television can bring such a freshness to things." She professed to be content to be working mainly on TV instead of feature films. "For me, there is no difference in terms of the work and I'd choose always to work in television. It's now the more important of the two forms. Television is doing subjects you could trot around to film offices for three years and not find financing for."

Redgrave was somewhat perverse when she spoke of the series that was on against *Peter the Great*, the Joan Collins soap/sex epic *Sins*. "I thought *Sins* was much closer to real life than *Peter*," she said. "It was said to have been melodramatic; well, my grandparents were in melodrama, and what did that mean except that it was larger than life. Everything in *Sins* has happened; surely we have little trouble believing that. No, I considered it very seriously. It reminded me, in its own popularized way, of Zola and de Maupassant. It was all there—corruption, greed, murder. Excellent in every way."

In her first scenes in *Peter the Great*, Redgrave looks wicked and imperial as she plays with a little dog. Her skin is ultra-pale under her black eye makeup and she barely has any eyebrows and her forehead looks imposingly high. Redgrave backs up this vivid visual impression with the haughty regality of a woman raised from birth to be royal. Challenged by Prince Feodor (Omar Sharif), she spits out, "Oh, you, *you* . . . you won't permit it?" as if she's never heard anything so absurd. The series loses a lot of life once Sophia is locked away in a monastery, but she gets out for one or two more scenes of power-grubbing before being driven off to the Arctic. This is not a deep or complex performance from Redgrave, but it is full of drive and color.

# Second Serve

*Playing for Time* producer Linda Yellen offered Redgrave the most challenging role of her career in 1986: transsexual doctor and tennis pro Renée Richards in a television film called *Second Serve*, which had a screenplay by Gavin Lambert and Stephanie Liss based on Richards's memoir. In this part, Redgrave would have to play many scenes as a biological man, and she would have to suggest all the various stages of Richards's development both before and after he had his operation to become a female. A tall order, especially on a twenty-day television schedule, and even with an expert director like Anthony Page attached.

Redgrave turned down the role at first, fearing it would be an exploitative film on Richards's life, but she trusted Yellen enough to accept the part, and she found something to identify with in Richards. "Renée is a very courageous woman," Redgrave said. "And the story is not about transsexualism but about all the social problems she had to face. The press witch-hunted her, but it only increased the admiration and warmth people felt for her."

Yellen had been trying to get the film made for almost a decade. "Even five years ago, it would have been too freaky," she said at the time. "I'm sure in today's society there will be people who are turned off by it, but society has been exposed in the last five years to unisex heroes—Boy George, Michael Jackson—and cultural unisex dressing. I think the women's movement also helped popularize that androgyny."

Reading Richards's memoir, Redgrave had been taken aback by her own prejudices regarding what she thought of as normal or healthy, and she worked hard to come to a deeper and more nuanced understanding of gender. She threw herself into preparing for the part, cutting off her hair and shaving it at the forehead into a widow's peak. She met with many transsexuals to discuss their lives, but Redgrave didn't meet Richards herself until after the shoot was finished. She latched onto an accurate idea of her as a kind of radical romantic, and this idea gave her the psychological clarity she needed in a role filled with potential traps and unclear byways.

In this period Redgrave was continually drifting toward a kind of androgyny in her work, always cutting off her hair and embracing her epic size not just as a woman but as a human being. "She really freaked out when she saw herself made up with all the changes because she'd never realized how much she looked like her father," Yellen said of Redgrave on set. "It's unbelievable. In his early movies, as a young man, he was her spitting image." This physical shock and link to her father Michael offered Redgrave another key to understanding Renée's torment.

Before her operation, Renée's name was Richard Raskind. Her original last name was changed to Radley for the film because Richards wanted to protect her son and her father. Richard Radley is a successful ophthalmologist, and we first see him in *Second Serve* taking off scrubs after an operation and walking into the New York cold.

Redgrave narrates in a voice pushed as low down as it can possibly go, and it does sound overly hoarse sometimes. This voice is the one element that gives Redgrave a bit of trouble, but there are moments when it is eerily like a man's voice: foggy, hidden, highly repressed. As we watch Richard play tennis, it's clear that Redgrave has entirely transformed herself physically into a very boyish young man. Redgrave's long arms and large hands are a persuasive visual help here, but this first section of the film still requires a large leap of faith for both actress and audience.

Richard shaves his face in a hotel room in a brisk, contemptuous way that makes us see how much he *hates* this facial hair, and after he's done he puts on women's clothing and goes out on the street in heavy makeup. Redgrave almost never wears much makeup on screen, and so when her Richard walks out in drag with lots of mascara around the eyes, he looks uncannily like a biological man reaching for femininity. Yellen suggested that Redgrave wear brown contact lenses for the role, and this change of eye color brings with it a suggestively destabilizing effect. Sometimes in *Second Serve*, it's possible to forget that we are watching Redgrave at all.

As she charts the confusing back-and-forth attempts of Richard to become Renée, Redgrave's imagination is stretched almost to the breaking point, but it never breaks because she holds fast to her notion of Renée as a seeker of a kind of gender utopia. This is a performance based on transformation, but the transformation keeps shifting all the time because Richard is a hybrid person struggling mightily to bring all of his male contradictions into the relief of some kind of female order.

When she is playing Richard, Redgrave moves like a man would but never in a clichéd way and never in a way that would suggest too strongly that masculinity is mainly learned behavior, which could have been an escape route for tackling this aspect of the role. Instead, she steers clear of any didactic points such as this and stays grounded somehow in the many sides of this person's complicated needs and longings. Her Richard is always reclining, staring off into space, and dreaming about a life that his body won't allow him to live. Richard chooses the name Renée for the inner woman inside of him partly because the name Renée in French means "reborn," and that's what he wants to be.

Redgrave's Richard is really an imprisoned woman, and when he finally yells at his traditional psychiatrist (Martin Balsam) you can see the lifelong fight he has waged against this woman who is begging to emerge and live. Redgrave's Richard does seem to genuinely love his first girlfriend and has good sex with her. Was he a lesbian? Or a transvestite? Redgrave puts these questions to rest when Richard tells the psychiatrist that he knows how to make love to a woman because he is trying to do what Renée might like, a mind-blowing thought that lets us know just how Byzantine human sexuality can be.

Balsam's psychiatrist character suggests that Richard grow a beard, and this beard sidelines Renée for about a year until Richard is inducted into the army and has to shave it off; at this point, it's clear that this painful story has its comic side. Redgrave doesn't neglect the humorous here, hinting at it especially in Richard's scenes with his male friend Josh (William Russ), but it is never emphasized. What's funny in these scenes is the blatant signifiers of gender and societal norms, not Richard's struggle.

Within the limitations of this standard television-issue movie, Redgrave crafts her ultimate outcast heroine fighting for inner peace, a woman who packed a lot of living into her one life on earth. When Dr. Benjamin (Jeff Corey) is sympathetic to Renée's plight and promises to help her be born with hormone injections, Redgrave opens up Richard's blocked, cloudy face so that it looks like the sun is shining on it and bursting out of it for the first time, a miraculous moment.

No less miraculous are the tricky scenes where Redgrave's Richard has started to become Renée but isn't quite there yet. It's worth stepping back for a moment to consider what's in play here. We have Redgrave, a biological woman, playing a biological man who feels like a biological woman inside and begins to make a gradual transition. It's in these scenes of the transition that Redgrave is in particularly dangerous territory, where being a little vague about any moment-by-moment choices could prove disastrous.

Transsexuality is still a confusing issue for many people today and was even more so in 1986. Redgrave must shine a light on it and hold firm to every detail of her conception of both Richard and Renée. Yellen found herself confronting her own prejudice while they were filming. "When we were making this movie, a handsome young man, who is now an attractive woman, decided to have the operation and finalize the deed," Yellen said. "Suddenly, we wanted to stop it. We thought it was crazy. There was a terrible urgency. We were calling Renée, we were calling doctors, anything we could muster to stop it." Even the makers of this progressive film were marked by prejudice.

Redgrave makes razor-sharp, precise decisions in the scene where Renée is approached by an older man and asked to dance. Her facial expressions reveal exactly how nervous and how hopeful she is as Renée gets up from her table. For the first time, Renée feels like the dream she has always had of herself, but some of Richard is still clinging to her body language, and the dream turns violent on the dance floor when a man calls her a queer and starts a fight. When this happens, it is *Richard* who responds physically, not Renée, yet it is Renée who eventually resurfaces to take the blows when her wig is ripped off.

This scene is so imaginatively acted by Redgrave that if you really think about what she's doing, it takes the breath away. Only the greatest actor could possibly understand the flux of identities getting all mixed up here, and only Redgrave has the skill and the daring to go so far out on a limb while still hitting every emotional nuance with pinpoint accuracy as well as enormous sensitivity.

When Renée goes into a doctor's office in Casablanca to have her sex-change operation, it is clear to her and to us that she is still too much Richard to go through with it, and so she drops the forms she was filling out and leaves in a confused rush, an ungainly, lost, tragic figure, an awkward mess in sloppy women's clothes, neither here nor there. Richard marries and has a son, and this part of his life is rushed over in the film. After divorcing his wife, Richard declines and Renée finally begins to take over. She wears more natural makeup now, and Richard's diffident masculine mannerisms begin to get dropped or subsumed.

Renée finally finds the confidence to go through with the sex-change operation she has wanted her whole life, and Redgrave gives us a brief, grueling look at the pain she endured after the surgery, feeling it intensely, letting out a few grunts of total agony that come straight from her gut. We're far past imagination now and into what looks more like channeling than what usually passes for acting. The film doesn't get into exactly what the operation entailed. "You could ask what happened to the penis and what about the vagina," said Yellen. "I would like to have explained that, but we couldn't. There was so much to tell. The story could have been much longer. You could do two hours just on one episode of her life."

Renée makes a new start for herself in warm California, and Redgrave now shows us the final side of her character, a somewhat butch woman, definitely a woman, but one who can call upon a refined masculinity whenever she wishes. In the first scenes in California, the femininity Redgrave finds for Renée is still slightly fragile, newly born and newly tried out, but she gains in confidence when she starts playing tennis again. Renée finds a male lover, and there's a very moving moment when Redgrave lies in bed after her lover kisses her and gently raises her fist into the air in a sort of wistful memory of masculinity, a kind of good-bye to Richard, who is now in his proper place.

After fighting a court battle to be able to play tennis as a woman, Renée went on to coach Martina Navratilova, and she kept her doctor's practice, too. In the last scene of *Second Serve*, Renée takes her young son for an outing and tries to explain her life to him. She talks about fishing, something that he understands. "It's hard for a free fish to understand what a hooked fish feels like, isn't it?" she asks. This is boilerplate writing, but Redgrave makes it a concluding grace note in favor of empathy, her lifelong and career-long project, which reached its highest peak in this performance. She was nominated for an Emmy and won mainly positive reviews. "Once again, Miss Redgrave can be found taking chances that few actors could attempt or endure," wrote John J. O'Connor in the *New York Times*.

Yellen was not happy, however, about Redgrave's reported political stance on Israel at this point. She told the *Los Angeles Times* that she would never hire Redgrave again. "I was just really appalled this time," Yellen said. "She had made a point about not mixing politics with this film. She even wanted me to sit in on some of the interviews because she didn't want to answer political questions. She seemed to have mellowed. I left her on a Wednesday, and she must have gone out the very next day and made these anti-Israel statements. And I started getting the same crazy rash of phone calls I did six years ago." Both Yellen and Richards were Jewish and pro-Israel.

# The Classics
# and Peggy

n this period of artistic renaissance, Redgrave tested her mettle against two essential roles, making a second try at Shakespeare's Cleopatra opposite Timothy Dalton in rep with *The Taming of the Shrew*. The personal relationship between Redgrave and Dalton was nearing its end, but Redgrave did not recognize that yet, and so there were some sorrowful and uncomfortable feelings between them as they worked together. Having trouble with her Cleopatra, which she was playing in a long blond wig, Redgrave consulted Corin, who advised her to read Prosper Mérimée's *Carmen* and play the role more like a gypsy.

Speaking of their *Shrew*, Dalton said, "I don't think there's anything wrong with its subject matter at all, fundamentally. It's saying that true love exists when two people get to know each other. If they fall in love with each other superficially on surface appearances, it's going to fall apart." According to most reviews, Redgrave played her final speech of submission on a note of perverse sexuality, as if she got a sensual kick out of submitting to a man she loved. The company still had difficulties as they played in Wales, but they won fine notices for both plays by the time they acted in London at the Haymarket Theatre.

With Tom Wilkinson as her Pastor Manders, Redgrave next played Mrs. Alving in Ibsen's *Ghosts* at the Young Vic, a play about heredity and disease that she had chosen because many of her friends then were fighting against AIDS. Redgrave even learned a bit of Norwegian to better understand Ibsen's intent, and she had the Young Vic commission a literal translation of the text and hire a Norwegian scholar to help the cast check every line against the original.

"There was thunderous applause as soon as the curtain fell," says film scholar David Melville Wingrove, who saw Redgrave in *Ghosts* when he was a student. "Then Vanessa came out to take a bow and the applause actually stopped. Not because her performance wasn't brilliant, but because she still looked like a woman who's been forced to help her son commit suicide. In floods of tears, dripping with sweat, shaking from head to foot. How on earth could we applaud that? So she stood there in silence for a moment or two until we reminded ourselves that this was, after all, acting—and the applause started up again, twice as loud as before."

Proving her versatility on film, Redgrave gave a loose, sexy performance as agent Peggy Ramsay in the Joe Orton biopic *Prick Up Your Ears* (1987), carefully written by Alan Bennett and carelessly directed by Stephen Frears. The film takes pains to present the symbiotic relationship between playwright Orton (a perfect Gary Oldman) and his eventual murderer Kenneth Halliwell (a shrill Alfred Molina) as a kind of marriage, set off against the musings of Orton's biographer John Lahr (Wallace Shawn), and this has the effect of dampening and over-explaining Orton's life and work.

Frears allows some of the actors in small roles to overplay, and he views Orton's sexual adventuring clinically, but Redgrave works beautifully with Oldman in their scenes with each other, and together they create a bit of fun in the middle of what is too often an overly serious, digressive movie. "We tried to make *Prick Up Your Ears* in the early 1980s, and we failed," Frears said. "One of the reasons we failed is because we couldn't cast it. Gary Oldman said that I'd met with him for it then, but he must have been too young when he came in before. We couldn't raise the money to make it in the early '80s, and that proved to be a blessing."

Frears was friends with Lahr and Bennett, and excited by Lahr's book. "The idea of someone having a secret life like that was so interesting," Frears said. Bennett continued to work on his script through the mid-eighties until they were ready to film. "We weren't making it for very much money, so there weren't conditions imposed on us. Gary Oldman so physically resembled Orton. I can't remember why we chose Vanessa. I think Wally Shawn was coming over and saying, 'I suppose you'll get Vanessa to play Peggy,' and I said, 'Yes?' And he said, 'It's such an obvious idea.'"

It was not an obvious idea physically, as it had been in the casting of Oldman as Orton. "Peggy was not at all like Vanessa, she was a little sort of birdlike woman," Frears said. "But she was a sort of poetic dreamer. Well, dreamer's the wrong word, because she was actually an agent and sort of hard-nosed. She got writers who she represented to write better and to be sort of true to themselves in some way. A lot of my friends, she had a tremendous influence on them. And she was very funny and very eccentric."

Simon Callow had a romantic friendship with Ramsay, and when she asked him if Redgrave had been any good in *Prick Up Your Ears*, Callow replied, "She missed you by a mile." Intrigued, Ramsay said, "What do you *mean*?" Callow said, "She played you as all benevolence, radiating kindness and sweetness and light." To which the spiky Ramsay replied, "Good God. Has she ever met me?" Clearly Ramsay was more of a sharp Maggie Smith type in life, but Redgrave makes her own legato version of Peggy into something quite special.

Redgrave's casting in this film has resonance not only to her own status as a symbol of Swinging London but also her turning-a-blind-eye relationship to the gay life of her father and Richardson. In this film, at least, Redgrave got to cast a naughty-amused glance on promiscuous gay male sexuality and also got to display the kind of sophisticated understanding of these men that she might not have possessed herself when she was a young girl in the 1960s. All in all, even though it's very much a supporting role, this is one of her most satisfying and memorable screen performances, allowing her much leeway for spontaneous behavior and solemnly campy intonations.

Redgrave's Peggy enters *Prick Up Your Ears* looking on apprehensively at the crime scene. She enters the small apartment of Orton and Halliwell backwards, as if to be tactful even after their deaths. It's clear that her Peggy likes putting people on and giving them pleasure when she sits down with Lahr to talk about Orton. Speaking about men with men and what they get up to sexually, Peggy slowly stretches out one of her legs to feel the material of her own stocking. In her memoir, Redgrave mentioned seeing the actress Geneviève Page make a similar gesture which, as a girl, she felt was the ultimate in sophistication, and so she saved it up and used it here for her portrait of this stylish woman. Peggy calls everyone "dear," and she's the only one who bothers to be kind to Halliwell, who is left in the lurch after Orton's success as a playwright and proves impossible to get rid of.

There's a lovely moment here when Peggy saves an awkward social situation during an unsuccessful art opening for Halliwell's collages. Not many people have shown up to the opening, and Halliwell's nerves are on edge. Peggy has bought one of his pieces, a screen, and Joe has told her that she doesn't need to buy it, but she insists, very sweetly, that she likes it, and maybe she actually does. Halliwell explodes at an unsympathetic patron, in the most embarrassing possible way, and Peggy gently takes his arm and says, "I love my screen," as if nothing has happened. In a moment like this, Redgrave makes being kind to someone who desperately needs it seem like fun. Not just the right thing to do, but fun. It's one of her greatest moral moments on screen, this kindness to the freakish and miserable Halliwell, and it's wrapped up in Peggy's pleasure in all people, her pleasure in being alive.

Peggy is one of Redgrave's most purely sensual characters, always feeling her own body and enjoying the tactility of life. She reaches out and lightly strokes Orton's bottom when he shows her a cheap coat he bought for her, and in Lahr's kitchen, Peggy stands and poses in her expensive clothes to show them off. Sitting down to eat, she speaks about Joe's first sexual experience as recorded in his diary: "Joe came all down the man's raincoat," she says matter-of-factly, then purrs, "Lovely melon," to Lahr's wife (Lindsay Duncan), as if the long-ago tawdry sex and the juicy food had an intimate relation to each other. You can see why Peggy loved Joe, and why she was a kind of dream agent for him. The film itself could use more of her presence and less of Lahr's theorizing about the central relationship.

"Bennett, perversely, gives his best lines to Vanessa Redgrave, who makes of Peggy Ramsay the combination of nurturing mother and battling businessman that every writer dreams of for an agent," wrote Dave Kehr in the *Chicago Tribune*. "As Orton's sister, mixing Joe's and Kenneth's ashes together as her brother requested in his will, frets that she may have spooned in more of one than the other, it's left to Redgrave to observe, 'It's a gesture, dear, not a recipe'—a line that carries more of Orton's remorseless spirit than anything *Prick Up Your Ears* allows him to say."

Redgrave made three trips to Russia in 1987. She and her remaining comrades viewed the political thaw of this time with enthusiasm, seeing it as a definitive end to Stalinism, and she took books by her hero Trotsky to distribute to the Russians she met. Back in London, she read the simultaneous translation for a play from Russia that had impressed her, *A Day Lasts More Than a Hundred Years*, turning down a role in a Woody Allen film to do so (*September* {1987}, presumably, in which case she was well out of it).

As a member of the tiny Marxist Party with Corin and Healy, Redgrave continued to support the Palestinians as led by Arafat and Khalil al-Wazir, deputy commander of the Palestinian armed forces, who was believed to be an architect of several terrorist attacks against Israeli civilians. Either not believing this or choosing not to believe this, she mourned al-Wazir's assassination on April 16, 1988.

Our greatest actress is capable of the greatest blunders, and the alleged comedy *Consuming Passions* (1988), in which she is top-billed, contains the very worst Redgrave film performance, bar none. Forty or so minutes into this embarrassing picture, Redgrave makes her first appearance, over-made-up, wearing a shaggy wig, and sporting a tattoo on her arm. Her accent is perplexing. Is it Italian? Cockney? Italian Cockney? The accent is all "z" and "sh" sounds, whatever it is, and it's just as bizarre as the rest of her work here.

"The point about the character is that you should wonder about her all the time, you should never be quite sure she is what she says she is," Redgrave explained, claiming that she was going for a Maltese accent. "I have the impression of a woman with extremely grubby hands, who has worked extremely hard to make her way up from nothing. There's something in her history you just can't place. She seems to be London but she isn't London. She seems to be Mediterranean but she isn't quite Mediterranean. She's a kind of no-man's land." Redgrave's Mrs. Garza is supposed to be a nymphomaniac, and she beats a tambourine as she humps the hapless Graham (Freddie Jones). Redgrave can't do this kind of vulgar sketch-comic stuff. It's a part for Lynn, and they definitely got the wrong sister for it.

"I laughed when I first read it," Redgrave said while she filmed this monstrosity. "I laugh when I come to work reading my part, and I laugh every time I hear Freddie Jones saying those incredible lines. I haven't worked with a script that's so good as this through and through. I didn't want to change a single thing, and that's very, very rare." She even discerned a political element in it. "I would prefer the audience to decide for themselves what it's about," she said, "but even just hearing the story, you see it's got the blackness of our times in it. It seems to me a very sharp social and political comment on our society today."

Just as much care and wayward thought went into her worst film performance as it did into her best. "For instance, I decided she's had some fantastically ferocious bleachings and has got a lot of very black roots," Redgrave said. "But it was Peter Owen, the hairdresser, who translated that into the right kind of wig. And his decisions in turn influenced my portrayal, because the hair suggested someone concerned with her image, yet pretty ruthless at the same time, because she doesn't care that much if the image isn't complete. She's in such a race to get ahead, working so hard at it, she just doesn't do her hair every two weeks."

"I do a lot of preparation, but I don't plan," she said. "I don't decide in advance how something ought to be. I let the other characters, the situation, the room, the actual physical circumstances of that particular moment tell me what I should be doing. I let the invention come, without thinking about it—in fact, I don't even invent it. It's hard to explain, but really very straightforward. It means you behave as if you were that person in that place in real life."

In October 1987, the U.S. Court of Appeals found in Redgrave's favor on her civil rights claim against the Boston Symphony, but she was still having trouble with employment. In February 1988, the *New York Times* reported that the Pepsico Summerfare Festival had cancelled a production with Redgrave where she would have read a simultaneous translation in English of a Soviet play, *Tomorrow Was War*. Christopher Hunt, the director of the festival, said that it was a mainly budgetary consideration but that he had other "concerns." Hunt had asked the advice of Peter Sellars, the director who had opposed Redgrave's firing by the Boston Symphony, who was staging *The Marriage of Figaro* in that festival.

"Obviously, Chris knows how I feel," Sellars said in the *Times* piece. "He knows I testified in the Boston Symphony trial and that I think this is a totally unacceptable thing to do." It was relayed that Hunt had cancelled the production because of "budget constraints, lack of a suitable site, questions about security, and a threat to block the production from a source he refused to identify." On August 31, 1988, the First Circuit Court reversed itself on her BSO case, and her last appeal in the case was denied on January 23, 1989.

"Convoluted debates about comity, federalism, and certification determined the outcome in *Redgrave*, but the procedural circumstances were so unique that the actual holding may be of interest primarily to federal court scholars compiling footnotes on odd miscarriages in certification procedure," wrote Marjorie Heins in her lengthy article on the case for *The Boston Law Review*.

There have been some legal cases that have tried to use the "Redgrave defense" based on her arguments at these trials. "Regardless of how new assertions of the Redgrave defense are resolved," wrote Heins, "and whatever factual showing the courts eventually require or balancing tests they impose, the dicta in Redgrave v. BSO has . . . handed a new weapon to private corporate defendants in civil rights and employment discrimination cases." So Redgrave had provided a new weapon, at least, with which to fight injustice. This case was clearly one of her worthiest fights. "She told me that winning that case was the most important event in her life," *Playing for Time* producer Linda Yellen said, "even more important than having her children."

# Orpheus

I n her high noon of 1966, Redgrave had made a brief but memorable silent cameo as a smiling Anne Boleyn in Fred Zinnemann's film of Robert Bolt's *A Man for All Seasons*, which won an Oscar for Paul Scofield's Thomas More, and in 1988 she took on the Wendy Hiller wife role to Charlton Heston's Thomas More in a new version of the play for television. It was shot in a speedy eighteen days.

Heston had wanted to perform the lead in the Zinnemann film, so he leaped at the chance to direct himself in the role and restore most of the cuts to the play, like the character of The Common Man (Roy Kinnear) who addresses the audience directly. Heston felt Scofield had been too astringent as More, and he labored to play the part with more warmth. He rightly said of Redgrave, "She does a wider stretch of parts, and she takes more chances than any actress alive," and the conservative Heston said he didn't mind that Redgrave "makes Jane Fonda look like Herbert Hoover."

"I can think of no living actress who has undertaken the range of parts Vanessa has," Heston said. "Not just Shakespeare and the Greeks, but Ibsen, Shaw, *bad* Tennessee Williams {*Orpheus Descending*}, a musical, and, to my great good fortune, a couple of parts with me."

This new *Man for All Seasons* would seem merely unnecessary if it wasn't for Redgrave's bizarre and misjudged performance as More's wife Alice. Since Alice had been born in Yorkshire, Redgrave wanted to play her with a West Country accent, but Heston felt that this accent would be too difficult for American audiences to understand. When Heston and producer Peter Snell showed her some footage they'd already shot, she said, "Oh no, that won't do," and she tried another more Northern accent instead.

She speaks very loudly in the film and shouts "Argh!" like some lady pirate and makes all kinds of broad gesticulations with her hands. Obviously she should have dropped this accent idea entirely. She often sounds like she's been dubbed, or like she's been possessed, and when she isn't talking strangely to others she's wrinkling up her face and even chattering quietly to herself.

Heston was admiring of the fact that she chose to play Alice as "an embattled shrew," but it's a performance all given in goonish exploding lurches, and it's worth asking why Redgrave chose to play this illiterate but strong-minded woman as a kind of childish simpleton. "It's a lion I married," Heston says to her in her last scene, but she seems less like a lion and more like a schizophrenic llama. All in all, with this demented performance and the dire *Consuming Passions*, 1988 was a low point in her acting career where her worst ideas seemed to prevail.

After organizing a concert and conference in Moscow to oppose the Israeli occupation of the West Bank and the Gaza Strip, Redgrave next played Nora Melody in a production of Eugene O'Neill's *A Touch of the Poet* with Timothy Dalton at the Young Vic and the Haymarket Theatre.

"After the Haymarket Shakespeare season," Dalton said, "Duncan Weldon Management asked Vanessa and me what else we might like to do in the West End, and after a great deal of reading and searching around, Vanessa remembered *A Touch of the Poet*, which she had once been asked to audition for in America. As soon as Vanessa gave me the script, I knew that we had to do it . . . the miracle for us is that no one in London had ever tried it before.

"Although it's a commercial production, Vanessa and I were very keen to restart it at the Young Vic because seat prices are so low that you really do get a young student audience," said Dalton. "As soon as we started rehearsing, all the problems of the play, its focus on the Irish immigrants to America in the last century, its length, and its detailed references to American politics of the period, seemed to get ironed out by the sheer strength of O'Neill's poetry. It's a play that grows all the time you do it."

The director David Thacker, who had directed Redgrave in *Ghosts*, was hired to direct this O'Neill revival. "Vanessa was very keen to open up the extent to which the play is dependent upon an understanding of Irish history," Thacker said. "Without Vanessa's interventions in that way, one might not have been quite as focused on that."

"If we want to understand anything of now, we have to understand the history that produced the now," Redgrave said. She felt that her "strength as an actress" was due to "the fact that I am very conscious of the necessity of finding out the history that produced the subject of whatever I am working on." It was by all accounts a production of O'Neill's play that emphasized its Irish themes, even employing live bagpipe music off-stage and during intermission. Thacker thought that Redgrave's work in *A Touch of the Poet* represented "a definitive performance for all time. Who'd want to see anyone else play it?"

"Redgrave's initial entrance in the play was staged in a way that did not elicit applause in the performances I witnessed," said the production's dramaturg William Condee. "She entered unobtrusively, shuffling through a side door. Applause may also have been dampened by disorientation and shock at her appearance: the usually dazzling Redgrave had sagging breasts (after much experimentation, lentils worked best), greasy gray hair, a heavily lined face, and padding so as to look overweight. While Redgrave's verve and sparkling eyes were unmistakable, it was a marvel to watch the extent to which she transformed herself. She truly gave the illusion of being spent, overweight, and weighed down with years of work and turmoil."

Elizabeth Marvel, a major American stage actress, was hugely inspired by Redgrave in this play. "I had one of those lightning bolt experiences," she said. "I saw Vanessa Redgrave in *A Touch of the Poet*, and I sat, like, two rows away from her, and that's when I knew. That's what happened. I saw her, and I was so fascinated—it was like watching Harry Houdini escape from the milk bottle, or whatever his famous trick was. It was magic to me. And I wanted to learn how to do that."

Redgrave then settled in to rehearsing the part of Lady Torrance in Tennessee Williams's problematic *Orpheus Descending*, under the direction of Peter Hall. She played the role three times in England, brought the play to Broadway in 1989, and filmed it for television in 1990. It was an immense personal success for her.

The theater, and this play in particular, acted as a kind of renewal for her. She liked the challenge of "compelling the attention of 700 people with 700 problems and preoccupations who are probably wishing they'd come to the theater another night. What's so special about the stage is that in the space of two and a half hours, the actors, the author, and the audience are all three creating something that will not ever happen again in quite that way. When the conditions are right, when the play is really good, when the actors are really listening to each other and to the audience, you get this wonderful, contradictory feeling that it's all occurring for the very first time."

"Tennessee was always dreaming of her as Lady Torrance," says James Grissom. "You never get over the rejected love, which is what he called plays of his that didn't succeed. He said to me, 'There's got to be a way we can get *Orpheus* right. I still love that play and believe in it.'"

Redgrave felt that Lady Torrance was the most difficult theater role she had attempted up to that point, and she needed all of director Peter Hall's encouragement and guidance to pull it off. As so often before, she also called on the help of Tony Richardson. Redgrave had been playing the part with an American accent, and Richardson insisted that she was mad not to use an Italian accent for the role. He thought that the play was impossible, but he very much wanted Redgrave to succeed in it.

When she tried the Italian accent for Hall, he told her to keep it and stated that something was releasing in her that was Lady that hadn't been coming out before. Her son Carlo was in a bad car accident during the early run of the play, but she was able to carry on with it.

Frank Rich wrote a rave review of the London production that ran in the *New York Times*: "Will homebound Americans ever see it? One can hardly assume so; Miss Redgrave, whose vocal support for the Palestine

Liberation Organization is repugnant to many, has been conspicuously absent from our stages since the Boston Symphony Orchestra cancelled her engagement as a narrator for Stravinsky's *Oedipus Rex* in 1982. In the meantime, Americans are missing the creative prime of the greatest actress in the English-speaking theater."

The actress Imogen Stubbs saw her in the production and later said, "Vanessa's character, Lady, had to have an Italian accent. Accents are not her forte (I had accent classes at RADA and was hot at spotting good or bad accents). This one was a mixture of Italian, Welsh, and Pakistani. But as I sat there, I became totally caught up in her performance. At the end, she had been utterly broken. She sat on stage with one leg out—like a broken doll—diminished and defeated. That could have looked like a rehearsal idea but it was devastating. At the curtain call it felt inappropriate to clap.

"Vanessa acts out of instinct—she is an incredibly risky actress," said Stubbs. "I don't know if it is strategic or how her heart takes her. . . . She has greatness—charisma, daring, insanity. It is not even technically controlled. You know when an actor is cheating. But Vanessa has that element of catharsis. She is a great role model. I have worked with her and sometimes her decisions in rehearsals are mystifying: she has eccentric, extraordinary, not-to-be-analyzed instinct. I learned from her. She pushed me and made me braver."

When she was offered a Broadway run for *Orpheus Descending*, Redgrave agreed at once. She loved the play and the production, but she also wanted to prove that she could act on an American stage without protests throwing everything off.

Before going to America for *Orpheus*, she played three months at the Apollo Theatre in London in Martin Sherman's *A Madhouse in Goa*, a pair of one-acts that opened to poor-to-mixed reviews. Redgrave got good personal notices and developed an enduring friendship with Sherman, drawing the retiring playwright into her world of activism and benefits.

Robert Ackerman, the director of *Madhouse*, got a dose of her obstinacy in rehearsal. Both he and Sherman saw Redgrave's character Mrs. Honey as a faded Southern belle, but she latched on to a second-act description of her character as a "crusty old dame" and ran with it. "She started talking in this gravelly voice, took on a masculine persona," Ackerman said. "She wore a baseball cap and pedal pushers. She is supposed to ring a little dinner bell, but Vanessa opted for a cowbell. At first we were rather put off. I argued she was heading in a totally wrong direction. But Vanessa can be very convincing, and because she is one of the greatest actresses alive, she can make you believe anything she does is beyond brilliant."

But Ackerman's enchantment with her reputation and her sheer Vanessa-ness fell away during the tech rehearsal. "Holy shit," he thought. "She's dreadful." Though he had been fine with her work in the rehearsal hall, on stage she seemed to be playing a caricature. Finally Redgrave stopped, broke character, and admitted, "Bob darling, I feel totally fake." Ackerman told her to just get through the rest of the rehearsal and then took her out to dinner with Sherman. They talked to her about their idea of the role and she mainly listened quietly, taking their words in. They were to open in two days, and she had gone so far down the wrong track that they all worried the damage was irreparable.

The day of the opening, Ackerman came into Redgrave's dressing room and she showed him a soft white wig she had found, a small white fan, and a matronly dress she had bought that morning from a Marks & Spencer department store. She was going to go on that night in a totally new characterization of her role. Ackerman told Redgrave he thought that she was very brave. "You have to be," she told him, "when you're that stupid."

"She loves the process," says James Grissom. "It's like you want to say, 'Stop with the journals!' I said to Alec Guinness once, and I prefaced it by saying Vanessa was far more talented, of course, but I said in rehearsal it sounds like Vanessa is like a British version of Shelley Winters, and Alec said, 'Oh, that's very good.' He and John Gielgud would say that they were too old to rehearse with Vanessa forty years ago, let alone at the point they were at then."

Redgrave was billed as "Sister Crucifix" in *Breath of Life* (1990), a film set in a TB sanitarium that involved a love story between Franco Nero and a former ballerina played by Lucrezia Lante della Rovere. In one scene, Redgrave's nun adds a sensual touch to the film by draping herself in part of the ballerina's gold chiffon costume.

She then came to New York with *Orpheus Descending*. Redgrave made journalists who wanted to interview her sign an agreement that there would be no political questions and that she was to be given a copy of the interview to vet it. Speaking of this document, Redgrave said, "It provided a basis for mutual trust, and, I dare say, it protected those journalists who wanted to write something decent and objective but were told by their editors to 'get' me." The only person she was protecting, of course, was herself, but Redgrave was as bold and unprotected as ever on the stage in the very romantic *Orpheus*.

Rich reviewed the production again when it was on Broadway: "The fusion of Vanessa Redgrave and Tennessee Williams is an artistic explosion that was bound to happen, and the wonder is that we had to wait until Peter Hall's revival of *Orpheus Descending*." Rich had trouble with some of the re-cast American actors in the production, particularly Tammy Grimes as the sheriff's wife, but he agreed, as most writers did, that Redgrave had made a personal triumph in this role against all odds. The other actors didn't faze her, nor did the problems in the script itself. She had decided to commune with Williams, and she had made it into a kind of spiritual event. Williams might have laughed uproariously and appreciatively at her notoriously broad accent, which was exactly the right non-realistic choice for this material.

Not everyone was entranced by her work in this play. She received some bad or merely bewildered reviews, but that's to be expected when an actor is working as far out on a limb as she did as Lady Torrance. The line between a superb and an awful performance can be very thin, and Redgrave walked that knife-edge line at every moment she played in *Orpheus*.

Redgrave filmed this production of *Orpheus Descending* for the TNT cable channel in 1990, again under the direction of Peter Hall and with most of the original stage cast joining her, including her leading man Kevin Anderson. It was a tough shoot for Redgrave, six days a week where she was in practically every scene and giving her all. "I am very, very glad we are doing this film for TV," she said. "Tennessee always wrote for film. If ever a film tries to take away most of his dialogue, because films are supposed to have less dialogue, you immediately lose what makes him wonderful for film—that is, his stories and the way they develop and the characters' thoughts and situations. This is very far from being a film of the stage production. This is bringing it to completely new life."

George Manasse, the producer of this TV *Orpheus*, was impressed by Redgrave's physical commitment to Lady. "She damaged her knee on Broadway and had microsurgery on it," he said. "I was slightly concerned, but yesterday she had a scene on her knees and I came in and she was kneeling on the concrete floor. There is tremendous dedication there."

Asked why she wanted to do *Orpheus* to begin with, Redgrave gave a characteristically lofty answer: "The story tells, and the particular characters show, an extraordinary understanding of the situation of dispossessed people. The Sicilian dispossessed can't find jobs or keep their families together and have to immigrate to America to find a life. They can't find the life here and become trapped. This situation comes together with the situation of the Indian people and the black American people and the situation of poor white sharecroppers, which is a reflection of the vestiges of a feudal society still there in the South at the time he wrote it. We are talking real history, and you have to know that real history to appreciate it when you are studying what he wrote."

The film serves as a valuable record of both her own outstanding performance and the production itself, which Hall directs gracefully and intelligently, bringing out the grotesque elements of Williams's almost impossible play without ever going too far with them. "That's the way Tennessee was," Redgrave said. "He'd laugh his way like a maniac through the most tragic situations, and that's life, you know? That's life, too. And he did laugh, it seemed inappropriately, it seemed to people sitting in the audience. He could see the farce in the middle of horror."

We first see Redgrave's Lady Torrance in a car with her hated husband Jabe (Brad Sullivan), and her eyes are proud, for Lady sets great store in her own pride. Redgrave's Italian accent takes some getting used to, particularly when she shouts at people; this shouting makes her voice sound shrill and the effect is almost absurd. Her very extreme, risky accent probably worked much better on stage. In many ways this is a major theater performance played on a large scale and transferred to film without enough modifications for the intimacy of the camera.

Redgrave's Lady has blond hair and brown eyes (she wore brown contact lenses and had her hair dyed). She talks to herself and is always letting out a cascading laugh that goes "Who-do-who-who-who-who-ha-ha!"

This laugh acts as a release valve from tension and bears no relation to genuine mirth.

After listening to Anderson's Val talk about a bird with no wings, one of Williams's most lyrical monologues, Redgrave hits a note of pure longing when Lady sighs and says, "I'd like to be one of those birds." In her first scenes with Anderson, Redgrave allows Lady to be somewhat passive but furtively alert to the pull of Val's sexuality. Her accent can seem too forceful when Lady is upset, but the vulnerable, apprehensive look in her eyes is just right for the role.

In the scene where Lady tells off her former lover David Cutrere (Lewis Arlt), Redgrave holds her large hands on her hips and then whips her hands around her face and body to give Lady the courage to keep talking. Her bold physicality works in this scene because Hall has his camera at a discreet distance from Redgrave, but when Val confronts Lady and hurts her feelings, Redgrave's face is filled with epic, quivering, humiliated, childlike hurt, and though it comes from a genuine place, it's meant to be seen from the second balcony of a theater. It's too much for a film close-up.

Still, Redgrave is perfect for this material because she is able to play it on an almost entirely abstract plane without too many merely human behavioral choices, and Hall films her with love when Lady takes her clothes off to go to bed with Val. In this moment of actual physical nudity, the daring of both actress and character meet.

Redgrave is a sensual actress, but rarely a sexual one. The blunt force of sexuality usually frightens her. Redgrave approaches sex indirectly, abstractedly, as an idea of release, never as a fact or a joy or a goal, but she lets her guard down here for Williams, who saw sex as a kind of communion and salvation. Redgrave's persona almost always seems above the merely sexual, but she lets herself be naked and needy in this Williams play and drink from the cup that Val offers her.

Redgrave's portrayal of Lady's hectic grasp at happiness in the last scenes is as vivifying as it must have been on stage, even if the camera is again too close and sometimes gets in the way of her full-bodied "Italian!" performance. Lady's father used to make money with a dancing monkey until it dropped dead, and now Lady keeps repeating what he said at the chimp's last performance: "The show is over, the monkey is dead!" Redgrave even puts on a full monkey mask at one point, which is almost too much, too literal, but she purifies Williams's most outlandish impulses here with her own noble, queen-like vitality.

In these final scenes Lady has become wild and sweet and willing to fight for life, and the only word for Redgrave's acting here is *exalted*. When Lady is shot down dead by her husband, Redgrave does an immensely pained death fall to the floor, reaching out to us like a dancer, and as the life leaves Lady's face, Redgrave somehow manages to look like a corpse. We aren't just watching an actor play a death scene but a womanly life force caught short by death. The show is over, the heroine is dead.

# Lynn

t the start of the 1990s, Redgrave worked for the first time with
her sister Lynn in a production of Chekhov's *Three Sisters* at the
Queen's Theatre in London. Vanessa played Olga, Lynn was
Masha, and Corin's daughter Jemma played Irina.

After Lynn had moved to America in the early 1970s, she and Vanessa had lost touch. In the late seventies, Lynn was outspoken about
the misgivings she felt over the Workers Revolutionary Party and how it
had affected both Vanessa and Corin. "When her revolution comes, and
it does, and I were in her way, I'm sure she'd walk right over me," Lynn
told *60 Minutes* in 1978. "It would upset her, I think, but it's 'onwards,
brothers, to the final goal.'" Now was a time, though, for rapprochement.

Vanessa was stimulated by Robert Sturua, their director for the
Chekhov play, and the production was a success for all three Redgraves.
"The director Robert Sturua told us if we didn't make everybody in the
audience think of their own lives and what they were doing with them—
and maybe feeling quite uncomfortable about that—then we would have
failed," Vanessa said admiringly.

There were off-stage tensions, however, when Vanessa strongly came
out against the American Gulf War in a speech at a rally in Barcelona,

Spain on January 13, 1991, where she called for "the withdrawal of U.S., British, and all imperialist troops from the Gulf. We must uncondition- ally defend Iraq against American, British, or Israeli troops." Later, in an advertisement she placed in the *New York Times*, Vanessa clarified: "I unconditionally oppose the Iraqi invasion of Kuwait." A wary Lynn sought to distance herself from her sister's political dramatics.

Lynn's career had been somewhat spotty, usually for personal reasons. "I was the child of whom nothing was really expected," Lynn said. "Van- essa was the child of the family—being the oldest—of whom everything was expected. And she surpassed any possible expectations. My aspira- tions were treated with amazement and sort of suppressed shock because basically our parents were very nice people who didn't want to show their shock. I saw it. I saw the shock."

And she in turn was shocked when she read her father's memoir and discovered just how shocked he was that Lynn was going to pursue a career in acting as well. "I had no idea of it because his stock in trade, to me certainly, was to greet things with a noncommittal sort of look," Lynn said. "His great communication was in his work."

Lynn's first film success had been *Georgy Girl*, a movie as ungainly and galumphing as her title character, a large, lovable type who is set upon by rich James Mason, a dirty old man who offers her a contract to be his mistress even though he sees her as a kind of daughter (he employs her father). *Georgy Girl* had first been offered to her older sister. "The rumor was that Vanessa had torn up the script and threw it into the river Tiber," Lynn said later, with a laugh. "I don't know if it's true, but that was the rumor." Maybe this was not something Lynn felt comfortable asking about.

*Georgy Girl* is quite similar in look and feel to Vanessa's *Morgan*, and even more all-over-the-place, riding along on a catchy theme song and Lynn's essential good nature, which is besmirched regularly, especially when she is made to kiss Mason in weirdly icky close-ups. Lynn and Mason had an affair off-camera, but you'd never know it from their work in the film. Vanessa is unthinkable in the role, and if she did throw the script into a river, she was right to do so.

At one point, Vanessa and Lynn were up for the same role. "Both Lynn and I auditioned for Hal Prince for the first production of *Cabaret* in

London," said Vanessa. "I got into round one and promptly never heard a word again. Lynn got to round one and a lunch with Hal Prince, but Judi Dench got the role, and Judi was fantastic in it. So I wouldn't have felt bad if Lynn had got it. I would have wished I'd got it! But I wouldn't have felt bad if Lynn had got it, and I certainly didn't feel bad when Judi got it. As long as someone's good in something we don't get, but they've got to be good!" she said, and laughed. The Redgraves finally snagged this plum role when Vanessa's daughter Natasha made the greatest success of her career playing in the Broadway revival of *Cabaret* in the 1990s.

Lynn did a short blackout sketch in Woody Allen's *Everything You Always Wanted to Know About Sex But Were Afraid to Ask* (1972), and played the title role in *The Happy Hooker* (1975). Her career often encompassed a peculiar mix of low and high culture. She would appear in something called *Disco Beaver from Outer Space* (1978) and then do some Shaw on television, or a *Love Boat* episode followed by a TV production of *Antony and Cleopatra* with Vanessa's long-time lover Timothy Dalton. She was most famous for Weight Watchers commercials, forever singing "This is living!" on TV, and she also played on several TV series, getting into Vanessa-like trouble on one of them when she wanted to breastfeed her baby on set, was fired, and took the producers to court.

In so many ways, Lynn is like a funhouse mirror version of her sister or a reaction to her, and she's helplessly likable even in her worst films. "It was always 'Corin's the brain, Vanessa's the shining star, oh and then there's Lynn,'" Lynn joked. At her best, she was just as open as Vanessa, but far more intimate and life-sized, and she certainly enjoyed the chance to be silly. In the 1980s, on television, it was possible to watch Vanessa at Auschwitz or undergoing some gruesome ordeal and then flip the channel and see Lynn singing and camping it up in a Weight Watchers commercial. They served as a kind of balance for each other.

When Lynn ventured into Vanessa territory with a TV-issue movie like *My Two Loves* (1986), where she tactfully played a lesbian, it was notable that her non-heroic character says things like "I just want to slide by and enjoy life," and was cozy in the closet because she didn't want to be a "sacrificial lamb." Unthinkable sentiments for Vanessa, both on screen and in life. Lynn had her day as an older character actress, playing a lead romantic role in *Shine* (1996) and scoring an Oscar nomination for her very funny, very Hungarian housekeeper in *Gods and Monsters* (1998). And she did a straight-to-the-camera monologue at the end of *Kinsey* (2004) that showed just how much skill and focus she had developed over the years.

Lynn and Vanessa worked together on screen for the first time in a television remake of *What Ever Happened to Baby Jane?* (1991), and they make an odd fit with this material, which was played for melodrama and camp anger by Bette Davis and Joan Crawford in the original 1962 movie about has-been sisters. It's like putting Dorothy and Lillian Gish in the roles when what it really needs to go for dead-on stunt casting would be a sister act like Joan Fontaine and Olivia de Havilland tormenting each other.

Instead of a Hollywood death-match spectacle, the Redgrave sisters simply play their roles to the best of their considerable abilities, and there isn't a moment that feels like personal exploitation. Even when Vanessa's Blanche Hudson watches one of her old movies on television, we don't see a real Vanessa Redgrave movie from the 1960s (Crawford watched herself in *Sadie McKee* {1934}), but a middle-aged Vanessa herself in a blond wig acting out one of Blanche's trashy old romance films.

"I was principally excited to work with Lynn, not because she's my sister, but because she's a wonderful actress," Vanessa said when they were promoting the film. Lynn felt the same way. "If Vanessa were a terrible actress, I wouldn't have been thrilled to work with her at all," Lynn said. "I would just be wanting to invite her to tea."

It was acting work, fittingly, that brought them together after such a long hiatus from each other. "Doing *Baby Jane* and *Three Sisters*, this is the longest consecutive time that I have been with Vanessa since we grew up together," Lynn said. "So we haven't had enough years together to get on each other's nerves."

"There's a problem in just finding things with two great parts for women," Vanessa said. "Let alone two great parts for women who bear a remarkable resemblance to each other in one way or another. So we've always felt that we probably had to play sisters. In the two projects that we've got back-to-back, we're playing very different sorts of sisters, but I don't suppose many of those opportunities will come again."

When the casting of the roles was questioned, producer Bill Aldrich said, "I think people expected Vanessa to play Baby Jane. And that's why I wanted Lynn to play her." Vanessa agreed with this idea right away. "I thought that was absolutely perfect," she said. "I knew Lynn would be quite extraordinary in this part. There wasn't a question in my mind as to who should be who as soon as the idea came up."

"There are things that Lynn and Vanessa do and say—and looks that they give one another—that only sisters could give," Aldrich said, "only sisters who've known each other for over forty-seven years, and have shared terrible tragedies and wonderful highs together. At the end of some takes, they would stare at each other and then hug each other and cry. Actors don't do that. Sisters do that." Or Redgrave sisters do that.

"I think we did feel that," Lynn said. "We had a childhood where my relationship with Vanessa was unique in that we never fought. Vanessa was a sort of storybook sister to me. There is a bond between us that I feel very, very strongly." Vanessa was very much the older sister, serious, careful, majestic, the boss. Lynn was forever the little sister, apt to be overlooked, honest, jolly, open. Both of them shared a certain impulsiveness, but that impulsiveness went in drastically different directions.

Lynn spoke about her sister's difficulties in securing parts all through the 1980s. "It was sort of horrifying that she was blocked from work for a long time, where her work, it seemed to me, spoke for itself," she said. "Her political beliefs are poles apart in many cases from things that I believe, though sometimes we cross paths. But I think the longer things went on, it was a sort of self-fulfilling prophecy. And when, thank goodness, the producers of *Orpheus Descending* said, 'We're going to put it on because of her wonderful performance in England,' nobody stormed the theater."

There had never been any real career rivalry, Lynn insisted. "As unbelievable as it may seem, a rivalry, a hatred, a moment of wanting to kill the other one—all of which are natural to most sisters—never happened. We're people of an advanced age now. It's not going to happen."

This version of *Baby Jane* belongs solely to Lynn, who really outdoes herself, biting into every aspect of her outlandish, flashy part, making expert transitions from pathetic child to dangerous, mentally unbalanced drinker. Her Jane and Vanessa's Blanche joke like sisters in the first scenes, reminiscing and talking at the same time, and they both emphasize the love that Jane and Blanche have for each other, a quality that is totally missing from the famous Davis/Crawford standoff. The film goes out of its way to capture the seedier side of Los Angeles and makes its smartest revision by turning Victor Buono's mother-dominated character in the original into the outright gay Billy Korn (John Glover), a video store clerk and putative talent manager who flatters Jane out of some money (Lynn plays many of her most exposed, vulnerable moments with Glover).

When the confrontation scenes start to occur between the sisters, Lynn holds back a bit and Vanessa seems uncomfortable playing Blanche's manipulation of Jane. While Lynn's performance stays steady and comes to an almost surreal climax when Jane tries to do a cabaret act and gets thrown out of a club (Lynn wears her old *Smashing Time* {1967} outfit), Vanessa doesn't seem to know what to do with all of her scenes of bed-ridden victimization, which the masochistic Crawford ate up greedily.

In the climactic beach scene, Vanessa plays her final monologue through chattering teeth. This is an accurate physical choice, for Blanche is freezing and has been starved, but it gets in the way of the scene's emotion. The movie was treated as unnecessary, which it is, and Vanessa is not at her best in it, but Lynn's layered, outstanding performance deserves to be remembered.

Redgrave guest-starred on the TV series *The Young Indiana Jones Chronicles* as a mother who speaks briefly of war and romance in London in 1916, and then she played Empress Elizabeth in another Russian costume miniseries, *Young Catherine* (1991), where the location filming no doubt gave her more opportunities to distribute books by Trotsky to any Russians at hand.

In *Young Catherine*, which ran in two parts on TNT, Redgrave made for a bullying Empress, sometimes dressing in male drag, maternal and steely by turns. "I have thrown people into dungeons in chains—for *life*—for *less*!" she explodes at one point at Marthe Keller, who plays Catherine's mother—as ever, she makes for uniquely believable royalty. Felled by illness during production, Redgrave was looked after by Franco Nero, who was also in the cast, and still a remarkably loyal presence in her life. She then took on one of her most complex roles on film.

# The Ballad of
# the Sad Café

Carson McCullers's novella *The Ballad of the Sad Café* is one of the weirder bits of Southern Gothic written in the last century, and its ultimate meaning remains obscure. It deals with the slightly cross-eyed, mannish Miss Amelia, who stands six feet two inches tall. Miss Amelia is a hard, unlikable character, engaging in frivolous lawsuits and tyrannizing the small town she lives in until she meets Cousin Lymon, a hunchback dwarf who claims to be a distant relation.

Something like love for Cousin Lymon softens Miss Amelia's mean disposition, and she opens a café just to please him. The café is a success, and the ground-down townspeople are given a bit of pleasure by it until freed convict Marvin Macy comes back to town. The good-looking Macy, who had delighted in breaking and humiliating virgin girls years before, had fallen in love with Miss Amelia and married her. Following a half-hour of unspecified activity on their wedding night, Miss Amelia had thrown Macy out.

Cousin Lymon falls in love, in a way, with Macy, or at least with the idea of him, and the narrative builds to a brutal physical fight between

Macy and Miss Amelia that ends with Miss Amelia's hands around Macy's throat. Just as she is about to win the battle, Cousin Lymon flies through the air and attacks her, insuring that she loses. After Lymon and Macy wreck her store, Miss Amelia is last seen as a face staring out of a boarded-up window, her hair grown out, her love destroyed.

"*Ballad* must be the first time in Anglo-Saxon literature that a woman writer discusses precisely how it is that a man can love a woman for her masculine qualities," Redgrave said. "Miss Amelia, because of the way she's been brought up as a man, and as a laboring, farming man, cannot reciprocate either as a man or a woman. She finds it totally repellent that Macy should seek to give her his physical love. It's something she knows nothing about and is as disgusted by as any Southern belle would have been in the 1860s who didn't know about the facts of life. The only difference is that she's capable of knocking him out for six when he tries it, which very few Southern belles would have done."

Edward Albee did an adaptation of this material as a play starring Colleen Dewhurst in the early 1960s, parceling out some of McCullers's ideas on love and life to several subsidiary characters. Redgrave has never appeared in an Albee play, whereas her closest rival Maggie Smith starred in several revivals of Albee works through the '90s and '00s. Great as Albee is, he is too deeply pessimistic for Redgrave's taste.

Albee's play was used as a basis for the film of *The Ballad of the Sad Café* that was directed by actor Simon Callow in 1991. Callow found the play too talky and cut some of the dialogue and the role of the narrator, which had been played by Roscoe Lee Browne. Albee himself had very clear ideas about the material, which he offered to producer Ismail Merchant:

> For the film to succeed to McCullers's intentions it must bring a mythic quality to the relationship. It is not the story of a shy, sexually repressed, mannish woman set on by a brutish punk. It is the story of two people who, however unclearly to themselves they may comprehend it, are engaged in a bizarre "grand passion"—the one real chance in their lives for something very special—the one opportunity for them both to fully realize themselves. It is this quality, this awareness which reaches toward the mythic, and makes what

happens when Marvin Macy comes back so poignant, so inevitable, and the stuff of true tragedy. It is this which is missing from the screenplay. As it is now, a punk gets rejected and comes back and does his dirty work. That is not what McCullers intended, is not what I intended, and is not what the screenplay should be offering us.

Redgrave was considering playing Miss Amelia when Merchant took her to dinner along with fifty Russian actors she had brought over to London. Callow remembered that the vodka flowed and many speeches were given, and when Merchant asked Redgrave to play the part outright, she was at a great flushed-faced height of exaltation. "Why not?" she cried, joyfully throwing back her head and laughing with what Callow called "roguish joy."

Sam Shepard was originally set to play Marvin Macy, but he backed out at the last minute, and Keith Carradine took the role right before they were due to start shooting. Callow's film of *The Ballad of the Sad Café*, shot in and around Austin and Seguin, Texas, came and went from theaters quickly, and it remains his only movie as a director to date. Reviews of it were generally negative. Though it isn't entirely successful, it remains a more than honorable stab at extremely difficult material, and Redgrave was certainly the only casting possible for Miss Amelia, with her unusual height, her androgyny, and her ability to pretend her way into even the most unlikely situations.

"It was all very, very difficult indeed because Cork Hubbert, who was playing Cousin Lymon, wasn't really an actor at all, he was a stand-up comedian," says Callow. "I was very uncertain, because I was a first-time director, and I had to direct Cork very, very carefully."

Callow approached working with Redgrave with much anticipation. "I was waiting to see what Vanessa felt about the character, and so on," he says. "And I think, as quite often happens with Vanessa, she only found out herself as time went on. So at the beginning we were all a little bit tentative, and curiously enough that gave a kind of wonderful quality to her work, a kind of delicacy."

As always, Redgrave let her ideas about her role carry her down some odd byways. "I think what happens with Vanessa when she works on a part is that she is groping towards a kind of rationalization of the part, or a concept of the part, and she slowly begins to get it," says Callow. "She said to me one day while we were working that she had been re-reading the novel and suddenly it was staring her in the face that Miss Amelia must be Native American. And I said, 'Why do you say that, Vanessa?' and she said, 'Because she has an herb garden, and she must be in touch with the spirits,' and so on. And she said that obviously we were going to have to re-shoot everything we had done, because obviously she couldn't be blond, she would have to dye her hair black. And I said to her that we just couldn't do that because we had no money at all for it."

This movie is the rare occasion when actually seeing the interactions between literary characters serves to clarify the source material, and this is no small feat considering how odd and private McCullers's story is. The film begins with a scene of a chain gang swinging their pickaxes and singing, and it also ends with this chain gang, which serves as the bewildering coda of McCullers's tale. The picture that Redgrave makes in her first scenes is of whip-smart Frankie Addams from McCullers's play *The Member of the Wedding* all grown up physically yet stunted emotionally and intellectually. When she changes out of her overalls and wears a red dress in the café, Redgrave even looks like Julie Harris's Frankie did in the film of *Member of the Wedding* when Frankie tries on a bridal party dress that is too big for her.

"In a film, much more than in a play, there are no absolute interpretations," says Callow. "You just take the actor you have and the quality that they bring and the response that they have, you have to shape that accordingly into the general narrative. Vanessa had a tremendously strong sense of this kind of alienated woman with her own inner life. A lot of the things you see in the film were absolutely her ideas, like Miss Amelia wearing that red dress once the café has opened. Vanessa imagined that this dress was a dress that Miss Amelia's mother had once worn."

Miss Amelia's tyranny in the film is restricted to one darkened scene where she takes away a much-needed sewing machine from a poor family as payment for a debt; otherwise, we see little of her hardest edges. Redgrave's conception of the role is much more romantic than McCullers's is, yet this has the effect of bringing out the writer's buried themes about love more clearly.

"Vanessa did a lot of research among the Carson McCullers papers, and she found various things that gave her a further clue into the character," says Callow. "She's always thinking, she's always working to make it absolutely fresh and completely new and original, sometimes, it seems, at the expense of what seems to be on the page. She is a completely inspired kind of actor, and sometimes her inspirations might mislead her."

When his friend Peggy Ramsay asked Callow if Vanessa was mad, he said, "Oh completely." "Stupid?" Ramsay asked. "No, not at all," Callow said. "Intelligent, then?" she asked. "Intelligent with a poet's intelligence, not that of a scientist," he concluded.

Redgrave's Miss Amelia moves slowly through swamp water like a noble, dumb animal, and Callow's camera seems transfixed by her harsh face. Redgrave even manages a slight suggestion of Miss Amelia's crossed eyes when she starts to feel love for Cousin Lymon, taking boyish pleasure when he wiggles his ears for her and exploding in a delighted laugh after he does it, like someone let out of prison and breathing fresh air.

Lymon insists on bringing some excitement to Miss Amelia's solitary life. They go to see *New York Nights*, a movie starring Norma Talmadge, and thrill to its car chases and gunfire. Miss Amelia is willing to humor Cousin Lymon, but she has no need for adventure as he does, and Redgrave exactly catches the strangest moment in the story: Miss Amelia reacts with puzzlement when Lymon envies the fact that Macy has been in jail, as if jail was more interesting (or more honest?) than their lives in town.

Callow indulges in some evocative low-light visual effects, and he saves up some impressive deep-focus shots for key moments, like when he frames Macy's face in extreme close-up on one side of the composition while Miss Amelia struggles up the road to the church to get married on the other. He's very attentive to his players and gets excellent work from the hard-to-restrain Rod Steiger as a preacher who gets to deliver McCullers's own thoughts on the lover and the beloved, and how "the state of being beloved is intolerable."

"We had a very difficult cameraman, just an impossible and temperamental and destructive cameraman, which sometimes happens," says

Callow. "And he was difficult with Vanessa and was quite rude to her sometimes, and this upset her very much, but it probably added, in the end, to the success of her performance. She would use whatever was going on to inform her work. I remember she would sometimes have occasion to call Tony Richardson to ask how to handle this impossible cameraman, and Tony gave her practical advice on that.

"Vanessa very much made herself part of the community, she involved herself with all the extras, she made the little herb garden all on her own, she made great friends with Miss Amelia's donkey, and she was much loved by everybody on the film," says Callow. "As you know, Vanessa, perhaps more so then than now, was tremendously immersed in Marxism and the study of Marxism, and she would very often on the set be found with a copy of a text by Engels or Marx or Trotsky or Lenin, and she would be making notes on it almost like a schoolgirl would, making sure that she understood all their points carefully. She was immersed in that at the time, but she didn't talk about it much, it must be said, in terms of her work, but that's what was going on in her life."

Callow patiently stays on Redgrave as she works through Miss Amelia's anger, which can feel a bit too much like mugging, though this surface-deep quality is clearly part of her character conception. There's a lovely moment when she tells Lymon about an acorn she picked up from the ground after her father died where Redgrave puts a full, rippling laugh under the word "died" so that it comes out as "di-he-he-hied," negating the power of the word with her only weapon at hand, the feelings of the moment.

"It was perhaps a bit difficult for me to direct her at times because I am also an actor, and so I was very much aware of how extraordinary she was in what she was achieving for me," says Callow. "But I was perfectly able to suggest things to her. Her mind is working all the time. I tried to create an atmosphere where she could do what she needed to do. In fact, the performance she gave was not at all the performance I had expected, but she was so brave, it was really remarkable."

Redgrave's Miss Amelia is none too bright. Everything seems to confuse her, and Redgrave comes perilously close to a village-idiot quality at times, but these moments are part of the risks she's taking and always takes as an actress. In her best work, and Miss Amelia definitely counts among her best, Redgrave's performances are made up of almost nothing but risks. She has her ideas about her characters and she works them out then and there in the moment, and you're never sure where they will lead her. Her total immediacy, yoked to a huge imagination, is an exceedingly rare quality on stages or screens, and it makes Redgrave as much of a lovable, beautiful, Brando-esque freak as her Miss Amelia.

Surely Redgrave intuits that so much of McCullers's large pain over unrequited love is based in the impossible love a gay person might have for a straight person, and this is McCullers's link to her friend Tennessee Williams, who actually wrote *A Streetcar Named Desire* on the same table with McCullers while she wrote *The Member of the Wedding*.

Redgrave goes all out in Miss Amelia's bloody fight with Macy, putting herself into the most grotesque and ugly positions until she has him by the throat and her eyes fill with bloodlust as she strangles him. No stunt doubles were used for the fight. "The positions had to be very precise, and were blocked out just as you would a modern ballet," Redgrave said. "It should look very agonizing."

"I haven't felt any inhibitions at all about fighting a woman," Carradine said. "Perhaps it's because Vanessa is so towering in terms of accomplishments, not to mention her physical stature."

When Lymon attacks her and Macy wins the fight, Miss Amelia slowly gets up and then starts to cry like a child. "The fight scene was just grueling beyond belief," says Callow. "It was done in short sections, but nonetheless, this was a man beating up a woman with full pugilistic force. And Keith was skillful at remembering the specific moves, which sometimes Vanessa wasn't so great at because she was so much in the moment.

"So it was quite dangerous, and then the makeup artist would have to run in every time to increase the damage on their faces. It was both highly technical and highly emotional. And a little catastrophe happened when Cork Hubbert flew in to try to tear Vanessa away from Keith, because his flying rig broke and he fell to the ground. Fortunately he was all right, but it created a bit of tension on the set, and it fed the anxiety of the situation. It was a very tough five days or so of shooting."

Redgrave left the end of the fight up to chance. "She didn't do that cry she does in rehearsal at all," says Callow. "We had very little rehearsal, in fact, because the schedule was so tight. We would work a little on the set if we could. She said to me beforehand, 'Just let it run, let the camera run, because I don't know what I'm going to do, but something will come out.'"

Redgrave does not use the deep-seated grief she summoned up for *My Body, My Child* or *The Trojan Women* but chooses a more distanced, even theatrical sound of grief, the kind of grief that Olivier was famous for on stage, a larger-than-life howl that has as much to do with technique as with real feeling. It's the only choice for this outsized material, which last sees her Miss Amelia as a haunted face staring out of near total darkness, an emblem of an undervalued movie pledged to difficulty and far-out allegory, desperate for some kind of reconciliation or understanding of human suffering and contradiction.

"I remember saying at the wrap party, which was very emotional, that Vanessa was my equal collaborator on the film," says Callow. "Because she was so connected to the character, she had a kind of identification as a tall, slightly awkward woman. Not that Vanessa is in any way really awkward, but I think that she had felt at some point in her life that she was an outsider. She identified with Miss Amelia utterly. And she liked very much my idea that it was a fairy story by McCullers. It was something heightened, something not necessarily naturalistic or realistic."

# Howards End

Redgrave lost the plum lead role in the national tour of Peter Shaffer's *Lettice and Lovage*, a part that had been played by Maggie Smith, after protesting the first American Gulf War. She filed a grievance against the producers, one of whom was her own son-in-law Robert Fox, who was married to her daughter Natasha Richardson. The producers' decision, which the court upheld, was that after Redgrave's speech against the war in the Persian Gulf, a national tour could not possibly be financially successful.

This was clearly a case of blacklisting, even more so than in her case against the Boston Symphony. She had been engaged, she had voiced a political opinion, and she had been fired for speaking out. "It was quite clear to me and Equity that there was politics involved in the producers' decision," Redgrave said. "I can't agree with the arbitrator. But obviously we failed to prove our case." Julie Harris was given the role on the tour for Shaffer's play.

And so Redgrave played Isadora Duncan again, to much acclaim, in Martin Sherman's play *When She Danced*, which dramatized one day in the life of an older Isadora and her Russian husband Esenin. Isadora doesn't speak Russian and her husband doesn't speak English, and the play is about their struggle to communicate with each other. Redgrave still used the flat twang she decided on for the 1968 *Isadora* film, and though many questioned Sherman's play, most agreed that its star had made a kind of mystical communion with Isadora.

Redgrave, Sherman, producer Robert Fox, and director Robert Ackerman had made a trip to Russia to find the right actor to play Esenin and they settled on the charismatic Oleg Menshikov, who didn't speak any English himself. At one point on their trip, Sherman got himself locked in a restroom, which made Ackerman and Fox laugh uproariously. Redgrave pressed her face against the door and tried to calm Sherman down, telling him solemnly how terrible she thought his two friends were for laughing at his plight.

Tony Richardson was planning a production of *The Cherry Orchard* for Redgrave. Even though he was ill and tired as he talked to her about his ideas for the play, Redgrave noticed that his eyes still danced with the mischief she had fallen in love with in the 1960s. But he faded fast after she left him to play Isadora.

As Richardson lay dying in Los Angeles, Sherman would take Redgrave home every night after *When She Danced* and he would hold her hand across her kitchen table to comfort her. She flew out to LA on November 13, 1991, and Richardson died of AIDS-related causes the following day. Her first love, and perhaps the love of her life, was gone, taken by a disease that carried a heavy stigma at the time.

"He was of a generation that was private about all sorts of things," Redgrave said a few years later. "I didn't know about it until he was clearly ill." Casting aside personal sorrow, Redgrave chose to view speaking about his death as a chance to promote awareness. "The reason I am willing to talk about Tony is because ignorance is the biggest promoter of AIDS. . . . It could have been contact with a man or a woman or even a blood transfusion," she said. "I couldn't do anything to prevent his death. But we can do a lot to help and alleviate and prevent and educate."

"People say that because you knew he was going to die, it must have made it easier," Natasha Richardson said. "I don't think so. I don't think you are ever prepared for grief and how it affects you. There isn't any training for that. It did certainly change my attitude about death. I believe that anyone who is terminally ill and in agony and wants out should be given as much help as possible, the way we do with animals. They should have the right to die."

Redgrave's first major performance undertaken without Richardson's input and guidance was the pivotal role of Ruth Wilcox in *Howards End* (1992), an adaptation of E. M. Forster's novel that marked the height of Merchant Ivory's success as a producer-director team. Redgrave received her sixth—and to date last—Oscar nomination for this film.

"I always sound uncertain over things," says Ruth Wilcox in Forster's book. "It is my way of speaking." Forster goes on to describe Ruth's voice as "sweet and compelling," but with "little range of expression." A wife and mother who dearly loves her childhood home Howards End as a symbol of permanence, Ruth is a blurry, out-of-focus sort of person, "a wisp of hay, a flower," writes Forster. There is a mystery to her preoccupations and her silent brooding, and she inspires a feeling of love in the intellectual, forward-thinking Margaret Schlegel, who finds herself drawn into Mrs. Wilcox's world, which both entices and repels her.

As a film *Howards End* has many virtues, not the least of which is Richard Robbins's dramatic, driving musical score. Emma Thompson and Anthony Hopkins are both outstanding as Margaret and Mr. Wilcox (Thompson deservedly won an Oscar for Best Actress for her performance here). On the debit side, there are actors in smaller roles who feel amateurish, and James Ivory arranges scenes rather than directs them, so that moments between heavyweights like Thompson, Hopkins, and Redgrave come alive, but many others just lie there, waiting in vain to be animated.

The film begins with Redgrave's Mrs. Wilcox slowly wandering the grounds of Howards End, the train of her long dress dragging through the tall grass behind her. She looks in on her family through a window and then touches the branch of a tree, almost impatiently, which expresses a kind of insecurity. Mrs. Wilcox knows she is dying, and she hasn't told her family because she doesn't want to bother them. She is a deeply tactile person when it comes to objects, a romantic materialist, and Redgrave fully expresses the depth of her need to make physical contact, for this need has been a constant for herself throughout her career. Redgrave is always reaching out to touch things and people with her long-fingered hands, and in *Howards End* every touch feels like a kind of heartfelt good-bye.

"I like this character very, very much," Redgrave said. "There is another side, another element, in the Wilcoxes that comes out via Mrs. Wilcox, who was a Quaker originally. She represents an older England that still continues amid the newer traditions of the moneymakers, like her son Charlie. She's both one of the family and not of the family at the same time."

"*Howards End* was our ambitious film of that time, eight million dollars, and we could not get eight million dollars from anybody," said producer Ismail Merchant. "Americans never saw the possibility of this film being successful. . . . Orion Classics wanted to do it, but they only gave us a very small sum of money. We had to raise almost eighty-five percent of the money outside." Forty-five percent of the budget came from an enthusiastic Japanese investor and the rest from English sources.

"The casting of Vanessa Redgrave, all along, from the very beginning, I had wanted her in that part," said Ivory. "I thought she was *the* actress to play the first Mrs. Wilcox. And we kept sending her scripts, and this is the way it always is with Vanessa, because she travels around so much and has a million different things on her mind. You're never sure she's gotten the script, and you're not quite sure she's read it. Even though you've put it in her hands, you can't be sure she's actually read it. A lot of time passes, and it's always a bit vague as to whether she's read it, whether she likes it, whether she will do it."

"Jim's heart was set on Vanessa, and so was mine," said Merchant. "We sent the script, and then we went to tea at the Waldorf. . . . We were sitting there, and she had her four or five months of plans. She said, 'It is very difficult for me to come. And the money which you have offered is not enough.' So I said, 'What would you like?' And she said, 'Well, if you will double that amount, I will do it.' So I said, 'Okay, that's it, you said it, I will double your salary.'

"She couldn't believe it was instantly, spontaneously done, knowing that we had a small budget and that we had to struggle for every penny," said Merchant. "For her, I would do anything. If she says, 'Get me the moon,' I will get the moon for her. It might not be possible for people to get the moon, but I will do it."

The most eloquent defender of *Howards End* is writer and film professor Nick Davis, who notes the irony in the way that "the one-time symbol of British counter-cultural radicalism has crystallized onscreen the dreams and adorations of its know-nothing Edwardian regency."

Davis also notices how Ivory gradually strips material objects away from Mrs. Wilcox. When she plays her first scene with Thompson's Margaret, Mrs. Wilcox is surrounded by furnishings that act as a kind of protection for her. Redgrave speaks very slowly in this scene, so slowly at first that it feels like Mrs. Wilcox might be a little touched in the head, but by the end of the scene we can fully understand why Margaret is intrigued by her interlocutor's gorgeous, lambent vagueness.

"She has a slightly odd voice," says Tony Palmer of Redgrave. "It's not a beautiful voice by any stretch of the imagination. But she has an instinct for poetry and getting the rhythm perfect. She got that from her father Michael, who I worked with. You were never quite sure with either of them where the beat was going to come."

Redgrave's reactions are very strange here; she's on a completely different wavelength because Mrs. Wilcox is a special person, so old-fashioned and feminine in the most passive sense that she barely seems to exist. She shimmers at us and at Margaret like a long-forgotten promise. The effect is both touching and creepy.

Mrs. Wilcox has all of the prejudices of her age and class, but her halting delivery of reactionary attitudes about foreigners, London, and the roles of men and women displays a rare kind of charm. I first watched this film with my mother. When we came to the scene where Redgrave's Mrs. Wilcox was asked about women's suffrage at table and she replied, "I am only too thankful not to have the vote myself," my mother shifted pleasurably in her seat. It was clear to me that she felt the full Brechtian impact of Vanessa Redgrave, of all people, mouthing this line of dialogue. Redgrave's image off-screen actually helps her in this role for which she is so eminently suited in looks and bearing. She moves through a room here slowly and carefully, like an aged woodland creature about to be put down and gently aware of that painful fact.

Redgrave spoke of her own Howards End, an old fisherman's cottage kept by her mother Rachel. "She used to race down there after the theater with a basket of food," Redgrave remembered. "She cut the hedges, sowed the lawn, and planted the flowers. She bought it when she was thirty-five and had to sell it when she was seventy-three, when my father went on. That's a lifetime," she said.

Mrs. Wilcox loves her life, though she is "too apt to brood," she says to Margaret. What she broods about remains unknown, but it must have something to do with the past. She's on her way out, and she wants to leave something of herself behind, and so she leaves Margaret the deed to Howards End, but Hopkins's Mr. Wilcox sees this only as "a whim" of his late wife.

Mrs. Wilcox dies about forty minutes into *Howards End*, and she haunts the rest of the film. Should her memory be embraced, or must we reject her entirely? That's a question Forster cannot answer. Redgrave the political activist might insist we reject Mrs. Wilcox in toto. Redgrave the artist makes a more than full case for her.

# A Memoir, Margaritas, and Mrs. Dalloway

Redgrave played with Paul Scofield in Shaw's difficult, lengthy *Heartbreak House* in 1992 at the Haymarket Theatre in London. It was directed by Trevor Nunn, and surely it was good for her to do this particular play since she had been denied the opportunity to act in it Off-Broadway because of her Boston Symphony firing in 1982. "Redgrave has a field day playing a Bloomsbury free spirit before her time," wrote Matt Wolf in the *Chicago Tribune*. "Nunn stretches actors like no one else, so that even a familiar presence like Redgrave seems transformed. As for the play, it's long, exhausting, and mightily impressive. This new production is its match."

At this point in the early 1990s, Redgrave's film career took a dip into much smaller and often-unrewarding roles while her political activity, benefit concerts, and traveling only intensified. She was drawn, as were many at this time, to the people in Yugoslavia who were suffering under the terrors and ethnic cleansing inflicted by Slobodan Milosevic, and she made it her business to get that suffering reported and known while taking what she could as an actress.

Asked about the strain her political life had put on her career, Redgrave focused instead on the cost to her personal relationships. "I don't think I have lost anything, though I have lost a lot of work, but anyway, it's not the effect on me but on others that counts," she said. "It's been very difficult for the children, who often didn't see me for a long time. But I'm really glad that I stayed really close to the men that I've loved and the men who've loved me. I think it was rather wonderful of them to put up with me."

Timothy Dalton has spoken very little about his long-term on-again off-again love affair with Redgrave, which stretched out over a number of years from the early seventies to the mid-to-late eighties. "I've never talked about my relationship with Vanessa before," he said in 2007. "We have known each other for a long time. We worked on a movie called *Mary, Queen of Scots* and became friends. I don't feel it was because I thought her world was more colorful, and I wasn't ever caught up in it." Without Dalton and his provocative artistic opinions and challenges to her, personally and professionally, Redgrave spent most of the 1990s single and still determined to make a difference in the world.

Her filmography started to get cluttered, random, and difficult to track and sort out. As a retired missionary in the "why-was-this-made?" *Great Moments in Aviation* (1993), Redgrave has one good scene when colleague Dorothy Tutin confesses a long-standing secret love to her and she reacts with surprise and delight. It was never theatrically released in the United States and went straight to video, where it gained an even more unsuitable title, *Shades of Fear*.

The film was written by *Oranges Are Not the Only Fruit* author Jeanette Winterson, who based it on a short story she wrote called "Atlantic Crossing." She had meant the movie to be a kind of fairy tale, and she was unhappy with the results on screen. Harvey Weinstein, who bought the film for America, insisted that Winterson write a new ending, and this made her even more unhappy. "It is not the movie I thought we could make," she said.

With blondish hair and brooding demeanor, Redgrave acted in Spanish and English in Lita Stantic's Argentine drama *A Wall of Silence* (1993), playing a British filmmaker who wants to make a movie about a woman's "disappeared" activist husband. "An amnesty for the main leaders, it's an outrage," she says at one point, in English, clearly an actress who is looking all over the globe for outrages to report to us. Stantic's decent film was little seen outside of Argentina.

While working on the movie *Miss Mary* (1986) with Julie Christie, Stantic had been touched by Christie's love of Argentina and her wanting to know about the recent history of the country, and this inspired her to write a screenplay about an English woman coming to the Argentine. "What I wanted was to talk about memory, about a person who wanted to forget," Stantic said. "At times one wants to forget about the traumatic experiences one has had in life, and wants to say, 'Well, my life is beginning right now,' and it's not that way. . . . What makes me proud about this film is that I feel that many people who work on human rights identify with this film. History is recounted from within, no?"

"I couldn't dare to say that I never get into a pessimistic mood, because I'm human, and when bad things happen, for a moment or a couple of days I can fall into a depression like anybody," Redgrave said. "But I do know that it's a scientific fact that one infinitely small, subatomic change in one field will cause very great changes in another. A film, for instance, might be seen by very few people. But those few people having seen that film are already part of a process which can lead to a change." Which explains why she felt it was worthwhile to give her services to a movie like *A Wall of Silence*, which had so little chance of being seen by a large audience.

Having covered the military dictatorship in Argentina, Redgrave next covered the military dictatorship in Chile, taking what amounted to a bit part in the all-star disaster *The House of the Spirits* (1993), based on Isabel Allende's novel, which featured Meryl Streep as a porcelain-skinned Beautiful Soul with telekinetic powers, Glenn Close as a repressed lesbian dressed all in black, and Jeremy Irons howlingly miscast as a Latin American aristocrat. The short dash of Redgrave's emotional reality in her brief scenes puts the rest of the hapless players to shame. Streep later said that she shared pitchers of margaritas with Redgrave during filming, and they certainly needed all the help they could get in order to finish such a stinker.

Redgrave next went to Sicily to do a role as a nun in Franco Zeffirelli's *Sparrow* (1993). She played Sister Agata, a lady who has gone slightly mad because of a lost love, and Zeffirelli's sentimentality kept her a long way from the heights of her Sister Jeanne in *The Devils*. She then headlined an unappetizing TV chiller for Showtime, known as *They* and also *They Watch* and also *Children of the Mist* (1993), where she played a blind woman who harbors the souls of dead children in her home. They did not watch.

Starting in late November 1994, Redgrave played on stage with Eileen Atkins at the Union Square Theater in Manhattan in Atkins's play *Vita and Virginia*, which detailed the relationship between Virginia Woolf, played by Atkins, and Vita Sackville-West, played by Redgrave.

She had first met Atkins when they were young girls going on a holiday together with friends after appearing as walk-ons at Stratford-upon-Avon. At one point, Redgrave came back to their room with a stack of movie magazines and asked Atkins, "Why aren't we film stars?" Atkins responded, "Are you kidding? Look at us. We're serious actresses, and neither of us has tits." And so Atkins was impressed when she saw Redgrave become a film star in *Morgan* and *Blow-Up*, and she held on to the idea of one day working with her.

"I had only read *Orlando* and *Flush*," Redgrave said, speaking of her experience of Woolf's books before she began to work on *Vita and Virginia*. When producer Robert Fox offered her the role of Vita in Atkins's play, she professed to be "enthralled" by it, even though she had long had a prejudice against Woolf: "I just read the script and I knew that there was something truly remarkable that Eileen had abstracted from these two lives."

"It's really one long conversation," Atkins said. "They wanted us to stand at two desks, but Vanessa was the only one who got that it should be a long conversation." Redgrave observed, "If we put it mechanically, it would be as if David Hockney had photographed Vita at every moment of her entire life from the time she met Virginia to the day she heard that Virginia had committed suicide."

On Charlie Rose's talk show to promote *Vita and Virginia* with Atkins, Redgrave said, "I hoped that I would become a great dancer. I didn't realize that I was too tall. For a long time, that's what I wanted to be." In a spirit of fun, Atkins said, "I didn't become tall enough to be what Vanessa desperately wanted to be, which was a tiller girl, which is like a Rockette." Redgrave's face lit up in her foggy/merry way at the mention of this. "I trained as a classical dancer because that was second best, a paradise, but second best to being a tiller girl," Redgrave said, "where you flash your legs in complete unison with a lot of other girls! That was my big dream for a long time, it's true."

The promiscuous life force of Redgrave's Vita thawed out the timid frigidity of Atkins's Virginia on stage, and when Vita's son Nigel Nicholson saw Redgrave in the play, he told Atkins, "She's how my mother would have liked to have been."

"In life Redgrave is often aggressively unfashionable in her dress and her political views," wrote Laurie Winer in the *LA Times*. "She seems to feel extraordinarily comfortable, however, in playing Vita as elegance personified. . . . As she expounds passionately about whatever she experiences, her bangs fall boyishly into her stunning blue eyes, as if she knows she has beauty to spare. When she drapes her legs over the seat of a divan, she looks like a coltish, growing boy, like the ageless, timeless, pansexual Orlando, the character that Woolf created as a tribute to Vita." David Richards in the *New York Times* was not impressed with the play itself, but very taken with Redgrave's physicality and her lyricism:

Ms. Redgrave looks absolutely terrific. Her hair is auburn and cut in a bob, and the costumer, Jane Greenwood, has dressed her in Vita's habitual daytime attire: lace-up boots, riding pants, and a swoop of pearls. Striding about the stage, taking in great gulps of air, exuding enthusiasm with every stride and gulp, her Vita is just as Virginia describes her: "stag-like or racehorse-like." She's a vivifying force of nature who threatens to blow her frailer, dowdier companion off her feet. . . . Since Vita's husband was in the diplomatic service, she is forever traveling to far-flung Persia (or farther-flung Hollywood), from which she reports on the exotic sights, never failing to add how much she misses her dear Virginia. That gives Ms. Redgrave the evening's more rhapsodic passages, and she throws herself into them with abandon. After

Virginia sends her a copy of *Orlando*, Vita, who is the subject of the novel, exults that it is "the loveliest, wisest, richest book that I have ever read." Ms. Redgrave escalates her delivery with each adjective, then tops it off by concluding hyperbolically, "You have invented a new form of Narcissism . . . I am in love with Orlando."

Redgrave was doing many benefits and special readings and performances at this time, and she made certain that they were as helpful as possible. A source who assisted her at this point who wishes to remain anonymous says, "She's taken a lot of flak for her politics, but there's one story I have that says a lot about her, I think. She was doing a benefit for a young woman who was being held in a detention center. Vanessa was going to do a performance on her behalf, to raise money for her. I told her that she would have five hundred dollars on her debit card, and Vanessa said, 'Oh, but I need five thousand dollars!' And I said, 'Vanessa, why do you need so much money?' And she said, 'Well, I have to pay for the theater and the stagehands and the technicians and all that.' I said to her, 'I thought you were doing a benefit?' And she said, 'It wouldn't be a benefit if *they* had to pay for it!' People always say that she's humorless, but I don't think so. She was so much fun. She would jump up and down like a kid sometimes when something excited her."

"Humor is the last bastion of the bourgeoisie," her brother Corin loftily told his wife Deirdre, and surely Redgrave absorbed that attitude in her years with the WRP. When people mention "humor" in a person, what they often mean is an ability to laugh at yourself, which is not among Redgrave's virtues. They also mean, underneath, a sense of the absurd, which Redgrave also does not have. She can understand absurdity only on a theoretical level because she feels it as a kind of cynicism, and cynicism of any kind is anathema to her. "Although Vanessa was essentially terribly serious, there was an almost girlish side to her that was innocent almost to the point of naiveté," her sister-in-law Deirdre observed. Redgrave was certainly capable, in her private life, of moments of childlike gaiety and enthusiasm. This quality was also one of her aces as a performer.

Redgrave had published her memoirs in England in 1991, and now she brought the book out in America in a slightly cut edition that tends to get lost in causes, concerts, and long-winded, sometimes obscure thoughts on politics. In this book, as in her interviews, she is always stopping herself to judge, check, and qualify, and this can be irritating, moving, or comic by turns.

Her description of her brief dating relationship with Bernard Levin is classic elaborately humble qualifying Vanessa: "Alas for Bernard Levin (whose heart is now safely engaged elsewhere, and who probably thanks his maker a thousand times for saving him from a fate worse than death, if indeed he so much as spares a thought for his youthful folly), my heart, and soon my hand, was engaged to Tony Richardson." That's quite a mouthful, and proof that Redgrave is often most touching when she is trying to be funny.

When she focuses her intelligence on her work as an actress and her artistic collaborators, she can be quite illuminating, but her best insights into working with Antonioni or giving herself over to playing Renée Richards or Fania Fénelon are swallowed up by her torturous justifications for her political engagement and the internecine workings of the Workers Revolutionary Party. The book lacks a sense of proportion. Her mind refuses to stay on one track for long and enjoys wandering off into too much minor detail and flora and fauna. Reading it is probably much like watching her in rehearsal for a new role as she tries out her many different ideas.

What the book lacks is a director-like editorial figure to guide her. She gets several names and dates wrong, calling the BSO artistic administrator Bill Bewell instead of Bill Bernell, and her judge in the BSO case Robert E. Keaton instead of Robert Keeton. She says she filmed *Murder on the Orient Express* in 1975, but the film was released in 1974. Her account of the raid on the WRP school barely mentions Irene Gorst, and doesn't at all mention Gorst's specific allegations against Redgrave and her brother Corin. Instead of setting the record straight, Redgrave sweeps Gorst's claims under the carpet instead.

"I was surely glad when I'd actually finally finished it," Redgrave said of the book. She was hard on herself as a writer, as she always is on every aspect of her life, save some of her political views. "It's a difficult process," she admitted. "Because I've discovered that memory obeys—temporarily, at least, until you challenge memory—obeys your own wish as to what you want to remember and what you would like not to remember. Or perhaps sometimes you've even forgotten, but your memory's got it locked away there, and it can suddenly remind you of things that can be very painful to you indeed. And then to try to communicate that, if you're not a writer, which, although I write a lot, I am not a writer.

"My fundamental form of communication is to perform what others have created," she said. "Therefore, to write in a way that I don't just trot out banalities, which would be my normal way, to take time to think. I think my thoughts aren't totally banal in conversation, but in trying to describe a wonderful experience, I probably fall back to a kind of school-girl diary, if I just did what comes naturally . . . I had to go back to what I was needing to remember, needing to write about. . . . I did write what is in my book, I actually wrote it," she said.

Redgrave said that she had wanted to use photos in her book only of her family, her homes, and her pets, but not of herself. This idea was typical of her urge for aggrandizing self-effacement, her constant war between seeking the spotlight and seeking humility. She had to be persuaded by her publishers to use photos of herself in private and photos of herself in different roles.

"There are the facts—who said what, what happened—and then there's also the history of who the protagonist is and why he or she would have acted that way, or done or said a certain thing," Redgrave said, describing the way she went about writing her book. The memoir is cluttered with unnecessary facts, and her own perceptions of why she behaved the way she did are seen through a glass darkly. Though Redgrave said she wrote the book herself, it sometimes reads as if her brother Corin had a hand in it, especially in the political sections. Her connection with Corin was probably her deepest and most destructive personal bond, a mysterious kind of pact that cannot be easily explained.

In the icky thriller *Mother's Boys* (1994), where Jamie Lee Curtis's character attempts to seduce her own eleven-year-old son, Redgrave was called upon to play Curtis's mother. She reacts to Curtis with subtle apprehension in her first scene and then reappears to speak of her husband's suicide in a long monologue that Redgrave makes longer with several time-bending, overcome pauses. In her third and final scene, her wicked daughter smothers her with a pillow. *Mother's Boys* deservedly received wholly negative reviews, and many wondered how Redgrave had gotten herself involved in such a tawdry enterprise. Hopefully she was well paid for her time.

She found far more rewarding work in James Gray's debut feature, the moody *Little Odessa* (1994), where she played a Russian mother dying of a brain tumor. Gray was just twenty-five years old when he directed this film, and it inaugurated a distinctive and still-developing career that has already been celebrated with a French-printed monograph by critic Jordan Mintzer.

We first see Redgrave in *Little Odessa* in one of Gray's classically composed frames stretched out in bed and staring at the ceiling, her face abstracted and distant, suspended in time; she touches two fingers to her mouth to indicate that she wants a cigarette. Her son, played by Edward Furlong, hears her screaming in agony, and when he looks into her bedroom he sees his father (Maximilian Schell) grappling with her on the bed. We see her face upside down as she stares helplessly at her son, her eyes pleading with him not to look at her, a very primal, Oedipal sort of moment. In the scenes she has left, Redgrave makes us feel this woman's warmth with her youngest son and her worry over her older son (Tim Roth), who has taken up a life of crime. As in *Blow-Up*, Redgrave folds herself into a painterly work and subsumes her own needs for the needs of Gray's elegiac, solemn film.

*A Month by the Lake* (1995) was a rare vehicle of this period centered just on Redgrave, but it was too lightweight for her and she seemed uncomfortable, even gauche, in this touristy romantic comedy. Redgrave grabbed this leading lady role because it was so different from what she was usually offered. "I was excited that I was going to be able to play a real woman of fifty-seven who looks attractive and who falls in love and does all of the things that real women of fifty-seven do, but that we rarely see them doing in the movies," she said. Still, she knew that she was at her best in character rather than star parts. "I was lucky when I was seventeen or eighteen because I was so tall, I was always being given character parts of fifty-year-olds, wearing white wigs and putting lines on my face. So, to me, I'm carrying on doing the same thing."

She realized that her appearance was part of what she had to offer in her profession. "At some point, you have to make a decision as an actress whether or not you're going to try and hang on to your youth as long as possible or be a real actress and play any character, regardless of age," Redgrave said. "I always swore that I'd never do plastic surgery. But in 1985 I had something taken out of my eye bags. I did that then because I was having such bad luck being cast. I never did it before and I'm not going to do it again. But I won't put down anyone who makes any other decision."

Redgrave had also taken the role, in part, because it meant she got to shoot in Italy. "The first time I went to Italy was in 1950," she said. "You have to remember what England was like then. Dreadful cooking. We'd been badly bombed in the war. England was a very, very gray place. So to go to Florence and see it with your own eyes was amazing." To celebrate her mother Rachel's eighty-fifth birthday that year, Redgrave took her to Venice for three days and nights, along with her own daughters and their husbands. "We'd all been there before, but it just knocked us to pieces," Redgrave said. "We couldn't believe how beautiful it was."

Redgrave did a German accent in *Down Came a Blackbird* (1995), a television film for Showtime concerned with torture in Central America. Laura Dern played a journalist who had been captured by death squads; her boyfriend was killed, but she made it out alive. Redgrave's white-haired character is a survivor of Auschwitz who runs a clinic for survivors of torture. It was the last film made by Raul Julia, who played another patient at Redgrave's clinic.

With her brother Corin, Redgrave formed the Moving Theater, a politically minded collective that opened with her own production of *Antony and Cleopatra* at the Alley Theatre in Houston, Texas. Asked why she had founded the company, Redgrave replied, "We wanted to commemorate all the lives destroyed during the fascist occupation of Europe. Moving Theater is about how we can work with people of different nationalities on different themes." Each person in the troupe, from the actors to the set builders, got equal pay. Speaking of Corin, Redgrave said, "He can lift me out of the depths of despair at any given moment."

The Moving Theater staged such shows as *The Liberation of Skopje*, which was described as "an epic play about the resistance to fascism in 1940s

Macedonia." Staging a whole season of plays to celebrate the fifty years that had passed since the end of fascism in Europe, the company played to very small crowds and the Redgraves lost a lot of their own money. "We didn't get even half-full houses most of the time," Redgrave said.

Redgrave appeared briefly in a dark wig and Edwardian-era period clothing to introduce and wrap up her narration to an animated version of *The Wind in the Willows* (1995), reading the book to a group of children, and she did a sequel the following year, *The Willows in Winter*. She accepted a much larger paycheck than usual and wrinkled her nose not once but twice in the back of a cab with Tom Cruise in Brian De Palma's *Mission: Impossible* (1996), but this mega-commercial movie was so far from Redgrave's usual context that she can be forgiven for offering a sort of parody "Vanessa!" star turn, all "playful" spontaneity.

"I was rather pleased to play a rather wicked lady who was an arms dealer and British," she told *60 Minutes*, viewing it as a change from the usual image of an arms dealer. The part she played, Max, was originally written for a man, but Cruise suggested it might be fun to play these scenes with Redgrave, and his idea was taken up by De Palma.

"Is there some reason why Vanessa Redgrave plays an underground mastermind like the madam of a West End brothel?" asked Owen Gleiberman in his review of the film for *Entertainment Weekly*. The answer to that question was likely a mix of (a) to entertain herself, and (b) to connect sex and power, or at least wicked wrongdoing, for there was always a strong puritan streak in Redgrave.

For television, Redgrave played one of her rare oppressor roles as a bigoted grandmother who wrests away custody of her grandchild from her lesbian daughter (Valerie Bertinelli) in *Two Mothers for Zachary* (1996). It was based on a true story, and it has all the earmarks of a television-issue movie. Valerie Bertinelli is hardly an acting partner for Vanessa Redgrave, and casting Redgrave as a hard, low-class Southern woman is straining credulity to the breaking point.

"I had the privilege of working with Vanessa Redgrave, who played my mother," Bertinelli said. "I was in awe of her as a smart, talented, independent, political, outspoken woman. And she opened her arms to me and made it seem as if the work wasn't beneath her. We went out for margaritas one night and had a great time. Her passion for life and work impressed me."

Though her Southern accent is shaky, Redgrave makes a vivid physical impression in her first scene as a trashy, managing broad in oversized sunglasses charging into her daughter's house and wreaking havoc to get her grandkid. This woman is a selfish harpy, and in the second half of the movie Redgrave has nothing to do but keep sighing in relief as she wins and wins against her daughter in court. In her early scenes, however, she reaches out as far as she can imaginatively in order to understand the woman she's playing. Watch the scene where Bertinelli tells her mother that she's more than friends with her female roommate. At first, Redgrave smiles at her brightly, refusing to understand her daughter's meaning, and this feels very psychologically accurate, as does her uneasy, confused distaste when she finally says that their relationship is "unnatural."

In the midst of an old-time-melodrama scene where police are forced to yank Bertinelli's baby from her arms, Redgrave whispers, "She's makin' me look bad," which shows real insight into the way a woman like this would act and behave. She feels that what she's doing is necessary, and she won't be put off by appearances, even if the situation itself seems insanely against her on the surface. It's as if she's saying, "I know what this looks like, but I'm in the right!"

In need of money, Redgrave did only one expositional scene in *Smilla's Sense of Snow* (1997) as a religious fanatic in white clothes, glasses, and blue scarf. She looks like she'd like to do something with her character, but the script gives her no opening at all. She had always played small roles here and there, but at this point there were too many parts like this on film that made no use of her skills whatever.

*Wilde* (1997) is a plodding biopic of the famed wit, playwright, and martyr. There's little variation in Stephen Fry's performance as Oscar Wilde: he looks pained when he's sleeping with beautiful boys, he looks pained in court, and he looks very pained in prison. The film has one major point in its favor: Jude Law's acidic Lord Alfred Douglas. Law is ideal for the role, with his extraordinarily cruel, pretty face and his ripely sensual mouth that opens like a trapdoor when he's in a temper. Redgrave appears as Wilde's mother, a kind Irish bohemian type, wise and intuitive.

Of Redgrave's five films made in 1997, the keeper is certainly *Mrs. Dalloway*, a fluid, modest adaptation of Virginia Woolf's seminal modernist novel. The screenplay for the film was written by Eileen Atkins, Redgrave's partner on stage from *Vita and Virginia*. Enthralled with Woolf, Redgrave had wanted Atkins to write a film version of *Vita and Virginia*, but Atkins didn't think it would work for a movie. She suggested instead that someone should write a film version of *Mrs. Dalloway* for Redgrave.

"Vanessa said, 'No. You write it,'" Atkins said. "I had realized, you sort of don't say no to Vanessa. . . . I know a lot of people really are afraid of Virginia Woolf. If she did hate the movie, I pray she forgives me. But she must look at the good side of it and know that it will send a lot of people to read *Mrs. Dalloway* who wouldn't have done otherwise."

It was a difficult shoot. "We did the thing you should never do," said Atkins. "We started shooting without all the money in place. It was ghastly. After three weeks we ran out of money." They finally found the funds for the rest of the shooting through First Look Pictures and producers Lisa Katselas Paré and Stephen Bayly. "Some people thought this book was unfilmable, but [Atkins] made a great job of it," said director Marleen Gorris. "Everything is there that's important in the book, and it is quite close to the book."

Atkins had some disagreements with Gorris's working methods. "She wouldn't, for example, let the young actors watch the older ones filming," Atkins recalls. "I also was very concerned that connections between the past and the present be utterly, visually clear. Marleen, who is Dutch, insisted on much more voice-over than I would have liked. Europeans apparently like it much more than American or British audiences."

The film is well cast in some roles, but not in others: Rupert Graves tries hard as Septimus Warren Smith, a young man suffering from shell shock, but he's a fatally weak link in a role that needs to function as a sharp juxtaposition with Redgrave's Mrs. Clarissa Dalloway, a woman of great charm and weak will who spends a day planning her evening party and thinking of the past.

When Mrs. Dalloway hears of Septimus's suicide during her party in Woolf's novel, she is alarmed: "Always her body went through it, when she was told, first, suddenly, of an accident; her dress flamed, her body burnt." Mrs. Dalloway is a sensitive but cloistered woman, and it is only when she hears about the death of this young man that she makes a final leap into the sort of empathy that is Redgrave's *raison d'être* as an artist.

Mrs. Dalloway is described by Woolf as a bird, light-hearted yet somewhat inhibited, dressed in blue-green and "grown very white since her illness." In her first scenes in *Mrs. Dalloway*, Redgrave makes herself look exactly like this description in the novel. More importantly, when she speaks some of Mrs. Dalloway's thoughts on the soundtrack, these words never feel like narration or voice-over but like an actual, hushed, interior stream-of-consciousness.

In a soft blue coat topped by a soft yellow feathered hat, Mrs. Dalloway walks the streets of London to get flowers for her party, and Redgrave opens her face just enough to catch that exquisite note of insecurity and time-rushing-by fervor that is the essence of Woolf's style. She is in her starriest mode here, and this is a real star turn that suits the exploratory material to a T. Redgrave gets the sense of nostalgia that marks Mrs. Dalloway's memories on this day, and the sense of regret, standing in her well-appointed room and wondering if life is all over for her.

Mrs. Dalloway is hard and contemptuous with the bitter, religious Miss Kilman (Selina Cadell), a friend of her daughter Elizabeth (Katie Carr), and this sort of thing never comes easily for Redgrave, but luckily it doesn't come easily for Mrs. Dalloway either. When Mrs. Dalloway meets her old beau Peter (Michael Kitchen), Redgrave gives you the feel of Woolf's novel and the feel of this woman's delighted melancholy over the past all in a pause, in a stare. This is the kind of role that lets Redgrave soar right off of the earth and earthly interactions and right into a heavenly sort of ether, and so she goes higher and higher with this Woolf material in her head, like a liberated queen or goddess.

Redgrave can do practically anything as an actress, but she's more comfortable with poetry than with prose. You can put her in a kitchen, if you like, or an office, but she's more herself in a castle, a magic forest, or a drawing room in 1923 London as imagined by Virginia Woolf. Clarissa Dalloway wants to give everyone she knows one night when "everything seems enchanted," where they are thought amusing and liked by their fellow creatures. She views social life as a kind of healing art. When

Redgrave's Clarissa practices greeting her guests in front of a mirror, she's an actress preparing to give a perfectly controlled performance.

During the main party scene, we see Mrs. Dalloway receiving people at the top of the stairs, and Redgrave freezes her open-mouthed smiles until we can see how completely artificial they are; only a great actress would know that such total artifice can be the most heartfelt expression of a person's soul. Redgrave elongates her vowels for Mrs. Dalloway's greetings: "Ho-ow delightful to se-e-e you," she says to each passing guest, but inside of her head, in her internal monologue, Clarissa worries and frets: "I feel burned to a cin-der," Redgrave drawls hopelessly, and then, "It's a dis-ah-stah . . . my party's a dis-ahhh-stah."

Her Clarissa suddenly looks very pale in close-ups, as if the party is too much for her (for she has been ill, supposedly with heart trouble), and she grows even paler when she hears of the boy's suicide. Mrs. Dalloway goes upstairs and thinks about the boy who has jumped out of a window, and Redgrave stands silently and feels all of Woolf's shivery thoughts for her heroine, especially the crucial one: "I once threw a shilling into the Serpentine, but he's thrown his life away."

Screenwriter and ultimate Woolf devotee Atkins was pleased with Gorris's frankness about love. "Marleen couldn't resist having the young Clarissa and Sally kiss," she said, "which I thought was perfect and absolutely true to Virginia. People assume it is only because Marleen is gay, but Woolf was very interested in that tendency in adolescent girls, that undertow. Don't we all feel it?" *Mrs. Dalloway* is not a film that needed to be made, and it isn't even a good film, sometimes, but in the marriage of Redgrave and Woolf, it achieves moments of lyric power.

Asked if she felt very different from her somewhat limited, party-giving character, Redgrave said, "I was Mrs. Dalloway. I just knew her. I knew who she was, and although I'm a very different person living in a different time, there was no distance between us."

While she filmed *Mrs. Dalloway*, Redgrave was playing at the National Theatre in Ibsen's difficult late play *John Gabriel Borkman* with Atkins, who found that Redgrave was a rock during some troubles she had. "I was playing the wife of a bankrupt at the time in a London play," said Atkins. "Vanessa was an angel. I broke down once, and only because she was so nice to me. I couldn't stop crying, and I was scheduled to perform that afternoon. Vanessa took me to the theater's nurse to get some Valium and the nurse said, 'Just tell them you can't go on.' I said, 'Don't be stupid, woman. It's only going on that will get me through!' So Vanessa took me in a cab to her doctor and got me something so I could go on. I have to say I was bloody marvelous that afternoon."

Redgrave explained how she got in the mood for Ibsen's snowy drama of residual bitterness: "I'd found an old photograph of the house where my mother's father lived for six years as a little boy, after his father went bankrupt and they had all become very poor schoolteachers," Redgrave said. "And you know, the family house is very much part of the play. So every night I used to go to this photograph and just put myself into it and follow in my mind—walk up the country lane and open the door and smell the flowers that were there, the trees, the sounds I'd follow through the stone passageways, all in my mind. That was my preparation."

Her own imagination was still going full blast, and Redgrave expected that her audience's imagination could reach just as high. When told that the snow machine that was so important to the play's second act had broken down, Redgrave advised the stage manager, "Why don't you give me some sheets of white paper, and when I make my entrance, I'll tear them up into little pieces and throw them around the stage, and we'll have snow!" Observing her playing with her granddaughter Daisy in the snow, Atkins said that Redgrave "must be the best grandmother in the world," a mode tantalizingly suggested by her *The Wind in the Willows* films.

As the twin sister of Borkman's wife (Atkins), Redgrave received mixed reviews. "Ella is played by Vanessa Redgrave in a performance whose effectiveness is marred by a surfeit of distracting mannerisms and overdone changes of rhythm," wrote Paul Taylor in the *Independent*. "But, great actress that she is, there are moments when the aching desolateness of this dying woman and the avenging solicitude of her approach towards Borkman come across with power and simplicity."

Redgrave's need for money was ever pressing. "She hasn't got a penny to her name," said Katharina Wolpe, an English pianist and close friend of the actress. "She hasn't got a bean." Redgrave lived at this point in a spare two-bedroom walk-up apartment with a bare bulb in the foyer. She was so strapped for cash that she even shivered through a morning with a reporter from the *New York Times*, Frank Bruni, rather than dirty her one good winter coat, which she had just had cleaned. Self-denial was something she was practiced in, even something she welcomed. The touch of the martyr. She led Bruni from refugee shelter to refugee shelter, telling him all about the refugees from this regime and that regime, raising her fist in the air when she caught the eye of one of the refugees to give him hope and spur him on.

Redgrave told Bruni that she was making the same salary as she had made in the 1960s in spite of inflation, and she sought to connect herself with other workers, saying that the salary problem was a problem for everyone. "You name it: taxi drivers, shopkeepers, whatever. They're earning exactly the same in real value terms as they did in the 1960s," she insisted. "Imagine" by John Lennon, she said, was her favorite song, because she liked to imagine that there would be a time when there would be no countries.

Ben Brantley in the *New York Times* was harsh about her third version of Shakespeare's Cleopatra at the Public Theater in New York, calling the production "a portrait of an amiably dizzy, redheaded, and not terribly intelligent queen who does some wacky things (like pretending to be dead and throwing shoes at messengers), but only in the name of romance. Cleo may not be big on logic or an even temper, but she's as loyal as can be to that big lug, Marc Antony. Indeed, the subtitle of this jaw-droppingly bizarre production might as well be 'Stand by Your Man.'"

Referencing her first violent 1973 stab at the role for Tony Richardson, Brantley asked, "Whence cometh this transformation from virago to addled helpmate? Ms. Redgrave, arguably the greatest living actress of the English-speaking theater, has had a long time to think about Cleopatra since she first took on the role, deafening the critics of London with her screeches in the Richardson production. In 1986, again in London, she played opposite Timothy Dalton as a Cleopatra variously described as 'a volatile, witty sensualist' and an 'eccentric bluestocking.'"

In this production, Brantley felt like Redgrave had "wandered in from *Twelfth Night* or some other gentler comedy about the complications of love. . . . For all the descriptions in the play of this queen's perversity, there is none that quite matches Ms. Redgrave's singular interpretation of her." Perhaps Redgrave should have played Viola in *Twelfth Night* three times instead of Cleopatra. Judging from the reviews, it sounds as if her second attempt on the role with Dalton was the best, if still somewhat far off the mark.

Surely her starry-eyed third interpretation of Cleopatra had something to do with her leading man. She was enamored of David Harewood, her Marc Antony, and let him move into her flat for two years. "I gave him a place because he hadn't got anywhere to live," she said. "And I thought he was lovely and he thought I was lovely." Redgrave was thirty years older than Harewood. She insisted, all appearances aside, that their relationship was platonic.

"I don't like to give my ego a chance," she said. "I've got an enormous one, and I've got to keep it tamed and very, very silent, very low. I think one's ego comes out when one starts falling in love. Sooner or later it always does. If I can generalize just a little bit, you start getting jealous and possessive, and all sorts of troubles start that aren't there if you are just really good friends." At this point, she was beginning to sound like her '60s rival Jeanne Moreau when it came to her ideas on romance.

"I think men do find me a little frightening, and I'm sorry about that because it would be much nicer if they didn't," she said. "I wouldn't really like to frighten anybody unless they were a horrible person." She said that she was celibate at this point in the '90s. "I think I've always tended to be a sort of platonic person," she observed. "Look, I've slept on floors all over the world, with a multitude of different people, but we didn't have sex." And if someone approached her romantically? "Well, I have a bit of a tease and a laugh and try to make the person feel not put down," she said. Speaking of the ever-loyal Nero, she offered, "He is more than an ex because we really adore each other. Franco has gone on record as saying he would give me anything he had, including his life, were it necessary, and I would equally do anything I could to help him."

Halfway into Henry Jaglom's sub-Robert Altman *Déjà Vu* (1997), Redgrave makes an appearance in a group scene sitting next to Anna Massey. She gamely tells a story from her own past about the girl who sang "The

White Cliffs of Dover" in the hospital for her; she even sings a bit of that song for the camera. Jaglom's films are mainly improvised, and it feels natural that Redgrave would be up to the challenge of that.

"Jack Nicholson, in my first film, *A Safe Place* [1971], he's said to this day he's never been as much himself," said Jaglom. "What I do is try to get the fullness of their character up on screen rather than have them play some separate character from themselves. But Jack's work comes from a similar creative background, whereas Maximilian Schell comes from a completely different one. Or Vanessa Redgrave, for instance. It's a wonderful process if you can get people to open up areas, especially when they are really skilled, really talented actors who have always worked one way—off of a script, off of a literary narrative, more from the outside, and to get them to drop some of that protection, and use the spontaneity of what they're feeling and what their impulses are in a different kind of way."

The queen of spontaneity, Redgrave fits herself into Jaglom's casual context and also transcends it with her star power. She's at her very best in this film, especially when she muses that an illusion is "the scent of something real coming close." This movie also marked a collaboration for Redgrave and her mother, Rachel Kempson, who says of Vanessa here, "She is a bit strange." Kempson shares one scene with her daughter in which they embrace, and this is as lovely a moment as the one between Michael and Vanessa in *Behind the Mask* forty years before.

Redgrave was forced to deal with the outright trashy in the ludicrous television miniseries *Bella Mafia* (1997), where she played a Mafia wife emeritus bent on vengeance ("Hell hath no fury like the women of *Bella Mafia!*" blared the ads), a "Mama" surrounded by younger hams like Jennifer Tilly and Illeana Douglas. "Every rose has a thorn," she says quietly at one point, in that hard "r" American accent that makes her sound like she's from Mars. In one inadvertently hilarious scene done in an overhead shot, Redgrave's Mama learns the identity of a bloody corpse and then bangs its head against the floor to show her displeasure. Most of the reviews joked that the film was an offer we could refuse.

Redgrave taught a master class for five theater students on April 29, 1998 at Mount Holyoke College in Massachusetts. She was gentle with them, starting in on any suggestions with the careful words "The thought occurs that maybe you could . . ." and often exclaiming "Lovely!" as encouragement. She told them to try "for a feeling of complete sponta-neity" but warned that much work needed to be done before they could be so instinctive. "If it is a play by Ibsen or Chekhov, you have to spend *ages* on the text before you ever get to working on your character," Redgrave said. "To do even a simple line like 'I have no faith' you must ask yourself if there's ever been a moment in your own life when you've felt like this."

She compared mining a script to mining for coal. "When it comes to acting, you can't take even the simplest statement at face value," she said. "As an actress, you must know where a line like 'I'm a seagull' comes from. You must pursue the answer to that question. And ask others what they think it means; it needn't always be you who works it out." She wanted the actors to "take two sentences and really think about them. Ask your-self 'What's the key question?' When you go into one thing really deeply, you'll find that very often everything changes." Finally, she said, "Direc-tors get unhappy when it takes time, but passions, emotions, events have their own rhythm."

Bills still needed to be paid and benefits still needed to be paid for. *Deep Impact* (1998), a millennium-approaching disaster movie, had Redgrave as a chatty mother to Téa Leoni for a few scenes, and Maximilian Schell, Robert Duvall, and Morgan Freeman were also on board, which is a lot of heavy-weight talent showing up for such piffle. In the first shot of Paul Auster's *Lulu on the Bridge* (1998), we see the topless photo of Redgrave that was used to advertise *Isadora* next to pictures of Josephine Baker, Louise Brooks, and the star of Auster's movie, Mira Sorvino. Saxophonist Harvey Keitel is gazing at these photos, and then the camera pulls back so that we see that they've been tacked above a urinal.

In the film itself, Redgrave plays Catherine Moore, a former actress turned director, and when Keitel asks her why she gave up acting, Cath-erine pauses to consider this for a moment and then tells him that "beauty fades." She's more comfortable, she says, not being seen through the eyes of a director. It's an uneasy moment, but Redgrave gets through it gracefully, and she makes a convincing director when Catherine creates a new movie version of G. W. Pabst's *Pandora's Box* (1928). "I wanted all the people that are in the film, and I asked them," Auster said, a popular novelist making his first movie. "Many of them I knew—that was my casting technique."

On January 8, 1999, at the San Carlo Theater, Redgrave recited and sang, in Italian, the title role in the three-hour oratorio *Eleanora*, about the revolutionary Eleanora Fonseca Pimental, a Portuguese noblewoman who was executed for her beliefs in 1799. Surviving bits of this performance show Redgrave at her most commanding, an artist who seeks to cross any barrier of language or country or time period to speak directly to anyone who might be watching her.

For Tim Robbins's diverting *Cradle Will Rock* (1999), which deals with Orson Welles staging Marc Blitzstein's controversial musical, Redgrave was one of the more colorful of the ensemble as a dotty countess and arts patron, but she didn't have enough to do to make an impression. "I'm having a ball," she insisted. Redgrave liked her ebullient character, comparing her to Leonie, her sexy wife in *Morgan*. "In a way, Leonie is a younger countess, or the countess was the grandmother of Leonie—or the mother of Leonie," she said, trying to get it right. "The countess wasn't a member of the project, just a passionate admirer and supporter, so I wasn't part of that period of preparation. I would have loved to have been, but I was doing something else, I can't remember what it was.

"Tim invented the part for me—wasn't I lucky?" Redgrave said. No matter how small the role, she gave some thought to it. "The countess is English, she married a count who died or whatever, and then an American steel magnate. I have my own stories about her: She has little parts of Decca [Jessica] Mitford—I chose Decca because she was in love with the arts—and Vita Sackville-West. Vita, apart from being an immensely passionate and enthusiastic person, which the countess also is, was very different. But they came from the same social class. Incredible to think that Vita died a natural death in 1964, already an epoch away, but for me that's still within touch. But mind you, I feel in touch with the Elizabethan period too, and that's definitely out of touch from the point of view of physical acquaintances."

Redgrave felt at this point, years after the dissolving of the WRP under Gerry Healy, that she wasn't having problems being cast. "I have been through situations that were definitely blacklisting," she said. "But each time, there was a very big revulsion against blacklisting. At the present time, that's not the dominant issue at all." But she insisted that she was still working for change. "Everyone I know is doing important work in connection with many terrible situations, not just in war zones, but in inner cities," she insisted.

She did a cameo in her son Carlo's film *Uninvited* (1999), playing a character called Mrs. Ruttenburn, a schoolteacher. *Variety* felt she overplayed this role "in an incongruously comic vein." She then wasted her time in what she called "a weenie part" as a psychiatrist to Winona Ryder in *Girl, Interrupted* (1999), staring at the young star with an indulgent look on her face. She was billed as "Priestess" in *The 3 Kings* (2000), a little-seen Biblical drama filmed in Tunisia about the three wise men in search of baby Jesus, and appeared with Nero and Gérard Depardieu in *Mirka* (2000), a little-seen Italian film about the Bosnian genocide.

But she was still finding rewarding work on stage. In 1999, Redgrave appeared in a successful revival of Noël Coward's *A Song at Twilight* opposite Corin and his wife Kika Markham. Rehearsals for that play were said to be "tempestuous," with one screaming match in particular "emptying the room." There were problems with their director, the critic Sheridan Morley, who called Vanessa "incredibly boring, fatuous, and pretentious" and who hated her "terminally antiquated and irrelevant political views."

Morley's main problem with her was the very wellspring of her gift, her spontaneity. "This woman is driving me into an early grave," he wrote. "She never does the same thing twice." In return, Vanessa tried to be patient with him. "If I have ever been rude to you, I am sorry," she wrote him. "It's no excuse, but I get upset and fussed and can't work properly if things are not calm and thoughtful. I will certainly try my best to make them so. Sometimes *you* don't know how to make them so for lack of experience," she cautioned. Though he had spent his life writing about the theater, Morley had directed very little.

The play concerned Sir Hugo, a famous writer who is confronted by Carlotta, an old flame who threatens to reveal his homosexual liaisons. Coward, who played Hugo when it was first performed, insisted that *A Song at Twilight* was based on W. Somerset Maugham, but he knew enough about the subject as a closeted man of the stage himself.

Corin played Hugo and Vanessa played Carlotta, and surely it must have been strange for them to act in this play about the threat of homosexual blackmail written by one of their father's major male lovers. "Homosexual tendencies in the past?" sneers Carlotta at one point. "You're as queer as a coot and you have been all your life." Of their performances in *A Song at Twilight*, Nicholas de Jongh wrote in the *London Evening Standard* that "these Redgrave siblings act as if the play hits them where it hurts." He felt that Vanessa was like "a shot of bourbon for Coward's milk and water text."

At the end of *A Song at Twilight*, Corin's Hugo opened some letters to his male lover and wept over the lifelong denial of his sexuality. The lightweight play had been turned into a heavy-duty exorcism of both their personal pain over their father and Vanessa's pain over Tony Richardson, as well as a more universal plea for openness. It sounds like a most unlikely production undertaken on a dare for the thrill of doing something really dangerous, and it paid off for them, as Redgrave dares sometimes do.

The *Independent* wrote, "Vanessa Redgrave is almost shockingly girlish as the amusingly vulgar Carlotta and although her compelling combination of skittishness and earnest intent produces an occasionally awkward rhythm, she makes you believe that nothing in her performance has been planned." The *Guardian* felt that Vanessa had found some Ibsen in this Coward play: "She turns sexual melodrama into moral debate." And the *Financial Times* thought, "Vanessa Redgrave is magnificent as Carlotta, a rather vulgar has-been actress of sixty-something. She swigs vodka, illuminates her face-lift scars with a candle, snorts and guffaws in a splendidly embarrassing manner."

Vanessa laid flowers on a statue of Coward for his centenary, December 16, 1999. "In my first part for a London play he came to my dressing room and said to me something that I remember in all those bad times that you feel lacking in confidence or lose your way," she said. She wouldn't say exactly what Coward had told her, keeping it to herself. "He gave me a look and I saw in his eyes that all he cared about was truth and kindness," she said. "I think that's a wonderful thing and that is why I am here to celebrate."

Redgrave played Prospero in Lenka Udovicki's production of *The Tempest* in 2000 at Shakespeare's Globe Theatre. "I do want to find things for great actors, and Vanessa's a great actor, male or female," said Globe head Mark Rylance, who himself had taken on the role of Cleopatra for the Globe the year before. "Vanessa has always had a very passionate interest in people in exile and has often encountered people who are in that very situation that Prospero is in. I think she'll bring her experience of the world's troubles to the part."

Udovicki and her family had fled the Balkans in 1993 and Redgrave had put them up for seven months. Redgrave suggested to Rylance that Udovicki would be the best director for the play. "As an exile you have to establish yourself in a completely new environment without the usual references of family, place, and society, you have to rediscover yourself, ask yourself who you are," Udovicki said.

Redgrave did one of her most incomprehensible accents as Prospero, wavering toward Ireland and Scotland but winding up somewhere in between in a kind of United Nations brogue. "Querulous, scattered, and not a little cranky," wrote Kristen McDermott of Redgrave in *The Tempest* for *Theatre Journal*. "Such a Prospero was gratifyingly unconventional, although at times more low-key than one would wish from an actor usually so powerful. Redgrave's voice, low pitched, clear and flexible, nevertheless lacked the ringing command often inherent in the lines.

"Her Prospero's affection for Miranda was much more apparent than the character's anger over the past and his sinister anticipation of revenge to come. Redgrave chose an androgynous interpretation of the role that unfortunately robbed the character of the vengeful macho posturing that helps make his later reconciliations poignant."

"Since this actress prefers to play sufferers, saviors, and saints, she suppresses signs of Prospero's tyrannical tendencies and desire for vengeance," thought the *London Evening Standard*. "Her adieu to magic misses notes of regret and her rather monotonic speaking, in an accent crossed between Irish and Scottish, is sometimes unintelligible in the middle gallery."

The *Daily Telegraph* wrote, "There is almost always something wayward about Redgrave's performances, and on this occasion it is a totally bizarre accent that seems to flit at random from Mummerset to Ulster and from RADA to the United States." The *Independent* said, "Despite cutting a piratical figure, she moved through the proceedings with the air of a slightly embarrassed imposter." The *Guardian* wrote, "I've seen tougher, harsher Prosperos, but few so imbued with the spirit of charity."

That same spirit was alive off-stage, too, when she raised £2000 for the families of sailors who died after the sinking of the Russian Kursk submarine ship. At a news conference in Moscow, where she gave the families the money, Redgrave said, "When I heard about your men I was in the Globe Theatre and all I could do was think about you and your families. I want you to know that we made the collection because I knew you could think of something important that could be done even with this small amount of money. I understand, perhaps because all the men in my family were in the navy during the Second World War, that men in the navy are very special and mariners are perhaps the most special of all. We wanted you to know that ordinary people can't stop thinking about you . . . we won't forget you." There was nothing ordinary about her, of course.

Corin played with Vanessa in a 2000 revival of *The Cherry Orchard* in London directed by Trevor Nunn, who had wanted to work with Vanessa again after having such a fine time with her collaborating on Shaw's *Heartbreak House* in 1992. For the *Los Angeles Times*, Charles McNulty wrote of Corin in this production: "In his final elegiac moments with Vanessa, when the characters are scattering after the sale of the estate, the hope and heartbreak were superbly balanced and textured. For a brief moment, art and life seemed to blur as the Redgraves' fictitious brother-sister counterparts abandoned a cherished past for an unknown future."

In the *Observer*, Susannah Clapp wrote, "This play, Nunn's production makes clear, is about growing up—and failing to do so. Which is why casting the Redgraves is a triumph. Watching them, frolicking in middle age, clinging to each other in their family home, you see a couple whose past locks them together—and stops them from moving on. Corin Redgrave catches this creaky infantilism superbly. A garrulous fusspot, he mounts a rocking-horse to make a speech and tries to curb his tongue by buttoning up his lips, as a child does. His sister is—sometimes within one speech—unnerving, unconvincing, and dazzling. She mutters some lines with a voice so flat and faltering it's as if she can scarcely be bothered to speak. You realize only afterwards that you've been tricked into hearing them afresh. She semaphores distress hammily. And then she flashes illumination. Urging an up-and-coming entrepreneur to marry her adopted daughter, she all the while seduces him herself, as she slowly caresses his head."

Writing for *Theatre Guide London*, Gerald Berkowitz said, "There is a moment near the end of the Royal National Theatre's new production of Chekhov when Vanessa Redgrave, as the aristocrat who has lost the family estate, takes one last look around the room she is about to leave forever. Because the play is being done in the round, she actually scans the audience as she turns in a circle. But we don't see ourselves reflected in her eyes—we see the walls her character is seeing. Redgrave is one of the greatest silent actresses in the world, and that moment of absolute reality is almost worth the price of admission in itself. There's a similar moment earlier, when the memory of her dead child makes her change slowly from silent joy to silent (and then wailing) grief. . . . However foolish the woman, we experience her from the inside and believe her confusion, her pain, and even her blindness."

"For a long time I didn't appreciate him," Redgrave said of Chekhov. "I couldn't understand why, but I just found it too gentle, too elegiac, too nostalgic. I preferred Ibsen because it was harder and more savage. But when I played Arkadina in *The Seagull* in 1985, I discovered a capacity I hadn't found in a playwright before, of taking you inside the anatomy of human beings with all their different states of mind, above all into the 'opposites' which go on inside people." Interviewing Vanessa with her brother Corin, David Benedict observed that she was more volatile and spontaneous in his presence, whereas Corin took up her usual worried-thoughtful responses to questions.

When Blythe Danner, perhaps the definitive modern Nina in *The Seagull*, was asked if she would play in *The Cherry Orchard*, she spoke of this Redgrave/Nunn version. "After seeing that production I don't know if I even want to touch it because what they all did was so extraordinary."

# If These Walls Could Talk
2

A t this point in her film career it did seem like Redgrave was too often stuck in small roles that offered her little opportunity to create, but in 2000 she won her second Emmy and offered a master class in acting for the first segment, "1961," of the Showtime movie *If These Walls Could Talk 2*. "Her work is metaphysical," said writer-director Jane Anderson of Redgrave. "I swear to God, when she drops into character, her molecules get rearranged.

"When we first met before the shoot to talk over the script, I had no idea what I was in for," Anderson said. "Vanessa has a reputation for being a bit unpredictable at times. During the run of *Orpheus Descending*, she decided one night to make her entrance stark naked. I'm sure that the stage manager had a seizure in the booth, and her fellow actors probably dropped their lines along with their jaws. But this is what makes Vanessa so brilliant: her willingness to be exposed.

"She didn't want to wear any makeup for her role in my film—not even a base. The D.P. and the makeup person were baffled, and we all talked about getting her to change her mind. But she knew what she was doing. She didn't want her skin to be covered. She wanted the camera to have direct access to whatever miraculous things she was about to do with her face."

After the credits for "1961," we see Shirley MacLaine on a movie screen doing her climactic confession scene from *The Children's Hour* (1961), where she says that she's "guilty" of love for fellow teacher Audrey Hepburn. Some patrons in the movie theater walk out and a few boys in the back of the house laugh loudly. Redgrave's Edith Tree is watching this scene intently and holding hands with her lover Abby (Marian Seldes), but when the two women hear the boys' laughter, they stop holding hands. Outside of the theater when they pass these boys, they make sure to walk down the street at a distance from each other, an intensely moving image that expresses their shame and fear.

At home alone and safe from a prejudiced world, Edith and Abby are playful and loving with each other, a longtime, deeply happy couple. They bicker like couples do, and Redgrave makes sure to emphasize the affectionate physical intimacy between them (Seldes, an important theater actress, creates a wholly believable relationship with Redgrave in just a few minutes of screen time).

Abby has a stroke and falls from a ladder, and Edith takes her to the hospital. While waiting for word on her condition, Edith comforts a woman whose husband has had a heart attack. Because she isn't an official family member, the hospital staff won't let Edith see Abby, and so she continues to wait anxiously and patiently in the lobby. She isn't notified by the staff when Abby dies, and so Edith doesn't get to say good-bye to the love of her life. When Edith desperately asks for Abby, a sympathetic nurse tells her that Abby's body has already been taken away.

Abby has only one family member left, her nephew Ted (Paul Giamatti), and he calls to say he is coming to see the house with his wife Alice (Elizabeth Perkins). Edith guiltily takes down photos of herself and Abby from the walls before Ted and Alice arrive (we see that the picture frames have left their mark on the wallpaper). Ted is obviously a nice guy, but since the house is in Abby's name only, he is going to have to pay an inheritance tax. He gently tells Edith that she will have to move out.

Edith and Abby had been schoolteachers, and they had lived in a world of their own creating, as so many couples do. When this world is torn away from Edith, Redgrave reacts with slow incomprehension and then gathering anger, which has to be hidden. Edith is not a sharp person, and she only begins to realize the situation that she's in gradually. Alice is oblivious and insensitive to her; in this story's most sickening moment, she brightly tells Edith that she can pick one of Abby's bird figurines to remember her by. Redgrave shows Edith's helpless rage with one perfect gesture, punching a pillow on a couch when Edith knows that she's alone.

Edith hasn't even begun to mourn Abby, and now with her house and possessions being stripped from her she feels the full load of her sorrow and rushes to their bedroom to collapse on their bed. Maggie (Marley McClean), the young daughter of Ted and Alice, discovers Edith weeping in the bedroom like a wounded animal, crying, "My darling, my darling, my darling" into her pillow. This scene proves again that no one goes as all-out in a portrayal of grief as Redgrave can.

Yet Anderson found her rather lighthearted on the set. "She had me playing charades with her between setups," Anderson said. "She practiced irreverence because she knew it was death for an actor to take herself too seriously. She taught me that the deeper you have to go in the work, the more you need to come up for air and goof around. . . . There's a reason that the verb 'to play' applies to acting out a role.

"Our budget confined us to shooting in an actual house rather than a soundstage, so we were all crammed together in this very small room, crew and all. I was sitting by the camera, just a few feet away from Vanessa, watching her break down. I'm emotionally detached when I direct. But when the film started to roll, Vanessa let out a sob of grief that was so raw, so fierce, so real that I felt my own molecules get rearranged. She shook me to the core of my solar plexus, and after we checked the gate, I was still shaking. I ended up having to take a walk out to the trailers and have myself a good hard cry."

Anderson was particularly impressed by Redgrave's patience when she shot this scene. Though she has her faults, a starry temperament is not among them. "During the scene, a little girl walks into the bedroom, and Vanessa's character has an exchange with her," Anderson said. "We had to shoot the girl's coverage first so we could release her for the night. So Vanessa had to play the scene to an adult stand-in—a woman who was a little person. The woman was so in awe of Vanessa that she kept missing her mark and screwing up the takes, so Vanessa had to call up her grief again and again and again. When we were finally done, Vanessa was exhausted and the poor woman was a wreck. Most stars would have immediately retreated to their trailer without another word to this incompetent underling. But Vanessa looked the woman in the eyes, gently took her hand, and said, 'Thank you so much for working with me.'"

When Edith notices Maggie staring at her, she snaps right out of her tears and says, "What do you want?" in a very hard voice (maybe Redgrave used her frustration at the delays caused by the stand-in?). Maggie gives Edith one of Abby's handkerchiefs and then tries to make her feel better by saying that she can keep it. In the authoritative tone of the schoolteacher she once was, Edith says, "Little girl, it is not for you to say what I can and cannot have," but soon afterward she can see that her anger is of no use. What Edith has to withstand here on top of her loss of Abby seems almost too much to bear, yet she gets herself out of this abyss on their bed. With all the strength she has in her, Edith pulls herself together and goes in to have one final talk with Ted.

She sits down in a chair by a window and caresses the arms of the chair as if the arms are Abby herself. Her lover is gone from this earth, but Abby still lives in the objects that they chose for their home together, these objects that are being stolen from Edith. This is a key example of Redgrave's sensual, physical approach to acting; the touch of the chair gives Edith the courage she needs.

Ted never really knew his aunt, and so Edith tells him how kind she was to all living creatures. In the few moments she has left with Abby's nephew, the man who is taking her whole life away from her, Edith tries to make her lost lover live for him. In the middle of talking about Abby's kindness, Edith pauses briefly and then says "and *funny*," as if this is something she cannot forget to say about Abby (Seldes suggested all of these qualities in the moments she shared on screen with Redgrave).

After Edith gives the departing Alice a richly deserved dirty look, the story ends with Seldes singing "Bye, Bye, Blackbird" on the soundtrack, a song that has followed Redgrave from *Isadora* to *Julia* and on to this master class in the art of acting, the strongest narrative argument for gay marriage that has yet been made. "It's one of her most brilliant performances," her daughter Natasha said at the time. It is purely didactic, purely felt, and pure Vanessa Redgrave at her empathetic best.

# Chechnya and
# Lady Windermere

Our wandering actress heroine had a lead role in *A Rumor of Angels* (2000) as a gruff older woman who befriends a young boy. It was based on a 1918 novel by Grace Duffie Boylan, *Thy Son Liveth: Messages from a Soldier to His Mother*, a book where Boylan wrote about receiving messages via Morse code from her son after he was killed in World War I. In the film, Redgrave's character is grieving for a son she lost in the Vietnam War, and she helps her young friend grieve for his dead mother. A modest film on an icky/creepy subject, it received poor reviews, but Redgrave brought depth of feeling and careful detail to her role.

"How can God be so greedy?" Redgrave asks as the grandmother of a murdered little girl in Sean Penn's slow, self-serious *The Pledge* (2001). She plays her one scene with Jack Nicholson, but Penn frustratingly keeps them separate in shot reverse shot style, and though she tries with her eyes to make a large point about the suffering of children, her slightly campy accent doesn't help her make her case. There are entirely too many heavy-duty actors here playing small roles, from

Patricia Clarkson to Mickey Rourke to Helen Mirren, and so she gets lost in the shuffle.

Redgrave had fun with a hammy German accent narrating and presiding over the convoluted *Jack and the Beanstalk: The Real Story* (2001), a three-hour television movie directed by Jim Henson's son Brian that often felt more dogged than magical, then played with Crispin Glover and Margot Kidder in a disastrous Menahem Golan version of Dostoyevsky's *Crime and Punishment* (2002), which again confirmed her place on the marginal outskirts of filmmaking. The film was seized in a bankruptcy lien and has rarely been seen or heard of.

Talking about the making of this movie, Kidder said, "Golan is outrageous! He is really outrageous. I did a version, a very bad version, of *Crime and Punishment* that he directed in Russia, with Vanessa Redgrave and John Neville and John Hurt and Crispin Glover. Now, he was not a good director, but again, you had this humongous personality. Just this humongous, *humongous* personality, who took it upon himself to rewrite Dostoyevsky, and got very flustered whenever Crispin Glover would point out that the script was betraying the book."

Kidder had a death scene, but Golan cut it. "And so Crispin said 'Cut the death? You *can't* cut the death, it says right here in the book'—and he brings out this dog-eared copy of *Crime and Punishment* and Menahem says 'This book, I'm sick of hearing about this book. *I* wrote the *script!*'" Kidder remembered. "Which was just my favorite thing I've ever heard. I mean, it was just fabulous.

"And then he tried to cheat people, as Menahem will do," Kidder said. "There was some lawsuit going on where he'd taken some American ship that he'd rented, shot it full of holes for a movie, returned it full of holes, and said it had been shot up in one of the many Palestinian-Israeli skirmishes . . . I don't think I got paid for that, and everybody's checks bounced. And he told me I should have been honored to be working with Vanessa Redgrave, and that was true, but that didn't mean he didn't have to pay me."

On the London stage in 2002, Redgrave was at least properly paid for appearing with her daughter Joely Richardson in Oscar Wilde's *Lady Windermere's Fan* under the direction of Peter Hall, with real-life husband and wife John McCallum and Googie Withers. There was a bit more glamour for her in the theater, but not much. She had a grand dressing room, but you had to climb up five dark flights of stairs to get to it.

"Wilde would still provoke society today," wrote Hall in the *Guardian*. "He was bisexual and, while preferring his own sex, still managed to love his wife—and to father and worship children. One of the themes of *An Ideal Husband* is bisexuality." Redgrave said, "It's so wonderful to be working with Oscar Wilde's words. I have never acted with my daughter before so it should be interesting."

Richardson was glad to work with her mother. "I always regretted not having worked with my father," she said. Asked about her upbringing, she said, "I went through the classic thing of having difficulty squaring what I read in the papers with the reality of having that desperate desire to be normal that all teenagers have, but then, what's normal? That was normality for me. This whole thing about my family and the tradition, I mean, what family? I lived with my sister and my mum, who was a working single mum. And I saw my dad in the school holidays." Speaking of Richardson's upbringing, Vanessa said, "I wanted my children to be able to be independent, free to get on with their lives." During rehearsals, Richardson laughed and said, "She's a bit of a show-off on stage—more of a natural exhibitionist than me."

By most accounts, Redgrave emphasized the drama of Wilde's play rather than the comedy. "My mother is known for her experimenting in rehearsals," Richardson told the *Independent*. "There are legendary stories about her suddenly deciding during the first preview that her character is Caribbean. In rehearsal for *Lady Windermere*, all of a sudden she made the decision that her character should be Irish. Later on, she apologized for not knowing her lines, and I replied: 'No problem, but if you spring that Irish accent on me again, I'll kill you.'" She admired her mother's fresh approach to the theater. "Doing *Lady Windermere*, I've learnt how Mum is still so dedicated. She is fascinated by detail and still has the hunger of someone who's just out of drama school.

"Mum loves working with the family and has proposed it many times in the past, but I've always held off because it didn't seem right," Richardson said. "When you come to the table, you want to be sitting there in your own right. I also worried that we might argue. We have always been incredibly close, mixed with times when we've clashed. There is no doubt that if your mother is the greatest actress in the world, that sets you a pretty high benchmark, but we all want to be judged on our own merits. I realize people will make comparisons with my mother, but that's not my concern."

"Redgrave defies all convention by playing Mrs. Erlynne not as some swaggering voluptuary but as a gracious, humane woman whose mission is to prevent her daughter repeating her mistakes," wrote Michael Billington in the *Guardian*. "When the upright Lady Windermere asks Mrs. Erlynne what she has to do with her, Redgrave replies 'Nothing, I know it' in tones that would break the heart of a stoic. And in the final act Redgrave cunningly suggests that Mrs. Erlynne's social poise is a mask for her turbulent emotions."

Redgrave found herself yet again at the center of a political controversy when she posted £50,000 bail for Akhmed Zakayev, describing him at a press conference as "Chechnya's Laurence Olivier." Zakayev was a Chechen separatist who was accused by the Russian government of being involved in the hostage-taking and deaths of 120 people in a Moscow theater, a charge that Zakayev vehemently denied. Redgrave made sure that he could stay with her in London and not be brought to trial in Russia. "I'm his friend, I'm his guarantor," she said. "There's a load of people who care about the Chechen situation and care that there should be peace for Chechen people."

"I think everyone who knows the way things are in Chechnya, it's a very easy question to understand," Zakayev said. "There are several representatives of Chechnya who found themselves in the hands of the Russian authorities. Some of them simply disappeared without trace before any trial. Those who did get as far as being tried, and found guilty, they would then be sent to prison or to a camp, and there they would disappear. And I think that the same fate would await me."

He condemned the terrorist act in the Moscow theater. "Actions like that don't get us closer to our goals. On the contrary, they are putting off the day when we see the rule of law in Chechnya and democracy in Chechnya," he said. "If we're talking about terrorism in Chechnya, then there's one thing I think that has to be said: the Russian forces have been given a very specific task, right from the start of the second war, which is to destroy the Chechen nation. And what they're doing is terrorizing the civilian population. And those Chechens who have taken arms are, in their turn, terrorizing the Russian troops. So we're in a vicious circle, and there seems to be no way out of it unless someone intervenes from outside, and by someone I mean the international community."

As ever, Redgrave was magnetized to hellishly complex world situations like this, made up of vicious circles where it could be difficult, if not impossible, to tell who is in the right because no one is in the right, at a certain point, in such standoffs. As if the continuing Israeli-Palestinian conflict wasn't enough to keep her busy. And she continued to act. And presumably found time to have some kind of personal life too.

She used the same words for both struggles, saying she defended Chechnya's "right to self-determination" just as she had used those words over and over again for the Palestinians. Redgrave condemned the terrorist actions in Moscow. She said, "If there are no statesmen, no mediators on a high-up level, if these fail a population repeatedly over a period of years, people get desperate. The majority of people never turn to terrorism. But if there is anyone who has got a specific agenda, then you'll get young people responding to a call which leads to absolute horror."

For HBO, Redgrave played Clemmie Churchill to Albert Finney's highly convincing Winston in *The Gathering Storm* (2002). To prepare for the role, she read *Winston and Clementine: The Personal Letters of the Churchills*, which was edited by their daughter Mary Soames, and she also met with Soames.

"Mary begged me not to make her hair too perfect . . . not to make her look as though she had just come from a hairdresser," Redgrave said. "She explained to me the lady from the inner point of view, which is extremely important." Clemmie read all the newspapers she could in the morning, and Redgrave found this particularly telling. "You could tell from her letters she would have considered herself an absolute failure if she had neglected to read carefully and thoughtfully all the political information that was connected with the concerns that were utmost in her husband's mind and hers," she said. She took the role in part, she said, because it dealt with a period that was "certainly the defining period for all human rights legislation."

In the film, mostly Redgrave is just there to offer well-groomed support, but she has one fine scene. Churchill accuses Clemmie of selfishness and this makes her explode in anger, even going so far as to hurl a plate at him. When Clemmie has finished her tantrum, she flinches from what she's done and her arms go up to her face, protectively, before she charges out. It's a rare moment of realistic marital behavior in a too-simple, patriotic movie. "All intelligent people are confrontational," Redgrave insisted in a promotional interview for the film.

There was not much she could do with the Hallmark Hall of Fame sentimentality of *The Locket* (2002), though she does have a fine first scene where her nursing-home resident is lost in her own bitter thoughts. She gamely appeared as herself, with Jane Birkin, in one of the worst films ever made, *Merci Docteur Rey* (2002), which is worth seeing for Dianne Wiest's hammy performance alone, and which has to count as a favor to someone, unless Redgrave just flies around the world looking for the oddest possible shoots.

"Vanessa was intimidating at first because of her reputation as the greatest living actress, but in fact she was terribly easy to work with," said director Andrew Litvack. "It was funny how she insisted on playing such a mean and imperious version of herself. I kept saying, 'Vanessa, since you're playing yourself, we can make you nicer,' and she answered in the third person, 'Andy, Vanessa is not playing herself, she is playing a version of herself.'"

"The day we were shooting with Dianne, Jane, and Vanessa, there were lots of Russian political refugees on the set. . . . Both Jane and Vanessa are big on humanitarian causes, and rightfully so, and perhaps on some level they were, very nicely, trying to outdo each other. Then all of a sudden Jerry Hall arrived, bedecked in jewels for her costume fitting. . . . To see all these actresses, their respective refugees, and then this Texan in diamonds was like a scene from a Fellini movie," Litvack marveled.

Redgrave did some lolling on couches in the miniseries *Byron* (2003), where she played Lady Melbourne. In her scenes with Jonny Lee Miller's Byron, Redgrave gets across that Lady Melbourne is titillated by Byron underneath all of her stern disapproval. She also joined Cheech Marin, Carl Reiner, and Delta Burke in *Good Boy!* (2003), a film about talking alien dogs where she provided the voice of a character called The Greater Dane. And no, I did not make that up just to see if you were still paying attention.

At this very lowest point of her filmography, where she was actually asked to play a talking dog, Redgrave took on the most testing and difficult theater role of her career, the drug-addicted Mary Tyrone in a Broadway revival of Eugene O'Neill's *Long Day's Journey Into Night*. Within the same year. At this point, her unpredictability in picking projects begins to seem downright batty. But if money is needed, then you have to take whatever is offered you, even *Good Boy!*, and then the Mount Everest of Mary Tyrone. That range of work is why many of our best actors might be driven more than a little crazy.

# Long Day's Journey
# and The Fever

*Long Day's Journey Into Night* played on Broadway, after Eugene O'Neill's death, with Fredric March, Florence Eldridge, Bradford Dillman, and Jason Robards, who remembered that Tennessee Williams had been so overcome on the first night that he had charged toward the stage during the curtain call, trembling with emotion and admiration for what O'Neill had achieved. It is a memory play "written in tears and blood" about O'Neill's own family and all families. It is maybe the greatest of all American plays.

Katharine Hepburn played Mary Tyrone in a 1962 film version of the play with Ralph Richardson, Dean Stockwell, and Robards, and this movie directed by Sidney Lumet, with its poetic black and white cinematography by Boris Kaufman and its edgy André Previn music, is for many people the definitive version of the play. All four actors outdo themselves, but it is Hepburn who stakes her claim as one of our greatest actresses in a performance that blends technical skill, savage anger, and an overarching morbidity that runs excitingly against the grain of her accepted movie image. This was the underside of Hepburn's cheery, can-do spirit, expressed most dangerously in the scene where her youngest son (Stockwell) tells her that he is dying and she reacts by slapping him in the face.

Hepburn's performance begins on a slightly artificial note, but the first scene of the play as written is weak and desultory in comparison to what is to come. Hepburn digs deeper and deeper into this woman's relentless passive aggression, her romantic daydreams, and then her final drugged retreat back into her early convent years before she became so unhappy. Hepburn was proud of this performance, and she had every right to be. The role is full of traps and self-pitying jags, but she guides you over them with all the strength of her intelligence, which is formidable, and when that is not enough, her intuition. It's a plunge into darkness, and Hepburn comes out of it on the other side like a runner who has finished the longest, toughest marathon of her life with time to spare.

Redgrave had a strong cast to play with in *Long Day's Journey*: Brian Dennehy as James Tyrone, Philip Seymour Hoffman as Jamie, and Robert Sean Leonard as Edmund. The director of this production, Robert Falls, had worked with Dennehy on a successful revival of *Death of a Salesman* and had directed Dennehy in a production of *Journey* at Chicago's Goodman Theatre. Falls wanted to bring the show to Broadway, and he knew that he needed a star cast.

"I offered it to Vanessa," said Falls. "She couldn't do it. And it was after that that there was this investigation—which became very public and I think somewhat messy—surrounding Jessica Lange, who had done the play in London with producer Bill Kenwright. Kenwright claimed he had the rights to do the play. Completely unconsulted by me, Jessica's name became attached to the project." This was eventually sorted out when producer David Richenthal revealed that he alone had the rights to produce *Journey* on Broadway, and he and Falls wanted Redgrave for Mary.

"One of the greatest performances I ever saw in the theater was Vanessa doing *Touch of the Poet*, in which she played the wife Nora—a production at the Young Vic about seventeen years ago," said Falls. "As I said, I made an offer a couple of years ago, and she was very interested, but she had family and professional commitments for about eighteen months. And when I went back to her, she basically said 'Great.' I always think of her as fearless. I think she lives her life on the edge. And it was interesting to meet her and see a sort of shyness, modesty, a humbleness. Not the slightest hint of a diva or a grand lady of the theater. Much like her politics—what I've read about—she has the common touch. Her politics are her humanity, and her humanity is such that everyone is treated the same, be it a director, producer, intern, or taxi driver." Redgrave had six weeks of rehearsal after she accepted the part.

I saw a preview performance of this *Long Day's Journey* filled with critics right before it opened and was fully prepared for the merging of the greatest actress of our time with the greatest role, but from Redgrave's first scene, I sensed there was going to be trouble. She chose to play the opening moments in a way that suggested that Mary had already begun to completely unravel. Redgrave would throw her head back and get lost in a sort of silent laughter until Hoffman's Jamie knew for certain that Mary was back to taking her morphine, her "poison." This was a striking scene and it began the play strongly, but it had the effect of a poker player showing all their cards all at once. For the next four hours, Redgrave had nowhere left to go.

Her Mary often spoke of her hands and how ugly they had become, and Redgrave would sometimes start to drum her large fingers on any available surface as if she were playing the piano, which was part of the training of Mary's convent days. This was an interesting physical choice, but in the performance I saw, it felt mechanical, not fully felt. As the play went on and on, I sank back into my seat as I watched Redgrave walk through scene after scene. She was never the kind of actress who could get by on technique alone, and she failed continually here, for hours and hours. Worse, she seemed to know that she was failing, and this awareness only added to the pain of watching her.

The writer James McCourt saw her in this play and said that she was "indicating" throughout, and that was sadly true the night I saw her. At the end, when she came out for the curtain call, the look on her face was ashen and embarrassed. She seemed to be saying, "Why are you applauding?" My theater companion, the actress Sarah Milici, said afterwards, "I don't think she got enough love in rehearsals."

Yet Redgrave received rave reviews in most quarters. Ben Brantley in the *New York Times* called her work "a performance that will never leave the memory of anyone who sees it. . . . Good old pity and terror, the responses that Aristotle deemed appropriate to tragedy, are seldom stirred on Broadway these days. But Ms. Redgrave elicits them again and again as Mary wanders restlessly through the long day of the play's title, dispensing blame and love, cold lies and scalding truths. You understand on a gut level why O'Neill, when writing this autobiographical play six decades ago, was said by his wife Carlotta to emerge from his study gaunt and red-eyed, looking ten years older than he had in the morning. . . . This is Ms. Redgrave's best work in years and among her best ever."

But John Simon in *New York Magazine* wrote, "Vanessa Redgrave's Mary Tyrone is weird and fluttery, by turns childish and hysterical, untrustworthily unpredictable from the start. It is admittedly hard to convey the dichotomy of this lovable but ruinous character, best captured in my view by Martha Henry, Constance Cummings, and Geraldine Fitzgerald. The highly accomplished Redgrave gets some details right, but the overarching mental unstableness she exudes is so excessive as to make one wonder whether she is playing or being unhinged."

Dennehy said that she was giving the performance of the decade, and Redgrave eventually won a Tony award for her Mary. To be fair, I have talked to several people who saw her in this play and apparently she could be drastically different on different nights. One friend of mine told me that he saw Redgrave do the play around the time her mother Rachel died, and he said that she was extraordinary that night, unforgettable. Unfortunately, it isn't financially possible for most of us to see a play more than once, and the experience of watching Redgrave fail for four hours in the performance I saw of *Long Day's Journey* was so upsetting that I wouldn't have thought to go back and try again.

Coming out of the theater, I was met by a brightly smiling girl who handed me a card and said, "Tell us what you think of the play!" Not the production, but the play itself. In the lobby, they were selling merchandise, copies of the play, yes, but also *Long Day's Journey Into Night* T-shirts. It wouldn't have been surprising if they had been selling Mary Tyrone action figures, with tiny morphine syringes sold separately. Surely Redgrave of all people looked askance at such merchandising as she entered and left the theater every evening.

While she worked on this O'Neill play, Redgrave had had to deal with the illness and death of her mother Rachel, who had been living with her. Redgrave spoke about watching Rachel swim when she was an elderly woman, and telling her mother that she was beautiful. Rachel glanced around timidly, as if she didn't believe her daughter. "I could see why Michael couldn't believe his luck when she told him they ought to be married, and why her lover adored her for over thirty years, until he died," Redgrave said.

Rachel had played parts on stage as a young woman that Vanessa might have played: Juliet, and Ariel in *The Tempest*. As an older woman, she had had her own successes on television, particularly in the series *The Jewel in the Crown* (1984). She was ninety-two when she died in 2003 while Redgrave played Mary Tyrone. Though her own career had persistently taken a back seat to the work of her husband and then her children, Rachel had carved out her own particular space, yet the feeling remains that she could have done far more.

She happily admitted in her 1986 memoir *Life Among the Redgraves* that she had never had a strong enough ego to really push herself to the forefront. And so she remained mainly in the background, supporting her family in life and sometimes on stage and screen, making sure that everything was running smoothly. "She suffered from her lack of security, making room for my father's career," Lynn said. But Rachel hung on to her love of Shakespeare's Juliet, reciting a Juliet speech when she was ninety years old at the wedding of Lynn's daughter Pema.

During the time Rachel lived with Vanessa toward the very end of her life, they became extremely close. It had never been easy being the wife of Michael, or the mother of Vanessa and Corin, but Rachel handled all difficulties with very becoming grace and tact. She was a strong and unwavering light and support for her family.

Familial closeness could lead to professional missteps. Redgrave appeared with her daughter Joely on ten episodes of the television show *Nip/Tuck* from 2004 to 2009, and it was painful to see her so out of place and so trapped in such a badly written TV show context, trying to speed her way through all the contemporary vulgarisms in her dialogue. It would be good to forget that we ever heard Vanessa Redgrave utter the line, "You were thinking of me while you were masturbating into my granddaughter's panties?"

Richardson, who had recommended her mother for the part on the show, said that her father and mother had taught her to be independent, "which invokes strong-mindedness and opinions. So when our opinions clash, they can clash big time." Lost in reverie as they were being interviewed, Vanessa observed, "I was just imagining Tony [Richardson] rubbing his hands and saying, 'Oh, there's a drama.' I think a teenager has to be rebellious. I don't think it's possible to be anything else if you're going to grow to be yourself." Their relationship as mother and daughter had changed and shifted. "First there's the rebelling, then we were lucky to be friends, and now I often feel more parental and protective of Vanessa," Richardson said.

Redgrave predictably spoke out about the usefulness of plastic surgery for reconstructive purposes when she gave interviews about *Nip/Tuck*, and she forthrightly admitted to the work that she had had done to remove bags under her eyes in 1985, "though they came back again," she said. Her beauty, of course, had always come from the openness of her blue eyes, and that is the kind of beauty that does not fade. She disagreed with her character's assessment of beauty as power that fades after forty "because that's to confuse beauty with youth," she said. "It is true that youth has its own special beauty. So it's very hard to play this character with those views."

Speaking of her own face, Redgrave said, "I've got a sort of face that responds to whatever is going on inside me. And I'd like it to stay that way. I don't want a face that won't respond, that won't wrinkle, no furrows in my brow. I've got a great big trench on my forehead in between my two eyes. That's life's wear and tear. As I'm an actress, I think that's fine. Although I had my stage of modeling and doing beauty magazines and so on, it was a different era, and I enjoyed that. I never quite believed if anyone told me I was beautiful."

"I think she regrets that she was not there, really, for our childhood," Richardson said. "A difficult price to pay was not spending any time, really, with my children," Redgrave said. "At the time, I didn't understand that any moment of a relationship between two individuals . . . especially with children, being involved with your children's life *and* being involved with children in every other country in every city . . . not keeping your family selfishly as a unit that exists only for its own sustenance, but reaching out to other families, refugee families or families in great need stuck in camps . . . I didn't realize that they're interlinked. So I saw hardly anything of my children. But they've grown up to be wonderful human beings and seem to have done okay. I've made many mistakes, but I don't regret them if I've been able to learn from them."

Family connections proved far more fruitful with *The Fever* (2004), an adaptation of Wallace Shawn's play directed by her son Carlo Nero that aired on HBO. Redgrave is front and center here in challenging, complex material, playing a well-off bourgeois woman who starts to have pangs of conscience about her place in the world. Shawn himself did *The Fever* as a monologue, performing it at first in various apartments in Manhattan. When he did it in 2007, the play was preceded by a champagne reception, which led to uncomfortable resonances for the audience after he started delivering his text on liberal guilt.

"In the case of *The Fever*, it's a passion," Redgrave said of this project, distinguishing it from the many movie jobs she took for money only. "I consider it my testament, my personal testament. . . . What responsibility does this character bear for the terrible violence and poverty and suffering in the world? The character was aware to the extent that they would be generous with donations, philanthropy, but not beyond that.

"By the time I read it, I wanted to do it myself, and I did it myself on a Sunday afternoon and evening performance at the Chelsea Arts Center in London," Redgrave said. "I became convinced it could be a film. I've known Wally for many, many years, and I spoke to Wally about it and then I spoke to Carlo about it. They met up, but Wally didn't think it could be a film, but he put up some of his own money for Carlo to write a preliminary draft, and when Carlo brought it back to Wally, he got very excited and thought, 'Oh, maybe it could be a film, I see what you're getting at.' So he began writing and he and Carlo worked on the script. . . . They got into the cinematic visual dynamics.

"*The Fever* examines this psychological thing of, you think you're nice, you think you're generous . . . I like to think I'm a quite nice and generous person," Redgrave said. "We like to think of ourselves that way. We would like to be good people, and we're maybe humble . . . but we each have a role in allowing a situation to continue in which more and more children, especially children, are starving and live in poverty in the United States, are illiterate . . . as well as in the developing countries, but these countries are *not* developing.

"If you want to deceive yourself into thinking that you're a thoroughly good-hearted, courageous person who gives generously via philanthropy, that's not the point. The point is how blind any of us can be, I can be, under certain circumstances. . . . She is struggling with herself all the way through . . . and we can become quite horrified with some of the things we actually think which might be getting in the way of our becoming really humble people without our ego of wanting to be seen as the special person."

Clearly the film of this major Shawn play confronted Redgrave with many of the personal and political issues she had been facing her whole life. She was being made to look at herself, but she also, like the character she was playing, had certain blind spots. The tension between wanting to be "the special person" and wanting to be truly humble is the main conflict of Redgrave's life, if not her art. And in her art, in *The Fever*, she was finally allowed to deal with this personal conflict in the best possible material, which she chose for herself.

"Although I'm not the character that I play," she said, "it's my testament because you see me go through this as well as this character. They're different but they're together. You see me somewhere in there, each person can decide where I am." She spoke of having had the experience of being under gunfire and in war zones for UNICEF. "Nevertheless, that doesn't exempt me from self-examination," Redgrave said. "She reaches a catharsis of humility, of recognizing her place in the world."

There were technical challenges, particularly for the many scenes when Redgrave speaks directly to the camera, which is much different from speaking to a live audience in a theater. "I've never played direct-to-camera," Redgrave said. "I learned a lot. I learned how difficult it is. And I had to learn the most important thing, which is to be really, really close to your inner self, and not act."

One of the many fascinating things about Redgrave doing Shawn's *The Fever* is the fact that she approaches her role from a viewpoint of total sincerity. Because of who she is and what she believes off-screen, the ironies of Shawn's play come through even more strongly because of her idealistic conception of her own role in the world in relation to this character, who at one point reads Marx's *Capital* in her well-appointed bed. The character cannot penetrate some of Marx's formulations in the early part of his book, but she is struck by his anger when writing about the exploitation of child labor.

Like so many people, like Redgrave herself, this is a person who needs to have an emotional connection to unfair economics before she can start to question buying a beautiful coat for a low price and what that low price entails. This is a woman in expensive clothes and fancy hair who listens to Beethoven with hard, consumerist eyes, but she reaches a crisis point and goes to a poor country that is riven by war because she starts to feel empathy, and this relates back troublingly to Redgrave's lifelong empathy for her often-oppressed characters.

In Shawn's *The Fever*, empathy is seen as a kind of disruptive force, and the lack of it can be comic, as when Redgrave's character sees a production of *The Cherry Orchard* and suddenly can't remember why she is supposed to weep over a rich woman forced to give up her estate and go live in an apartment in Paris.

In the film's best scene, Redgrave (who is only called Woman in the credits) goes to see a former lover who starts to complain angrily about his father's death and how the hospital couldn't help him; he mentions that six nurses were there trying to keep his father alive. Helplessly, Redgrave makes a connection between this elderly man being kept alive and out of pain in the best way that modern civilization can buy and the people who are being kept on torture tables, surrounded by people making sure that they die in the worst possible physical agony. This woman's former lover is offended by her words. To speak a truth like this is to disturb the complacency of bourgeois society. More upsettingly, to care for one selfish person and offer them words of comfort because you love them, or once loved them, is seen as a joke and an indulgence in the face of the much worse suffering of others you do not know.

Nero breaks up Redgrave's monologue to the camera with a lot of animation and extended scenes where Redgrave listens to guest stars like Michael Moore (uncomfortable) and Angelina Jolie (effectively salt of the earth), but he comes back to just her talking to the camera in the build-up toward the end, where she tries to justify her own life with a flurry of self-deceptions and selfish reasoning. The writing gets itself into a bit of a muddle at this point, mainly because Shawn has gone so far out on a limb that there's no way he can possibly resolve the issues he has brought up. And so he reaches for and ends on a more existential kind of dread, where Redgrave's entitled Woman breaks down and starts to wonder if a person's beliefs really matter at all.

*The Fever* offers a very nuanced examination of Redgrave's lifelong empathetic impulse, her feeling that everyone is the same, and by the end of the play, and the film, it feels like non-selfishness is a dilemma that can only be shaken off by retreating back into self-justifying lies. Redgrave beautifully balances all of the ideas here and purifies them through her own glowing sense of purpose, so that this version of *The Fever* has more solid hope than Shawn might have intended, and that's not a bad thing.

Speaking about working with his mother, Nero said, "It was very natural and straightforward because we both have mutual respect. I certainly have respect for my mother not only for her work as an actress or an artist but also for her incredible campaign for human rights. So really, I myself take a very keen interest in these issues. It was an intense collaboration. We listened to each other. We're really all part of something bigger than ourselves; that's how natural it felt, not to say that there weren't difficulties along the way. It's not always strawberries and cream, but we kept focused on the objective."

# The Year of
# Magical Thinking

n *The Keeper: The Legend of Omar Khayyam* (2005), a preachy film about the Muslim oral tradition of storytelling, Redgrave appears briefly, unflatteringly photographed, and croakingly lingers over some lines of Khayyam's *Rubaiyat*. It was directed by a young Iranian-born lawyer from Houston, Texas, Kayvan Mashayekh, who spent many years trying to get the movie together. Some of the film's grosses went to a children's charity. For Redgrave, it was basically acting as social work.

More than an hour into *Life Is a Buffet* (2005), also known as *Short Order* in Britain, Redgrave is seen from the back at a bar, drinking and smoking a cigarette, and she does a monologue about a fool who wanted to be immortal and was in some Vincent van Gogh paintings. The writing isn't much, but Redgrave is riveting with it, opening up her face and punctuating pauses with her haunted blue eyes. The camera lingers over her gorgeous, delicately lined face and long hair as she smokes and talks in her halting, slightly absent, croaky voice. It's just magic. Redgrave has never done anything quite so glamorous as this small bit at a bar; in this movie, she touches some of the sexual allure of the mature Jeanne Moreau.

Redgrave has been a serious smoker for most of her life, which is why her voice lowered so precipitously. As a young woman, she said she liked to smoke "for the pleasure of the moment when the match produces friction and flame." But later on in life she fretted about this pleasure. "It sets a bad example, and I hate to be a bad example," she said. "I'm an absolute addict. I only started smoking because I read a newspaper article when I was twenty-four in which Françoise Sagan was asked what she had for breakfast. What did she have? A cup of black coffee and a Gauloise." Drawn to the sound of that, Redgrave picked up smoking and never stopped.

Vanessa and Lynn joined in support of Natasha Richardson in the Merchant Ivory film *The White Countess* (2005), a poky, old-fashioned costume piece about stranded former Russian aristocrats. It was shot on a low budget in Shanghai. Asked about working with Vanessa and Lynn, Richardson said, "I loved it. I just wish we'd had more to do together. I think we all felt we were up against it a bit, so there was a wonderful sense of camaraderie. We have the same vocabulary and the same sense of humor, so the few weeks they were there it was so lovely to be together and work together, then go back to the hotel at the end of the day and eat Chinese food and drink wine and talk about the next day's work."

Vanessa enjoyed finally getting to go to China. "I had an invitation to go there on a cultural exchange in 1967, but I didn't get there—I changed my mind in Moscow," she said. "I thought—but it was a delusion on my part— that I could save my marriage if I went back to Italy, where my husband was. So I missed China to save my marriage, but I didn't save my marriage. But that was okay, because we loved each other to the end."

Playing a woman forced to work in a dance hall, Richardson has striking moments of fragility, and at one point, when she cries, her nose runs for quite a while, just as Vanessa's did in that endless close-up in *Camelot.* Lynn does an expert portrait of a character bound up in hard, unforgiving pragmatism while Vanessa hovers in the background most of the time, letting Lynn dominate as she did in *What Ever Happened to Baby Jane?* But Vanessa has one scene that shows her full talent. In bed one night, her head covered with a cloth, her character talks about visiting the consulate. It's imperative, she says, that she wear her one remaining sign of position, an expensive hat. In the consulate she swans right in and the hat has transformed this broken woman back into a grand dowager. All she needed to become Russian royalty again was to put on this hat. Magic again. Great acting.

During a soundcheck for an interview about the film for NPR, Vanessa intoned, "I have no feedback" in her oracular voice, and Lynn joked, "You *are* a superior being!" Asked about their current relationship, Vanessa said, "We can talk to each other very intimately about whatever is on our minds." Lynn reminisced:

> When I was a little girl, Vanessa was a dream sister. She'd make me little toys out of a shoebox, almost like a stage set, with little windows, and illustrated little books for my dolls. I remember one Christmas, I collected little glass animals . . . and Vanessa was given a very beautiful, long-legged sort of Bambi. And I went in carrying my little collection of glass animals, and I went into her bedroom and sort of skirted around the subject of deep envy for her Bambi. And she gave it to me. And then I dropped it. And I've never forgotten this, because she was so kind and so dear about it. I knew she loved her Bambi too, but she knew it meant so much to me that she gave it to me. I feel like we've come back to that sisterhood we had as quite young children. This became particularly true three years ago when I was diagnosed with breast cancer, and much of my recovery from that was due to Vanessa.

In 2005, Redgrave played in Euripides's *Hecuba* in a production for the Royal Shakespeare Company, her first work with them in some forty years. She did it in London and then at the Kennedy Center and then at the Brooklyn Academy of Music, and she saw the play as relevant to the loss of habeas corpus during America's so-called war on terror.

Reviewing her in London, Michael Billington wrote, "Redgrave is very good at grief and supplication—as she kneels before Odysseus begging for her daughter's life, she tugs at the heart. But the difficulty with Euripides' play is that it requires Hecuba, after discovering her son has been killed by his Thracian protector Polymestor, to turn from victim to tyrant. It is a switch that tests the mettle of any actor, and one Redgrave simply fails to make. In the play, Hecuba, aided by the Trojan women, blinds Polymestor and kills his two sons. But Redgrave, even as she stands over the children's corpses, suggests less a gloating infanticide than a dismayed district nurse. Where Clare Higgins, who played Hecuba at the Donmar, was monotonous in grief but outstanding in revenge, Redgrave is the precise opposite."

When she played it at the Kennedy Center, Peter Marks wrote in the *Washington Post*: "Redgrave's bearing is an asset here. Is there any actress more persuasive as royalty? Hers is a vigorous physical performance. Taller than almost everyone else onstage, she bends and twists and folds her body in grief: truly, a great personage brought low."

Responding to her *Hecuba* at BAM, Howard Kissel in the *New York Daily News* found that he did not like the translation: "Tony Harrison, the British poet who adapted *Hecuba*, often uses modern turns of phrase, which undercut the tragic mood. Moreover, he has politicized it. The Greeks are referred to as 'the coalition.' (Get it?) And the vengeful Trojans at one point are called 'terrorists.'" Michael Feingold in the *Village Voice* was not impressed by Redgrave's "throaty, toneless muttering of the title role."

Reading her theater reviews of the last thirty or so years, many of the less specific notices merely iterate the fact that Redgrave is a great actress and say little about her actual performance. She reached a point very early where her reputation as an actress was practically unassailable, and many critics never bother to judge what she is actually doing and achieving and not achieving in certain roles.

Speaking about *Hecuba* to CNN, Redgrave said, "I think the point today, whatever anyone's views about the war, I think that the main issue is justice. What is the basis of democracy? It is access to law, it is the rule of law, it is the upholding of judicial review. It is the upholding of habeas corpus.

"The only way that you can find out if someone has committed an evil act is to charge them and put them on trial," Redgrave said. "That's the only way that humanity has found, and it's found some major progressive steps along the way and America led the way on that. And that is why millions of people looked to America and should be able to continue to look to America for that.

"How can there be democracy if the leadership in the United States and Britain don't uphold the values [for] which my father's generation fought the Nazis, [and] millions of people gave their lives against the Soviet Union's regime, didn't they?" she said. "Because of what? Democracy. And what democracy meant. No torture, no camps, no detention forever or without trial, without charges. In solitary confinement. Those techniques which are not just alleged, they have actually been written about by the FBI. I don't think it's being far left—I hope that I'm wrong to consider that it's far left to uphold the rule of law."

She told her interviewer Bob Costas that she had one big role she would like to attempt: "I would like to play Constance in *King John*. That's another play in which the playwright, Mr. Shakespeare, has expressed his horror at what war does to people."

Costas asked her an important question on this broadcast: "Do you accept the notion that even though the settlements and other aspects of Israeli policy are subject to dispute, those policies were undertaken in response to Arab and Palestinian aggression and terrorism, and if the Israelis could be sure that would go away, they would roll it back to pretty much the pre-'67 borders?"

Redgrave answered, "We have seen quite clearly, let alone what my Israeli friends who lead the fight for human rights for the Palestinians and in Israel, we have seen that the Israeli people want peace, and they have voted many times that the Palestinians should have their rights and land and we know that the Palestinians have a right to that. I think we have to look at some of the very important judgments that the Israeli high court and international high courts have made on the question of this wall and so on. Hopefully a number of politicians are going to try and make sure and the media can help in that, of course, by helping publicize the efforts and the actual words of people who are striving for peace. I hope very much that both the Israelis and the Palestinians will have their rights and will have peace, but again, you have to have the rule of law."

Her opinions on recent films were eccentric, to say the least. "It's one of the greatest films I have ever seen," she proclaimed of *Meet the Fockers* (2004). "Brilliant acting, brilliant script, brilliant story. I think it should have won the Academy Awards last March, with all respect to all the films that did get it. Comedy is the most difficult of anything to do and [it is] a brilliant comedic story that has all sorts of insights to what goes on in our world and what goes on in families and what goes on in individuals. I thought all of them were brilliant." She admitted, "I am fixated on the Fockers."

Redgrave's appetite for stage work was still keen even if her energy for it might have been flagging, and she had not forgotten political engagement, of course. In 2005, while playing in *Hecuba* and doing small roles in films, she formed the Peace and Progress Party with Corin, but it was clearer than ever that such things were mainly theatrical gestures toward change. Still and all, she was willing to support and even, in some instances, bail out of jail detainees at Guantanamo Bay, which she repeatedly called "a concentration camp."

In a long interview of this time for the *Observer*, a paper that had been her nemesis in the past, Lynn Barber wrote about Redgrave in the harsh tone that seems to be a dominant mode of the British press, but she actually managed to get something different out of Redgrave. Barber did not approach her in the credulous and sometimes-sycophantic way journalists had been listening to her in recent years. This interview had conflict and drama and offered much insight into Redgrave.

"Journalists usually describe Vanessa Redgrave's flat in Chiswick, west London, as 'modest,' which made me expect some dismal shoe-box," wrote Barber. "Actually it is quite large and very prettily decorated with good antiques and also, when I went, dozens of fabulous flower arrangements sent for her sixty-ninth birthday. There is a big, almost country, kitchen at the back that is obviously equipped for serious cooking. The whole place feels more cheerful than I expected. But it is 'modest' in London property price terms and therefore proof, if any were needed, that she puts her money where her mouth is—into political causes."

Barber noticed that Redgrave was limping because she was waiting for a second hip replacement; this operation delayed the opening of *Hecuba* in London. When Barber said that it must be daunting coming into the Redgrave family in any way, Vanessa replied, "Well, you never know, do you? I mean from my point of view I always think how nice it must be to know us! Because we're fun." Barber was skeptical: "Are they?" she wrote.

"I must say it never in a million years occurred to me that the Redgraves might be fun—I always pictured them weeping and raging and arguing and making each other sign petitions.

"I keep trying to make her smile because she looks lovely when she smiles," Barber wrote, "but it is uphill work: she seems to think it is her duty to be serious. . . . Politics seems to be her default setting—you can ask a question on almost any subject and she will veer off into the plight of the Chechens, the Bosnians, the Iraqis—so many people, so many plights, I lose track and occasionally wonder if she does, too."

At this point the interview became a kind of one-act play where Redgrave was confronted with her lifelong fear: ordinary, provincial self-interest. Barber wrote: "I tell her: 'I know it's very frivolous and bad of me, but . . .' and she chuckles, 'Well, be frivolous and bad if you want to be!' 'But,' I continue, 'you have to realize that there are selfish people like me who just don't care about the rest of the world.' She is genuinely shocked: 'You're not one of them! Are you one of them? I don't think so.' 'Yes, I am,' I insist. 'I don't care what's happening in Kosovo, I really don't. I care a lot about what happens to my family and friends, so I'm not entirely selfish. But I sometimes think it's easier to worry about people on the other side of the world than to worry about people you know.' She is obviously hurt, and says, almost tearfully, 'Well, obviously that's how it seems to you. I don't find any of it easier.' She seems so distressed that I apologize, but she urges me on—'It's all right. It's okay. Don't worry.'—even while she dabs her eyes."

And then Barber asked the big question. She asked Redgrave if she regretted her involvement with Gerry Healy. Redgrave considered this seriously for a moment. And then she said, "Hmm. You really are pitching in the whole bag, aren't you? I never, ever regret what I have learned and I've learned from many people. I learned about history from Gerry Healy to a depth and precision that I would never have done otherwise." When pressed about Healy further by Barber, Redgrave got angry and said, "I won't discuss this anymore." Healy was obviously a touchy subject. Even at this late date, she could still never admit to herself or anyone else just how bad he had been.

Mainly, she said, her political focus was now channeled safely into her role as a UNICEF ambassador, a link to her old fellow ballet student

Audrey Hepburn. "I do believe that good theater is essential for keeping society human and humane and sane," she said. "I came to realize that in Sarajevo—that the arts are fundamental to human existence and human resistance and to keeping humanity and saving children." Barber sneered at that: "It is as if she can never allow herself to say, 'I do this because I like it, because I'm good at it'—everything has to be for the greater good of humanity. It is infuriating but, I suppose, by now incurable." Barber's blatant admitted selfishness is a bridge too far, but Redgrave's incessant search for suffering in the world is a bridge too far in the other direction. This collision between their two extreme viewpoints was as revealing of Redgrave as any interview, or even any role, she has ever done.

Redgrave took a split-second job as a bug-eyed nun in the children's film *The Thief Lord* (2006), the sort of non-part that can only have been meant to pay the bills. Given a small amount of screen time as Peter O'Toole's abandoned wife in *Venus* (2006), Redgrave seizes the opportunity to act with the lyric O'Toole and makes strong, bold choices to fill in the sketch of her part. She wears black, squarish glasses and a loose, cozy sweater; when she lets O'Toole into her home, she's holding a cat in one hand and a cane in another. He goes into her kitchen to cook them some food, and she shouts that he's on television (he's playing an elderly actor). Looking at the image of O'Toole's younger self in an old movie, Redgrave's wife character marvels at how handsome he once was. The camera takes in O'Toole's stung reaction.

"And there's that woman who took you away from us," she says, as an actress comes on her TV screen. He says that their food is burning, and she turns back to him violently and says, "You will burn, Maurice!" emphasizing each word for maximum weight. After this outburst, she looks slightly out of breath, as if she knows she's gone too far but she can't resist the urge to stick it to him. Later she will hold his head when he bows it in sadness in her kitchen. After his funeral, she gives the young girl he was semi-courting a venomous look. This is barely a performance, just a few stray pieces of dialogue and opening for movement that Redgrave takes up and fuses together into a totally convincing, troubling portrait of a limited first wife filled with unreasoning anger.

Off-screen she reunited with Franco Nero and participated in a commitment ceremony where he placed a ring on her finger. "It just seemed a wonderful thing to make our own particular commitment and exchange rings," she said. "We danced and had a bonfire and fireworks and exchanged rings and everybody brought a gift, a poem, a dance, a piece of music."

They weren't legally married because Redgrave wanted to "stay clear of all the money business," but Nero had waited for her, in his way, for thirty-five years, and now he finally got her for keeps. "I think I'm terribly lucky, terribly lucky," Redgrave said. "We had never really separated. We had plenty of times when we weren't speaking to each other or when we were shouting at each other. Mostly the worst times were when we were not speaking to each other."

But now Redgrave accepted the love of this simple and beautiful man, a man who salved some of her rougher edges and complications. Her rekindled love for Nero was taken up as a heartwarming story by the press. This was a facet of Redgrave's sense of romance that appealed to a wide audience, unlike many of her political stances. "We did it the best way possible, in my view," she said. "Which is that you don't enter into a legal agreement, which I think spells trouble." Her face would soften with happiness when she spoke of Nero. "After forty years, you know who you love and respect," she told *60 Minutes*. "And I do love and respect him very much."

"When you rediscover love, it's even stronger," Nero said. "It's not physical anymore, it's something deep." Speaking for herself at this point, Redgrave said, "You're not impatient to turn somebody into something they're not. You just love them for who they are." They had not mellowed, though. "We fight every moment—but in a nice way!" Nero said.

"Our kind of marriage ceremony wasn't the kind people consider to be normal, which I consider to be abnormal," Redgrave said. "It was a personal pledge, which was lovely. We have no other commitment to each other. We know that we love each other and that's not going to change."

She appeared on TV in *The Shell Seekers* (2006), based on the Rosamunde Pilcher romance novel, which had previously been filmed in 1989 with Angela Lansbury. Once again, Redgrave was praised in reviews while the production itself came in for negative appraisals. In 2007 on Broadway, Redgrave took on a 90-minute one-woman show based on Joan Didion's *The Year of Magical Thinking*, a memoir about the loss of her husband, John Gregory Dunne.

After her book was published, Didion also lost her daughter Quintana in 2005. For the play version of the book for Redgrave, Didion added a final segment about her daughter's death. The producer Scott Rudin first approached Didion and persuaded her to make the best-selling book into a play, and he approached Redgrave's daughter Natasha and told her that he wanted Vanessa to do this part. Natasha immediately called her mother and told her, and Redgrave slowly accepted this responsibility.

"I was working for Daryl Roth, who was producing *The Year of Magical Thinking* with Vanessa," says James Grissom. "I was down in Chelsea, and this spectral image came at me, like something out of *A Christmas Carol*, and I thought, 'Which ghost is this?' It was Vanessa. She was dressed like she was ready to do *Mother Courage*. Walking around lost, like a stoned person. It was like if a bird flew over her she would go, 'Oh, look . . . a bird. . . .'"

"Vanessa is vaporous," Grissom says. "She'll say, 'I'll be in New York in November,' and you'll ask, 'When?' and she'll say she'll be in New York in November four years from now. I always wanted to talk to her about her work, but she's famous for saying, 'I don't remember.' It could be something incredible, but she'll say she doesn't remember."

Speaking of collaborating with Didion, director David Hare said, "We agreed on most things, but most of all on the casting. The literal-minded may have found it hard to understand why we wanted Vanessa Redgrave. She's so tall, they said. She's so English. But Vanessa had long been part of Joan's life, a country member at least of the Malibu club. She understood the territory. I mean no disrespect to any American when I say we cast the actor we knew would perform the play best, the one with the most profound access to the feelings of the character and a consummate flair for the phrasing of the words."

"Somewhat late in the process, we asked ourselves why the play had been written at all," Hare said. "We were sitting in the Booth Theatre, probably at an afternoon rehearsal during the preview period, watching

Vanessa up on the stage telling us once more about her moody Irish husband and her beautiful, volatile daughter. The author and director had one of those psychic moments at which two people think the same thing. Joan pointed one of her spidery fingers at the stalls. 'Wouldn't this be better,' she asked, 'if it were less about me? And more about them?' Next day, she inserted the blazing admonishment with which the play opens."

Didion's play begins with these words: "This happened on December 30, 2003. That may seem a while ago but it won't when it happens to you. And it will happen to you. The details will be different, but it will happen to you." Redgrave delivered them simply, and they had an almost menacing effect, but, as in *Long Day's Journey*, she showed all her cards at once, so that there was nowhere left to go afterward, no layers to be unpeeled.

There was a disconnect in sensibility between Didion's small-scale, elliptical prose persona and Redgrave's epic romantic size. Didion's writing about politics has often been cool and conservative. She famously wrote in *Slouching Towards Bethlehem*, "If I could believe that going to a barricade would affect man's fate in the slightest I would go to that barricade, and quite often I wish that I could, but it would be less than honest to say that I expect to happen upon such a happy ending." Redgrave, of course, has practically lived at those barricades all her life.

"I remember saying to David Hare, 'I'm not supposed to be playing her, am I, because I don't see how I could possibly?'" Redgrave said. "And he said: 'No way.'" She told the TV program *Theater Talk*, "I'm like a violin, and David and Joan are playing me." John Lahr wrote in the *New Yorker* that seeing her play Didion was "rather like seeing a falcon impersonate a sparrow."

"Even sitting on a chair with hands folded, Vanessa Redgrave looks like she's just come down from Olympus," wrote Jeremy McCarter in *New York Magazine*. "Silver-haired, wearing an off-white blouse and gray skirt, she seems otherworldly: placid as stone and spectral as a ghost. When she speaks in *The Year of Magical Thinking* . . . she often has a faraway, distracted look: It's like she's bringing bad news from Delphi."

Redgrave approached Didion and her text with reverence. "Once in a while, I've suggested perhaps we might not need one line," she said. "I pose it very hesitantly, as I would if I were talking to Ibsen." Redgrave also likened Didion to Virgil and Shakespeare.

"For me the whole motor force of the play is that Joan is in enormous fear and panic as to whether she will be able to save her daughter's life when her daughter's father isn't there to support her," Redgrave said. She felt that this play about grief would touch all the people in the audience who had lost someone.

There were four films in 2007, none of which made good use of Redgrave. The best that can be said of her role as a villainous media tycoon in the Vinnie Jones thriller *The Riddle* is that it only required her to play two scenes. Former football star Jones said, "Vanessa Redgrave is the business. She asked me to be a patron of her charity afterwards, and I agreed. Only I can't remember what the charity is called." *How About You* cast Redgrave as a bitchy, racist former actress in an old-age home who's given to wearing turbans. There's a scene in front of a mirror where another character trims her nose hairs, and at this point it's best to "draw the veil," as Ruth Gordon used to say.

*Evening* was a sentimental movie version of Susan Minot's much darker novel. Redgrave spends most of her scenes in bed, dying majestically, while Claire Danes plays out her character's youth in flashback. Her daughter Natasha played her daughter on screen. "Seeing her lying on that bed, in that room, I mean, she was heartbreaking to look at anyway," Richardson said. "There were times it was very, very hard to hold it together, because it does make you think of all those things, projecting to the future and thinking back to the past. It made me think of the moment my father was dying. I'm sure she was thinking about how it was when her mom passed away, a couple of years before."

Natasha spoke very insightfully about her mother's gifts: "What's always different about my mother is that there's always something unexpected about her work, because she's sort of fearless. She loves to take so many risks in her work, and sometimes it doesn't work as well because she takes that risk. But when she hits it, then it sort of is just incandescent."

Asked about her relationship with her mother, Richardson said, "There was a period of her life when she was very politically active, and that took her away from us. It's a difficult subject to talk about because I know it's something that she regrets very much now, that all that came before her children. But her children have entirely forgiven her, because she is a great mother."

As Manohla Dargis noticed in her *New York Times* review, it doesn't seem like Danes and Redgrave could possibly be the same person, for Danes twitches with discomfort throughout, whereas Redgrave "gives the impression that she'd rather swallow a grand piano than surrender the spotlight." Redgrave got to share a scene with Meryl Streep, whose own daughter Mamie Gummer played Streep's character as a young woman. "I just had the one scene, and I was nervous again," Streep said. "It was something to me. I think about it. I still think about it."

As the "Older Briony" in the costume movie *Atonement*, Redgrave was asked to play a small role much like her father Michael's stunted part in *The Go-Between* (1971), and she approached her concluding monologue with honest, if unrewarded, feeling. "I always had Vanessa in mind because I worship the water she walks on," said director Joe Wright.

Teased about the little-girl hairstyle that characterized the young Briony (Saoirse Ronan), the eighteen-year-old Briony (Romola Garai), and Redgrave's Briony at seventy, Wright joked, "The hair, well, you know, I mean, it's an extraordinary feat of Briony's to be able to maintain that hairstyle for seventy years, especially in this day and age, but, er, she did!" Describing her character, Redgrave said, "It is her story as she sees it, as she wants to remember it, as she doesn't want to remember it, as she wishes she didn't have to remember it."

Redgrave was billed as "Sky News reader #2" in an Australian thriller starring Travis Fimmel called *Restraint*. The film was shot in 2005 but only released in 2008. Supposedly she played a radical anarchist named Hannah in a German TV film called *Ein Job* (2008). The film's language is listed as German, so presumably she acted in this language. She is also credited in a 2008 Swedish movie called *Gud, lukt och henne*, which translates as *God, Smell and Her*. It's at a point like this that even the most zealous Vanessa-phile has to be stopped in their tracks for a breath and a "huh?"

Redgrave played *The Year of Magical Thinking* again in 2008 at the National Theatre in Britain. Talking about doing this play about grief again, she said, "It is always wonderful coming back after a good big gap," she said. "The only analogy I can think of is when in your life you reconsider some period and suddenly see it in a different light, so you are seeing things you didn't see at the time, which can only be beneficial. Whether one likes it or not."

After the death of her mother, she had been given three performances off in *Long Day's Journey Into Night*, which she felt was "monumentally understanding" of the producers. When asked if she used her grief in her work, Redgrave said, "You are not playing yourself, so the object of the exercise is to put yourself into someone else's shoes. But of course, stepping into someone else's shoes often kicks off memories. That is what happens to an audience in a play—they are assisted in stepping into other people's shoes. And if the play is really good, they start thinking about themselves in their own shoes."

Speaking to Charlie Rose about the process of collaborating on *The Year of Magical Thinking*, Didion said that Redgrave had to be quicksilver in her emotional changes, and Redgrave likened it to skiing, though she said she had only skied once in her life. "But there are rocks and trees and things like that, and once you start, you have to negotiate and you have to be thinking very fast," she said. "The difference of course with skiing is that you're alert on a journey, and you carry inside you all the different zigzags of this journey. . . . David crafted this work with Joan so wonderfully, and we were all working together."

Redgrave said that she was very careful about Didion's all-important sentence rhythms; even an extra "and" or "the," she said, would throw these rhythms off. She described her own experience of death, having lost Tony Richardson and others. "But I have not, thank God, lost one of my daughters or sons."

She spoke of how some societies allow for extended periods of grief, but many modern societies do not. "Circumstances don't allow you to," Redgrave said. "I have lost quite a lot of people very close to me and it was always at a time when I felt I couldn't break the commitments I had made."

# Natasha

Redgrave's daughter Natasha Richardson had been closer to her father Tony for most of her childhood. Natasha saw herself as "a caregiver" to him, and often cooked for his large parties (cooking would always be a major interest of hers). "She would literally go down to the market at St. Tropez, bring back boxes of food, and suddenly there would be roast lamb and potatoes for thirty people," said Fiona Lewis, a friend of the family. Natasha was comfortable talking to all of the adults around. "She was never considered childlike in any way," Lewis said.

Tony Richardson's social life often seemed to be one long party, and he enjoyed not just party games but staging theatricals. He once did a production of *Gypsy* at home with a young Joely in the title role. The young Natasha played Mama Rose after the Milanese transvestite who was going to play the part developed laryngitis.

As a little girl, like Vanessa, Natasha wanted to be a ballerina. "I was always dressing up in fancy dress, and I loved visiting movie sets," she said. "For me, it was like going to Disneyland, seeing my mother in wonderful costumes and my father directing." After her parents divorced, she dreamed of getting them back together. "I remember thinking when

I was seven or eight, if I save up all my pocket money and send red roses to my mother, pretending they're from my dad, would that do the trick?"

Natasha later spoke of a crucial exchange with her mother. "When I was about ten or eleven I said to my mother, 'Is my Papa gay?'" Richardson remembered. "She said yes. I remember being very upset by that . . . it was completely a closed door. It was something he never talked about. . . . It was a strange mixture of being very private about it but public too. It's very hard to explain. It's not as easy as somebody being in the closet because he didn't hide it." Asked about gayness and complicated sexuality, Richardson laughed and said, "It seems to run in my family!"

When she wasn't with her father as a girl, and with Vanessa off campaigning for the WRP, Richardson dreamed of a more settled existence. At the age of ten, her favorite TV show was *The Waltons*, a series about an ideal family life. She was left very much alone, taking care of things for herself and her sister Joely with the aid of a nanny, and as a teenager she took to overeating a bit and became insecure about her appearance. Natasha would look after Vanessa just as well as she did her father. "Who's the mom and who's the daughter in that family can get to be a perplexing business," said agent Sam Cohn.

After her mother's speech at the Academy Awards in 1978, Richardson took some flak. "I remember being in a physics class at school and a kid pointed at me and said, 'Your mother is a Commie,'" Richardson said. "I ran away and collapsed in tears. I've never been tough in that way. It hurt." And her mother was unable to console her daughter. "Her focus seemed to be elsewhere, on the politics, which seemed to me to be the very thing causing the problem," Richardson said. "It was painful, but we've since worked it out between us. And I respect her."

When both of Vanessa's daughters entered into the family business, they got opposing messages at first. "We didn't have to be actresses," Joely Richardson said. "Mum begged my sister and me not to be actors. She said, 'Please be anything but.' And my father was direct. He said, 'Act!' So we had two different role models."

As a father Richardson took the same tough approach to his daughter Natasha as he always had when he was acting as a mentor to Redgrave. "You've got a lovely voice and a lovely quality on stage, but that isn't good enough," Richardson told his daughter when he saw her perform in *A Midsummer Night's Dream*. "I'm going to mark up a copy of the script, which I want you to read, think about, and get to work." This hurt Natasha's feelings at first. "I was just devastated," she said. "I thought, 'How cruel can you be.' In retrospect, it was the kindest, best thing anyone had ever done for me. I did study his notes, and by the end of the run, my performance was entirely different."

She studied at the Central School of Speech and Drama, just as her mother had, and she made her professional debut with her mother in *The Seagull* in 1985. "I don't know if at the time I was ready for it," Richardson said later. "At the time I was so terrified of the whole nepotism thing. I hated being thought of as just my mother's daughter, as well as being intimidated by her as an actress because she is such a great actress."

When her father came to see her in that play, which he had also directed Redgrave in years before, "he was just sort of beaming afterwards," Natasha said, "and so effusive in his praise that I knew it was really meant, coming not only from a father that I loved, but a director whom I totally respected. You know, when you look at the body of my father's work, not all of his films were great, but some were downright brilliant, and almost always, the performances were top-notch. John Gielgud credited my dad with teaching him to act on screen."

Natasha also said that she learned a lot from her mother's example. "She's just totally inspiring because she's one of the greatest actresses that's ever lived," Richardson said. "Her absolute dedication to the pursuit of truth and her emotional life and her transparency. I learned an approach to work through her, which helped me, which was reading Stanislavsky for the first time, which was the key that opened the door for me. So I owe her an enormous amount."

There were expectations placed on Richardson as Vanessa Redgrave's daughter. "I think it was particularly difficult in terms of my mom, because of other people's perceptions when I was starting out," Richardson said, "because you want to quietly work away and make your own name and place for yourself. Having a famous parent can sometimes result in a level of attention you feel that you don't deserve and you don't want, and comparisons, so it was [like] carrying a card around your neck for a while." She felt that actors were born, not made. "I do think that acting's a vocation," she said. "It's something you don't have a choice in. When I hear people say 'I want to be an actor,' I always think 'Well, if you are one, you will be.'

"The last thing you want is to ride any coattails, because you don't want people to be accusing you of nepotism," Richardson said. "You want to be able to learn and practice, and not to be thrown into a spotlight before you're ready for it. It's tough to be compared to a great actress and a great beauty. It makes you feel very inadequate, really." Richardson sometimes found auditioning tough-going. Some directors would see her, she said, for the sole purpose of "treating a Redgrave like shit."

Asked about the idea of a Redgrave family dynasty, Richardson was blunt: "I love my family and I feel privileged to come from it. But sometimes there's an idea that it's like royalty in some way. What a load of crap. We're a family of working actors. It's like coming from a family of carpenters or plumbers who work in the family business, generation after generation, that's all. Because it's acting it makes it more public, but we're worker bees, not royalty lying back on the couch. It's a really tough profession that has big perks and big privileges, but you also have to constantly expose yourself to rejection, criticism, and humiliation."

After a few television appearances, Richardson made her proper film debut as Mary Shelley in *Gothic* (1986), a typical Ken Russell biographical extravagance, small and silly, but enough to give an impression of how well she held the screen. Tony Richardson called it "a terrible film which Natasha survived, miraculously."

It was in two films for director Paul Schrader, *Patty Hearst* (1988), about the kidnapping and brainwashing of the American heiress by the Symbionese Liberation Army in the early 1970s, and *The Comfort of Strangers* (1990), an adaptation of an Ian McEwan novel, that Richardson did her finest work on screen.

"When I first met Natasha, while casting *Patty Hearst*, I was quite simply dazzled by her," said Schrader. "Not just her beauty and lineage, both undeniable, but by her intelligence and fearlessness. She was very talented and very smart. I told her she'd won me over, but now we'd have to win over the producers and backers, since she had never had the lead in a film before. So we did a screen test—and that was that. It was clear that she was the actress for the role."

In the first moments of *Patty Hearst*, we hear Richardson's voice on the soundtrack saying, "There's little to prepare you for the unknown," and then we see a montage of photos of young Patty and photos of her growing up. This opening of the film has a tabloid kind of thrust to it, but once Patty is kidnapped and subjected to Maoist mind-control conditioning, the film retreats into a spare, locked-down style entirely from her point of view.

For the first third or so of *Patty Hearst*, Schrader puts us in Patty's position, locked in a closet with almost no light and air while confusing revolutionary rhetoric is hurled at her. Patty sleeps constantly, her body giving up, and we start to feel what it might be like to be brainwashed and broken down over a long period of time. Whenever she is out of the closet, Patty is blindfolded, and the group forces her to do things like push-ups and firing guns with the blindfold on. Finally she hears, "Take your clothes off, Patty," and her sexual servitude begins. At this point Richardson's Patty has retreated into total passivity.

Schrader's choice to film everything from Patty's perspective in the first third is a risk that starts to pay off once we see her become a revolutionary named Tania; at this point, we viscerally understand that she has no choice in the matter. And it is also at this point that Richardson is allowed to take over, filling in Patty's emptiness with a kind of feral nihilism hovering above a kind of wasted flatness of affect—when told to smile, her attempt is chilling.

Patty ventures even further into nihilism when she realizes that no one from the outside is even trying to help her: "They didn't even try to take us alive," she says in horror after one of the group's criminal jobs (Richardson employs the twanging American accent that her mother used in *Isadora*, and it suits this character). Patty realizes that no one cares for her, and her world has narrowed to a life with no options at all. She just sort of hangs around, solitary, going through the motions as Tania.

When the FBI arrests Patty, she pees her pants, and when they insist on accompanying her to change them, the film makes a connection between the Symbionese Liberation Army and law enforcement. For Patty Hearst, getting caught was just moving from one prison to another, and her lawyers are just as domineering as the members of the group who kidnapped her. When her mother and sisters visit her, Patty folds to the ground. Almost all of her memories are gone.

A battery of crude psychiatrists works Patty over, and she is convicted on robbery charges and does years of jail time. In her final scene, Patty says, "Fuck 'em, fuck them all," and Richardson refuses to lighten or vary the tone of this difficult role in order to give herself, or her audience, some relief. In this story, there is no relief. (Thankfully, John Waters has helped to give this very depressing tale a happy ending by casting a cheerfully revitalized Hearst in several of his films).

Richardson admitted that she only spoke to her mother at this point when they "were in the same place at the same time," and she added that Vanessa was "the actress I admire most in the world." After filming, Richardson met Hearst for lunch, and they found they had something in common. At one point Hearst exclaimed, "You don't know what it's like to be surrounded by ideologues twenty-four hours a day," and Richardson replied, "Yes, I do."

Two years later, in Schrader's *The Comfort of Strangers*, Richardson again offered a remarkably glamour-free study in passivity in a Hitchcock-like narrative. "I found the story and screenplay quite disturbing," Richardson said. "I like to do things because a story speaks to something inside me. This didn't do that." Schrader talked her into doing the project, which was scripted by Harold Pinter. "I really like working with Schrader and I thought, 'Well, hell, a Harold Pinter script, Schrader is going to direct, and it's got this great cast, and we're shooting in Venice,'" Richardson said. "I can't turn this down."

She found working with Pinter an exacting and mysterious process. "He's very precise in how he works," she said. "He wants you to stick to the script, and he doesn't work in a psychological way, which I do. When I'm playing a person, I have to feel what makes them tick, and I asked him to tell me the story of these people, why they got involved. Pinter said: 'I don't work that way, I've never worked that way and I'm not going to start now!' He gives you no clues."

In her two Schrader films, Richardson staked out a claim for herself as an actress of shy integrity. She knew that she would never escape the comparisons to her mother, and her reaction to this was both smart and intuitive—she found her own place as an actress by pursuing more subterranean emotions than her mother usually did. They were the kind of emotions, based in repression, that had been the chief characteristic of her grandfather Michael's work, and there are many links between Michael and Natasha, not least their common exposure of nerves and the more furtive varieties of human fragility, which run like supportive tributaries to Vanessa's huge gestures of empathy and imaginative leaping.

Richardson received a Tony nomination in 1993 and made a big success in a Roundabout Theatre revival of Eugene O'Neill's *Anna Christie*, another difficult role to put across in a difficult play. Part of the impact it had was due to the fact that she fell in love with her leading man, Liam Neeson, and their sexual chemistry charged and vitalized the old-fashioned material.

"Natasha Richardson . . . gives what may prove to be the performance of the season as Anna, turning a heroine who has long been portrayed (and reviled) as a whore with a heart of gold into a tough, ruthlessly unsentimental apostle of O'Neill's tragic understanding of life," wrote Frank Rich in the *New York Times*. "Yet Miss Richardson could not triumph without the sensitive partnering she receives from Liam Neeson.

"Miss Richardson, seeming more like a youthful incarnation of her mother, Vanessa Redgrave, than she has before, is riveting from her first entrance through a saloon doorway's ethereal shaft of golden light," wrote Rich. "Her face bruised, her eyelids heavy, her slender frame draped in the gaudy fabrics and cheap jewelry of her trade, she is the tattered repository of a thousand anonymous men's alcoholic lusts and fists."

Her director David Leveaux said, "The miracle is that Natasha Richardson *is* a great actress in the making. Sir Michael was great. Vanessa is great. It's very unlikely that you'd get another great one, not just a cheap imitation." In her dressing room, Richardson tacked up a print of Edvard Munch's painting *The Scream*. It gave her the feeling she needed to play Anna Christie.

Richardson was married at the time to producer Robert Fox, brother of James and Edward, but she divorced him to marry Neeson. "It was not an easy time when I met Liam, because I was married," Richardson said. "And my marriage . . . things weren't good. So the timing of meeting Liam, working with him, what happened between us, and that becoming public knowledge in conjunction with my marriage falling apart, was kind of bad timing. So what can I say? Obviously I fell very much in love with him. And it is scary when someone has the reputation of everyone or a lot of women also falling in love with him. But I'm pleased that women fall in love with him, because I know why."

Neeson had been involved with several famous women without committing himself to them fully. "She pushed all the right buttons," Neeson said of Richardson. "Certain people push one or two. But she pushed buttons I didn't even know I had." In New York, Richardson felt more her own woman, and far freer of the long shadow of her family. She was married to Neeson in 1994, and they had children soon afterward. "I had my boys eighteen months apart," Richardson said. "Of course, we didn't plan on having back-to-back babies. But life almost never goes according to plan."

As Neeson's career in movies flourished, Richardson was able to joke, "I've spent half my life trying to get away from being Vanessa Redgrave's daughter, and now I've got to get away from being Liam Neeson's wife." They were a low-key couple. "It has been my choice to live under the radar," she said. "I recall, as a child, being chased with my mother by photographers after her separation from my father—and being very scared. So Liam and I fulfill our professional obligations, but don't want to take it further."

Her own career on film settled into fairly unrewarding roles as she raised her sons, but on stage was a different matter. In 1998, she had the greatest triumph of her career as Sally Bowles in a stage revival of *Cabaret*, again for the Roundabout, and won a well-deserved Tony for her work.

"You think you can do something in your imagination, and you have an empathy with it, but then I thought, 'I can't sing these songs,'" Richardson said. "I can dance with friends, but dancing on a stage is a whole other thing. . . . In this production, and my interpretation of her, she's a lost girl who's going down at the end, not a triumphant survivor."

It took her a while to get her nervy characterization set. "I didn't feel I was in control, and I felt very nervous and frightened," she said. "I had to find the confidence to play this part for an audience. I needed every single preview and more." Her mother came to a preview and gave her two key bits of advice: to look into people's faces in the audience and not the stage lights, and to treat Sally's fur coat as her most treasured possession. "She was absolutely right," Richardson said.

Working against the memory of Liza Minnelli's razzle-dazzle Sally in the Bob Fosse film of *Cabaret* (1972), Richardson returned this character to her outsider/loser roots in the original Christopher Isherwood source material, *The Berlin Stories*. Sally has an affair with the bisexual Clifford (John Benjamin Hickey). When asked about the relation of this material to the union of her parents, Richardson said that it "resonates in all sorts of ways, some of which I'm aware of, some of which I'm not. I mean, my dad never said to me, 'I'm gay,' or 'I'm bisexual.' Yet it was never a hidden thing. I don't know, is that denial or total openness?"

Richardson knew about her father's other life early. "I think I was about eleven when I found out, when it really hit home," Richardson said. "I'm ashamed enough to say that I was shocked and upset. Children don't want their parents to be different from all other parents."

Again the *New York Times* review said she gave "the performance of the season." She had reinvented Sally just as she had reinvented Anna Christie. In film that survives from that production, particularly in her last song, Richardson reaches out, with both clarity and rawness of emotion, for the terror that Michael brought to his "The Himmler of the Lower Fifth?" scene in *The Browning Version*. I didn't see Richardson live in *Cabaret*, but the footage of her performance that can be viewed sometimes on YouTube is enough to convince me of its bravery, its brute-force anger, and its completely ravaged vulnerability; her faltering "genteel" diction is particularly haunting. Sheila O'Malley, one of the best writers on acting today, wrote a tribute to Richardson in this play:

> In the final moments, as the pace of the song started to pick up, Richardson, violently trembling, started reaching her arms up and out to the light (only she could barely manage it because

of how much she was shaking: she looked incredibly thin and fragile), screaming, on tune, yes, but not pretty, nothing you want to listen to for pleasure, "Life is a cabaret, old chum/only a cabaret, old chum/and I love a cabaret." She held the last note, arms up, and as it went on and on, rasping, un-pretty, the wail of a woman who was swirling down never to emerge again, her face took on the look of the screaming figure in Edvard Munch's famous painting.

Richardson's film work continued in disappointingly trivial movies like *The Parent Trap* (1998) and *Maid in Manhattan* (2002), as if the randomness of her Aunt Lynn's career was creeping in. "I've had the opportunity on stage to play some incredible women," Richardson said. "But I feel I haven't had that part on film yet."

She played on stage in Patrick Marber's *Closer* in 1999, and in 2003 she took on her mother's favorite Ibsen role, *The Lady from the Sea*, with real success. There are certain plays that seem to just belong to this family: *As You Like It*, *Saint Joan*, and *The Seagull*, most definitely, but also *The Lady from the Sea*. Richardson, however, had deliberately avoided doing *As You Like It*. "The only part I didn't want to try was one my mother did, which was a very famous Rosalind in *As You Like It*," she said. "It was apparently one of those legendary performances in English theatrical circles where a glaze goes over the eyes, a hush over the room, when they talk of Vanessa Redgrave's Rosalind. I've always felt that that's one road I'm not going down."

In 2005, she offered her rather down-to-earth Blanche DuBois for the Roundabout Theatre in *A Streetcar Named Desire*, with John C. Reilly, a natural Mitch, miscast as her Stanley Kowalski. Blanche is an ideal role for Vanessa, which she never attempted, unfortunately. Vanessa would most likely have emphasized the part's most fantastical, moth-like qualities, whereas Richardson went as far in the opposite direction as she could. Her Blanche was sturdy and even sensible, a bit snooty, good-humored, trying to adapt to circumstances, and this approach worked until the character was meant to unravel completely. The final clash with Stanley had no impact, mainly because there had been no connection, sexual or otherwise, made between her Blanche and Reilly's Kowalski.

In January 2009, Richardson did a benefit performance with her mother of Stephen Sondheim's *A Little Night Music* that was meant to pave the way to a production of that musical. On March 16, 2009, Richardson fell on soft snow during a beginner's skiing lesson at the Mont Tremblant Resort in Quebec. She sustained an injury to her head. She laughed after falling and was lucid for a while after the accident, and so paramedics and ambulance were sent away and told they were not needed.

Richardson refused medical attention twice and returned to her hotel room. Three hours later, suffering with a headache, she was taken to a hospital in Saint-Agathe-des-Monts. She was then transferred, in critical condition, to a hospital in Montreal. This was about seven hours after the accident. From there, she was flown to Lenox Hill Hospital in New York, on life support. It's clear from all reports that the resort did everything to help Richardson, but she didn't realize the seriousness of her head injury until it was too late.

"Natasha is off skiing," Redgrave told her friend Loretta Brennan Glucksman the day before this happened. "I don't understand. She doesn't even like to ski." Redgrave was called to the hospital in New York. Before the life support was turned off, it was reported that Redgrave sang "Edelweiss" to her daughter, a song she had sung at Richardson's first wedding (this was later disputed by Joely Richardson). Redgrave briefly fainted. Richardson was pronounced dead on March 18. The cause was given as an "epidural hematoma due to blunt impact to the head." If she had been treated for this right away, doctors could have saved Richardson, but too much time had elapsed between the accident and treatment.

"I have been thinking about the times I spent with her since I heard the news of her tragic accident," said her co-star in *Cabaret*, Alan Cumming. "And the strongest memory I have is of her laughter, her unmistakable throaty laugh. I think that's a great way to remember someone."

In 2010, her cousin Jemma said, "Tasha lived her life to the full. She embraced every second of every day. She wrung the juice out of life. She celebrated friends and family. She was a centrifugal force, she kept us in contact. Relationships and friendships happened because of her. It was the way she lived her life, rather than the manner of her death, that taught me so much. She always had plans. She loved setting a dinner table. She was a mover and shaker."

After Richardson's death, Redgrave was scheduled to do a benefit performance of Didion's *The Year of Magical Thinking*, but it was postponed and then rescheduled for October 2009. "Instinctively you want to withdraw, but you know you have given your word and you must stick to it," she told the *Telegraph*. "The people you are working with are very understanding and very supportive in all sorts of ways. But it's very difficult."

Asked about performing this play after her loss, Redgrave said, "It seemed to me that I'd understood the role to the best of my ability at the time. But when I performed it after Natasha's death I realized I hadn't understood anything at all. This time it was completely different. I wouldn't do it again." Speaking of her lost daughter, Redgrave said, "Tash, she was the merriest. She was always more full of laughter than anyone else."

# On Top of the Mountain

On April 6, 2010, Corin Redgrave died of cancer. Less than a month later on May 2, 2010, Lynn Redgrave lost her long fight with breast cancer. These two deaths, coming so soon after the unexpected death of her daughter Natasha, placed a heavy burden on Vanessa, who was expected to promote the fluffy *Letters to Juliet* (2010), where she has a lot of screen time and gets to share some scenes at the end with her partner Franco Nero but mainly has to support the young star, Amanda Seyfried, hardly a rewarding task.

Corin had emerged again as an actor after his long time in revolutionary politics with a performance at the Young Vic as Shakespeare's Coriolanus in the late 1980s. He also won acclaim for his performance in Tennessee Williams's *Not About Nightingales*, which had a New York run in 1999. Vanessa herself had found that unproduced play while she was doing *Orpheus Descending*. "Corin is like a man who has suddenly decided to cultivate his garden, having let it run down," said Simon Callow, who appeared with Corin in the film *Four Weddings and a Funeral* (1994). "He's still a very clear and convinced Trotskyist. But whatever it is that has relaxed in him has enabled him to release all these possibilities."

His sister Lynn saw a change in Corin after so many years buried in the WRP and in the service of Gerry Healy. "I went to see him as Rosmer," Lynn said, speaking of a production of Ibsen's *Rosmersholm* in 1992, "and there were all those things again that he was so wonderfully as a young actor; suddenly, he was free."

"There was a period when Corin was blacklisted," Vanessa said. "There was a period when I was blacklisted. It's very frustrating if you can't get work and you're out of work. How do you pay your bills? It's not a question of frustration; it's a question of being demented." Vanessa's talent was so formidable, so majestic, that it could not long be buried by her politics. Corin didn't have that star quality she had, and so his talent was indeed buried as a man in his younger and middle years.

Asked in 1999 if he finally felt that he was in his prime, Corin sounded a lot like his mountain-climbing sister Vanessa when he said, "We shall see whether, after all, this is one of those plateaus where you've climbed a great height, and yet there's always something beyond. Hopefully, there's always something beyond." When his daughter Jemma had told Corin that she had decided not to join the Royal Shakespeare Company, he told her, "Oh well, always stand by your rotten decisions."

In 2005, Corin did a notable *King Lear* for the RSC. When he was thirteen, Corin had seen Michael play Lear: "I learned to love the sound of Shakespeare from my father," he said. "Like John Gielgud, he had an effortless command of the rhythms, cadences, and stresses of blank verse. But it was my mother who taught me to love Shakespeare's stories."

Corin also scored in one-man shows as Anthony Blunt, Kenneth Tynan, Oscar Wilde, and Dalton Trumbo, a quartet of men who expressed his own sharply divided artistic and personal character. A heart attack in 2005 had affected his short-term memory, so Corin read the Oscar Wilde show from a script. At his funeral, the very ill Lynn won some laughter when she told about how, when she was a girl, Corin had taught her how to climb trees but not how to get down from them.

Lynn had explored her relationship with Michael in a self-written one-woman show, *Shakespeare for My Father*, which played 274 performances on Broadway in the 1993/1994 season. At first Vanessa was afraid to go and see it, but she finally went about six months into the run and was deeply impressed. Backstage she told her little sister, "You gave me a window into your soul and also gave me a window into Dad's." Their mother Rachel was a big fan of the play, going to see it every Saturday night when Lynn played it in London.

In 2000, Lynn suffered much embarrassment when her long-time husband John Clark revealed that he had fathered a child with her personal assistant Nicolette Hannah, who had married and divorced their son Benjamin. But she rallied and won awards and acclaim for her 2003 Off-Broadway performance as Miss Fozzard in one of the monologues that made up Alan Bennett's *Talking Heads*. It provided an ideal role for the cheeky Lynn, who played a retiring sort who finds that she enjoys the attentions of her foot-fetishist podiatrist. She acted in this play while undergoing chemotherapy, and she said later that it was "doctor theater" for her. No matter how drained she felt before going on, when she hit that stage all her adrenaline came back to her. All during her fight with cancer, Lynn found a staunch ally in Vanessa, who comforted and took care of her sister whenever she could when they were both in New York.

Before her death, Lynn did another self-penned play about her family, *Nightingale*, about her maternal grandmother Beatrice, and she collaborated with her daughter Annabel on a book of photographs chronicling her chemotherapy. As she grew older, Lynn was as forthcoming as ever about everything in her life: chatty, warm, unguarded. As always, very much the opposite of Vanessa, who exists on some other, untouchable plane. She was buried in Saint Peter's Episcopal Cemetery, near her mother Rachel and her niece Natasha.

"I miss my sister very much," Redgrave said. "She and I were very close. We were more or less the same age, had been through this and that. I always adored her. Having lost Lynnie, losing Tash and Corin, makes you appreciate the lives of others much more preciously, because you never expect them to die. Nobody expects it, even if things don't look good."

"It's a privilege to work with Vanessa," Franco Nero said after filming *Letters to Juliet* with her. "I think she's the best. When I say the best, I tell you she's the *best*. She has an incredible talent and we all know that and she's a great woman." He acknowledged that she could be difficult.

"Sometimes she's a little bit stubborn and I have to find a way to convince her to do something."

Nero insisted on putting a line into one of their scenes. In the film, Redgrave tells him she's sorry she's late (their characters, once lovers, haven't seen each other in many years), and Nero says, "When we speak about love, it's never too late." After Nero and Redgrave heard that this scene had been cut, they called the studio and got it reinstated.

Redgrave told friends and family that she needed to take it easy for a bit, but she soon found herself in a long run on Broadway in Alfred Uhry's modest play *Driving Miss Daisy* opposite James Earl Jones. Well into the run, she agreed to an interview with Patrick Healy of the *New York Times* and mostly deflected his questions about how she was doing personally, but toward the end of their talk, speaking of losing a loved one, she said, "Two days feels the same as two years or twenty years or 200 years, except you don't live that long."

Interviewed by Charlie Rose, Redgrave spoke of the enjoyment of putting over this small play in relation to her labors in *Long Day's Journey Into Night*: "You're not dragged into a hole as Eugene O'Neill drags you—and it's a mighty important hole—to do four hours of *Long Day's Journey Into Night*, no actor is going to be thrilled every moment that they step on that stage."

The James Earl Jones/Redgrave revival of *Driving Miss Daisy* was a hit, and it had steep ticket prices, with some tickets costing well over a hundred dollars. When asked to participate in a scheme to drive up ticket sales, Redgrave demurred. "This sounds to me like Broadway buffoonery!" she cried, according to Michael Riedel's *New York Post* column. "I am not interested in Broadway buffoonery!"

And so two major stars activated a solid, modest play. Even John Simon liked the result: "The acting is simply superb. That is if the vast talents of the cast can be called simple. They are tried and true performers who bring ultimate artistry well beyond mere craft. From Redgrave, it is a kind of sublime mugging and gloriously projected, perfectly Southern speech, going from chilly hauteur through sassy incandescence to bone-deep humanity."

I did not see this production, but clips from it on various TV shows indicated that Redgrave was giving an extremely broad, busy performance.

"It's hard to tell where her character's flintiness begins and the brisk apathy of a slumming stage doyenne begins," wrote Scott Brown in *New York Magazine*.

The play was a financial success. A member of the creative team for this show who wishes to remain anonymous says, "Like a lot of older actors, she had a list of things she wanted to make her more comfortable at the theater. She wasn't really right for the part, in all honesty. And she wasn't very social. She doesn't do well in groups. At the opening night party, Vanessa walked in, took a quick look around, and walked right back out again."

Redgrave received a BAFTA fellowship from Prince William on February 20, 2010, and her deep bow to the prince before accepting the award caused much comment. Redgrave had come a long way, it seemed, from the woman of the 1970s who had predicted that Britain was about to become a military dictatorship. Considering that she had spent most of her life calling for the abolition of the monarchy, this gesture was viewed with much surprise by the press, but of course it is always best to expect the unexpected from Redgrave.

Andrew Anthony wrote a critical piece about her acceptance of the award for the *Observer*. In the comments section, one observer noted, "As she went down to gobble, sorry, *curtsy*, before the Next in Line to the Throne and voiced respect and admiration for his Mum and Dad tonight, I just couldn't help remembering those wonderful Equity meetings when she and the other WRP Trots tried taking over the union and demanding a workers state etc. blah blah blah. . . . Well, Vaness, now that you're ensconced deep in the establishment's castle, how about unbolting the gates so that we workers can surge in and take over at last?"

In 2011 in the UK, a low-minded book was set to be published about the Redgraves. After excerpts from this book were published in the *Telegraph*, Joely Richardson came to her mother's defense in a published editorial in that same newspaper that had the hurt, judicious tone of Corin's book about Michael. In early June of 2011, I interviewed Richardson on the phone for a play she was doing in New York, *Side Effects*. I was told not to ask about her family. We spoke of the play and of acting in general, but even this was difficult. I had the feeling that if I asked her about the weather, it might upset her.

I made a huge mistake in saying that I admired the piece she had written in the *Telegraph* defending her family against the book. I then asked her if she had anything more to say about the matter; if not, we didn't have to speak of it. This was met with such a pained silence that I felt very sorry for even mentioning it. I had wanted to maybe broach the subject of doing a more respectful book on Redgrave myself, but there was no way of crossing that bridge now. Richardson said in a small voice that she only wanted to talk about the theater. When I asked for some thoughts on her mother's work, she was unresponsive. She said she hadn't seen *The Devils* or some of the other films I mentioned. I asked about some of her own film work she liked best, and she mentioned *Sister My Sister* (1994), a version of the story that inspired Jean Genet's *The Maids*.

I was supposed to see *Side Effects* that night, but I got a call from the press agent saying that Richardson was upset with me, that she had spoken to her agent and her manager, and she wanted me to sign something about not using the interview for syndication purposes, or something along those lines. I suppose I shouldn't have been surprised, since this was the way Vanessa had dealt with the press for most of her life, but I was saddened that I had mucked things up with her so thoroughly. I told the press agent that I wouldn't write the piece at all so that we wouldn't have any more trouble.

The next day, weirdly enough, I got a cheery, upbeat voicemail from Richardson saying that she didn't know why she had gone so far back in time when talking about her favorite film work. She said that she had also enjoyed playing Wallis Simpson on TV and playing the young Queen Elizabeth I to her mother's older Virgin Queen in the yet-to-be-released *Anonymous* (2011).

I emailed the press agent to ask what was going on, and as I waited for his answer, I found *Sister My Sister* online and watched it. It was an excellent film, the best version of this story I had ever seen, and as the self-loathing older sister, Joely Richardson was superb: sensitive, empathetic, making a case for a girl who was driven to incest and the bloodiest of murders. She was on the same level as all the other Redgraves at their best, a level where no human being is too damned, damaged, or eccentric for our imaginative sympathy.

I wouldn't have signed any papers before or after an interview even for Vanessa, but I also had sympathy for Richardson and the situation she found herself in. Her sister Natasha could sometimes be too placid in her screen roles, and Joely sometimes has the opposite problem in her work when she picks one emotion and hits it too hard, but at their best they had both continued the family tradition. Joely even took on Ibsen's *The Lady from the Sea* on the London stage in 2012, proving again that certain plays really do belong to the Redgraves.

At the 2011 Tony Awards, where Redgrave was nominated for Best Actress for *Driving Miss Daisy*, she received a heartfelt standing ovation when she came out on stage with co-star James Earl Jones. During Neil Patrick Harris's opening musical number, which revolved around the idea that Broadway wasn't just for gay people anymore, he briefly talked to Redgrave in the audience and asserted that she was heterosexual, whereupon she looked annoyed and mouthed, "How do you know?" Part of this response has to do with her humorlessness, of course, her inability to go along with a joke for a silly musical number, but another part might have been her deeper anger over being the subject of a scurrilous trash biography in her native country.

There were several more films of this time where it was necessary to play a game of "Where's Waldo?" or "Find Vanessa!" She followed her daughter Joely once more into a subpar project, the science fiction mini-series *The Day of the Triffids* (2009) for TV, playing an evil nun who sends people out to be monster-plant food. She was credited in a film called *Eva* (2010) from Romania, but I have yet to spot her in it, and I've seen two different versions of it, though she is supposed to be the older Eva (this film recently vanished from her IMDb page).

She appeared briefly in Julian Schnabel's *Miral* (2010), which dealt with a Palestinian girl (Freida Pinto) caught up in the Israeli-Palestinian conflict, and she lent support to the solemn *The Whistleblower* (2010), where Rachel Weisz played a journalist who uncovers sex trafficking in Bosnia. In that movie, Redgrave is just a token presence of good intentions, speaking up for the U.N. on screen as she did in most of her interviews. Even when the roles were minuscule, it was clear that Redgrave still liked to throw her weight and experience behind films that involved some kind of social issue. She did *Driving Miss Daisy* again in London, where she again received mostly fine personal reviews, but Susannah Clapp in the *Observer* wondered why Redgrave and Jones were "mugging it up" in this play, "as if they didn't have better things to do."

*Anonymous*, directed by Roland Emmerich, is a lightweight film on a large subject—the actual authorship of Shakespeare's plays—and it offered no serious case either for or against, but it did offer the spectacle of Redgrave unusually cast as the elderly Queen Elizabeth I, forty years after she played Mary, Queen of Scots on screen. She herself gamely said she had long doubted that Shakespeare was the man we know from Stratford. "Whoever Shakespeare was," she said, "he wasn't a little ordinary yeoman who headed back to Stratford after he had his fun. . . . I'm quite certain that he was a quite exceptional aristocrat who had to keep totally quiet and needed Shakespeare as cover."

On her first entrance, Redgrave makes an odd, dotty impression, as if the Queen has started to unravel a bit mentally. When she watches the Shakespeare plays, Redgrave's Queen wears a totally open expression, reacting like a child to each new action on stage. With her ladies in waiting and men of the court, her Queen can be brusque and irritable, vain and capricious, and toward the end of the film, Redgrave seizes the idea that the Queen is a kind of actress herself as she vividly dramatizes the court intrigue around her for willing listeners.

This is a bold, imaginative, kaleidoscopic performance that captures all kinds of opposing nuances in this complex woman. The film that houses this performance does not deserve it, but it made clear that Redgrave was still capable of working at her full capacity on screen at this late date. Certainly her work here suggests what an exciting Elizabeth she would have been at greater length. Given an adequate script and more time, she might have put the monotonously predictable and merely steely screen and TV Virgin Queens in the shade.

She described the queen's life as a "black hole in some respects, with gleams of sunlight . . . when she was age three, her father raised her to the heights, and crowds adored her. And then when she was a teenager, she was in the tower and expecting to be executed. . . . She was the monarch of a despotic regime, which is the same thing as a totalitarian regime.

"It's very interesting, the fractures in this extraordinary creature, of whom there have been some writers who have given much insight," Redgrave said, "and I only hope that I've been able to respond to Roland and the script sufficiently to be able to give a little glimpse of that.

"I was so excited because I've always wanted to play Elizabeth from the time I was about nineteen, and finally . . . I got to play the old Elizabeth and I was very thrilled about that, because I've always been fascinated by her, young and old," she said.

During an interview for the film, her daughter Joely said, "I see bits of me in Vanessa. And I think actually that you do see bits of yourself in me." But Redgrave said, "No, I don't." Joely persisted: "We have talked before how there are definite similarities." But Redgrave wasn't having it. "Thank God I don't see myself in you!" she said, seeming to put herself down. "Stop it! We are similar and different at the same time," Richardson said. "We are," Redgrave said finally.

"I had hoped to play all the roles for women in Shakespeare, and I didn't get to play a lot of the roles," Redgrave reflected, "but it's hard to see a six-footer playing Juliet, I guess, unless the rest of the cast is six foot three. So I knew I would never get to play Juliet. I would have loved to have played Viola. And I never played Ophelia, but Natasha played Ophelia." She had forgotten her brief stint as Viola at the Shaw Theatre in 1972, but it is a shame she never played that particular role again.

An unexpected Shakespeare role did come her way, this time on film. George Bernard Shaw once mischievously wrote to Vanessa's grandmother Margaret: "What!!! So Michael is *your son*? I must re-write *Coriolanus* for the two of you." And so it was perhaps fated that Redgrave finally played this particular Shakespearian role on screen, Volumnia, the mother in Ralph Fiennes's film adaptation of *Coriolanus* (2011).

"I am not interested in just playing roles that are like me," Redgrave said. "I wouldn't be an actress if I were not interested in trying to understand every kind of human being, present or past. I didn't know if I would be able to play Volumnia. This is a woman whose son descends through her from generations of fighters and leaders for the Roman republic. I don't come from a line of military families. But Ralph assured me he believed I was the only person right for the role.

"I have to identify from the inside," she said. "As an analyst I might be able to say different things, but as an actress I have to identify in a deeper way than in terms of adjectives like 'strong' or 'weak.'" Asked at this point if art should be political, she said, "Art should be free to be what it wants. It should speak out for what it wants, political or not. If you say art should be political, you are shutting out at least half the world. Maybe three-quarters. Some of Shakespeare's plays have been refused by dictators who saw them as threats; some have been welcomed by dictators who thought he was supporting them. As a matter of fact, Shakespeare is much more human than that, much less political than that, although he certainly understood the political struggles of his time.

"I found it difficult to play a woman glorying in her son's battle wounds," she admitted. "I found it difficult to put myself into the skin of a woman who would not cry if her son were killed. I had to take the road of entering a woman whose parents, grandparents, great-grandparents have all been military men. It is a different mindset." The role of Volumnia was not one she had ever thought of for herself. "It was never a part that I wanted to play, and more important than that, when I read the script my imagination got blocked," she said. "I didn't think I could play her, but I wasn't going to refuse working with Ralph."

Alas, the film itself proved something of a letdown, made in the shaky handheld style favored by cinematographer Barry Ackroyd, clearly hampered by budget constraints and more seriously hampered by Fiennes's inexperience as a film director. He himself gives a fine reading of the title role, one of Shakespeare's most complex and demanding lead parts, but scenes that would be best played in long shot are done in extreme close-up, so that Fiennes's declaiming is far too in-your-face, and Redgrave is similarly undone by several moments when the camera is basically on top of her as she speaks the verse. When the domineering Volumnia madly attacks one of her son's enemies, the scene is shot handheld in such a confusing way that it's impossible to judge what choices Redgrave is making as an actress because we can barely piece together one bit of her behavior to the next.

Redgrave's first scene is her best, where Volumnia speaks to her daughter-in-law (Jessica Chastain) with her eyes avid and obscenely hungry and hard with bloodlust. It's such a strong opening gambit that Redgrave has nowhere to go; again, she has impatiently shown us all her cards at once. Her voice is downright gravelly here, and the camera films her harshly at close range with very little makeup.

Redgrave's interpretation gets muddy by the halfway point, and in her last long scene she fails to get across this woman's pride, need, and mastery of her own son—she just points at him and narrows her eyes and generally looks lost and tired. Volumnia is a Maggie Smith role, really, not a Vanessa part, but it's a shame that her strong showing in the first scenes has so deteriorated by the end. The great monument of her face and body were beginning to seem worn down by cares and grief. This is what life had done to one of the most beautiful of all human faces.

She was honored by the Academy of Motion Picture Arts and Sciences in November of 2011. "I thought I must be dead, and somehow present at a memorial," she said to the *Telegraph*. "There are two words that are always used about Vanessa: she has courage and she has massive radiance," said Eileen Atkins at the event. "And I think that comes from her true belief that basically mankind is very good. She believes in humanity. And not many people do."

At the tribute to her more than fifty years in film, host David Hare said she had the "ability to make thinking look fun, to lend glamour to thought as much as to feeling. In her performances there is an interior quality which has been much remarked . . . the sense that the emotion or conviction is drawn up from a deep, almost inaccessible place. But less remarked is the shine she then puts on it. It is as if she both draws light and reflects it."

When she spoke about her preparation for playing Renée Richards in *Second Serve*, Redgrave quite unguardedly said, "I was really ignorant, I've always thought maybe I'm bisexual and I've never tried it out," at which point Meryl Streep merrily volunteered from the audience to help her experiment. Two of her first loves, her father Michael and her first husband Tony Richardson, were bisexual but leaning toward gayness. Part of still loving them, perhaps, was in wanting to feel what they felt, in the empathetic way that she functioned as an actress at her very best in *Second Serve*.

Redgrave was still unrepentant about her time with the WRP. "The period of time in which I was in that political party, which had followed being in the Labour party, which I had done a lot of campaigning for in the sixties, what interested me in this particular party, the Workers Revolutionary Party, was the enormous amount of study," she said. "Study of history and philosophy. Although I've never asked enough questions, I've had to learn to ask questions. It began to feed questions that were teeming in my brain, and I'd never found anybody who could answer them."

"I would be surprised if she really re-evaluated her role with Healy now," says Tim Wohlforth. "I know she changed her politics. Especially around Sarajevo and things like that in the 1990s, she did a very heroic job, trying to help and performing there and all that. That was post-Healy and that was *her*, I think, you know. She found a political voice then that I think really suited her. But I would be very, very surprised if she would go back and think what she did with Healy was wrong. She would just think that she'd moved beyond that and that it was a different situation now."

In her early seventies, she no longer called herself a Marxist. "I was learning," she stressed. "Perhaps at the time I wrote it [her memoir] we were still all using labels too readily, about oneself as well as about other people. No, I wouldn't call myself a Marxist. But I think that Marx made a very great contribution to philosophy." As ever, she deflected questions about herself and tried to make her answers more general. Redgrave was still doggedly pursuing a kind of humility because she knew that her basic personality was filled with justifiable ego and the need to demand attention.

In her art, her urge to make a difference was justified and lavishly repaid devotion. In the arena of politics, this urge led her into areas that were certainly none of her real business. "There is definitely a dramatic angle attached," said Lynn of Vanessa's politics. "Perhaps it is the ultimate in being center stage." Many people have tried to come up with psychological reasons for her tenacious political struggles, but the root cause has long been surpassed by a lifelong commitment that can only be called obsessive and that can only be called her own.

Speaking of her radical politics, her former son-in-law Robert Fox said, "It's very, very unrelenting." What had been a phase for her *Julia* co-star Jane

Fonda had been a constant forge for Redgrave. "She's stuck her neck out and changed politically," said her daughter Natasha in 1998. "Her politics are much less black and white. She concentrates most of her efforts on the plight of refugees and UNICEF and the concerns of children. To me, she's some kind of saint for all she does for people. She's had the courage of her convictions, always. People think she's very intimidating and tough, but she's not. She's very generous and very vulnerable." James Ivory commented, "There was a time when she was more with-a-clenched-fist, urging revolutions. Maybe the change comes with age, where you have less energy to spend climbing up on all kinds of barricades."

It is easy to want to blame Corin for first involving her in the WRP, but the blame for her mistakes, as for her considerable achievements, must lie squarely within herself. The censorious queen in her might not always want to admit to that, but the best personal part of her, the part that strives so constantly for humility, would have to accept the record of her own personal and political shortcomings as well as the glory of her artistic achievement, through which she accomplished what she had always wanted, justice or at least a fair hearing for all, even the pitiable, even the damned.

"I would say that Vanessa is as unhappy with her 'grand dame of the theater' title as I am as the godfather of social enterprise," says John Bird. "Neither of us likes being spittles of capital. But unlike many I know, I think she always tried her best. Unfortunately the intellectual tools were never forthcoming."

The major American novelist and children's writer Paula Fox wrote in her 2011 memoir *News from the World* that a child must be taught the difference between good and bad behavior, but once the child is aware that they are doing something good in order to think that they are a good person, they must be told to stop. This seemed to me, when I first read it, an unnecessarily strict standard for behavior. After all, no matter what it does to the child's character, the good the child does, for vanity or for other reasons, still gets done.

Fox's very tough judgment, I think, applies to Redgrave and what she has tried to achieve in her political engagement. From the early 1990s onward, Redgrave found proper channels for her impulses to help those in need, but still at considerable cost to herself and to those around her. She was a professional do-gooder, and she might also be called a professional meddler. There is doing good and there is the vanity of knowing you are doing good, and Redgrave is smart enough to make that distinction but often helpless to let it stop her from speaking out of turn and holding press conferences about far too many disparate issues and struggles.

In 1969, Redgrave said, "Why are so many millions of people forced to live such miserable lives when a few like myself lead such lovely ones? I've never come up with a satisfactory answer." Guilt over being her extraordinary self has never left her. "I have never wanted to have to do any of this," Redgrave concluded, of her lifelong activism, in 2013. "Of course, I wouldn't want there to be a reason to have to."

Redgrave had stayed true to theater as well as to film, and as an older woman she realized the full value of both. "When I was younger, I'd thought of theater as a bit of a luxury, that other emergencies came before that," she said. "But I came to understand that was something of a puritan attitude—that art without censorship, opening doors to all people, even if their governments were in conflict, was fundamental to the existence and defence of civilisation."

Some of her positions, however, were lifelong. "I don't want Israeli artists to be kept out," she said. "I think the Israeli government is abominable to the Palestinians but I want to work with Israeli artists and with Palestinian artists, too." Speaking at the New York Society for Ethical Culture about the Israeli blockade of the Gaza Strip in 2008, Redgrave tried to keep cool but at one point furiously declared, "All the great powers have an urgent interest in the maintaining of this conflict, all of them!"

Before her untimely death, Redgrave's daughter Natasha had given her mother a small change purse to save for a rainy day, but Vanessa was constitutionally incapable of doing so. She saw her work as a calling still. "All the arts, whether it's paint on canvas or sculpting, dance, singing, modern, classical, acting, are absolutely vital to the resistance of human beings both to war, to horror . . . the arts stop society from going rotten and mad, basically," she said.

Grieving her lost daughter, Redgrave told the *Telegraph* that she carried with her a postcard a friend had given her. It was an image from an illuminated manuscript from the fourth or fifth century from the British Museum of two figures separated by a river. One is a man in a red gown and the other is a woman seen only as an outline. "It's about a man whose wife has died—she's on the other side of the river," Redgrave said. She bought lots of copies of the postcard. "I send them to people I'm very, very fond of," she said. Speaking of how she changed after her daughter's death, Redgrave said, "What people say reverberates differently. Everything that happens, there's a different sound, a different look. One sees with more perception. One considers more. One doesn't feel impelled to rush precipitously.

"I used to be a big diary writer, but I haven't written for quite a while, and Joely, my second daughter, has been urging me to write again, to write to Natasha in my diary," she said. "And I said to her, 'I know you're right, but I can't bring myself to do it.' I literally cannot do it. Although I knew she was right, I knew. But to write to my daughter and not be able to hear back, to leave a message for her and not have her ring me back, it's still a very, very hard thing. . . . It changed my world, because it isn't usual that the mother survives and the daughter dies, except in horrible situations like war or Gaza.

"I still find it very difficult, of course. I found it difficult when my mother died, but I knew she had to. I was grief-stricken and missed her desperately, because she lived with me for the last few years of her life. But you accept that—even if you rebel spiritually because you can't bear your mother to have gone. Nevertheless, you know this has to happen, with old age. But when your daughter dies, it's so unacceptable, particularly when it's not expected in any shape or form. Actually it's pretty terrible if it is expected."

She still had money that needed to be made, for herself and her causes. Her grandfather Roy had died penniless, and her father Michael had died with no savings in the bank, but these men had spent their money mainly on themselves, whereas Redgrave ceaselessly gave her money to others. She lived now in a smallish two-bedroom flat in Hammersmith, "mortgaged up to the hilt," she told the *Telegraph*, so that she had to take pretty much anything offered to her.

She did a horror film, *The Last Will and Testament of Rosalind Leigh* (2012), guest-starred as a lesbian Supreme Court judge on the USA series

*Political Animals* with Sigourney Weaver, and played opposite Terence Stamp in *Unfinished Song* (originally titled *Song for Marion*) (2012), where these two beauties of Swinging London got a chance to sing.

"We are talking about a national treasure," Stamp said of Redgrave. "But the fact is I had worked with her in the theater, I had done Ibsen with her at the Round House Theatre about fifteen to twenty years ago and I had no reservations about her as an actress. But as a person, I found her kind of political views a bit tough. She asked me more than once if I would look after the donkeys at the Young Communist Fair, and I said 'piss off.'"

Stamp found that Redgrave had been changed by time and grief. "When I walked onto the set of *Song for Marion*, I saw her and I realized that within the space of twelve to fifteen months prior to the day we met, she had lost her daughter, her sister, and her brother, and I don't think I had ever seen anybody as fragile," he said. "I just thought to myself, I mustn't be careless with her, I have got to behave really well with her, and of course, and this is only my assumption, but my feeling was that she had done what great artists do, she kind of put her grief into the character, but it was kind of tethered to the very best part of her."

Redgrave gave a searing performance of elderly loneliness in her son Carlo Nero's short film *The Call Out* (2013) but was just one of the stars in *Lee Daniels' The Butler* and *Foxcatcher*. She was still capable of surprising choices. Redgrave elected to do Jesse Eisenberg's play *The Revisionist* at the venerable but small Cherry Lane Theatre in Greenwich Village from mid-February to mid-April of 2013, most likely for very little money. "It was so good, so good—and I knew that I wanted to do it straightaway," Redgrave said. "Terrific writing is what excites you. There are some wonderful writers, but there's also a lot of terrible writing, and quite a bit of it seems to come my way."

She would not give her specific thoughts on the play to the press beforehand. "I want audiences to come in not knowing anything about the play except who's in it, the names of the characters, and where it takes place. I want them to be able to go into what is, in fact, a fresh micro-cell of life." Eisenberg had waited for a while to catch her, and he was nervous. "The first two rehearsals, I was very worried that we would find flaws in [the play] and I was nervous that she would find those and drop out or something," he said.

Her part in *The Revisionist* required her to speak Polish fluently, and so Redgrave took language tuition at the Kosciuszko Foundation on the Upper East Side of Manhattan. Her role was sometimes written in broken English. Redgrave felt that with every dropped "a" or "the" in one of her lines that "a rhythm vanishes and a truth vanishes."

I saw *The Revisionist* the night before it opened, on February 27, and though I had read about how good Redgrave was in the play in previews, nothing prepared me for the major, full-scale, awe-inspiring performance she gave that night. "Vanessa is immensely excited by the script of *The Revisionist*, which she accepted as soon as she read the play," said the last line of her condensed bio in the program, which only mentioned her most recent Broadway work.

Redgrave played Maria, a Polish woman who is excited over a visit from her distant cousin David (Eisenberg), a young, self-absorbed writer. David only wants quiet to finish an overdue manuscript. Maria is a survivor of the Holocaust who lost all of her relatives to the Nazis and values family above all else.

Redgrave spoke with a thick Polish accent, and it might have seemed cartoonish if it had been used by any other actor, but from her it sounded right because everything else about her work was so extreme, so that her accent needed to match that extremity. Her Maria wore glasses and long bangs that covered a lot of her face, and she walked with a stoop that made her seem physically closed-off. Redgrave actually made herself seem small in the first scenes, which is not something she's been able to accomplish in any of the other work of hers I have seen. But as the play went on, she started to open Maria up and reveal to us who she was within the confines of her small apartment cluttered with family photos.

"With every inch and item of that apartment Ms. Redgrave seems to be on terms of intimacy that come only with decades of acquaintance," wrote Ben Brantley in his review for the *New York Times*. "Woe to him who, like David, tries to commandeer that space for himself. Maria's home isn't just her castle; it's her fortress and her asylum."

In a scene where David asked her about her childhood, Redgrave's Maria spoke of it casually at first, but when the full horror of her early memories hit her, Redgrave got up and staggered across the set, landing up in the kitchen, where she stood motionless in front of her refrigerator. After a brief pause for regathering, she pulled her hunched shoulders up and as far back as she possibly could. In that single resolute gesture, Redgrave expressed the entirety of this woman's private and valiant life.

There were more wonders to come, none more unforgettable than the scene where Maria let a younger man (Daniel Oreskes) shave her legs. Gradually, overwhelmingly, Redgrave made Maria seem like a young beauty letting herself enjoy the naughtiest of sensual pleasures. "Whispering and chiding in unintelligible but unmistakably gleeful language, and laughing with the sybaritic delight of someone indulging in a special treat, Ms. Redgrave spins a complete and compelling vision of one woman's world, as familiar to her as it is exotic to us," wrote Brantley. "And she occupies it with an assurance that makes us feel like humble, highly privileged trespassers."

To put it in another more technical way, what Redgrave was doing in this scene was fusing the most intimate Actors Studio private moment exercise with the external size and authority of her own English theatrical training, which made for a truly gobsmacking and probably unprecedented mixture of these two usually separate and warring schools of acting. Very rarely do you feel in the theater, or anywhere else, that you are in the presence of greatness. It was clear to me and to everyone else in that small space that we were indeed in the presence of something otherworldly, something more than we get 99% of the time when we confront any artistic endeavor.

Eisenberg's play gave Redgrave all the tools she needed to take off into the stratosphere, and he himself made a good staccato partner to her most inspired legato inventiveness. "She's so amazing," he said while they were in rehearsal. "She could break up with you and you'd want to hear it again." *The Revisionist* was a kind of thwarted love story between David and Maria, and Redgrave made the very most of the moments when she reached out to Eisenberg physically: caressing his hair, stroking his feet when he unexpectedly and obliviously stuck them in her lap, grabbing him up in an intensely needy, unbreakable hug when they were talking and drinking together.

Speaking of Eisenberg, Redgrave said, "He reminds me of Shelley. I don't know if I can put it into words. A very inquiring mind, interested in everything and everybody. This is quite unusual. A very unique quality as an actor too." Eisenberg related, "She normally says Gielgud. She sometimes will call me that in rehearsal. 'John . . . I mean, Jesse.' It's embarrassing, really."

Redgrave raced home right after the play. "Not because I don't like Jesse, but I race home for home reasons," she said. Eisenberg said, "We're both here very early, so we see each other here. I don't have anything else going on." And then Redgrave told him, "Exactly. That's the life."

Redgrave's Maria was a woman who had lost all of her family quickly and violently. Toward the end of the play it was revealed that she had made up her family connection to David because she wanted a new family so badly. In a performance studded with unforgettable physical behavior, the most memorable was the way Redgrave handled Maria's most treasured possessions, the framed photos of a family that wasn't even really hers.

It seemed as if this theme of a lost family struck the deepest chord within Redgrave, and it led to yet another superlative performance, one of her finest of all in a career already crowded with varied achievements. Having given it, she made another bold theater choice and floated off to London to play an elderly Beatrice to James Earl Jones's Benedick in Mark Rylance's production of *Much Ado About Nothing* at the Old Vic in September of 2013.

"I don't know what Beatrice is saying half the time and I'm working very hard to find out," Redgrave said before they opened. "Maybe we will be a disaster. I don't think so, but we might." Speaking of the perspective her age gave her, Redgrave said, "You see things differently from far up above than you do living in the streets of the world." The production received poor reviews, but it proved that she was still up for a dare. And she found time to film a Christopher Hampton story, *The Thirteenth Tale*, for TV. And while you've been reading this paragraph, Redgrave has probably filmed another cameo in a film in some faraway place.

# Coda

One critic (Howard Kissell in the *New York Daily News*) thought Redgrave played Cleopatra in 1997 "as a tomboy, the shock of red hair atop her makeup-free face an homage to either David Bowie or Tom Sawyer." During the 1980s and '90s especially, Redgrave was always toying with her own androgyny, going for masculine effects aided by her height, by short or even shaved hair, and by unisex clothing. Our greatest actress, she wanted to be all people and all sexes, and all nationalities, too, trying out a cornucopia of accents, sometimes with extremely bizarre results. "She dominates situations, exuding a charismatic power with which she controls people's attention," observed her sister-in-law Deirdre. "Like a blond Amazon, she towered above us. Six feet tall and as blue-eyed as her father, she had an almost masculine presence, as though in another life she would have been wielding a sword."

Two of her very best screen performances, *Second Serve* and *The Ballad of the Sad Café*, were pitched in the nether reaches of the male gender, where she moved in stages from male to female. When she chose to highlight the purely feminine, as she did so wonderfully in *Howards End*, she could seem so fragile and spacey that the gentlest breeze might blow her away.

She could be boyish but never manly. There is something about Redgrave that has always seemed eternally adolescent, no matter her age.

There is no doubt that Redgrave has reached as high up creatively as any actor ever has, and she has sometimes fallen as far, too. Just look at her bad film acting one-two punch from 1988, *Consuming Passions* and the remake of *A Man for All Seasons*, and you'll see that only our greatest actress could be capable of work so outrageously misguided. Even in the smallest, most unrewarding bit parts, she never seems merely tired, never seems to be just biding her time. Her mere presence commands attention. Even in *Mother's Boys*, even in *Bella Mafia*, there are moments when the camera just seems to gape at this splendid creature, walking into a room like some vast ship at full sail moving into harbor.

As a young woman, Redgrave said, "Perhaps at the end of my life people will say, 'That old girl certainly tried doing a bloody hell of a lot, didn't she?'" Her repertoire in the theater has been wide-ranging and always unexpected. She might focus on a major playwright, but not on the play you might expect of her. A natural for the perverse Hedda Gabler, she never played that role but made Ibsen's lesser-known *The Lady from the Sea* a trademark part and performance. A perfect Alma for *Summer and Smoke*, she instead latched on to one of Tennessee Williams's most difficult plays, *Orpheus Descending*, and somehow pulled it up to her level and triumphed in it in London and on Broadway.

She's covered most of Chekhov, done Greek tragedy, Brecht, Shaw, Wilde, and Noël Coward, and hurled herself at Shakespeare. She defined his Rosalind for all time, took on his shrew Katherine twice, made one unhappy stab at Lady Macbeth, and tried three times in all to be his Cleopatra, but she was never Ophelia, only briefly Viola, and she was too tall, she thought, for Juliet. Some felt she was phenomenal as Mary Tyrone on Broadway in Eugene O'Neill's *Long Day's Journey Into Night*. Others felt she walked through the part, as if O'Neill's Irish pessimism was too much for her own naturally hopeful nature. Redgrave will do battle, but she wants to win. She cannot fully function in a defeatist play, however great it may be.

Already one of the most sensitive and empathetic of all artists, the sorrows of Redgrave's later years often brought her to a visual point of static grandeur and silent, agitated remembrance. The harder and more frightening edges of her politics were sanded away, for the most part, until she spoke for more general human rights as represented by UNICEF.

Redgrave made it to the very top of the mountain of human conscious-ness creatively, and what she has seen and what she has shown us will continue to be of enormous value. The human cost of this artistic moun-taineering is there on her face as an elderly woman, and the personal cost, too, for she reached that height only by risking and daring the fathoms-deep sorrows and nothingness of the ocean floor, too.

Of her perseverance in the face of loss, Redgrave said, "You have a will to live. Even if at the same time it seems very attractive just to give up." Giving up is not a luxury that she has ever allowed herself. That is part of being an Englishwoman of her time, place, and class, and it might be said that it is also part of being a Redgrave, but Vanessa has surpassed all others in her family and in her profession when it comes to sheer stubborn survival and blistering anger at injustice and all-encompassing tenderness for others that does not flag or waver.

She will never go soft, but she will never get too hard. That's the wonder of her work. "You can see the weather on her face," said Eileen Atkins. "You can see every emotion passing across like a cloud." Redgrave has said that when she really clicks with a role, there is not even the smallest gap between herself and the woman she is playing. Her commitment to being that woman is total.

"All great English actresses stand in her shadow, and they know it," says Tony Palmer. "Judi Dench, who I know very well, would say that, I think. There's no envy or jealousy or spite about it, or anything bitchy, and this is a bitchy profession. You don't hear bitchery about Vanessa profession-ally. You know, people get cross about the Workers Revolutionary Party and all that stuff, but not professionally. When Vanessa is in a play in the West End, you see all the other actors and actresses there just watching her, and learning. And maybe we've forgotten Maggie Smith, but I think even Maggie would go along with what I've just said."

"Vanessa enters right into the mythic and the archetypal, and I think that's what she's very much trying to do as an actor," says Simon Callow. "Many English actors are very rigorous intellectually, and they chart the path of the character, and they often inhabit the thoughts of the character. I think that Vanessa isn't as interested in that. She is more interested in entering into these archetypal states. You could almost say, if you wanted to be quite grand about it, that she's almost a kind of Jungian actress, whereas most actors are Freudian actors. Above all, Vanessa is an intuitive artist, and she lets her imagination respond in ways other actors do not."

Redgrave is the most warm-blooded of all actresses, outstripping heavyweight competitors like Maggie Smith and Meryl Streep with the depth of her need to communicate with us and shake us up, confront us, and soothe us. During the curtain call for *The Revisionist*, Redgrave was still very much involved in the disruptive emotions of her character. In photos taken at the opening night party for that play, Redgrave looked radiantly happy, like a girl out of drama school having her first real part and real success, triumphantly unscathed, pledged to her art through all disaster. She looked like the heroine she always wanted to be.

This is the most transparent of faces. It is overwhelming in its Italian sun of joy and consistently fretful and querulous whenever Redgrave feels she needs to do what she considers to be the right thing, even if this means—or *especially* if this means—that she risks not being liked or even being outright hated. Those blue eyes of hers could still be playful in old age, but they could also be foggy and baleful and wounded. She is committed, martyr-like, to feeling ever-fresh and instructive pain for us while amply suggesting all the escape routes and tactile pleasures that can make the worst of life endurable. At this point in her career, she has nothing left to prove and everything to give. "Now and then of course I do think: 'I'm going to die,'" she said, during the run of *The Revisionist*. "It will probably take me by surprise."

On April 25, 2013, I ventured out to the West Village to see if I might ask Redgrave one question as she was leaving the Cherry Lane Theatre after one of her final performances there in *The Revisionist*. In all of her film work, above all else, the scene where she lets out a cry of agony when told her child must die in *The Trojan Women* stood out for me as her most extreme choice and her most characteristic moment. It has haunted me ever since I first saw it.

I waited outside for about twenty minutes. There were three other people waiting, one of them a stocky young Latino man with a very sweet face who was holding a poster of *The Year of Magical Thinking* that he wanted Redgrave to sign. When I asked him why he was there, he said, "I like that she puts in her two cents even if people hate her for it. I like that."

Redgrave wandered out of the theater in a dazed sort of way, and we shyly gathered around her. As she was signing programs, I said, "May I ask you, when you did the scene in the film of *The Trojan Women* when you let out that large cry, was it your idea to do it like that, or was it the director's idea? It's so moving, and I've always wanted to know how you did it." Redgrave looked me straight in the eyes for several moments, and her face was ghostlike, kind, ethereal, wistful. She looked almost apologetic as she slowly said to me, "I don't remember. . . ."

# Notes

## Introduction

p. 2     "Sometimes, I'll be watching": Frank Bruni, *New York Times*, Feb. 16, 1997

p. 4     "It is easy to know": Deirdre Redgrave and Danaë Brook, *To Be a Redgrave: Surviving Amidst the Glamour*, Simon and Schuster, 1982, pg. 62

p. 4     "She's always been the same": Michael Coveney, *What's On Stage*, April 14, 2008

p. 4     "I choose my roles carefully": Deirdre, pg. 50

p. 5     "It's a kinky part": Peer J. Oppenheimer, *Herald-Journal*, May 5, 1968

p. 5     "Literally all my family": Joan Dupont, *New York Times*, May 21, 1999

p. 6     "If there existed something": James Grissom, *Follies of God* website

p. 6     "I'm lucky": Charles Champlin, *LA Times*, Feb. 22, 1986

## Michael: Mask or Face

p. 8     "I know I am": Donald Spoto. *The Redgraves: A Family Epic*, Crown Archetype, 2012, pg. 9

p. 8     "He preferred to be": Margaret Scudamore notebook, 1955, Victoria and Albert Museum

p. 10    "The two years": Spoto, pg. 32

p. 10    "Too many people": Ibid.

p. 11    "There were moments": Michael Redgrave, *In My Mind's Eye*, Little-hampton Book Services Ltd, 1983, pg. 89

p. 11    "a moderate success": Rachel Kempson, *Life Among the Redgraves*, E.P. Dutton and Co, 1986, pg. 110

p. 11    "She was the most romantic person": Spoto, pg. 45

p. 11    "Edith always had": Sheridan Morley, *The Great Stage Stars*, Harper Collins, 1986

p. 11    "I am shallow, selfish": Simon Callow, *Guardian*, May 14, 2004

p. 12    "She understands so much": Spoto, pg. 85

p. 12    "She always felt very": *Backstage West*, 1998

p. 12    "Someday I'll bind you": *Gielgud's Letters: John Gielgud in His Own Words*, Orion, 2004, pg. 64

p. 12    "It's silly": Spoto, pg. 107

p. 12    "very wonderful": Lynn Barber, *Telegraph*, May 2, 2004

p. 13    "Michael, being tolerant": Ibid.

p. 13    "They had a long marriage": Peter Marks, *Washington Post*, April 5, 2009

p. 17    "I don't see why not": Philip Hoare, *Noël Coward: A Biography*, University of Chicago Press, 1998, pg. 393

p. 17    "Redgrave is a great actor": *Conversations with Losey*, Michel Ciment, Methuen, 1985, pg. 146

**Vanessa: A Great Actress is Born**

p. 19    "I think it's true": Bob Costas, CNN, June 18, 2005

p. 20    "To actually see": Ibid.

p. 20    "My father was": Charlie Rose, June 20, 2007

p. 21    "I began acting": *Vanessa Talks with Farouk Abdul-Aziz*, 1978

p. 21    "Vanessa grows": Spoto, pg. 93

p. 21    "Later on": Aziz

p. 22    "Corin and Vanessa": Spoto, pg. 123

p. 23    "I learned to continue": Aziz

p. 23    "The great contemporary": Bob Costas, CNN, 2005

p. 23    Drowning story: Jack Hamilton, *Look*, May 2, 1967

p. 24    "Don't worry": *Time Magazine*, March 17, 1967

p. 24    "My parents and I": *Backstage West*, 1998

p. 25    "a bit of the touch": Lynn Barber, *Observer*, March 18, 2006

p. 26    "When he heard": *Telegraph*, Oct. 8, 2011

p. 27    "Sweets for the sweet": *Letters to Juliet* promotional interview, 2011

p. 30    "I said to my parents": Charlie Rose, June 20, 2007

p. 30    "my eyes": BBC, Radio 4, Woman's Hour, Oct. 3, 2005

p. 31    "I do not understand": Michael Redgrave, *In My Mind's Eye*, pg. 222

p. 32    "Vanessa is great": Ibid., pg. 218

p. 32    "I was told": Mark Lawson interview, BBC, May 30, 2011

p. 32    "He trained me": Aziz

p. 32    "He worshipped her talent": Corin Redgrave, *Michael Redgrave: My Father*, Fourth Estate, 1996, pg. 154

**Rosalind and Tony**
p. 34    "I prefer the word": Lawson, BBC interview
p. 34    "We are the sprigs": Damien Bona, Mason Wiley, *Inside Oscar*, Ballantine Books, 1996, pg. 394
p. 34    "How exciting": Spoto, pg. 189
p. 34    "I learned": Aziz
p. 35    "My father": Ibid.
p. 35    "When I say intimidating": Ellen Gamerman, *The Wall Street Journal*, Oct. 23, 2009
p. 35    "Most people": Lifetime Intimate Portrait
p. 35    "She was just dreadful": Spoto, pg. 190
p. 36    "Dare to be big": *Life*, Oct. 27, 1967
p. 36    "I will never find": Spoto, pg. 179
p. 36    "I idly asked": http://www.mckellen.com/writings/tribute/100407cr.htm
p. 36    "like some kind": Simon Callow, *Charles Laughton: A Difficult Actor*, Fromm Intl, 1997, pp. 254-255
p. 36    "so startlingly": Ibid., pg. 257
p. 37    "I only pray": Spoto, pg. 201
p. 37    "For various reasons": Chris Hastings, "The Secret Fiance Dropped by Vanessa Redgrave," *The Sunday Times*, Sept. 13, 2009
p. 38    "The director": Jack Hamilton, *Look*, May 2, 1967
p. 38    "The Redgrave girl": pg. 277, Gielgud Letters, pg. 277
p. 40    "I saw a production": Peter Stanford, *Telegraph*, July 14, 2012
p. 41    "I knew that": Lifetime Intimate Portrait
p. 42    "How long": Spoto, pg. 214
p. 42    "I was on tour": *The Redgraves*, Biography Channel
p. 43    "Tony discovered me": Jack Hamilton, *Look*, May 2, 1967
p. 43    "Difficulties started": Spoto, pg. 218
p. 43    "I remember thinking": Spoto, pg. 214
p. 44    "Lynn is better": *New York Times*, Dec. 18, 1966
p. 44    "She just switches": *Time Magazine*, March 17, 1967
p. 44    "extraordinarily guarded": Deirdre, pg. 62
p. 44    Peggy Ashcroft: Lawson, BBC
p. 45    "splendid": John Gielgud, *Sir John Gielgud: A Life in Letters*, Arcade Publishing, 2011, pg. 309
p. 45    "I was thrilled": Aziz

**Swinging Vanessa**
p. 47    "I first met Karel": Fintan O'Toole, *New York Daily News*, Feb. 12, 1998
p. 48    "He had this patience": *London Review of Books*, Dec. 12, 2002

p. 49   "Vanessa's just sensational": Peter Evans, *Daily Mail Online*, Feb. 26, 2010

p. 49   "Before, men never spoke": Ibid.

p. 49   "Tony came back": Deirdre, pg. 151

p. 50   "Tony Richardson told me": Williams interview with James Grissom, 1982

p. 50   "Tony later apologized": Don Bachardy to DC

p. 51   "We knew that Jeanne Moreau": Ibid.

p. 51   "I think that's what Tony": Ibid.

p. 52   "Lots of gossip": Richard Burton, Chris Williams (editor), *The Richard Burton Diaries*, Yale University Press, 2013, pg. 128

p. 52   "I think she was": Bachardy to DC

p. 52   "He placed": William Mann, *Edge of Midnight: The Life of John Schlesinger*, Billboard Books, 2006, pg. 86

p. 52   "There was always drama": Bachardy to DC

p. 53   "I had to construct": Catherine Stott, *Guardian*, Jan. 1, 1969

p. 54   "It's about Vanessa": Web of Stories interview with Williams, http://www.webofstories.com/play/11303

p. 55   "I adore her": *Herald-Journal*, May 5, 1968

p. 55   "I like the protagonist": Aldo Tassone, "La storia del cinema la fanna i film," from *Parla il cinema italiano*, edited bv Aldo Tassone, Milan: Il formichiere, 1979

p. 57   "It is fresh": *The Architecture of Vision*, University of Chicago Press, 2007, pg. 91

p. 58   "I was in a West End play": Aziz

p. 59   "Dad, I've found": Joshua Logan, *Josh, My Up and Down, In and Out Life*, Delacorte Press, 1976, pg. 196

p. 59   "She was so extraordinary": Ibid.

p. 59   "Do we really": Logan, pg. 200

p. 59   "I've got a wonderful idea": Ibid.

p. 59   "I learned later": Ibid.

p. 59   "I was walking": Logan, pg. 177

p. 60   "So help me God": Logan, pg. 208

p. 60   "a pretty woman": Michael Feeney Callan, *Richard Harris: Sex, Death and the Movies*, Anova Books, 2004, pg. 177

p. 60   "My girlfriend got": Ibid.

p. 61   "The feeling": Ibid.

p. 61   "Everyone howled": Logan, pg. 208

p. 61   "maddeningly perverse": Ibid.

p. 61   "Isn't it marvelous": Ibid.

p. 63   "In our first two months": Harris bio, pg. 174

p. 63   "Actors are": Peter Evans, *Daily Mail Online*, Feb. 26, 2010

p. 64   "The Christmas Day": Christopher Isherwood, *The Sixties*, Harper Perennial, 2011, pg. 434

p. 65    "I don't know": *Daily Mail Online*, Feb. 26, 2010
p. 66    "She has lyricism": Boston College Law Review, 1989, Volume 30, Issue 5, Number 5, Article 2
p. 66    "We were in the process": Simone Signoret, *Nostalgia Isn't What It Used To Be*, Penguin Books, 1979, pg. 346
p. 67    "I remember it": *Telegraph*, Feb. 22, 2010

**Isadora**
p. 69    "All my lovers": Peter Kurth, *Isadora: A Sensational Life*, Back Bay Books, 2002, pg. 432
p. 69    "It is an American voice": Ibid., pg. 339
p. 69    "What mankind": Ibid., pg. 505
p. 70    "If I had been a man": Ibid., pg. 532
p. 70    "Isadora's end": Ibid., pg. 555
p. 71    "a disaster": *LA Times*, Sept. 15, 1985
p. 72    "The thing about dancing": Aziz
p. 73    "The choreographer": Oprah Winfrey, *O Magazine*, Dec. 2007
p. 74    "There will never": Barry Paris, *Louise Brooks*, Knopf, 1989, pg. 480
p. 75    "In *Isadora*": Aziz
p. 77    "That Maggie Smith": Deirdre, 180-181
p. 77    "I am in awe": Bob Costas, CNN, 2005
p. 77    "dressing room fracas": *People Magazine*, March 10, 1975
p. 78    "One spends": *Playboy*, April 1969
p. 78    "She does have": Michael Coveney, *What's On Stage*, April 14, 2008
p. 79    "When women say": Ann Pearce, *People Magazine*, Nov. 27, 1978

**Trojan Women and Devils**
p. 80    "A thrill to look at": A. Scott Berg, *Kate Remembered*, Berkley Trade, 2004, pg. 290
p. 80    "I don't know": Ibid.
p. 81    "I drove three hours": Rex Reed, *New York Observer*, July 7, 2003
p. 81    "For me": *Photoplay Film Monthly*, Feb. 1971
p. 83    "I see Andromache": *Women's Wear Daily*, Nov. 24, 1970
p. 83    "I saw his last film": *LA Times*, Sept. 2, 1970
p. 84    "We always do this": Ibid.
p. 84    Brass kiss: Deirdre, pg. 154
p. 85    "I wrote the script": Ingrid Pitt interview, http://www.ingridpitt.net/biography/ken-russell-2.html
p. 85    "I know originally": *Hell on Earth* documentary, 2002
p. 85    "All detail": Derek Jarman, *Dancing Ledge*, University of Minnesota Press, 2010, pg. 100
p. 86    "Rushes are": Ibid., pg. 102
p. 88    "It looked like": *Hell on Earth*

p. 88     "It's about the degradation": *Guardian*, April 28, 2011

p. 88     "It was fairly exhausting": *Hell on Earth*

p. 89     "In the end": Ibid.

p. 89     "They've been exploited": Ibid.

p. 90     "Ken's attitude": Ibid.

p. 90     "Some of the younger girls": Ibid.

p. 90     "A lot of the cut scenes": Ingrid Pitt interview

p. 90     "The wilder scenes": Derek Jarman, *Dancing Ledge*, pg. 102

p. 91     "You see the film": Parkinson TV interview, 1973

p. 91     "This is the way it happened": *Photoplay Film Monthly*, Oct. 1971

p. 91     "It's a very": *Hell on Earth*

p. 91     *"The Devils* is my favorite": Ibid.

p. 91     "I think every director": Ibid.

p. 92     "The films Ken made": BBC News, Nov. 28, 2011

p. 92     "I am even more": *The House Next Door*, Aug. 4, 2010

p. 92     "I shot *Mary, Queen of Scots*": Glenda Jackson to DC, June 24, 2013

p. 93     "The Redgraves were": Ann Pearce, *People Magazine*, Nov. 27, 1978

p. 93     "I never cared for Mary": Katharine Hepburn, *Me*, Ballantine Books, pg. 235

p. 93     "I loved playing": Will Lawrence, *Telegraph*, Oct. 8, 2011

p. 94     "I had continued to act": Aziz

p. 94     "The minute you realize": Deirdre, pg. 148

p. 94     "I wouldn't be": *New York Times*, June 19, 1971

p. 94     "I'd known of the Workers Revolutionary Party": Jackson to DC

**Keeping Left**

p. 95     "At Christmastime": Annie Ross to DC, July 30, 2013

p. 97     "I have always loved": Deirdre, pg. 180

p. 97     "cheap wine": Lynn Barber, "She's got issues," *Observer*, March 18, 2006

p. 97     "Corin impressed me": Bob Pitt, *The Rise and Fall of Gerry Healy*, Chapter 9

p. 98     "At the time": Tim Wohlforth to DC, May 8, 2013

p. 98     "I was trying": ICA Talks, 1991

p. 99     "I was shocked": *The Rise and Fall of Gerry Healy*, Chapter 9

p. 99     "Healy to me": Tim Wohlforth to DC

p. 100    "I asked her": Norman Harding, *Staying Red: Why I Remain A Socialist*, Index Books, Jan. 2005, pg. 213

p. 100    "But I need you": Adam Higginbotham, *Telegraph*, April 17, 2012

p. 101    "That BBC TV series": Gerri Kimber to DC, June 22, 2013

p. 101    "It was typical": Deirdre, pg. 72

p. 102    "Healy could really": Tim Wohlforth to DC

p. 102    "When Vanessa arrived": Charlton Heston, *In the Arena: An Autobiography*, Berkley Trade, 1997, pg. 482

p. 102   "Well, at least Lady V": Ibid.

p. 102   "She had an icy": Charlton Heston, *In the Arena*, pg. 484

p. 102   "Vanessa was doing": Shirley Knight to DC, July 1, 2013

p. 103   "Commitment to the party": *Guardian*, Feb. 18, 2000

p. 104   "Tony said": *Christopher Isherwood, Liberation: Diaries 1970-1983*, Harper Collins, 2012, pg. 417

p. 105   "They started in on me": *On the Edge: Political Cults Right and Left*, Dennis Tourish, Tim Wohlforth, M E Sharpe Inc, 2000, pg. 165

p. 105   "One has to say": *True Spies*, Ep. 2, BBC

p. 105   "Sometimes she can be very rude": Ibid.

p. 106   "With Irene Gorst": Tim Wohlforth to DC

p. 106   "I had to take her": Norman Harding, *Staying Red*, pg. 219-220

p. 106   "Norman Harding worked":  John Manix to DC, June 19, 2013

p. 106   "I have a couple": Tim Wohlforth to DC

## Ellida and Julia

p. 108   "Vanessa used to be": Paul Gardner, *Viva*, 1976

p. 109   "I don't think much": Ibid.

p. 109   "Vanessa Redgrave is controversial": This Richardson comment turns up constantly in press articles on Redgrave, but I have found no original source for it

p. 110   "Her face appeared naked": Peter Hall, *Peter Hall's Diaries*, Oberon Books, 2000, pg. 451

p. 110   "One of the five": Don Bachardy to DC

p. 110   "She brings an atmosphere": Simon Callow to DC, August 12, 2013

p. 111   "The person who": Fred Zinnemann, *Fred Zinnemann: An Autobiography, A Life in the Movies*, Scribner, 1992, pg. 223

p. 111   "It is believed": Ibid.

p. 111   "She would portray herself": Gabriel Miller (ed.), *Fred Zinnemann Interviews*, University of Mississippi Press, 2004, pg. 156

p. 112   "There is a quality": Jane Fonda, *My Life So Far*, Random House, 2006, pg. 364

p. 113   "I can't really emphasize": AMPAS tribute, Nov. 14, 2011

p. 114   "I got to know": Tony Palmer to DC, June 16, 2013

p. 115   "It is marvelous": Zinnemann memoir, pg. 224

p. 115   "Healy was the one": Tim Wohlforth to DC

p. 118   "As my friend Jane Fonda": George Haddad-Garcia, *Mandate*, Nov. 1979

p. 118   "To have been given": George Haddad-Garcia, *After Dark*, Oct. 1979.

p. 119   "do not represent": *Inside Oscar*, pg. 550-551

p. 120   "I am the Zionist hoodlum": *Inside Oscar*, pg. 551

p. 120   "Basically, she's right": Ibid.

p. 120   "What are these": Ibid.

p. 120   "she went on": Lumet testimony, Boston Symphony Case

p. 120   "I felt sorry": *Inside Oscar*, pg. 551

p. 120   "This is disgusting": Ibid.

p. 120   "I thought about": Ibid.

p. 121   "I had the opportunity": AlfarouqChannel, YouTube, uploaded July 13, 2011

p. 124   "Actually, I have": George Haddad-Garcia, *After Dark*, Oct. 1979

p. 124   "Before we began shooting": William J. Mann, *Edge of Midnight*, pg. 62

p. 124   "Vanessa is without question": Ibid., pg. 465

p. 124   "I thought her politics": Ibid., pg. 466

p. 125   "Vanessa and John": Michael Childers to DC, June 7, 2013

p. 125   "I shall never complain": Charlton Heston, *In the Arena*, pg. 276

p. 126   "I would deliver her": John Bird to DC, June 17, 2013

p. 127   "She caught": Derek Jarman, *Dancing Ledge*, pg. 214

p. 127   "We drove up": Derek Jarman, *Dancing Ledge*, pg. 215

**Playing for Time**

p. 128   "I do not accept": http://en.wikipedia.org/wiki/Fania_F%C3%A9nelon

p. 129   "I wasn't aware": *New York Times*, Sept. 28, 1980

p. 129   "If this attack": Miller testimony, Boston Symphony Court Case

p. 129   "We all had": Unpaid Film Critic, March 29, 2011

p. 129   "They would have": *People Magazine*, Oct. 6, 1980

p. 129   "They wanted their": Ibid.

p. 129   "Vanessa may have": *Sydney Morning Herald*, Feb. 7, 1982

p. 129   "I personally don't": Knight to DC

p. 130   "Joe was on": Melanie Mayron to DC, July 31, 2013

p. 130   "I don't know what": Knight to DC

p. 131   "When we were driving": Mayron to DC

p. 131   "Vanessa and I": Knight to DC

p. 131   "She didn't really": Mayron to DC

p. 133   "I tried to treat": *New York Times*, Sept. 28, 1980

p. 136   "It was the": Knight to DC

p. 136   "That's why Joe": Mayron to DC

p. 138   "I may have a driving": George Haddad-Garcia, *After Dark*, Oct. 1979

**TV and the Boston Symphony Case**

p. 139   "She carries on": Derek Jarman, *Dancing Ledge*, pg. 215

p. 140   "I had several points": John Duka, *New York Times*, April 11, 1982

p. 141   "I was a very": Tony Palmer to DC

p. 141   "I sat through": Gielgud letters, pg. 443

p. 142   "I took Storaro": Tony Palmer to DC

p. 143   "Tennessee would": James Grissom to DC, June 16, 2013

p. 143   "If I'm not good": Peter Evans, *Daily Mail*, Feb. 26, 2010

All further quotes in this chapter are taken from *Boston College Law Review*, Volume 30, Issue 5, Number 5, 9-1-1989, "Vanessa Redgrave versus Boston Symphony Orchestra: Federalism, Forced Speech, and the Emergence of The Redgrave Defense," by Marjorie Heins lawdigitalcommons.bc.edu/cgi/viewcontent.cgi?article=1901.bclr

### The Bostonians
p. 151  "Her voice": Frank Bruni, *New York Times*, Feb. 16, 1997
p. 153  "People called": Stephen Whitty, *The Star-Ledger*, Feb. 15, 1998
p. 154  "Christopher Reeve was": Heins article
p. 154  "I've seen a chameleon": Michelle Nguyen, *Daily Bruin*, Feb. 17, 1998
p. 154  "He always": Spoto, pg. 57

### Michael
p. 157  "He was what": *Christian Science Monitor*, May 28, 1993
p. 157  "He does what": Simon Callow, *Guardian*, May 14, 2004

### Healy's Ouster
p. 159  "Many women": *Workers Press*, December 6, 1986
p. 159  "wholesale sexual corruption": *The Rise and Fall of Gerry Healy*, Chapter 11
p. 159  "Vanessa Redgrave was": Ibid.
p. 159  "Not all of the women": Ibid.
p. 160  "neither for": Norman Harding, *Staying Red*, Index Books, pg. 252
p. 160  "cannot be separated": *News Line*, June 11, 1985
p. 160  "I don't care whether": Ray Moseley, *Chicago Tribune*, Nov. 10, 1985
p. 160  "demented middle class women": Ibid.
p. 161  "My friends in England": Tim Wohlforth to DC
p. 161  Slaughter figures: *News Line*, Nov. 20, 1985, cited in "Healyism Implodes," *Spartacist* No. 36-37, Winter 1985-86
p. 161  "they were only": WRP 1985: The Death of a Political Cult, RCL briefing 2, 1988, http://www.marxists.org/history/erol/uk.hightide/wrp.htm
p. 161  "I have always thought": Anonymous source, June 20, 2013
p. 162  "The WRP never received": *Telegraph*, July 25, 2004
p. 163  "There were political issues": *On the Edge: Political Cults Right and Left*, Dennis Tourish, Tim Wohlforth, pg. 169
p. 163  "Staying with Healy": Tim Wohlforth to DC

### Features Again and TV
p. 164  "I'm conscious": Charles Champlin, *LA Times*, Feb. 22, 1986
p. 164  "It's in theater": *LA Times*, March 19, 1985
p. 165  "She says": Spoto, pg. 284

p. 166    "I would have given": http://www.emanuellevy.com/oscar/
oscar-politics-vanessa-redgrave-2/)

p. 166    "There is still": Fox Butterfield, *New York Times*, Oct. 28, 1984

p. 166    "But after I": Ibid.

p. 166    "In the scenes": Ibid.

p. 167    "I was so enthusiastic": *Conversations with Losey*, pg. 386

p. 168    "In my experience": Ibid., pg. 387

p. 168    "I thought it was": Ibid., pg. 388

p. 168    "We repainted it": Ibid.

p. 168    "The days were": Ibid.

p. 170    "This isn't a": Morgan Gendel, *LA Times*, January 16, 1986

p. 170    "It was a chance": Charles Champlin, *LA Times*, Feb. 22, 1986

## Second Serve

p. 171    "Renée is a very": Charles Champlin, *LA Times*, Feb. 22, 1986

p. 171    "Even five years ago": Kenneth R. Clark, *Chicago Tribune*, May 11, 1986

p. 172    "She really freaked out": Ibid.

p. 174    "When we were": Ibid.

p. 175    "You could ask": Ibid.

p. 176    "I was just really": Howard Rosenberg, *LA Times*, May 12, 1986

## The Classics and Peggy

p. 177    "I don't think": Timothy Dalton chat group, July 2002

p. 178    "There was thunderous": David Melville Wingrove to DC, June 29, 2013

p. 178    "We tried": Stephen Frears interview, The Orton Collective

p. 179    "She missed": Simon Callow, *Love Is Where It Falls*, Fromm International, 1999, pg. 238

p. 181    "The point": Benedict Nightingale, *New York Times*, Sept. 20, 1987

p. 183    "She told me": *LA Times*, May 12, 1986

## Orpheus

p. 184    "She does": *LA Times*, Jan. 2, 1990

p. 184    "I can think": Charlton Heston, *In the Arena*, pg. 537

p. 185    "an embattled shrew": Ibid., pg. 538

p. 185    "After the Haymarket": Sheridan Morley, 1988, The Timothy Dalton Chat Group

p. 186    "Vanessa was": William Condee, *The Eugene O'Neill Review*, 12.2, 1988

p. 186    "If we want to": Ibid.

p. 186    "Redgrave's initial entrance": Ibid.

p. 186    "I had one": Kathryn Walat, Theatre Communications Group Interview

p. 187    "compelling the": Benedict Nightingale, *New York Times*, Sept. 20, 1987

p. 187    "Tennessee was always": James Grissom to DC

p. 188    "Vanessa's character": *Guardian*, May 7, 2010

p. 188    "She started talking": Tish Dace, *Martin Sherman, Skipping Over Quicksand*, McFarland, 2011, pg. 116

p. 189    "She loves": James Grissom to DC

p. 190    "I am very": Susan King, *Sun Sentinel*, Sept. 24, 1990

p. 191    "She damaged": Ibid.

p. 191    "The story tells": Ibid.

p. 191    "That's the way": Mark Lawson interview


**Lynn**

p. 194    "The director Robert Sturua": David Benedict, *Guardian*, Sept. 16, 2000

p. 195    "the withdrawal": Richard Bernstein, *New York Times*, Feb. 8, 1991

p. 195    "I unconditionally": Ibid.

p. 195    "I was the child": Rick Du Brow, *LA Times*, Dec. 16, 1990

p. 195    "The rumor was": *The Redgraves*, Biography Channel

p. 195    "Both Lynn and I": Mark Lawson, BBC

p. 196    "It was always": Paul Taylor, *Independent*, Dec. 6, 2011

p. 197    "I was principally": Mark Dawidziak, *Chicago Tribune*, Feb. 16, 1991

p. 197    "If Vanessa": Ibid.

p. 197    "Doing *Baby Jane*": Ibid.

p. 197    "There's a problem": Ibid.

p. 198    "I think people": Rick Du Brow, *LA Times*, Dec. 16, 1990

p. 198    "I think we did": Ibid.


**The Ballad of the Sad Café**

p. 201    "*Ballad* must be": Matt Wolf, *Chicago Tribune*, June 9, 1991

p. 201    "For the film": Mel Gussow, *Edward Albee: A Singular Journey*, Simon and Schuster, 1999, pg. 211

p. 202    "It was all": Simon Callow to DC

p. 204    "Oh completely": Simon Callow, *Love Is Where It Falls*, Fromm International, 1999, pg. 238

p. 204    "We had a very difficult": Simon Callow to DC

p. 206    "The positions": Matt Wolf, *Chicago Tribune*, June 9, 1991

p. 206    "I haven't felt": Lorraine LoBianco, Turner Classic Movies site

p. 206    "The fight scene": Simon Callow to DC


**Howards End**

p. 208    "It was quite clear": Mervyn Rothstein, *New York Times*, August 20, 1991

p. 209    Sherman in Russia: Sherman bio, pg. 120

p. 209    "He was of a generation": Geordie Greig, *The Tatler*, Feb. 2001

p. 209    "People say": Denis Hamill, *New York Daily News*, March 15, 1998

p. 211    "I like this character": Matt Wolf, *Chicago Tribune*, June 9, 1991
p. 211    *"Howards End* was": Criterion DVD, Featurette, "Building Howards End"
p. 211    "The casting of Vanessa": Ibid.
p. 211    "Jim's heart": Ibid.
p. 212    "She has a slightly": Tony Palmer to DC
p. 212    "She used to": Dave Kehr, *Chicago Tribune*, May 11, 1992

## A Memoir, Margaritas and Mrs. Dalloway

p. 215    "I don't think": *Vanity Fair*, Dec. 1994, pg. 31
p. 215    "I've never talked": *Daily Mail*, Feb. 24, 2007
p. 215    "It is not": Jeannette Winterson, *Great Moments in Aviation*, Vintage, 1994, pp. xiv-xv
p. 216    "What I wanted": Haden Guest, Harvard Film Archive, Fall 2009/Winter 2010
p. 216    "I couldn't dare": Fintan O'Toole, *New York Daily News*, Feb. 12, 1998
p. 217    "Why aren't": Wendy Mitchell, *Screen Daily*, Nov. 14, 2011
p. 217    "I just read": *LA Times*, Feb. 15, 1994
p. 217    "It's really": Ibid.
p. 217    "If we put it": Ibid.
p. 218    "She's how": Ibid.
p. 219    "She's taken a lot of flak": Anonymous source to DC, August 29, 2012
p. 219    "Humor is the": Deirdre, pg. 174
p. 219    "Although Vanessa": Ibid., pg. 153
p. 220    "I was surely glad": Charlie Rose, Jan. 10, 1995
p. 221    "There are the": Diana Jean Schemo, *New York Times*, Dec. 27, 1994
p. 222    "I was excited": Amy Longsdorf, *The Morning Call*, Oct. 15, 1995
p. 223    "We wanted": Joey Guerra, *Daily Cougar*, 1995
p. 224    "We didn't": Adam Higginbotham, *Telegraph*, April 17, 2012
p. 224    "I had the privilege": Valerie Bertinelli, *Losing It: And Gaining My Life Back One Pound at a Time*, Free Press, 2008, pg. 171
p. 226    "Vanessa said": *New York Times*, Feb. 15, 1998
p. 226    "Some people": Ibid.
p. 226    "She wouldn't": Ibid.
p. 228    "Marleen couldn't": *LA Times*, Feb. 15, 1998
p. 228    "I was Mrs. Dalloway": Fintan O'Toole, *New York Daily News*, Feb. 12, 1998
p. 228    "I was playing": *LA Times*, Feb. 15, 1998
p. 229    "I'd found": *Backstage West*, 1998
p. 229    "Why don't you": Ibid.
p. 229    "must be": Ibid.
p. 231    "I gave him": *The Tatler*, Feb. 2001
p. 232    "Jack Nicholson": More Than Meets the Mogwai, Jan. 2, 2008

p. 232  "The thought occurs": *College Street Journal*, Volume 11, Number 30, May 8, 1998
p. 233  "I wanted all": Stephen Garrett, *Indiewire*, May 21, 1998
p. 234  "I'm having": Joan Dupont, *New York Times*, May 21, 1999
p. 235  "a weenie part": CNN, June 18, 2005
p. 235  "tempestuous": Michael Thornton, *Daily Mail*, August 27, 2009
p. 235  "incredibly boring": Ibid.
p. 235  "This woman": Ibid.
p. 235  "If I have ever been": Ibid.
p. 236  "In my first part": BBC News, Dec. 16, 1999
p. 236  "I do want to": *Reading Eagle*, January 19, 2000
p. 237  "As an exile": Paul Majendie, *Athens News*, May 30, 2000
p. 238  "When I heard": BBC News, Nov. 3, 2000
p. 239  "For a long time": David Benedict, *Guardian*, Sept. 16, 2000
p. 239  "After seeing that": Frank Rizzo, *Hartford Courant*, June 24, 2012

**If These Walls Could Talk 2**
All Jane Anderson quotes: Jane Anderson, *Backstage*, July 20, 2011
p. 244  "It's one of": *The Advocate*, Nov. 7, 2000

**Chechnya and Lady Windermere**
p. 246  "Golan is": Nathan Rabin, *The Onion*, July 7, 2010
p. 247  "It's so wonderful": *Telegraph*, Feb. 8, 2002
p. 247  "I always regretted": Ibid.
p. 247  "I wanted my": Ibid.
p. 247  "She's a bit": Ibid.
p. 247  "Mum loves working": Nadia Cohen, *Daily Mail*, Feb. 21, 2002
p. 248  "I'm his friend": David Williams, *Daily Mail*, Dec. 7, 2002
p. 248  "I think everyone": David Frost interview, Jan. 5, 2003
p. 249  "If there are no statesmen": BBC, Radio 4, Woman's Hour, Oct. 3, 2005
p. 249  "Mary begged me": *The Seattle Times*, August 26, 2002
p. 250  "Vanessa was": Loann Halden, *The Weekly News*, July 8, 2004

**Long Day's Journey and The Fever**
p. 253  "I offered it": Robert Simonson, *Playbill*, April 24, 2003
p. 254  "indicating": *City Paper*, Feb. 4, 2004
p. 256  "She suffered": *Washington Post*, April 5, 2009
p. 257  "which invokes": William Keck, *USA Today*, July 12, 2004
p. 257  "I was just": Ibid.
p. 257  "First": Ibid.
p. 257  "because that's": BBC Radio 4, *Woman's Hour*, Oct. 3, 2005
p. 257  "I think she": *People Magazine*, Dec. 12, 2005
p. 257  "A difficult price": Charlie Rose, June 20, 2007

p. 258    "In the case": Ibid.

p. 258    *The Fever* examines": Charlie Rose, 2007

p. 259    "Although": Ibid.

p. 259    "I've never played": Oliver M. Pulumbarit, *PDI Entertainment*, Oct. 24, 2008

p. 261    "It was very natural": Ibid.

### The Year of Magical Thinking

p. 263    "for the pleasure": Jack Hamilton, *Look*, May 2, 1967

p. 263    "It sets": Stuart Jeffries *Guardian*, Sept. 9, 2011

p. 263    "I loved it": Alex Simon, *Venice Magazine*, Dec. 05/Jan. 06

p. 263    "I had": Barber interview

p. 264    "When I was": NPR, Dec. 20, 2005

p. 270    "It just seemed": Charlie Rose, June 20, 2007

p. 270    "stay clear": Ibid.

p. 270    "We did it": *Telegraph*, April 17, 2012

p. 270    "When you rediscover": Alexis Chiu, *People*, July 7, 2010

p. 270    "You're not": Ibid.

p. 270    "We fight": Ibid.

p. 270    "Our kind of": Tim Teeman, *New Straits Times*, June 7, 2013

p. 271    "I was working": James Grissom to DC

p. 271    "We agreed": *Guardian*, April 4, 2008

p. 272    "If I could believe": *Slouching Toward Bethlehem*, Farrar, Straus and Giroux, 2008, pg. 208

p. 272    "I remember": Sarah Crompton, *Telegraph*, April 19, 2008

p. 272    "Once in a while": Boris Kachka, *New York Magazine*, March 18, 2007

p. 273    "For me": Sarah Crompton, *Telegraph*, April 19, 2008

p. 273    "Vanessa Redgrave is": Lina Das, *Mail Online*, Sept. 15, 2007

p. 273    "Seeing her lying": Diana Saenger, About.com, June 5, 2007

p. 274    "I just had": AMPAS tribute, Nov. 14, 2011

p. 274    "I always had": Georgie Hobbs, *Close-Up Film*, 2007

p. 274    "The hair": Ibid.

p. 274    "It is her story": Mannythemovieguy, Dec. 14, 2007

p. 275    "It is always wonderful": Sarah Crompton, *Telegraph*, April 19, 2008

### Natasha

p. 276    "She would": Elisabeth Bumiller, *New York Times*, March 15, 1998

p. 276    "I was always": David Wallace, *LA Times*, March 28, 1991

p. 276    "I remember thinking": Steve Daly, *Entertainment Weekly*, July 31, 1998

p. 277    "When I was": *The Advocate*, Nov. 7, 2000

p. 277    "Who's the mom": Amy Clyde, *New York Magazine*, Feb. 15, 1993

p. 277    "I remember being": *Telegraph*, Oct. 8, 2011

p. 277    "We didn't have": Ibid.

p. 277   "You've got a lovely voice": Denis Hamill, *New York Daily News*, March 15, 1998

p. 278   "I don't know": Ibid.

p. 278   "he was just": Alex Simon, *Venice Magazine*, Dec. 2005/Jan. 2006

p. 278   "She's just totally": Diana Saenger, About.com, June 5, 2007

p. 279   "treating a Redgrave": Amy Clyde, *New York Magazine*, Feb. 15, 1993

p. 279   "I love my family": Denis Hamill, *New York Daily News*, March 15, 1998

p. 279   "a terrible film": Patricia Freeman, Kristina Johnson, *People Magazine*, Oct. 17, 1988

p. 279   "When I first met": Erin Broadley, *LA Weekly*, March 19, 2009

p. 281   "were in the": Patricia Freeman, Kristina Johnson, *People Magazine*, Oct. 17, 1988

p. 281   "You don't know": Ibid.

p. 281   "I found": David Wallace, *LA Times*, March 28, 1991

p. 282   "The miracle": Amy Clyde, *New York Magazine*, Feb. 15, 1993

p. 283   "It was not": Denis Hamill, *New York Daily News*, March 15, 1993

p. 283   "She pushed": Patrick Huguenin, *Daily News*, March 19, 2009

p. 283   "I had my": Ibid.

p. 283   "I've spent half": David Patrick Stearns, Obit, March 19, 2009

p. 283   "You think": Charlie Rose, June 1, 1998

p. 284   "I didn't feel I was": Elisabeth Bumiller, *New York Times*, March 15, 1998

p. 284   "resonates in": Steve Daly, *Entertainment Weekly*, July 31, 1998

p. 284   "I think": Jerry Tallmer, *The Villager*, March 25, 2009

p. 284   "In the final moments": Sheila O'Malley, *The House Next Door*, March 20, 2009

p. 285   "I've had": Steve Daly, *Entertainment Weekly*, July 31, 1998

p. 285   "The only part": Denis Hamill, *New York Daily News*, March 15, 1993

p. 286   "Natasha is": *Telegraph*, March 20, 2009

p. 286   "I have been": *The Examiner*, March 19, 2009

p. 286   "Tasha": Kate Kellaway, *Observer*, July 10, 2010

p. 287   "It seemed to me": *Telegraph*, Feb. 22, 2010

**On Top of the Mountain**

p. 288   "Corin is like": Matt Wolf, *New York Times*, Feb. 21, 1999

p. 289   "I went to": Ibid.

p. 289   "There was a period": Ibid.

p. 289   "We shall see": Ibid.

p. 289   "Oh well": *Observer*, July 10, 2010

p. 289   "I learned to love": *Guardian*, April 6, 2010

p. 290   "You gave me": *Washington Post*, April 3, 2009

p. 290   "I miss my sister": Tim Teeman, *New Straits Times*, June 7, 2013

p. 290   "It's a privilege": *Letters to Juliet* promotional interview

p. 292   "Like a lot": Anonymous source, Feb. 28, 2013

p. 295   "Whoever Shakespeare": Anthony Andrew, *Observer*, Feb. 20, 2010

p. 295   "black hole": *Anonymous* press conference, April 29, 2010

p. 296   "I was so excited": Rob Carnevale, *Time Out London*, Oct. 26, 2010

p. 296   "I see bits": *Telegraph*, Oct. 8, 2011

p. 296   "I had hoped": Mark Lawson, BBC

p. 296   "I am not interested": Stephanie Bunbury, *The Age*, Feb. 11, 2012

p. 297   "I found it difficult": BBC, Jan. 12, 2012

p. 297   "It was never": Shelby Hill, *The Vote*, Dec. 5, 2011

p. 298   "There are two": *Independent*, Dec. 6, 2011

p. 298   "ability to make": Ibid.

p. 298   "I was really ignorant": Wendy Mitchell, *Screen Daily*, Nov. 14, 2011

p. 299   "The period of time": Mark Lawson, BBC

p. 299   "I would be surprised": Tim Wolhforth to DC

p. 299   "I was learning": Mark Lawson, BBC

p. 299   "There is definitely": Karen S. Schneider, *People Magazine*, March 11, 1991

p. 299   "It's very, very unrelenting": Frank Bruni, *New York Times*, Feb. 16, 1997

p. 300   "She's stuck her": Denis Hamill, *New York Daily News*, March 15, 1998

p. 300   "There was a time": Stephen Whitty, *The Star-Ledger*, Feb. 15, 1998

p. 300   "I would say": John Bird to DC

p. 301   "Why are so": Patricia Bosworth, *New York Times*, May 4, 1969

p. 301   "I have never wanted": Andrew Edgecliffe Johnson, *Financial Times*, April 26, 2013

p. 301   "When I was younger": Stephanie Bunbury, *The Age*, Feb. 11, 2012

p. 301   "I don't want": Ibid.

p. 302   "I used to be": *Harper's Bazaar*, Feb. 4, 2010

p. 303   "We are talking": Ellie Seymore, Feb. 14, 2013

p. 303   "It was so good": Adam Green *Vogue*, Feb. 2013

p. 303   "The first two": John Williams, *New York Times*, April 9, 2013

p. 304   "a rhythm vanishes": Andrew Edgecliffe Johnson, *Financial Times*, April 26, 2013

p. 305   "She's so": Stuart Miller, *Playbill*, March 2013

p. 306   "He reminds me": John Williams, *New York Times*, April 9, 2013

p. 306   "I don't know": *Telegraph*, Sept. 13, 2013

## Coda

p. 307   "She dominates situations": Deirdre, pg. 60

p. 308   "Perhaps at the end": Patricia Bosworth, *New York Times*, May 4, 1969

p. 309   "You have a will": Tim Teeman, *New Straits Times*, June 7, 2013

p. 309   "You can see": Stephen Whitty, *The Star Ledger*, Feb. 15, 1998

p. 309   "All great English actresses": Tony Palmer to DC

p. 309   "Vanessa enters": Simon Callow to DC

p. 310   "Now and then": Tim Teeman, *New Straits Times*, June 7, 2013

# Index

4-14
d
9-18-14 5